Your Ultimate Companion to 100 Essential Shows

Edited by Alan Appel with Sue Tuttle and Karina Reeves
Introduction by Matt Roush

SASQUATCH BOOKS
SEATTLE

Printed in the United States of America
Published by Sasquatch Books
Distributed by PGW/Perseus
15 14 13 12 11 10 09 08 07   9 8 7 6 5 4 3 2 1

Cover design: Scott Taylor/FILTER/Talent
Interior composition/design: Scott Taylor/FILTER/Talent

Library of Congress Cataloging-in-Publication Data

I heart TV: your ultimate companion to 100 essential shows /
edited by Alan Appel with Sue Tuttle and Karina Reeves ; introduction
by Matt Roush.
    p.cm.
        Includes index.
        ISBN 13: 978-1-57061-526-9
        ISBN 10: 1-57061-526-8
  1. Television programs—United States—Plots, themes, etc. 2. Television programs—United States—Dictionaries. I. Appel, Alan. II. Tuttle, Sue. III. Reeves, Karina.

PN1992.3.U5I25 2007
791.45'750973—dc22
                         2007021918

Sasquatch Books
119 South Main Street, Suite 400
Seattle, WA 98104
(206) 467-4300
www.sasquatchbooks.com
custserv@sasquatchbooks.com

Contents

Contents

Contents

Introduction

We are what we watch.

Not that there's anything wrong with that—as they once said on some super-popular TV show. If you've picked up this book, it's because you, like the TV GUIDE editors who've contributed to this volume, must love television enough to take it to heart.

You probably can't imagine life without TV. Who would want to? In every TV fan's life, there are shows, characters, episodes, milestones that resonate with our memories of who we were and may have helped us become who we are.

Even 30-odd years later, I can't hear the familiar themes of *All in the Family*, *The Mary Tyler Moore Show*, *The Bob Newhart Show* or *The Carol Burnett Show* (each represented in this book) without conjuring up the vivid smell of butter melting on the stove to coat the popcorn—this was before microwaves—that my mom would pop in a pressure cooker as we nestled in for a Saturday night of classic '70s comedies. Yes, once upon a time there was great TV on Saturday nights, not just reruns.

How times have changed. How we've watched TV has changed as well—thanks, YouTube!—but what stays the same is our deep, passionate feelings toward the shows we treasure the most. Back in the day, there weren't message boards or Internet fan sites to feed our obsessions. But if you think the intensity of *Twilight Zone* fans was any less than that exhibited by more modern followers of *The X-Files* or the new *Battlestar Galactica*, you're seriously mistaken.

How strongly do people feel about their favorite TV shows? You should come visit TV GUIDE sometime when we're compiling—or, should I say, arguing over—one of these lists. There was plenty of healthy debate about what to include in this book's roster of 100 enduring classics from TV's past and present. (What do you mean, *Dark Shadows* didn't make the cut?)

What unifies these eclectic choices, ranging from *Friends*-size phenoms to cult items like *Buffy the Vampire Slayer* and *Veronica Mars*, and covering a trajectory from TV's earliest days to the most recent episode of *Grey's Anatomy*, is that there's something in each of these shows that strikes a powerfully personal chord.

The tributes you're about to read aren't definitive scholarly essays, although each entry includes informative "extras" about the show in question. Rather, these are mash notes, love letters if you will, idiosyncratic salutes to TV landmarks that were of their times, of our life and times, but also, we think, for all time. These shows reflect the culture of the moment, and in many cases helped shape the culture of the future. Where would the TV comedy be without *All in the Family*, or the adult TV drama without *Hill Street Blues*?

How cool, for instance, to trace the generational development of cutting-edge comedy from Sid Caesar's *Your Show of Shows* in the '50s through *Rowan & Martin's Laugh-In* in the '60s to the shock waves of *Monty Python's Flying Circus* and *Saturday Night Live* in the '70s all the way to *South Park* and *The Daily Show* of today.

We often tend to idealize earlier eras of television, but as you comb this list, you'll see that every TV age has been golden in one way or another. You simply had to be there. And to watch. And remember.

We did and we still do, and it's our privilege to share and celebrate these unforgettable shows of then and now with you.

Matt Roush
Senior TV Critic, TV GUIDE

All in the Family

By Greg Evans

Broadcast History: CBS, 1971–79
Runtime: 30 minutes
Genre: Sitcom

America heard Archie Bunker before it saw him.
The voice came booming from the other side of the front door of what over the next decade would become our home away from home—704 Houser Street in Queens, New York. He was bellowing at Edith, of course, with a volume that seemed to drown out anything else on television. The greatest comic creation of the day was a loud man in a very loud time.

"Socialist propaganda, pure and simple!" That's what Archie was ranting about that first night, January 12, 1971, when he made his entrance onto *All in the Family*'s set, a living room as worn down as the rest of the country. Because America *was* worn down—by a war abroad and a seeming torrent of socially divisive issues at home. What we weren't tired of—not yet, anyway—was arguing about it all. The passions of the day had raised barely a whisper in the sitcoms on view. Not everything was as vacuous as *Hee-Haw* (the show that preceded *Family* that night), but even the better comedies such as *Room 222*, *The Courtship of Eddie's Father* and *Julia* had only tiptoed around (or simply ignored) the bitter holdover issues of the turbulent 1960s.

America was ready for Archie Bunker.

"Meet the Bunkers" (the first episode) began quietly enough. After Archie and Edith sang "Those Were the Days" over the opening credits, the show introduced young marrieds Mike and Gloria Stivic—he liberal, she liberated, by 1971 standards anyway. The kids were planning a surprise anniversary brunch for Gloria's parents. Typical situation for a situation comedy.

Enter the parents, and exit typical. Archie, played by Carroll O'Connor in a career-defining performance, was upset that Edith (Jean Stapleton, every bit her co-star's equal) had interrupted his lazy morning. That this stalwart of blue-collar America made his debut grousing about,

> **Did You Know?**
>
> Producer Norman Lear originally wanted Mickey Rooney to play the part of Archie Bunker.

well, just about *everything*, was only the first hint of the groundbreaking series to come. Archie, it was clear from the start, was one angry man. Angry at his wife, angry at his son-in-law, angry at his church, angry at his job on the loading dock, angry at a country he no longer understood. As much as anything else, he was angry at another Sunday ruined. You didn't have to be a bigot to identify with that. He was, in fact, what series creator Norman Lear called "the bigger-than-life epitome of something that's in all of us, like it or not."

My dad (no stranger to anger there) once wondered how *All in the Family* got away with deriding the very people who made up a large part of the television audience. Particularly on the issue of Vietnam, America, circa 1971, had as many Archie Bunkers as Mike Stivics, probably more. Remember, Richard Nixon won in a landslide the year after *All in the Family* debuted.

So was the series' enormous success— 19 Emmy Awards, four spin-offs, two spin-offs of spin-offs and the No. 1 rated show for five of its nine seasons—all a liberal Hollywood plot? Certain hosts of today's right-wing shoutfests might think so. (Haven't heard Archie Bunker's voice lately? You're not listening.) I suspect a couple other elements at play. First, there was the sheer novelty of the show's topicality—it made the more madcap *Laugh-In* and *The Smothers Brothers' Comedy Hour* seem tame by comparison. Watching *All in the Family* become a cultural touchstone was exciting, even if you didn't agree with its point of view (and make no mistake, it *had* a point of view—and it wasn't Archie's). But much more important, the show was funny. Laugh out loud, phone your friends funny. The first four or five seasons were as good as sitcoms get.

Some background. *All in the Family*, the first and best of producer Lear's string of hits, was built for controversy. The history of the show is TV legend. Lear, inspired by a British sitcom called *Till Death Us Do Part*, found the perfect entertainment to explore the issues that divided the nation: race, war, feminism, religion, Watergate, hippies, gays, the economy. Putting Archie— the bigot that liberals always suspected lurked within conservative blue-collar America—under the same roof as long-haired Mike (the knee-jerk meathead of every Republican's nightmares), Lear was able to present both sides of every story. If the deck was stacked against Archie, he at least had the good sense (and secret heart) to love the females of the house: daughter Gloria, a young woman keeping step with an even younger women's movement, and Edith, the soul of the household and the series. More about Edith later.

The elements of success were there right from the start. Few sitcoms—not *Seinfeld*, not *M*A*S*H*, not *The Mary Tyler Moore Show*—have debuted so fully formed. That January Tuesday of 1971, viewers—relatively few of them, in those first weeks—saw everything that would push the show to TV's heights. Archie said "stifle" and "dingbat" and "meathead," all words that would soon enough grace countless buttons and posters and bumper stickers. He mixed up his malapropisms ("up there in his ivory shower"). He said "spics" and "spades" and "black beauties" and other epithets not otherwise heard on the airwaves. "You're the laziest white man I've ever seen," he told his son-in-law, one of the lines that scored an unprecedented amount of sitcom controversy.

Then there was the cast, one of the best in TV history. Sally Struthers as Gloria, adorable and girlish without playing dumb. Rob Reiner's Mike, his passion not yet strident, his love for Gloria, Edith and maybe even Archie smoothing over his youthful impatience.

And of course Archie and Edith. Relatively unknown despite years of character parts, O'Connor and Stapleton were so right for these roles, and seemed to play them so effortlessly, they immediately achieved the ultimate TV success (and curse): They *became* their characters. Audiences would never really accept them in any other roles.

By the series' end in 1983, a neighborhood of memorable characters had come and gone: Irene and Frank Lorenzo, Barney Heffner, Stretch Cunningham and, mostly notably of course, George, Louise and Lionel Jefferson. The Jeffersons were so popular they got their own series, which took the black family from Astoria to a deluxe apartment in the sky of Manhattan's Upper East Side.

One of the series' best episodes gave rise to another spin-off. "Cousin Maude," which aired December 11, 1971, featured the unforgettable Bea Arthur as Edith's headstrong cousin, a New Deal Democrat who could match Archie put-down for put-down. Her series, *Maude*, itself birthed another spin-off when *Good Times*, starring Esther Rolle as Maude's former housekeeper Florida Evans, debuted in 1974.

All that begetting took its toll. By Season 5, the cast seemed tired, playing to the audience, exaggerating their most identifiable character traits for easy laughs. O'Connor, Reiner and Struthers broadened their performances to vaudeville shtick, while Edith devolved into a sainted simpleton. (Watch the first few episodes and you'll be struck by how droll and less screechy Stapleton's performance was.) By the time Reiner and Struthers left the show in 1978, *All in the Family* was long out of ideas, reduced to third-rate sitcom doctoring. Was anyone surprised when a long-lost, cute-as-a-button niece showed up on the Bunker doorstep?

Classic Episode Close-Up

"Two's a Crowd"
(Original telecast: February 12, 1978)

Archie and "the Meathead"—one on one. In this memorable episode near the end of the series' eighth season (and only a month before the Stivics left the show), Archie and his liberal son-in-law, Mike, find themselves accidentally locked in the storeroom of Archie's saloon. It's an ideal setup for verbal sparring, especially after both guys turn to a whiskey bottle for solace from the wintry night . . . and from one another. They vent hostilities in a seriocomic encounter that ultimately yields to a poignant interlude: Archie's touching reflections of his childhood and memories of his father that lead Mike to feel pity and grudging respect.

A new name (*Archie Bunker's Place*), a new setting (a tavern) and new characters (none worth noting) would follow, but nothing helped. Still, the show and its loyal fans didn't deserve what producers cooked up in 1980. Stapleton wanted out, so the writers obliged by killing off Edith. When the 1980–81 season opened, Archie was coping with his grief (apparently by overacting and wearing too much pancake makeup) but the comedy never recovered. The show limped away in 1983, a drunk who'd stayed too long at the corner bar.

But let's not dwell on closing time. In its prime, *All in the Family* forced TV to grow up, made us laugh and think, and treated us like adults. It was loud and boisterous and smart and really, really hilarious. TV comedy has rarely lived up to that standard since, and maybe never really topped it. Those were the days, indeed.

Cast:

Carroll O'Connor *Archie Bunker*, **Jean Stapleton** *Edith Bunker*, **Sally Struthers** *Gloria Bunker Stivic (1971–78)*, **Rob Reiner** *Mike Stivic (1971–78)*, **Danielle Brisebois** *Stephanie Mills (1978–79)*

Ally McBeal

By Tim Holland

Broadcast History: FOX, 9/8/1997–5/20/2002
Runtime: 60 minutes
Genre: Comedy-drama

When *Ally McBeal* burst onto the scene in the fall of 1997 it was like finding a new best friend. A sexy, smart and seriously funny new best friend. David E. Kelley's quirky dramedy is one of those rare series that is populated with full-blooded, lived-in characters that viewers identify with from the get-go. Or at least viewers who have experienced the pangs of lost love, insecurity and loneliness, or the joys of new love, contentment and companionship. What makes Ally, a wistfully idealistic lawyer, so relatable is her willingness to be vulnerable and blunt and self-centered. "You know what makes my problems bigger than everyone else's?" she says. "They're mine!"

Ally (perfectly embodied by Calista Flockhart) is an attorney at Cage, Fish & Associates, a Boston law firm populated with eccentric co-workers who spend as much time gossiping and talking about their chaotic personal lives as they do interviewing clients and appearing in court. Frequently their chatter takes place in the firm's unisex bathroom, and it more often than not centers on Ally's love life—or lack of one. Although Ally frequently triumphs in the courtroom, her personal life is an ongoing disaster. One of her biggest struggles involves feelings she still has for her first love, Billy (Gil Bellows), a childhood friend and former lover who just happens to be a colleague and is married to Georgia (Courtney Thorne-Smith), a beautiful litigator at Cage, Fish & Associates.

Of course, Ally isn't the only borderline neurotic around. John "The Biscuit" Cage (2001 Emmy winner Peter Mac Nicol), one of the firm's two senior partners, is brilliant but insecure and often channels Barry White to gain confidence in approaching women. The other senior partner, Richard

Preview Review
September 13, 1997

Premise: A young, Harvard-trained lawyer takes a job working for a money-hungry former classmate, only to discover that her ex-boyfriend is working for him, too.

We Say: David E. Kelley (*Picket Fences* and *Chicago Hope*) has created another intelligent, incisive and quirky show. Voice-over narration and fantasy sequences are given a fresh spin to capture the world through the eyes of a wistful but wry young woman, played with idiosyncratic charm by Flockhart. Last minute changes to the pilot—like the addition of *Melrose Place* veteran Courtney Thorne-Smith as Gil Bellows' bride—should add even more intrigue to the plot.

Fish (Greg Germann), is a sexist moneygrubber prone to spouting "Fishisms," so-called words of wisdom, such as "Helping others is never more rewarding than when it's in your own self-interest." Their secretary, Elaine (Jane Krakowski), is a gossipy sexpot; Nelle (Portia de Rossi), nicknamed "Sub-Zero" for her icy demeanor, is, nevertheless a blonde bombshell; Ling (Lucy Liu) is the resident snob; Jennifer "Whipper" Cone (Dyan Cannon) is an aging but still voluptuous judge; and Renee (Lisa Nicole Carson) is a deputy DA and Ally's trusted roommate.

Another appealing aspect of Ally is her vivid imagination. She routinely engages in Walter Mitty–like fantasies that offer voyeuristic views of her private thoughts. Not surprisingly, many of them involve sex and take place in unusual places, such as a coffee cup. Sometimes Ally's life rivals her naughty imagination, like the time she got down and dirty in a car wash or shared a passionate lip-lock with Ling. But none of her fantasies equal the one involving her ticking biological clock, which is represented by a dancing, diaper-clad baby. The computer-generated image quickly became a pop-culture phenomenon.

The show's breakout success and its 1999 Emmy as Outstanding Comedy Series drew top-flight guest stars, such as Tracey Ullman (who nabbed her own Emmy as Ally's wacky therapist), Jacqueline Bisset, Taye Diggs, Dame Edna Everage, Farrah Fawcett, Anne Heche, Bernadette Peters, Christina Ricci and Bruce Willis. Some of Ally's memorable suitors included Robert Downey Jr., Jon Bon Jovi and Jesse L. Martin. Her parents were played by Jill Clayburgh and James Naughton.

Music was a vital part of the series and music stars routinely popped up. Los Angeles–based singer Vonda Shepard achieved popularity playing herself as the regular headliner at a bar where Ally and her cohorts hung out after work. Mariah Carey, Chubby Checker, Macy Gray, Al Green, Elton John, KC and the Sunshine Band, Gladys Knight, Barry Manilow, Randy Newman, Boz Scaggs, Sting, Tina Turner, Loudon Wainwright and, of course, Barry White all made appearances.

Since the series was built upon Ally's insecurities and her seemingly unrelenting quest for Mr. Right, the show appealed to a generous cross-section of women, but it alienated others. Feminists condemned Ally, along with her microminis, for being too fragile, too loony and too wrapped up in her search for self-worth—and a man. But none of that kept Ally from plowing forward in her never-ending pursuit, even if she and we knew that every

TV and Film Connections

Spin-off: *Ally*

one of her relationships was likely doomed to failure. As Ally once gloomily observed, "The real truth is, I probably don't want to be too happy or content. Because, then what? I actually like the quest, the search. That's the fun. The more lost you are, the more you have to look forward to. What do you know? I'm having a great time and I don't even know it."

Unfortunately, viewers themselves were having far from a great time as the series seemed to lose its bearings in its third season (Billy's divorce, hallucinations, brain tumor, death). Robert Downey Jr. was brought aboard to enliven the fourth season, and he did until his real-life legal troubles forced him from the show. As with many series created by David E. Kelley (*Picket Fences, Chicago Hope, The Practice*), *Ally* gradually devolved into a murky shadow of its former self. (In 1999 an edited half-hour version of the series that cut most

> ### Did You Know?
>
> Creator David E. Kelley's original choice for the role of Ally McBeal was Bridget Fonda.

of the courtroom scenes appeared, but vanished after three months.) The series lost its freshness and spontaneity, and became increasingly bizarre with outrageous story lines. The final one focused on the arrival of Maddie (Hayden Panettiere), a 10-year-old girl who was the result of Ally's egg donation to an infertility program. Ally took in the orphaned girl and they moved to New York City as the series concluded.

"Men are like gum," Ally once said. "After you chew they lose their flavor." Ally could have been talking about the series itself. Like a stick of gum, *Ally* was fun to unwrap and sink your teeth into. And it was juicy as hell. But after a while the flavor evaporated and you had to spit it out. Kelley once told me in an interview shortly before *Ally* debuted that the series seemed like a five-year show to him. He was right. And he was wrong. It lasted exactly five seasons, but the good taste began to wane midway through its run. It was more like a two-and-a-half-year show.

But, man, those first 50-odd episodes. Sexy. Smart. And seriously funny.

Cast:

Calista Flockhart *Ally McBeal*, **Gil Bellows** *Billy Alan Thomas (1997–2000)*, **Courtney Thorne-Smith** *Georgia Thomas (1997–2000)*, **Greg Germann** *Richard Fish*, **Lisa Nicole Carson** *Renee (1997–2001)*, **Jane Krakowski** *Elaine*, **Peter MacNicol** *John Cage*, **Lucy Liu** *Ling (1998–2002)*, **Portia de Rossi** *Nelle Porter (1998–2002)*, **Robert Downey Jr.** *Larry Paul (2000–01)*, **James LeGros** *Mark Albert (1999–2001)*, **Regina Hall** *Corretta Lipp (2001–02)*, **Josh Hopkins** *Raymond Milbury (2001–02)*, **Julianne Nicholson** *Jenny Shaw (2001–02)*, **James Marsden** *Glenn Foy (2001–02)*, **Vonda Shepard** *Herself*

The Amazing Race

By Rochell D. Thomas

Broadcast History: CBS, 9/5/2001–
Runtime: 60 minutes
Genre: Reality competition

***WWE Smackdown!* makes kids want to wrestle.** *So You Think You Can Dance* makes people want to shake a tail feather. But *The Amazing Race*? Ah, this Emmy-winning CBS reality hit not only makes couch potatoes dream of hang gliding off the cliffs of Rio de Janeiro, eating scrambled ostrich eggs in a Tanzanian village or climbing glaciers in Iceland. It gives them the itinerary to do it.

Since its launch on September 5, 2001, the show that pits 12 border-hopping pairs against each other in a $1 million clue-collecting race around the world has infected millions with serious cases of wanderlust. Watch *The Amazing Race* and you not only want to see Mongolia, you want to taste it—and maybe even dig around in its trash a bit.

"*The Amazing Race* was the experience of a lifetime," *AR*10 star Mary Conley, aka one half of Team Kentucky, told TV GUIDE. And she meant it. Before being picked for the show's cast, the 32-year-old coal miner's wife had rarely traveled more than a couple hundred miles from her family's home in Stone, Kentucky. She had no clue how to go about getting a passport. Next thing you know she and her husband, David (who'd originally applied to be on *Survivor: Cook Islands*), found themselves racing through seven countries in two weeks as one of the lucky teams. Before they were eliminated in Madagascar, they got a driver's license in India, combed through oyster farms in Vietnam and swam across a bay in Mauritius. Sure, they had to return to their four-bedroom trailer fairly empty-handed. (Though ABC's *The View* later gave them a new car and a house, among other prizes.) But I envy the impressive collection of stamps they have in their passports. Lucky Kentucky.

See, that's another thing about *The Amazing Race*: It makes you want to see places the average American doesn't and, once you're there, it makes you want to do things the average tourist can't. Now, thanks to the live-each-day-like-it's-your-last adventures of host Phil Keoghan and his teams, it's no longer good enough to just visit Japan—you've got to "drive yourself," as *AR*9ers did, to the famed Fuji-kyo Amusement Park. You can't just go to Norway. You've got to make like *AR*6ers and roller-ski through rural Voss. In short: *The Amazing Race* starts trouble.

> ### Did You Know?
>
> If teams use up their allotted money, they may beg, borrow or earn money, but they must not break local laws in the process.

The Amazing Race

Case in point: Beijing, China. In Season 10, *Racer*s made like invaders and climbed up the side of the Great Wall to get their clues. ("It was the hardest thing I've ever done," Mary said.) For the record: The Chinese government will not let just anyone scale the side of the Great Wall. I know; I've been there. And while I was in Beijing touring one of its few remaining historic Houtong neighborhoods, my guide asked if I knew what the black circular clumps were that lined the passageways of one courtyard. I answered, "Oh, that's coal," as if I see it every day. He was shocked. "Most Americans don't know what that is," he said. I just smiled. Little did he know I'd seen it three weeks earlier on *The Amazing Race.*

That's how *The Amazing Race* gets ya: It makes you feel smart for knowing trivial things. But there is a dark side to the show. As anyone who's ever contemplated sending Phil an audition tape can tell you, the show has been known to make a person rank their relationships based on which ones could survive the competitive pressure. After all, it's not easy to, say, race against other teams to find a remote village in Oman where you'll have to dig through the hot desert sand to unearth a *shuwa* (an underground oven) filled with roasting lamb you'll then be too tired to eat. San Francisco hippies B. J. and Tyler did that in *AR*9. Could I do it with my friend Linda? No, she's too easily frustrated. How about my girl Quita? No, she'd stop to get her flirt on with some Bedouin and I'd have to ditch her in the desert. Lacey?

Preview Review
September 15, 2001

Eleven teams of two—best friends; male and female; couples of all ages; straight and gay; a mother and daughter—compete in a fast-paced global race, with limited funds and no maps. Told where to go but not how to get there, the teams are strangers in strange lands, navigating their way through exotic landscapes and cultures to reach their destinations. And there, further challenges await.

We Say: The *Survivor* network has outdone itself. Upbeat in tone and visually astonishing—those bungee jumps in the jungle gorges of Africa!—*Amazing Race*'s splendidly produced first hours are an exhilarating and amusing joyride that revive one's enthusiasm for the "reality" genre.

Too fast. My sister? Too slow. My mother? Please. After much debate, I discovered that I could only do *The Amazing Race* with either my friend Maria—who wouldn't have time—or my traveling buddy Hui Hwa, who, much to my surprise, wouldn't choose me. Apparently she's got this theory about how she and her sister, who argue all the time, would make for better television. Ouch.

Yes, it hurts. But when it comes to *The Amazing Race* you've got to think about those things because that show's been known to ruin relationships. Especially romantic ones. Just ask *AR*10's Peter and Sarah. Though they'd trained for Ironman competitions together, their budding love started to nose-dive after just three days together on the series. When they were later eliminated in Kuwait, Sarah, who fans will always remember as the girl with one leg, told Phil that her soon-to-be ex was "not a very nurturing or kind individual."

AR6's Adam and Rebecca also didn't survive the show. (Who knew the guy with the hair horns was such a crybaby?) And fans prayed that married cast mates Jonathan and Victoria would call it quits after the spa owner repeatedly berated his wife and shoved her in Berlin. (The troubled couple met with Dr. Phil shortly afterward to work through their issues.)

The whole Jonathan/Victoria debacle was a shame, too, because so many more deserving people would have done much better on *The Amazing Race* than they did. After all, thousands apply each season. Unfortunately only 24 are chosen. (More for *AR8*'s lame "Family Edition." But let's not count that.) The rest of us—people who've got wanderlust but lack the border-hopping funds—will just have to figure out how to do our own versions of the show. At least that's what I did. Thanks to Google and a little *Amazing Race* inspiration, I now know that if I want to put my hands (and feet and everything) in the air and hang glide like Peggy Kuhn did off Pedra Bonita Mountain in Rio, I can go to Lookout Mountain Flight Park in Georgia. Want to climb a glacier like Grandma Mary Jean did in *AR6*? Head on over to the Davidson Glacier in Haines, Alaska (90 miles north of Juneau). And about those scrambled ostrich eggs? You can mail order one from Arizona's Rooster Cogburn Ostrich Ranch. Sure, they're poor substitutes. But, shoot, a girl's gotta do what she's gotta do to tide her over to till the next season of *The Amazing Race*.

Cast:

Phil Keoghan *Host*

American Bandstand

By Sue Tiedeck

Broadcast History: ABC, 8/5/1957–9/5/1987;
    Syndicated, 1987–1988; USA, 4/8/1989–10/7/1989
Runtime: 60 minutes
Genre: Music/dance show

For anyone who grew up in the 1950s and '60s, American Bandstand was really the only place on TV to find pop music. Certainly there were other shows that featured music, but they were boring adult fare (think *Lawrence Welk*) or only had occasional rock acts like *The Ed Sullivan Show*. *Bandstand* was designed for teens—and younger kids who aspired to be them—and became a daily destination where we could hear the latest tunes, see our favorite singers perform (lip-synch, actually, but that was good enough for me) and learn the newest dances. It was on in the afternoon (when my dad wasn't home to control the set), and my friends and I would race home from school every day. Kids across the country did, too, but those of us who lived in the Philadelphia area felt a special affinity for the show.

What went on to become the longest-running music program in U.S. TV history began in Philly on October 7, 1952, on WFIL-TV as *Bob Horn's Bandstand*, a televised version of a popular local WFIL-AM radio show. Horn's first attempt to change format, a dull collection of early music videos, bombed, but he had a hit when teenagers were invited to a live daily dance party. (The original announcer, although he was unbilled, was Ed McMahon.) Horn was fired in 1956 and replaced on July 9 of that year by another local disc jockey, that nice young man who had just moved in around the block from me in Wallingford into what's still known 50 years later as Dick Clark's house.

Clark was charming, witty and had a real rapport with both the teen dancers and the performers. He was 26 at the time, with a boyish look and enthusiasm about him that, over the next 50 years, never seemed to change. He was clean-cut and enforced the dress code Horn had mandated for dancers on the show—ties for the boys and skirts for the girls. It helped lend an air of respectability to that culturally subversive and still-suspect rock and roll. Clark added features like dance contests and "Rate-a-Record" ("it has a good beat and you can dance to it"). During his first year, he persuaded ABC executives in New York to take *Bandstand* national, and it was retitled *American Bandstand* when it began airing on 67 stations on August 5, 1957.

It didn't really change too much from what we'd been watching in Philly. Kids all over the United States seemed to enjoy *Bandstand* as much as we always had and started watching in large numbers. So large, in fact, that ABC execs could have been forgiven for breaking into their own dance when mail started pouring in, averaging more than 15,000 letters a week, and even more when votes were sent in to choose the winners of the dance contests. That might not sound like much compared to the millions of votes *American Idol* now receives, but it was a huge number for those days—more than the network was getting for its highest-rated prime-time show, *Wyatt Earp*. Plus, remember that we kids actually had to beg a stamp from our moms and go to the mailbox to send our votes to P.O. Box 5, Philadelphia.

The larger audience also enabled Clark to entice more artists to appear. The guest list in the first national season alone reads like a who's who of the music industry of the day. It was also one of the most racially diverse of any TV show of the time, since Clark insisted on including black performers. The names included Perry Como, Andy Williams, Tony Bennett, Patti Page, Fats Domino, Sam Cooke, Paul Anka, Johnny Nash, the Everly Brothers, Patsy Cline, Johnny Mathis, Connie Francis, Jackie Wilson, Teresa Brewer and Bill Haley and His Comets. Such artists as Chuck Berry, Jerry Lee Lewis, Buddy Holly and Chubby Checker got their first national exposure, and careers were launched for a trio of local Philly guys, Frankie Avalon, Fabian and Bobby Rydell, who came with the added bonus of living close enough to fill in at the last minute if another guest dropped out. There was also a duo who called themselves Tom and Jerry; they went on to bigger fame when they started using their real last names: Simon and Garfunkel.

Area teens dreamed of dancing on the show, some traveling as far as 15 miles after school to wait in line outside the WFIL studios at 46th and Market. They all hoped to gain entrance to Studio B, the small, cramped area with the hard concrete floor (which explains why the girls usually wore sneakers or flats) where the magic happened. Getting in was big, but getting fan mail was huge, giving a dancer status as a regular, meaning they'd get in without waiting in line. The most popular regulars became minor celebrities with fan clubs of their own: Arlene Sullivan and Kenny Rossi, Bunny Gibson and Eddie Kelly, Pat Molittieri, Joyce Shafer and Frani Giordano, to name a few. Justine Carelli and Bob Clayton even went on to make two records together.

Did You Know?

Despite his teen heartthrob status, Rick Nelson never performed on the show.

Of course, not everyone could be that lucky. The rest of us had to be content with watching and dancing along at home. I recall watching *Bandstand* as an interactive experience for the most part, up on my feet, either singing along or mimicking the steps and trying to learn the jitterbug, the twist, the mashed potato, the limbo, the watusi, the stroll, or one of the other dances made popular on the show.

The show also had a major impact on the music industry because an appearance meant a huge boost to a singer's career and record sales. Dick Clark's influence grew as he continually looked for new records to play, and he became involved in music publishing and record distribution. He was forced to give up those interests as a result of the payola scandal of 1959, even though he maintained that he had never accepted payment for playing a tune on the air and was never charged with criminal behavior. ABC insisted that he choose between the show and the business, and he wisely chose the show.

In September of 1963, the show changed from a daily afternoon fixture to a weekly Saturday one. In 1964, realizing that much of the recording industry had relocated to Los Angeles, Clark decided to move the show there as well (thus killing my hope of ever appearing, since I reached the minimum age of 14 that year). But the popularity continued as even more artists appeared, such as the Beach Boys, Donovan, Sonny and Cher, Martha and the Vandellas, The Supremes, Smokey Robinson and the Miracles, and the Mamas and the Papas. As the times changed, so did the music and the styles of dance, and Clark tried to stay in tune with shifting trends, even weathering the psychedelic songs of the late '60s that just weren't meant to be danced to. The '70s brought a new style—disco—and that became the focus for a while, along with new stars like Bobby Sherman and John Travolta.

Top 3 Moments

- When it moved from Philly to California.
- When Dick Clark stopped aging.
- When MTV arrived.

For more, visit www.jumptheshark.com.

In the 1980s, MTV and then VH1 were born, along with some other music outlets, and *Bandstand*'s popularity finally began to wane, even though Clark kept showcasing the latest artists, including Prince, Madonna and Jon Bon Jovi. The plug was pulled in October 1987. *The New American Bandstand*, with host David Hirsch, aired briefly on USA in 1989, but it never really caught on, and an era came to an end.

Over the course of its long run, according to music historian Richard Aquila, more than 65,000 records were played while more than 600,000 in-studio teens danced to them. The show launched many careers and almost every major performer appeared (Elvis Presley, the Beatles and the Rolling Stones were notable exceptions). It spawned countless imitators, although none were as successful. Dick Clark was inducted into the Rock and Roll Hall of Fame in 1993 for his impact on the industry. He even produced a drama series about a girl who was a regular, *American Dreams*, an apt title that pretty much sums up the way several generations of kids and musicians felt about the series that was a piece of our lives for so many years. Kids today don't know what they missed.

Cast:

Dick Clark *Host (1957–87)*, **David Hirsch** *Host (1989)*

American Idol

By Damian Holbrook

Broadcast History: FOX, 1/19/2002–
Runtime: 60 minutes
Genre: Reality competition

It was never supposed to be this big.

Not that adaptations of foreign reality shows hadn't struck gold on these shores before. Sweden's *Expedition Robinson* did just fine as our *Survivor*. And Britain's *Changing Rooms* still works as *Trading Spaces* over here. It's just . . . a UK karaoke contest? On *Fox*?

No, that was where we went for such reality messes as *Bachelorettes in Alaska* and *Who Wants to Marry a Multi-Millionaire?* Trash, not talent.

I blame it on Kelly Clarkson. I also voted for her eight times.

Based on Britain's runaway smash *Pop Idol*, the Americanized version may be the closest thing we have to a shared TV experience. Like the moon landing with cheesy ballads. And since more people tune in to the competition each week than almost every other show that airs opposite it *combined*, the series also inspires a universal dialogue that spans age ranges, racial divides . . . even networks. And for those execs who have tried to imitate the elusive magic of *Idol* on your respective nets, we thank you. Now give up.

Debuting as summer fluff in June 2002, the first season hit the ground running with its combination of ear-achingly bad auditioners and annoying hosts Ryan Seacrest and Brian Dunkleman. Adding to the train-wreck allure were the judges: faded pop star Paula Abdul, gushing record producer Randy Jackson and Brit snit Simon Cowell, whose bracingly harsh critiques had turned the overseas edition into a must-see phenomenon.

The recipe worked and Fox had an instant hit on its hands. Before you could say "you're going to Hollywood!" the series had lined up its first round of Top 10 hopefuls and filled its schedule with thrown-together *Idol* specials and encore rebroadcasts that raked in the ratings. Even more addictive than the performances were the eliminations, thanks in great part to the fact that the results were in our hands—we voted for our favorites and tuned in to make sure they were safe.

By the time Kelly Clarkson and Justin Guarini headed to the first-season finale, nearly 50 million viewers had grabbed a seat to see which one would walk off with the grand-prize recording contract and a place in TV history. Since we all know what Miss Clarkson's been up to for the past

Did You Know?

As of January 2007, former *American Idol* contestants and winners had racked up an impressive 103 No. 1 songs, according to *Billboard* magazine.

four years, it goes without saying that my call-in votes were not wasted.

That fall her debut single, "A Moment Like This," debuted at No. 52, then made a record-breaking jump to No. 1.

Since then, the series has wisely remained as close to its original format as possible, making only minor (and well-chosen) tweaks. The chemistry-free pairing of hosts Brian and Ryan was undone, with only Seacrest remaining to take on the unflinchingly ornery Cowell in an escalating battle of the barbs that now resides somewhere in the vicinity of playground name-calling and latent homophobia. Guest judges became de rigueur in the second season, where the theme nights proved a literal killing field for songbirds who couldn't cut it with classics or love songs or whatever idea the producers could come up with each week.

Also added to the mix was almost half a season of auditions. Realizing that most folks fed off of the insults being hurled by the judges—who seemed to take turns being mean—Fox front-loaded each season with extended coverage of the national tryouts. By the time the competition actually starts anymore, other network shows have debuted, tanked, been reworked, canceled and replaced by something else that is most likely on its way out as well. Especially if it had the bad luck of being scheduled opposite this juggernaut.

Of course, with great popularity comes great potential for scandal and *Idol* has had no shortage of those. While giving us the ability to swing the axe via our call-in votes, the eliminations of several Season 3 performers led to cries of jammed phone lines and "power voting" by residents of certain spared singers' home states. Then there was the sordid controversy that hovered over the fourth year after Season 2 finalist Corey Clark—ousted for hiding his arrest on domestic-abuse charges—alleged that Abdul had coached him in and out of her bedroom. She remained mum, save for a scathing spoof of the situation on *Saturday Night Live* and a release calling Clark "a liar [and] an opportunist." He went on to become even less famous than he was before. It's funny how things work out, huh?

Oddly, as *Idol*'s ratings have grown over its five years, the careers it's spawned have been hit-or-miss. After two bangin' albums, Clarkson has established a place at the top of the pop charts, while Season 4 winner Carrie Underwood has stormed the country scene with her impressive debut release. Others, including Season 2 victor Ruben Studdard, his runner-up Clay Aiken and Season 3 diva Fantasia Barrino have met with middling success. Faring even worse have been the show's tenuous off-shoots like the dismal 2003 theatrical "From Justin to Kelly" and pretty much everything from the show's most famous (and tone-deaf) evictee, William Hung. Jennifer Hudson, a runner-up from Season 3, could be the one to outshine them all, having delivered a mesmerizing, Oscar-winning turn in the 2006 feature film of *Dreamgirls*, while the fate of Season 5's underdog champ Taylor Hicks remains to be seen.

Personally, I didn't vote for him.

Cast:

Ryan Seacrest *Host*, **Brian Dunkleman** *Host (2002)*, **Paula Abdul** *Judge*, **Simon Cowell** *Judge*, **Randy Jackson** *Judge*

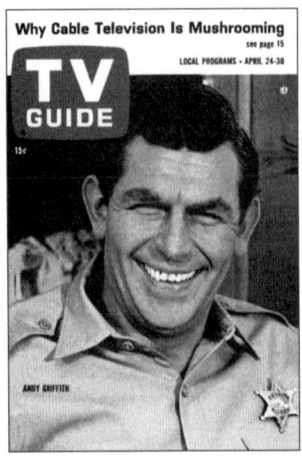

The Andy Griffith Show

By Tim Holland

Broadcast History: CBS, 10/3/1960–9/16/1968
Runtime: 30 minutes
Genre: Sitcom

The Andy Griffith Show is to TV what **It's a Wonderful Life** is to movies. George Bailey, Bedford Falls's most dedicated and revered citizen, embodies the simple but powerful message that every life is meaningful. George truly is "the richest man in town" because everyone (except, of course, Old Man Potter) loves him. He's the glue that holds the community together.

That's just what Sheriff Andy Taylor does in Mayberry, North Carolina. He's an unfailingly humble, decent and dependable go-to guy who just makes life better for everyone else. His deputy, Barney Fife, sums it up nicely when he says, "The people in [Mayberry] ain't got no better friend than Andy Taylor." Neither does the TV audience.

I grew up watching Griffith's show in the 1960s during its original eight-season run on CBS and I loved it. It probably didn't hurt that I grew up in South Carolina near a town not unlike Mayberry and that my dad was a dead ringer for Griffith. I can still relate to its characters' laid-back lifestyles, Southern-soaked hospitality and earthy mannerisms. Whenever I watch the series (which is often since my kids have discovered it on DVD and enjoy it as much as I do), it reminds me of home. But you don't have to be Southern or from a small town to appreciate *Andy Griffith*. Its warm appeal is universal.

A few years ago I interviewed Griffith and asked him why the show has endured as a classic. He said it's because "[the] central theme is love." Indeed, there's love for family, friends and one's fellow man expressed by a considerable number of endearing characters, led by Taylor himself, a widower and father to a young son, Opie (Ronny Howard). Andy is assisted in his parental chores by his lovable Aunt Bee (Frances Bavier) and assisted not so well in his law-and-order duties by his dependable but mostly inept deputy, Fife (Don Knotts). Other Mayberry regulars include barber Floyd Lawson (Howard McNear),

> ### Did You Know?
>
> At one point during the series run, one of the maps behind Andy's desk was actually a map of Nevada turned upside down.

town drunk Otis Campbell (Hal Smith), schoolteacher and Andy's future wife Helen Crump (Aneta Corsaut), Barney's girlfriend Thelma Lou (Betty Lynn), and grease-monkey cousins Goober (George Lindsey) and Gomer Pyle (Jim

Nabors, whose character was spun off at the end of the fourth season to head-line *Gomer Pyle, USMC*).

Yes, it's cherished for its genial humor and sunny optimism, but *The Andy Griffith Show* is also surprisingly shrewd and filled with lots of common-sense wisdom. Griffith made sure that each episode had a strong moral point. That doesn't mean that Andy, for all his virtues as loyal friend, respected town leader and compassionate father, is perfect. He's not. He's prone to impatient outbursts ("You beat everything, you know that!"), spreading gossip ("Barn, tell me the story about Myra Koonce") and fudging the truth, or as mountain man Ernest T. Bass likes to say, "Ask me no questions, I'll tell you no lies." But Andy's flaws make him all the more relatable.

One of the show's hallmarks is how effortlessly it shifted between comedy and drama, occasionally delving into serious themes and issues. One of its most memorable episodes, "Opie, the Birdman," opened the fourth season. Opie accidentally kills a mother bird with his slingshot. When Andy learns about it, he makes Opie, himself motherless, listen to the now orphaned baby birds outside of a bedroom window. The youngster quickly learns that being sorry doesn't always make things better so he takes on the responsibility of raising the nestlings until they are old enough to fly. When the young caregiver sets the birds free, he sadly notes that "[their] cage looks awful empty." His proud pa replies with one of my favorite lines from the series: "Yes, son, it sure does, but don't the trees seem nice and full."

> ## Preview Review
> ### September 24, 1960
>
> *The Andy Griffith Show* gives us a small-town rube named Andy, a widower, who, in his simple, homespun way, craftily outwits the city slickers every durn time (the test film was seen as a *Danny Thomas* segment last season). Andy is local sheriff, justice of the peace, newspaper editor and spouter of homilies (Andy, to reluctant bride who balks at going on honeymoon: "You can't stay here and send Wilbur off on a honeymoon alone. That's like puttin' a pig in a sty and takin' away the mud!"). This one is rife with relatives, too. Frances Bavier plays Andy's aunt; Ronny Howard his young son; Don Knotts is his deputy sheriff and cousin; and Elinor Donahue, as a pharmacist, is Andy's girl, in an antiseptic sort of way. *Debut: October 3.*

But, for me, the episode that perfectly captures the show's quiet charm—and its inspiring message—is "Man in a Hurry." In it, Malcolm Tucker (Robert Emhardt), a harried, big city businessman, is driving near Mayberry on a hot Sunday morning when his car breaks down. He walks into town and finds Andy coming out of church. Andy takes Tucker to see Wally, the town's mechanic. After Tucker describes the sound the car makes, Wally knows instantly what's wrong. However, Wally doesn't work on Sunday, forcing Tucker to spend the afternoon with the Taylors while novice mechanics Goober and Gomer try to fix the car.

Tucker suffers through a maddeningly quiet day with Andy, Barney, Opie and Aunt Bee. He can't understand why someone would waste a day sitting on a front porch just talking, strumming a guitar or rocking in a chair. "You people are living in another world!" he rants. But as the hours crawl by, Mayberry's relaxed way of life and the kindness of its citizens begin to affect him. When Gomer drives up in Tucker's repaired vehicle, the man in a hurry suddenly isn't ready to leave. He then claims to hear a disturbing noise in the engine and insists on staying the night so Wally can properly inspect the car the next morning. The episode ends with Tucker having fallen asleep in a rocking chair on Andy's front porch while attempting to peel an apple with one continuous slice.

> ## TV and Film Connections
> Spun off from *Make Room for Daddy*
> Spin-offs:
> *Gomer Pyle, USMC*
> *Mayberry R.F.D.*

More than 40 years later, Mayberry still casts the same down-home spell on viewers that won over Malcolm Tucker. The genuineness of the characters, the sly humor that flows from them, and their uncomplicated values get to you. And while the final three seasons without Don Knotts don't live up to its first five, *Andy Griffith* ended its eight-season run in 1968 No. 1 in the Nielsen rankings. (*I Love Lucy* and *Seinfeld* are the only other shows that exited on top.) Not bad for a series that spun off from an episode of *The Danny Thomas Show* in which Danny is pulled over for speeding by Sheriff Taylor. Unfortunately, the only ones who weren't won over by the series were the Emmy voters who, while giving the prize *five* times to Knotts and once to Bavier, never honored the show itself and never, inexplicably, even *nominated* Griffith.

In the end, does it matter? With or without the Emmy, *The Andy Griffith Show* has legions of faithful, adoring fans. Who can resist a series built on love that speaks to the worth of every individual and does so with such gently understated humor and sensitivity?

Cast:

Andy Griffith *Andy Taylor*, **Don Knotts** *Barney Fife (1960–65)*, **Ronny Howard** *Opie Taylor*, **Frances Bavier** *Aunt Bee*, **Elinor Donahue** *Ellie Walker (1960–65)*, **Howard McNear** *Floyd Lawson (1960–67)*, **Hal Smith** *Otis Campbell (1960–67)*, **Betty Lynn** *Thelma Lou (1960–65)*, **Parley Baer** *Mayor Stone (1962–63)*, **Jim Nabors** *Gomer Pyle (1963–64)*, **Aneta Corsaut** *Helen Crump (1964–68)*, **George Lindsey** *Goober Pyle (1965–68)*, **Jack Burns** *Warren Ferguson (1965–66)*, **Jack Dodson** *Howard Sprague (1966–68)*, **Paul Hartman** *Emmett Clark (1967–68)*

Arrested Development

By Tracy Phillips

Broadcast History: FOX, 11/2/2003–2/10/2006
Runtime: 30 minutes
Genre: Sitcom

I like the feeling of belonging to a club. It's validating and bonding, no matter how small the group. Being an *Arrested Development* fan was like being in a very exclusive club.

Arrested development, indeed. While it achieved that rare "cult status," the daringly different series suffered from viewer neglect and network mismanagement—culminating in cancellation after just three seasons—but it was far from a failure. It was, dare I say, a sitcom masterpiece.

It was in the opening lines of narration right there in the pilot episode, with the familiar voice that was instantly comforting, when I knew I was onto something I was going to love. It took only moments to decipher the source. Hey, was that the former Opie and Richie Cunningham? Why, yes it was! Oh, happy days. Ron Howard has grown into one of the most respected talents in Hollywood, and having his name attached to the credits as executive producer (and uncredited narrator) was endorsement enough for me. He is, after all, half of Imagine Entertainment along with Brian Grazer, a partnership that, besides making blockbusting, Oscar-winning movies, has quietly established a TV division that creates high-quality series, like *AD*, *Sports Night*, *Felicity* and *24*.

If Ron Howard is the godfather of the series, creator and writer Mitchell Hurwitz is its heart, soul and genius. Not that most of the Bluth family had much heart, but you laughed at (and therefore loved) them anyway, and that was the genius part. They could easily have been unlikable, those over-privileged oddballs.

The Bluths were a dynastic dysfunctional family, whose wealth was derived from a real-estate developing business, until the patriarch was busted by the SEC for fraud, and all assets were frozen—sending the never-worked-a-day-in-their-lives clan into independence (aka freak-out mode). The family's financial fall from grace brought them together, in a manner of speaking; they were forced to live in one of the company's model homes, a perfectly ironic location to launch the skewering of the needy and the greedy. There was mama Lucille the lush (Jessica Walter) and jailbird dad George Sr. (Jeffrey Tambor); level-headed family wrangler Michael (Jason Bateman) and his adorably awkward teenaged son, George Michael (Michael Cera); man-child "brother" Buster

(Tony Hale); not-so-magical magician Gob (Will Arnett); Michael's spoiled twin sister, Lindsay (Portia de Rossi), a rebel without a clue but plenty of causes (she's an activist for just about *anyone* causing opposition); her sexually ambiguous doctor-turned-aspiring-actor husband, Tobias (David Cross); and their precocious, pouty daughter, Maeby (Alia Shawkat). And I can't leave out the hilarious cast addition of their adopted Asian brother, Annyong (the family named him that because he kept saying it—it means "hello"). An entertaining ensemble of spot-on performers, there wasn't a weak one in the bunch.

The show's stabilizing force came from an unlikely source: the centerpiece of the gang, Jason Bateman (the superbrat from *The Hogan Family* and *Silver Spoons*). While he avoided the indignities of many a child star, he was still considered a comeback kid, and Bateman quickly proved to be—pardon the (totally warranted) cliché—a revelation. His deadpan delivery and impeccable timing combined with a reserved charm and handsomeness to put him at the top of everyone's talked-about list. I had an instant crush.

Word on the superb show got out *inside* the industry at least, and it developed such cachet, they had many willing participants for cameos: Claudia Schiffer, Thomas Jane, *Desperate Housewives* creator Marc Cherry, Harry Hamlin, Andy Richter, Frankie Muniz, Jamie Kennedy, Richard Belzer, John Larroquette, William Hung and Judge Reinhold. They also brought their friends and families along for the ride, including Ron Howard's *Happy Day* pals Henry Winkler and Scott Baio, both playing lawyers. Will Arnett's real-life wife, Amy Poehler of *SNL* fame, had a brief stint as "Wife of Gob"; and Bateman worked his family ties with sister Justine, who appeared as possible long-lost sister Nellie Bluth. They were only part of a guest-star parade that also included Liza Minnelli, Ben Stiller, Zach Braff, Heather Graham, Martin Short, Julia Louis-Dreyfus, Carl Weathers, Martin Mull, Ione Skye, James Lipton and Charlize Theron.

Did You Know?

Tobias's "nevernude" condition is a real psychological affliction known as gymnophobia, an abnormal and persistent fear of nudity.

Stars aside, what truly made this series shine was the quality, highbrow writing not often seen in TV today. You've got to admire a show that can successfully work in kissing cousins, Saddam Hussein and a broad range of other eccentricities (a stair car, a "never nude" phobia, a frozen-banana stand?) into its overarching plotlines. Smarter still were the inside jokes embedded in the dialogue, including self-mockery at their low ratings.

In its first year, the show took home the Emmy for Best Comedy. But viewers still tuned out like rebellious teens resisting wisdom-spouting parents; the more critics said, "You should watch this," the more the show was ignored. It didn't help that a panicked Fox, notorious for canceling promising-yet-underperforming shows, played musical time slots with the show, giving viewers another excuse to miss out on the funny—they couldn't find it even if they tried. After preemptions, reduced episode orders and ultimately fruitless interest expressed by Showtime and ABC in taking it over, the series was put to sleep with a few satisfyingly tied-up twists.

Perhaps there is this silver lining: In going before its time, *Arrested Development* at least went before it was creatively ruined. Like rock and movie stars taken in their prime—thereby reinforcing their legend—these memorable sitcom characters similarly live on, cherished. So, too, (on DVD) will the three perfect seasons of *Arrested Development*.

Cast:

Jason Bateman *Michael Bluth*, **Michael Cera** *George Michael Bluth*, **Jeffrey Tambor** *George Bluth Sr./Oscar Bluth*, **Jessica Walter** *Lucille Bluth*, **Will Arnett** *George Oscar "Gob" Bluth II*, **Tony Hale** *Buster Bluth*, **Portia de Rossi** *Lindsay Funke*, **David Cross** *Tobias Funke*, **Alia Shawkat** *Mae "Maeby" Funke*, **Ron Howard** *Narrator*

Batman

By Rich Sands

Broadcast History: ABC, 1/12/1966–3/14/1968
Runtime: 30 minutes
Genre: Action/adventure

The fact that ABC's campy *Batman* series was nothing like the brooding, humorless comic-book character it was based on may have been—and may continue to be—a sore spot to the hardcore fan. But the reality is, for most Americans, the flamboyant antics of Adam West and Burt Ward as Batman and Robin are the quintessential embodiment of the characters. Sure, the Dark Knight wasn't very dark during the show's 1966–68 run. In fact, this might be the most colorful incarnation in Batman's history: with brightly hued blasts of BAM!, POW! and THWACK! illustrating his smackdowns with an equally vibrant rogue's gallery, the show was a Technicolor typhoon.

A thumping Neal Hefti theme and outlandish plots helped, but it was an eclectic roster of guest-star villains who were largely responsible for the fun. Among those who found themselves foiled by the Caped Crusader were Burgess Meredith as the Penguin, Cesar Romero as the Joker, Vincent Price as Egghead, Ethel Merman as Lola Lasagne, Roddy McDowall as the Bookworm, Tallulah Bankhead as the Black Widow, Joan Collins as Siren, the Emmy-nominated Frank Gorshin as the Riddler, Milton Berle as Louie the Lilac, Zsa Zsa Gabor as Minerva, Victor Buono as King Tut and, of course, the twin bill of Julie Newmar, then Eartha Kitt as Catwoman. (Former Miss America Lee Meriwether played the feline fatale in a feature-film version of the series.)

Helping Batman outwit these outrageous foes were an endless array of gadgets (including Batarangs, a Bat shield, a Bat knife, Bat sleeping gas, a Bat Geiger counter and the cure-all universal Bat antidote), many stored in an indispensable utility belt. In his secret Batcave, nestled under stately Wayne Manor, he relied on a seemingly ahead-of-its-time Bat computer to help solve cases. And when Police Commissioner Gordon (Neil Hamilton) called or a Bat alert flashed, Batman and Robin could quickly jump to the atomic-battery powered Batmobile, one of TV's most iconic cars.

Given the initial intense interest in the show, and its twice-weekly airings (two-part episodes on Wednesdays and Thursdays for the first two seasons) it's not surprising that *Batman*—a Top 10 sensation in its first year—burned out on an accelerated schedule. In the fall of 1967 Batgirl joined the cast. In her skintight purple spandex and flaming red hair, the Dark Knight Damsel added some sizzle to the show. "I don't like to mess with success," *Batman* producer Howie Horwitz told TV GUIDE in 1967, "but we think adding a Batgirl freshens up the show. We figure we already got the kids, boys and girls, up to 8. But girls over 8 need someone . . . to identify with." Horwitz then pointedly added: "I rather think big boys will like to watch her, too."

Indeed, Batgirl—the alter-ego of Commissioner Gordon's precocious daughter, Barbara—was a spitfire, helping the Dynamic Duo fight crime and simultaneously exposing their general haplessness with the fairer sex. In one episode, after rescuing the pair from certain doom, she credited her success to "the one thing you couldn't possibly have in your utility belt, Batman: a woman's intuition."

Did You Know?

Before Julie Newmar was cast as Catwoman, Suzanne Pleshette was considered for the role.

But alas, even Batgirl wasn't enough and after three seasons the show was canceled. Thankfully for fans old and new the show has had a healthy life in syndication, even if it's not always on the same Bat time, same Bat channel.

Cast:

Adam West Bruce Wayne/Batman, **Burt Ward** Dick Grayson/Robin, **Alan Napier** Alfred Pennyworth, **Madge Blake** Aunt Harriet Cooper (1966–67), **Neil Hamilton** Police Commissioner Gordon, **Stafford Repp** Chief O'Hara, **Yvonne Craig** Barbara Gordon/Batgirl (1967–68)

Battlestar Galactica

By G. J. Donnelly

Broadcast History: Sci Fi, 1/14/2005–
Runtime: 60 minutes
Genre: Sci-fi

In 1978, the *Star Wars* sci-fi craze was in full swing and television wanted a piece of the action. ABC turned to producer Glen A. Larson, who created an ambitious, mythic space adventure called *Battlestar Galactica*. In it the survivors of a decimated civilization called the 12 Colonies search for a legendary planet—Earth—while trying to dodge a race of android predators. The only thing standing between this "ragtag fugitive fleet" and utter annihilation was a solitary interstellar warship called the *Galactica*.

Although the premise was good and the production values and special effects (by *Star Wars* whiz John Dykstra) top notch, *Galactica*'s potential was undermined by toothless drama, formula scripts and cardboard characters. Even as a kid I remember thinking that this was a series I wanted to like—I even had a toy Viper fighter at one stage—but it just didn't pack enough of a dramatic wallop. The result was a multimillion-dollar flop (the pilot alone cost a then unheard of $3 million) that limped through two seasons before completing its run as *Galactica 1980*. Star Richard Hatch—who played Apollo—continued to carry the *Galactica* torch, hoping to spark interest in a revival.

It finally arrived as a riveting 2003 cable miniseries that used the original premise as a springboard to examine complex political, moral and social issues. In 2005, *Galactica* returned as a full-fledged series with even Hatch signing on as a suspected terrorist with designs on President Roslin's office. The show's pale, almost chromatic photography seems to emphasize its penchant for gray areas. Similarly, dogfights in the vacuum of space are played out in stark fashion with minimal sound effects, further emphasizing the show's naturalistic tone.

> ### Did You Know?
>
> In his teens, star Edward James Olmos became lead singer in a rock band he named Pacific Ocean, which released a record in 1968.

This *Galactica* is a decidedly grim saga that portrays the Cylons as androids that rebel against their human creators, who are helpless to defend themselves after their computer defenses are sabotaged. Thanks to its obsolescence, the old ship *Galactica* manages to escape destruction. Its flinty commander, William Adama (Edward James Olmos), realizing the situation is hopeless, decides to save the humans that remain.

Unlike Lorne Greene's avuncular version, Olmos's Adama is blunt, pragmatic and doesn't put much stock in myths. His principal foil is Laura Roslin (Mary McDonnell), a minor cabinet official who ascends to the presidency after the government is destroyed. Although a shrewd and tough-minded leader, Roslin takes the spiritual beliefs of her people seriously and is convinced that she has been fated to lead the survivors to the mythical planet Earth. These two butt heads initially, but develop a deep-seated bond as the series goes on.

One of their biggest ongoing problems is that, in this version, the Cylons can infiltrate the *Galactica*'s ranks by taking human form, as in the case of pilot Sharon "Boomer" Valerii (Grace Park). In fact, virtually all of the original *Galactica* characters receive substantial makeovers. Carousing flyboy Starbuck—once played by *The A-Team*'s Dirk Benedict—is now a brash, brawling fly-*woman* (Katee Sackhoff). The new Apollo (Jamie Bamber) shares a love-hate bond with his father, Adama. The professional competence of executive officer Col. Tigh (Michael Hogan) is often at odds with his fondness for the bottle. Brilliant but cowardly scientist Baltar (James Callis)—whose negligence allowed the Cylon attack to succeed—is putty in the hands of sexy Cylon agent Number Six (Tricia Helfer), who resides in his brain!

TV and Film Connections

Remake of a 1978–80 series of the same name

Over the next three seasons, the crew endures one crisis after another as they try to stay one step ahead of the Cylons. Roslin is diagnosed with terminal breast cancer (she survives) and loses a presidential election to Baltar. Adama barely cheats death after Boomer guns him down on the *Galactica* bridge. Later, in captivity, Boomer gives birth to a Cylon-human hybrid, which Roslin tries to keep hidden from her. The *Galactica* has a surprise encounter with a sister ship from the Colonial fleet, the *Pegasus*, which Apollo takes control of after Six murders its commander. Baltar convinces the survivors to put down stakes on an uninhabited planet called New Caprica, which is soon conquered by the Cylons. Worse, several of the humans—Baltar included—collaborate with their captors. Eventually Adama comes to their rescue, but then has to deal with a divided fleet.

Galactica's parallels to real-life situations (including the war in Iraq) are chilling. Executive producer Ronald D. Moore said the series' re-imagining was inspired by 9/11 and it shows. This *Galactica* frequently addresses such sensitive issues as suicide bombings, prisoner torture and political radicalism. Yet the writers usually succeed in shining a sympathetic light on these space insurgents, whose main priority is the survival of their race. Even the Cylons aren't always cold-blooded—indeed Six seems to have developed a genuine affection for the duplicitous Baltar.

Battlestar Galactica, at its best, is a visceral, cerebral adventure that, like *The Twilight Zone* and *Star Trek* before it, adroitly uses the medium of science fiction to dramatize social issues. However, unlike those series, *Galactica* always maintains a high level of realism within its own universe. The series' combination of deft writing, strong characters and pointed commentary quickly drew an avalanche of critical acclaim that culminated in a 2006 Peabody Award. Certainly more plaudits are to come, along with more periods of struggle and sacrifice for the gallant crew. A spin-off called *Caprica* has also been proposed. It would chronicle life on the 12 Colonies before the Cylon attack.

Until then, we *Galactica* fans will have to be content to follow our favorite battlestar as it explores the biggest gray area of all: the universe.

Cast:

Edward James Olmos *Cdr. William Adama,* **Mary McDonnell** *President Laura Roslin,* **Jamie Bamber** *Capt. Lee "Apollo" Adama,* **Katee Sackhoff** *Lt. Kara "Starbuck" Thrace,* **James Callis** *Dr. Gaius Baltar,* **Tricia Helfer** *Number Six,* **Grace Park** *Sharon "Boomer" Valerii,* **Michael Hogan** *Col. Saul Tigh,* **Aaron Douglas** *CPO Galen Tyrol,* **Tahmoh Penikett** *Lt. Karl "Helo" Agathon*

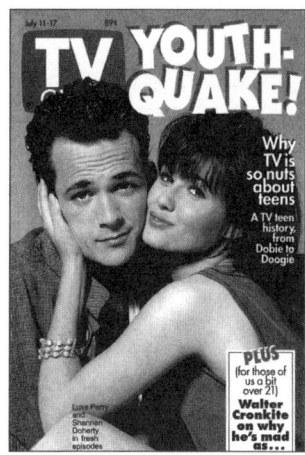

Beverly Hills, 90210

By Nerina Rammairone
Broadcast History: FOX, 10/4/1990–5/17/2000
Runtime: 60 minutes
Genre: Drama

In the fall of 1990, my attire consisted of faded jeans and an array of windbreakers. (The cold came early that year.) But what I wished, *really* wished, I could wear was that sexy scoop neck black bodysuit and wide white belt Brenda Walsh wore on *Beverly Hills, 90210*.

And it wasn't just the show's trendy threads I was drooling over. The fast cars, the sunny locales, the impossibly laid-back parents, the too-cool-for-school teachers and all that sex . . . who *were* these kids? Was this truly how the other half lived?

Reality or not, I couldn't get enough of Aaron Spelling's prime-time teen soap—and this middle-class Brooklyn girl wasn't alone. When it debuted on Fox on October 4, 1990, Spelling's series sent a ripple through every cafeteria in America. Trapper Keepers featuring the faces of cutie newcomers Luke Perry and Jason Priestley peeked out of every backpack. Cast shots hung in every locker. There were collector cards, lunchboxes, pillowcases and dolls. (Yep, I have one.)

Why the phenomenon? Because the legendary producer had once again mixed a magic brew. He took two wholesome kids from Minnesota, teen twins Brenda and Brandon Walsh, dropped them into the excess and glam of Beverly Hills and let them run amok. The result? A fish-out-of-water story with sex appeal. Spelling hand-delivered the much-desired 18-to-34 demographic to Madison Avenue, and Fox reaped the rewards.

But for us teens, it was all about the insanely rich and ridiculously beautiful brat pack at the center of the series:

Preview Review
September 15, 1990

"You make one false move and you're history." A line from a crime drama? No, it's just Kelly, a student at West Beverly High, telling a newcomer how things work at this school. The new student is Brenda Walsh, whose family just moved to Beverly Hills. Kelly continues: "I mean, if people saw you eating lunch alone today like that guy . . ." Brenda looks where Kelly is pointing. 'That guy' is none other than her twin brother, Brandon, the other new kid in school. Back in Minneapolis, Brandon was Mr. Popularity. Now they've transferred to a high school unlike any other in the world. Their classmates are the privileged children of celebrities and tycoons: Steve Sanders, for instance, is the son of a TV star. These kids drive Porsches, BMWs and Jaguars. Brandon and Brenda are in the fast lane—in an older economy car. Can they keep up? And do they want to?

boy next door Brandon Walsh (Priestley), his bad-girl-on-the-verge sis Brenda (Shannen Doherty), prom queen Kelly Taylor (Jennie Garth), tortured rich boy Dylan McKay (Perry), dork-turned-music producer David Silver (Brian Austin Green), jock Steve Sanders (Ian Ziering), nerdy newspaper reporter Andrea Zuckerman (Gabrielle Carteris) and virginal goofball Donna Martin (Tori Spelling). These high schoolers experienced everything we did, all the insecurities and angst, but they did it wearing Gucci. Their struggles, though hyper-stylized and set to a Top 40 soundtrack, gave us a voice. When Brenda had sex for the first time after the Spring Fling, parent groups protested. And we cried, "Wake up call!" Kids were—hello!—having sex. Teen suicide, violence, date rape, anorexia, drug abuse and alcoholism were on the rise. *90210* hit every one of those issues at a time when no other show dared. (OK, so those pat PSAs at the end of some of the "very special episodes" were a bit much, but at least the show had a conscience.)

> ### TV and Film Connections
> Spin-off:
> *Melrose Place*
> (which spun off *Models Inc.*)

And *90210* did it without sacrificing all the delicious drama—and, let's be honest, cheese—that comes with being a soap opera. To keep the momentum of the show's saucy story lines going Fox, in a genius move, ran original episodes throughout the summer of 1991. There wasn't a single person I knew who didn't tune in to watch Dylan and Kelly give in to their attraction and ultimately hook up in the pool of The Beverly Hills Beach Club.

In the years that followed the show lost some key players (bye-bye, Brenda) and gained a sense of humor ("Donna Martin Graduates!"). New cast members came along to stir up trouble: Jamie Walters, Tiffani-Amber Thiessen, Jason Wiles, Vanessa Marcil, future double Oscar winner Hilary Swank. And music guests rocked the Peach Pit After Dark. (Color Me Badd, what's become of you?)

> ### Did You Know?
> The show's original title was *The Class of Beverly Hills*.

On May 17, 2000, after 10 years, the series signed off with the wedding of on-again, off-again couple Donna and David. The college grads, minus, ironically, twins Brenda and Brandon, gathered to toast their pals and we did too. My friends and I got together for one last Wednesday-night rendezvous. We were college grads, too—some of us soon to be married as well. We said goodbye to the gang we had wished so much to be a part of. They laughed and they cried and they lived and they learned and they were, through it all, still friends. Apart from our ZIP codes, I guess we weren't that different after all.

Beverly Hills, 90210

Cast:

Jason Priestley *Brandon Walsh (1990–98)*, **Shannen Doherty** *Brenda Walsh (1990–94)*, **Luke Perry** *Dylan McKay (1990–95; 1998–2000)*, **Jennie Garth** *Kelly Taylor*, **Ian Ziering** *Steve Sanders*, **Tori Spelling** *Donna Martin*, **Brian Austin Green** *David Silver*, **Gabrielle Carteris** *Andrea Zuckerman (1990–95)*, **Carol Potter** *Cindy Walsh (1990–95)*, **James Eckhouse** *Jim Walsh (1990–95)*, **Joe E. Tata** *Nat Bussichio*, **Douglas Emerson** *Scott Scanlon (1990–91)*, **Mark Damon Espinoza** *Jesse Vasquez (1993–95)*, **Tiffani-Amber Thiessen** *Valerie Malone (1994–98)*, **Kathleen Robertson** *Clare Arnold (1994–97)*, **Jamie Walters** *Ray Pruit (1994–95)*, **Vincent Young** *Noah Hunter (1997–2000)*, **Hilary Swank** *Carly Reynolds (1997–98)*, **Lindsay Price** *Janet Sosna (1998–2000)*, **Daniel Cosgrove** *Matt Durning (1998–2000)*, **Vanessa Marcil** *Gina Kincaid (1998–99)*

Bewitched

By Greg Evans

Broadcast History: ABC, 9/17/1964–7/1/1972
Runtime: 30 minutes
Genre: Sitcom

I Dream of Jeannie. The Flying Nun. My Favorite Martian.

Fine lunchboxes, each and every one. But now about those shows . . .

To watch Jeannie or Sister Bertrille or Uncle Martin today, most likely on one of the various cable channels that exist so people of my generation can escape from any present-day misery, is to feel enormous pride in just how very, very much you've matured over the years. I know these were silly shows. I know that was their point. But I also know why the phrase "idiot box" took hold in the '60s.

You're thinking I'm a grouch, a man too old and bitter to appreciate TV's more fanciful pleasures. To which I say: *Bewitched*.

I fell in love with that show before Tabitha was born, back when I believed that a Scholastic Books paperback compendium of magic tricks would have me floating heavy household objects with the wave of a hand. I didn't bother to learn the lame card tricks after the book arrived in the homeroom mail, yet I didn't give up on *Bewitched*. Even after the new Darrin.

Years later (decades, actually), when the latter of the series' 252 episodes were aired in syndication, I was hard-pressed to dredge up any fondness for the show. The formulaic, endlessly rehashed plots were tiresome even by aging sitcom standards—just how many historical figures could be summoned to wreak havoc on McMahon & Tate, anyway? Dick Sargent—that new Darrin—was even more mirthless than I recalled, and given how worn out the show was, who could blame him?

And then, in June of 2005, Sony released *Bewitched*'s first season on DVD. Redemption, in beautiful black and white.

Bewitched debuted September 17, 1964, sandwiched on ABC's Thursday night lineup between *My Three Sons* and *Peyton Place*. Veronica Lake fans might have felt déjà vu—though not an adaptation, *Bewitched* looked more than a little like Lake's 1942 comedy, *I Married a Witch*, right down to the blond hair and impish beauty of its star, five-time Emmy nominee Elizabeth Montgomery.

The daughter of actor Robert Montgomery, 30-year-old Elizabeth

> ## Did You Know?
>
> Some viewers protested before the 1964 premiere of *Bewitched*, fearing that the show was going to promote devil worship.

and her producer husband, William Asher (who'd made his career as a director of *I Love Lucy*), were shopping around a script about a young bride who happened to be rich. Meanwhile, another producer, Harry Ackerman, had just hired a writer named Sol Saks to develop a series about a young bride who happened to be a witch. When Ackerman met with the Ashers, the project became *The Witch of Westport*. Later, someone had the wisdom to change the title to *Bewitched*.

Smart, mischievous, funny and sweet, Montgomery's performance was a charmer. The witch bride who's promised to give up magic for her loving, mortal husband, Samantha Stephens was a role that could have gone too cute, too dumb or both (take a look at *I Dream of Jeannie*). But Montgomery was too smart an actress for that. Especially in the early episodes, *Bewitched* was silly, of course, but also warm. There's a scene in the 1965 episode "A Is for Aardvark" in which Montgomery seems to be crying genuine tears as Samantha receives a simple, human gift—an inexpensive watch, some flowers—from Darrin. Few sitcoms of the day were as tender.

Preview Review
September 19, 1964

Bewitched has the lovely Elizabeth Montgomery as a young suburban housewife–witch who can make the crockery follow her around the kitchen instead of vice versa. Young husband Dick York, quite naturally, is confused by it all. For one thing, he has a mother-in-law who's the archetype of her class—she really is a witch, and like most mothers-in-law, she opposed the match from the beginning. "This nice normal boy," she thinks, might be a corrupting influence on her daughter. Despite her mother's warning that "He's probably prejudiced . . . ," the young witch breaks the news. Says York to a bartender sadly: "My wife's a witch; what'll I do?" Replies the bartender: "You should see *my* wife." *Debut: September 17.*

And Montgomery had help. Lots of it. As Darrin, the ad man frantic to keep his wife's secret a secret, Dick York played a character that should have been thoroughly unlikable—a stuffed, starched white shirt too unimaginative to grasp the wonderful possibilities of the magic life. Darrin *was* the 1950s, red-faced with panic and anger at the freaks and free spirits drifting through his suburban walls. Who could love him?

Samantha did, of course, and because York played him, the wifely devotion was easy to figure. The rubber-faced York, whose comic touch can't be praised enough, made Darrin seem like the kind of guy who really wanted to loosen that necktie and tell his overbearing in-laws to back the hell off, but, hey, times don't change so easily for everyone. York's Darrin was a decent, average guy in a very un-average decade. And he really, really loved his wife. He got lots of points for that alone.

Darrin also had a soft spot for the befuddled Aunt Clara and, on occasion, the practical-joking Uncle Arthur, two of the recurring characters that made *Bewitched* a showcase for some of Hollywood's most unforgettable character actors. Among them: Marion Lorne (the sweet Clara), Paul Lynde (who, as the bitchy Uncle Arthur, single-handedly introduced camp to America), Alice

Pearce (the first and best Gladys Kravitz) and David White (who, as Darrin's boss Larry Tate, was crucial to the show's adult appeal).

The list goes on: George Tobias as the henpecked Abner Kravitz; Mabel Albertson as Darrin's sour-faced mom; Maurice Evans, who brought his Shakespearean training to Samantha's hammy, tuxedoed warlock father; Alice Ghostley's Esmeralda; Kasey Rogers's Louise Tate; Sandra Gould (who took over as Gladys when Pearce died in 1966); Erin Murphy as little Tabitha. Could any other series of the time boast a roster of guest stars as eclectic (and transatlantic) as *Bewitched*'s Estelle Winwood, Mercedes McCambridge, Reginald Ower and a pre–*Brady Bunch* Maureen McCormick?

And, no, I haven't forgotten—I've merely saved the best for last. In 1964, Agnes Moorehead was one of Hollywood's more highly regarded character actresses, a veteran of Orson Welles' Mercury Theater Players best known for her performances in *Citizen Kane*, *The Magnificent Ambersons* and the radio classic *Sorry, Wrong Number*.

Not a lot of comedy on that résumé, which I think explains why the flinty Moorehead was such an inspired choice to play Endora, Samantha's mother. Endora wasn't exactly a children-cooking wicked witch, but she certainly was haughty, ultrasophisticated and loath to suffer fools (especially mortal ones) gladly. Her disapproval of the Stephens's mixed marriage embodied the comedy's central conflict, as Endora (that name came from the Book of Samuel's Witch of Endor, apparently chosen by the devoutly Christian Moorehead) conjured up all sorts of magical mischief for the hapless Darrin. As for Endora's own marriage (to the wandering warlock Maurice), surely it was TV's most worldly union, something just short of Noel Coward.

TV and Film Connections

Inspired a 2005 feature film of the same name

Spin-off: *Tabitha*

But even the urbane Moorehead couldn't stave off the show's inevitable decline. In fairness, *Bewitched* got more mileage out of its gimmicky premise than could ever have been expected. By the time Dick Sargent replaced York in 1969 (the show's sixth of eight seasons), *Bewitched* was just going through the motions. It would last three more seasons, until 1972, but its magical days were gone. And I don't think Sargent was entirely to blame. For me, the show lost something when it switched from black and white to color in its third season. This odd little gem of a sitcom—whose premise was retooled for 1977–78's *Tabitha*, which centered on the Stephens's daughter and starred Lisa Hartman and Robert Urich—went from winsome to garish then, its breezy little spell broken.

Cast:

Elizabeth Montgomery Samantha Stephens/Serena, **Dick York** Darrin Stephens (1964–69), **Dick Sargent** Darrin Stephens (1969–72), **Agnes Moorehead** Endora, **David White** Larry Tate

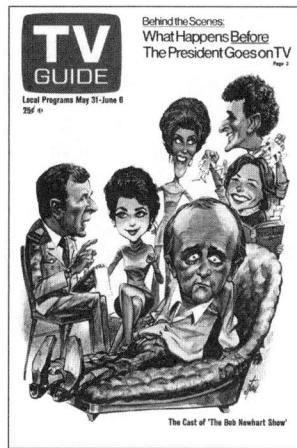

The Cast of 'The Bob Newhart Show'

The Bob Newhart Show

By Megan Walsh-Boyle

Broadcast History: CBS, 9/16/1972–4/1/1978
Runtime: 30 minutes
Genre: Sitcom

Let us pause to consider a candidate for television's longest underrated genius, and I say: What about Bob?

Part of possibly the greatest comedy lineup in TV history, from 1973 to '74, *The Bob Newhart Show* shared Saturday nights on CBS with *All in the Family*, *M*A*S*H*, *The Mary Tyler Moore Show* and *The Carol Burnett Show*. All of these series were Emmy winners and Top 10 hits, with one exception: *The Bob Newhart Show*. But that doesn't make this sitcom any less an enduring and beloved gem.

Newhart, with his impeccable timing and distinctively deadpan style, started out writing and performing skits on radio while keeping his day job as an accountant in Chicago. He received his big break with the release of his Grammy-winning 1960 album, *The Button-Down Mind of Bob Newhart*, which became the first comedy recording to top the Billboard LP charts (beating out Elvis Presley and the soundtrack to *The Sound of Music*). A 1961–62 variety series for NBC also titled *The Bob Newhart Show* garnered Newhart an Emmy (incredibly, the only one of his long and prosperous TV career) and a Peabody Award.

For the 1970s *Bob Newhart Show*, Newhart brought the famous stammering everyman shtick that endeared him to fans of his stand-up routine to the role of Chicago psychologist Bob Hartley. The serene Bob, surrounded by loony patients and needy friends, drew laughs as the straight man reacting to the craziness around him. The laid-back doc and his smart and sexy schoolteacher wife, Emily (Emmy nominee Suzanne Pleshette)—possibly the only character on the show saner than Bob—were in a very modern marriage. Bob and Emily were equal partners who were perfectly content to be childless while living in their fashionable high-rise.

Complicating life for them were ever-present neighbor Howard Borden (former *I Dream of Jeannie* sidekick Bill Daily), a childlike, divorced airline pilot who was always popping in on the Hartleys; and Bob's co-workers, self-centered swinging single orthodontist Jerry Robinson (Peter Bonerz, who went on to become a successful TV director for shows including *Murphy Brown*, *Home Improvement* and *Friends*) and wisecracking receptionist Carol Kester (Marcia Wallace, aka the voice of Mrs. Krabappel on *The Simpsons*). As for Bob's patients, seldom have head cases been more endearing, ranging from the meek and mild-mannered Mr. Peterson (John Fielder) to the sarcastic and neurotic Elliot Carlin (Jack Riley), a man who could drive even a psychologist crazy.

Created and produced by Lorenzo Music and David Davis, who had been writers on *The Mary Tyler Moore Show*, the humor was sly, sophisticated and, at times, wonderfully surreal. *The Bob Newhart Show* never insulted the intelligence of its viewers. It avoided slapstick and off-color jokes (it was the '70s, remember), instead relying on sharp writing and Newhart's self-deprecating and extremely likeable manner. "We were selling class and charm and wit," Davis said. And viewers were buying.

Newhart incorporated a trademark bit from his stand-up act, his one-sided telephone conversations; and his character's bedtime conversations with Emily showcased the effortless chemistry between Newhart and the charming Pleshette. One of their most famous exchanges wasn't on *The Bob Newhart Show*, but on 1990's final episode of his other long-running hit, *Newhart*, when Bob wakes up in bed with Pleshette's Emily saying, "You won't believe the dream I just had . . . I was an innkeeper in this crazy little town in Vermont," implying that the 1982–90 series was just a fantasy in the mind of the 1970s character. In 1997, TV GUIDE deemed this "unquestionably, the cleverest sitcom finale in TV history."

Classic episodes of *The Bob Newhart Show* include one in which Bob nearly falls down an elevator shaft and has thoughts of mortality. "Death Be My Destiny," No. 50 on TV GUIDE's List of the Top 100 Episodes of All Time, is a deft blend of the dramatic and daffy that has a great running gag about the correct name of the Grim Reaper, from Uncle Death to Old Father Time. "I felt icy fingers up and down my spine," says Bob of his experience. "That wasn't death," Emily reassures him. "That's Old Black Magic." Ranking No. 9 on that same list of 100 is "Over the River and Through the Woods," a memorable Thanksgiving episode (directed by James Burrows) that finds Bob and pals Howard and Jerry swigging grain alcohol while watching football on TV. Soon things get loco. Smashed, starving and facing a frozen bird, the guys consider cooking the gobbler at 2,000 degrees for

Did You Know?

Newhart agreed to do the show on two conditions: he and Emily were to have no kids, and he had to be a psychologist not a psychiatrist, so as not to poke fun at truly mentally ill people.

a half hour—but the oven only heats to 500. "Then we'll use four ovens," suggests Howard. That's when they decide to call out for Chinese food—to be precise, for "Moo Goo Goo Goo Gai Pan." And lots of it.

The Bob Newhart Show had the unfortunate luck to come along during a glut in quality sitcoms. (We should be so lucky to have such a problem today.) In 1977, the only year it was nominated for the Best Comedy Emmy, it faced stiff competition from *All in the Family*, *Barney Miller*, *M*A*S*H* and that year's winner, *The Mary Tyler Moore Show*. During its original run, *The Bob Newhart Show* maintained respectable ratings, placing among the Top 30 series its first four seasons. A new generation became familiar with the show in the 1980s and '90s through repeated airings on Nick at Nite and TV Land. The show even inspired a college drinking game, in which players chug beer every time a character utters the phrase "Hi, Bob"—which happens often.

In recent years, Newhart seems finally to be receiving his critical due. He was inducted into the Academy of Television Arts and Sciences Hall of Fame in 1993, and in 1996 TV GUIDE ranked him No. 17 among the 50 greatest TV stars of all time. In October 2002, Newhart received the Kennedy Center's fifth Mark Twain Prize for American Humor, and, in 2004, TV Land erected a life-size bronze statue of Bob Hartley in Chicago. Now in his seventies, he still tours and has widened his appeal with roles in movies like 2003's *Elf* and by guest starring on such TV hits as *ER* and *Desperate Housewives*.

It couldn't happen to a nicer, more understated and self-effacing guy.

Cast:

Bob Newhart *Bob Hartley*, **Suzanne Pleshette** *Emily Hartley*, **Peter Bonerz** *Jerry Robinson*, **Marcia Wallace** *Carol Kester*, **Bill Daily** *Howard Borden*, **Jack Riley** *Elliot Carlin*

Can you buy your way to an Oscar?

The Brady Bunch

By Donica O'Bradovich
Broadcast History: ABC, 9/26/1969–8/30/1974
Runtime: 30 minutes
Genre: Sitcom

Flash back if you will to those alternately tacky and turbulent 1970s. Polyester suits. Bell-bottom pants. Watergate. War protests. Lava lamps. Sexual freedom. And a sitcom that just won't go away.

Though the decade saw tremendous social upheaval, nowhere was that felt stronger than in the family structure. Divorce was becoming more commonplace and second marriages along with blended families were shaking up the traditional nuclear family. Television began to slowly reflect that change, which brings us to the benignly immortal series called *The Brady Bunch*. Sweet, charming and all so darn cute, the Bradys were sent by unseen forces from the television gods to force us into complete mindless submission. Dull suddenly became delightful.

The concept was simple: A widower with three young sons married a widow with three young daughters and lived happily together as one big family. It was a great idea for a sitcom and the possibilities for conflict and comedy were ripe. But creator Sherwood Schwartz, who had already given us the monumental *Gilligan's Island*, wasn't after family stress or discord; the name of the game was warm and fuzzy wholesomeness.

According to *The Brady Bunch Book* by Andrew J. Edelstein and Frank Lovece, Schwartz had worked on a story in 1964 called "Yours and Mine," about a widow and widower, each with kids, who marry. For various reasons, it wasn't picked up by any of the three networks and it stalled. By coincidence, the Lucille Ball–Henry Fonda movie *Yours, Mine and Ours* about a blended family had become a big hit in 1968 and interest at ABC for Schwartz's script piqued. The title was changed to *The Brady Bunch* and the show got the green light. He cast veterans Florence Henderson, Robert Reed and Ann B. Davis for the adult roles and after seeing more than 400 kids picked his final six for the parts.

> **Did You Know?**
> The only Brady kid to have a kissing scene was Bobby.

Set in a California suburb, *The Brady Bunch* debuted in 1969 to so-so ratings and not so favorable reviews. Why? It seemed even *these* kids were too unbelievable for TV. The Bradys, it appeared, had been shipped to us from a 1950s time warp where braces, measles and missing Kitty Carryall dolls were the biggest household problems. Where was the conflict about six growing (and possibly resentful) kids, two newly married adults and a housekeeper suddenly thrown together under one roof?

But though we chuckle now at the show's corny homespun obliviousness and tackiness—the hideous neon orange and avocado kitchen, the fake Astro-turf lawn, the cramped Brady bedrooms, the bad hair perms (both male and female)—there was something oddly comforting and immensely appealing about this family that made us eat it all up: saintly parents Mike and Carol, pimple-free siblings and a perpetually perky housekeeper like Alice. Architect Mike Brady (Reed) was always ready with a sensible parental platitude; the ever sunny and impeccably coifed Carol (Henderson) stayed patiently at home waiting for her brood to burden her with their day's lightweight dilemmas; Alice (Davis) was counted on to be court jester, house cleaner, cook and Brady champion (while herself seemingly never eating or sleeping).

> ## TV and Film Connections
> Spin-offs:
> *The Brady Brides*
> *The Brady Bunch Hour*
> *The Bradys*
> Inspired two feature films:
> *The Brady Bunch Movie* (1995)
> and *A Very Brady Sequel* (1996)

And let us not forget those kids! Depending on which sex you were, or your developmental bearing at the time, you always had your favorite: Greg (Barry Williams), the cool, dreamy eldest, who always felt the pressure to keep the siblings together; Marcia (Maureen McCormick), the gorgeous older daughter who never had a bad hair day; Jan (Eve Plumb), the neurotic middle daughter who, let's face it, we ALL related to; Peter (Christopher Knight), the happy-go-lucky middle child; Bobby (Mike Lookinland), the determined youngest brother who never could measure up; and cutie pie Cindy (Susan Olsen), who just smiled and lisped.

It became evident to viewers that the Bradys had no social or political awareness beyond the walls of their cheerful home. Theirs was a self-contained universe of innocent domestic problems solved within the half-hour allotted time (with the exception, of course, of the "very special" Grand Canyon and Hawaii three-part episodes). Yet, mysteriously, the series not only has endured in syndication, but in our collective cultural consciousness for more than 30 years.

So what exactly makes *The Brady Bunch* a classic? Back then, the folksy quality was charming in itself, but now the show has taken on mythic proportions of silliness that scream camp. We've come to find peculiar delight in and wait with baited breath for the moment when Jan utters the immortal "Marcia! Marcia! Marcia!" (in the episode "Her Sister's Shadow"); and "The Subject Was Noses" provokes the same guilty pleasure when Marcia gets hit in her perfect nose and utters the memorable "Oh, my nose!"

We also recall with fondness (and possibly some head scratching) the eclectic bunch of guest stars, from football's Joe Namath and Deacon Jones to TV icon Imogene Coca to young performers Desi Arnaz Jr. and Gigi Perreau. But no guest made a greater impression than Davy Jones of the Monkees in an episode about the kids trying to recruit him to sing at the school prom. Are you surprised that they succeeded? How could *any* fan of TV stars lip-synching rock songs not get moist-eyed seeing him sing his hit song "Girl"?

By the time the series went off the air in 1975, we began to learn much, perhaps too much, about the actors. In Barry Williams's book *Growing Up Brady*, he revealed that not only did he romance his TV sister Maureen McCormick, but had an even bigger crush on and went on an innocent "date" with TV mom Florence Henderson. We discovered that Reed, a well-regarded serious actor who had previously been a regular on *The Defenders*, was so unhappy about playing Mike Brady that he constantly fought with Schwartz about every single line he had. He ultimately refused to appear in what ended up being the last ever episode.

Brady mania was back when ABC created the ill-advised 1977 variety show *The Brady Bunch Hour*. Eve Plumb would have no part of it, but interestingly, Robert Reed accepted. From there, we were inundated with two Brady TV movies and various series spin-offs, including NBC's *The Brady Brides* in 1981 and CBS's *The Bradys* in 1990. Then the 1990s saw two feature films and an off-Broadway show that expertly parodied the Bradys' delightful dizziness. It just wouldn't stop. To this day, you can find cast members happily reminiscing about the series somewhere and continuing to cash in on their characters, either through performing, writing books or, in the case of Chris Knight, appearing in TV reality shows.

Top 3 Moments

• When Cousin Oliver came to town.

• Never jumped.

• Bad from Day 1.

For more, visit www.jumptheshark.com.

All Sherwood Schwartz wanted to do was create a series about a lovely lady, a man named Brady and their six normal kids; instead, he cooked up bland TV comfort food that new generations still consume in mass quantities. Sure, we may laugh at the Bradys, but we sure do continue to watch them, quote them and embrace them. Even as we take comfort that we are way cooler than they are, we also admire them in some way, as they rally around each other at the end of the day, or give each other support when a family member is in pain. So here's the story: If being there at the end of the day for one's family is corny, then, groovy, I'll take corny any day.

Cast:

Robert Reed *Mike Brady*, **Florence Henderson** *Carol Brady*, **Ann B. Davis** *Alice Nelson*, **Maureen McCormick** *Marcia Brady*, **Eve Plumb** *Jan Brady*, **Susan Olsen** *Cindy Brady*, **Barry Williams** *Greg Brady*, **Christopher Knight** *Peter Brady*, **Mike Lookinland** *Bobby Brady*, **Robbie Rist** *Oliver (1974)*

Buffy the Vampire Slayer

By Rochell D. Thomas

Broadcast History: WB, 3/10/1997–5/22/2001;
    UPN, 10/2/2001–5/20/2003
Runtime: 60 minutes
Genre: Fantasy

Warning: This essay starts with one mother of a grand, sweeping generalization. The author recognizes that. But said author is also making said generalization about herself and she promises not to sue. So, chill.

There are some things big black women just don't do: wear heavy metal T-shirts, see Bon Jovi in concert, campaign for the release of *Hee-Haw* Season 1 on DVD or use "übersuck" and "safe-drivery" in a sentence. I—a proud BBW—have committed two of those racial role-busting crimes. One I did with my Italian-American sister by another mother. (She knows who she is.) The other, well, for that one blame *Buffy the Vampire Slayer*.

In the seven years I spent vicariously patrolling the streets of Sunnydale with Buffy, I not only internalized such terms as "Hellmouth," "undead-American" and "vague up," I used them unironically in actual conversations. That's just the power *Buffy the Vampire Slayer* had.

Created by Joss Whedon, the cult-hit TV spin-off of the campy 1992 movie followed the night-prowling adventures of Buffy Summers (Sarah Michelle Gellar), a slight and sardonic teenaged Southern California girl the universe had tasked to secretly thin the vampire population and protect the world from all sorts of apocalyptic evil. "Into each generation a slayer is born," the narrator proclaims at the start of each episode. Written by Whedon and a zealous crew of linguistics-studying, language-loving scribes, *Buffy* not only got viewers to accept a reality where demons play cards, vampires order takeout and a blonde ex-cheerleader "saves the world a lot," it enabled grown folks like myself to embrace their inner teen speak. For better or for worse.

> ### Did You Know?
> Katie Holmes and Selma Blair were among the actresses considered for the role of Buffy.

Before the show debuted on March 10, 1997, I swear I was a normal college-educated adult, well on my way to dropping "like," "freaky-deaky" and the sarcastic, Valley girl–esque use of the word "much" ("Binge much?") from my professional vocabulary. Sure, I still verbed proper nouns ("Febreeze that for me.") and turned pop culture phrases into adjectives ("She was all 'I-pity-the-fool' about it."). But that was, like, weekend speak.

After a few seasons of *Buffy*, however, my verbal weekend wear became work wear and the next thing you know I was using "cryptic" as a noun (à la "Angel, drop the cryptic," as Buffy once said) and claiming things "übersuck." Some smart famous person once said something like, "If you want to change the way America thinks and speaks, write for television." True. In the seven years that Buffy lived, died (three times) and slayed in Sunnydale, the vampire love of her life, Angel, lost his soul and found it again. Her best friend Willow dated a werewolf then became a lesbian witch, and Xander jilted a vengeance demon. During the same time, it became perfectly acceptable for me to refer to a group of hardworking friends as a Scooby Gang, or to "overshare" and describe my misbehavin' dates as "manimals." Once I got excited over a project at work and quoted Anya's crazy line from the musical episode ("Once More With Feeling"), "Look at me I'm dancing pretty!" It's at times like that when I'm ecstatic to be working at TV GUIDE, where such outbursts are not only understood, they're a totally acceptable form of communication. But I digress.

Before you go thinking I'm weird, know this: I'm not alone in my use of Buffy speak. During the show's seven-year, two-network run, half a dozen books were published about its use. (Where was the Scooby Gang when I was desperately looking for dissertation topics in college?) In one of them, *Slayer Slang: A Buffy the Vampire Slayer Lexicon*, author and fellow obsessive series fan Michael Adams traces Joss Whedon's use of the word "much" back through 1989's teen flick *Heathers* to its southern California roots. He also crowns "-y" as "the ultimate slayer slang suffix" and goes on to cite at least 100 instances where Buffy and Co. memorably did the "-y" trick (e.g. bookwormy, broody, metaphory, stay-iny, veiny). Clearly Adams is a man after my own heart.

Classic Episode Close-Up
"Hush"
(Original telecast: December 14, 1999)

This quiet episode really caught everyone's attention during the 1999–2000 slaying season. In this innovative, dark and largely dialogue-free offering from creator Joss Whedon, Buffy and Co. are literally silenced by a mysterious force. "I was just trying to expand the use of TV as a visual medium," says Whedon, who was inspired by silent horror films. Whedon says the episode features "the scariest [villains] we've ever done." These beings, called the Gentlemen, steal Sunnydale's collective voice in order to harvest organs from the populace. With Sunnydale in a quiet riot, it's up to Buffy to bring in the noise.

Funny thing, though: *Buffy* wasn't a huge hit like *Seinfeld* ("yada, yada, yada") or *Friends* ("Could I *be* any more annoying?"). It won only one Emmy (for Best Makeup in 1998) and it never took home a Golden Globe. In fact, one of its highest-rated episodes (and one of my top five faves), the critically acclaimed "Hush," ironically had no dialogue and attracted less than seven million viewers—a fraction of what those other shows got on a normal basis. Therefore I should not easily be able to trace my use of the phrase "vague up" back to the show's premiere when Buffy asked her Watcher, Giles, "Gee, can you vague that up for me?" But I can. Heck, even members of my family who've never watched *Buffy* for complicated religious and/or simple vampire-show-hating reasons could. Case in point: During a visit home I accidentally drove over one of those cement parking-space divider things on my way out of the Family Dollar parking lot. You are not allowed to swear in my family. So, instead of yelling something profane I yelled, "Crappety-pop! That is *so* not the safe-drivery thing to do." "You sound like one of those kids on TV," my mother replied. And, laughing in the back seat, my younger sister rolled her eyes and said simply, "Buffy."

> ## TV and Film Connections
> Based on a 1992 movie of the same name
> Spin-off: *Angel*

Cast:

Sarah Michelle Gellar *Buffy Summers*, **Nicholas Brendon** *Xander Harris*, **Alyson Hannigan** *Willow Rosenberg*, **Charisma Carpenter** *Cordelia Chase (1997–99)*, **Anthony S. Head** *Rupert Giles (1997–2001; 2002–03)*, **David Boreanaz** *Angel/Angelus (1997–99)*, **Mark Metcalf** *The Master (1997)*, **James Marsters** *Spike (1999–2003)*, **Juliet Landau** *Drusilla (1997–98)*, **Robia LaMorte** *Jenny Kalendar (1997–98)*, **Harry Groener** *The Mayor (1998–99)*, **K. Todd Freeman** *Mr. Trick (1998–99)*, **Seth Green** *Oz (1997–2000)*, **Marc Blucas** *Riley Finn (1999–2000)*, **Lindsay Crouse** *Maggie Walsh (1999–2000)*, **Amber Benson** *Tara (2000–02)*, **Michelle Trachtenberg** *Dawn (2000–03)*, **Emma Caulfield** *Anya (1998–2003)*, **DB Woodside** *Principal Wood (2002–03)*, **Iyari Limon** *Kennedy (2002–03)*

The Carol Burnett Show

By Rebecca Paley

Broadcast History: CBS, 9/11/1967–8/9/1978;
    ABC, 8/18/1978–9/8/1979
Runtime: 60 minutes
Genre: Sketch comedy

The Carol Burnett Show lived way past its amazingly long and beloved 11 years on the CBS schedule. After the hugely popular variety show went off the air in 1978, endless reruns of a forlorn Eunice or a curtain-wearing Starlet O'Hara or segments of the soap spoof "As the Stomach Turns" inspired future generations of would-be comedians. Jim Carrey, for example, sent Burnett his résumé at the ripe age of 10; and *Will & Grace*'s Debra Messing admitted to a childhood spent "glued to the television watching *I Love Lucy* or *The Carol Burnett Show*."

"That girl can do anything!" Lucille Ball said about Burnett. And like Lucy, Burnett made an unlikely grande dame of TV (the two were actually friends and Ball threw Burnett her first baby shower). Raised in a dysfunctional family—first in San Antonio, Texas, and then in a small railroad apartment in Hollywood—Burnett was primarily cared for by her formidable, religious grandmother because her alcoholic parents often went missing. After she achieved some success in her 20s, Burnett ended up taking in her younger sister, Christine, still only a teenager.

On the road to success, Burnett had to rise above a poor childhood as well as overcome insecurity about her unconventional looks. "Long stringy brown hair, buck teeth," she told TV GUIDE in 1979. "Face it, I was not the one the football players looked at." Burnett didn't have the typical movie-star looks of someone trying to break into show business. Even her own mother encouraged her to stick to her childhood goal of a job in journalism, saying, "No matter what you look like, you can always write."

Perhaps because of her personal woes, Burnett took solace in the quirks of characters other than her own. "I can't be me," she told TV GUIDE in '61. "I don't think I'm funny as a person. Sometimes around people, I freeze up. I think they expect a lot more of me than's there."

If she felt shy as Carol Burnett, there's nothing she wouldn't do to get a laugh as one of the show's myriad characters. And boy, the number of characters Burnett and the writers had to cook up—to keep all those years of comedy fresh—is dizzying. From washerwomen to batty secretaries to little kids: you name it, and she played it. Bridging the new world of television with the old guard from motion pictures, Burnett spoofed everyone from Shirley Temple to

Mildred Pierce to Norma Desmond to Mary Poppins in hilarious send-ups of Hollywood classics. Most memorable, of course, was the November 13, 1976, spoof of *Gone With the Wind*, with Burnett as Starlet O'Hara draped in, well, drapes (complete with curtain rods) and co-star Harvey Korman as an enchanted Rat Butler. "That gown is gorgeous," Rat says. "Thank you," Starlet replies. "I saw it in a window and I just couldn't resist it." TV GUIDE ranked this the second Funniest Television Moment of All Time (No. 1 was a 1987 Johnny Carson *Tonight Show* segment with potato-chip collector Myrtle Young).

Not only the breadth of characters, but just about everything to do with *The Carol Burnett Show* is remarkable in terms of today's standards. Apart from the classic sketch comedy, this was a classy variety show that showcased top singers (Bing Crosby, Ray Charles, Perry Como and Ella Fitzgerald, to name a few) and other big-name guests such as Bob Hope, Rock Hudson, Jimmy Stewart (one of Burnett's idols) and Mickey Rooney. But comedy was its signature, and a tremendous amount of work and attention to detail went into creating those belly laughs. "Monday's a reading, Tuesday's for fitting, Wednesday's rehearsal, we block for cameras on Thursday, taping's on Friday," Burnett described a typical week in 1970. One imagines a circus pulling up its tent and reinventing itself every week.

Many years after the show ended, I interviewed Bob Mackie (the designer who not only put Cher on all the worst-dressed lists for her wacky Oscar outfits but also created the costumes for the Burnett series) and was amazed at the fact that each week he would start from scratch, sketching ideas, picking fabrics, draping and then fitting before tapings on Friday. Even Burnett put her comic talent toward the clothes. Mackie credits her with the pencil skirt that ditzy Mrs. Wiggins wiggled in throughout the years. Make it tighter, she told him, because it's funnier.

Despite a grueling production schedule, the ensemble cast made the show look like a party. Burnett's talented and faithful supporting actors known as "The Family," including Korman, Lyle Waggoner, Vicki Lawrence

---

TV and Film Connections

Spin-off: *Mama's Family*

Preview Review
September 9, 1967

Having won all sorts of awards and plaudits for her work with Gary Moore, and in specials with Lucille Ball and Julie Andrews (and in the short-lived *The Entertainers*), Carol Burnett finally has a series with her own name on the marquee. This show will resemble the old *Gleason* show in format, incorporating a continuing marriage skit within the fabric. Harvey Korman is Burnett's screen husband, in addition to working in most of the other comedy routines. There will also be such guests as Phyllis Diller, Trini Lopez, Pearl Bailey, Liza Minnelli and Mike Douglas. Naturally, the variety segment will include dance routines and general musical-comedy fare. The show is produced by Joe Hamilton—Burnett's real husband.

and Tim Conway, were always cracking each other up. They were genuinely having fun, and so were viewers. Along the way, the series collected 25 Emmys, eight Golden Globes and three People's Choice Awards. A retooled version of the series aired more than a decade later on NBC, but it's the long-running CBS original that we remember and cherish.

Cast:

Carol Burnett *Performer*, **Harvey Korman** *Performer (1967–77)*, **Lyle Waggoner** *Performer (1967–74)*, **Vicki Lawrence** *Performer*, **Tim Conway** *Performer (1975–79)*, **Dick Van Dyke** *Performer (1977)*, **Kenneth Mars** *Performer (1979)*, **Craig Richard Nelson** *Performer (1979)*

Cheers

By Ray Stackhouse

Broadcast History: NBC, 9/30/1982–8/19/1993
Runtime: 30 minutes
Genre: Sitcom

After working as a bartender for more than 20 years, I've gotten an idea of what goes into the making of a successful neighborhood watering hole. The best ones offer a welcoming place where you can get away, relax, grab a cold libation, keep to yourself—or not—watch some tube, catch up on the latest news and gossip, and enjoy the camaraderie and fellowship of your fellow imbibers. A truly *great* pub experience? That's where you can go where everybody knows your name, and they're always glad you came. Sounds familiar, right? That's the catchy theme of *Cheers*, the vintage sitcom about the Boston drinking establishment that aired on NBC from 1982 to 1993.

For more than a decade, it followed the antics of the bar's owner, employees and regulars, plus those who stopped in just to whet their whistles and found themselves caught up in the spirited goings-on. When the series first began, the owner and head barkeep was Sam "May Day" Malone (Ted Danson), an ex–Red Sox relief pitcher who left behind the Fenway Park boos and turned to dispensing booze. Handsome but not even remotely brainy, Sam was an inveterate womanizer, and though he was Cheers's proprietor, he was also a recovering alcoholic. Early on, his addle-brained sidekick and best friend was his former Red Sox coach Ernie Pantusso (Nicholas Colasanto), who went by the nickname "Coach" (although in one episode Coach said that he got tagged with the moniker because he never flew first class). He was also nicknamed "Red" once—because he had "read a book."

Besides Sam and Coach, the staff consisted of snippy waitress Carla Tortelli (Rhea Perlman), who doled out drinks with a shot of sass on the side, and Diane

Classic Episode Close-Up

"Rebound" *(Original telecasts: September 27, 1984, and October 4, 1984)*

It was the epitome of on-again, off-again sitcom romances when the series began its third season with the two-part "Rebound." In the wake of the argument that left his and Diane's relationship belly-up, Sam has fallen off the wagon. Coach begs Diane to return and she agrees, but there's a complication: She's afraid to tell Sam she has found a new love, pompous psychiatrist Frasier Crane. This episode marked Kelsey Grammer's first appearance as Crane, and he emerged as a solid cast member for the rest of the suds opera's 11-year run. Part 2 earned Glen and Les Charles an Emmy nod for writing.

Chambers (Shelley Long), a bubbly, cerebral grad student who, after being jilted by her professor paramour, took a job waiting tables at Cheers. Despite continuous sniping and antagonistic repartee, Sam and Diane engaged in an ongoing battle of the sexes, falling in and out of love and providing a romantic spark and sizzle that fueled the series until Long left the show in 1987.

Did You Know?

In high school, Diane was voted Girl Most Likely to Marry Into Old Money.

Other prominent regulars included Norm Peterson (George Wendt), a beefy beer guzzler whose arrival was always greeted with a resounding chorus of "Norm!" and a snappy exchange between him and one of the employees. "What's up, Normie?" someone would invariably say. One typical response: "My nipples, it's freezing out there." Norm's favorite drinking partner was mailman Cliff Clavin (John Ratzenberger). Originally, Ratzenberger auditioned for the Norm role, and when he felt that his tryout wasn't going well, he suggested to producers that they needed a blue-collar know-it-all. Ratzenberger was hired for a six-episode run, but proved so popular (and funny) that he was made a full-time cast member.

In 1984, fusty customer Dr. Frasier Crane, a pompous psychiatrist, joined the cast—a role Kelsey Grammer was to play on *Cheers* and in his classic spin-off series *Frasier* for the next 20 years. After Colasanto died in 1985, his replacement behind the taps was wide-eyed Indiana hayseed Woody Boyd (Woody Harrelson), who was just as intellectually challenged, probably more so, than the late Coach. Another addition to the cast was Dr. Lilith Sternin (Bebe Neuwirth), a starchy, buttoned-down fellow psychiatrist to Frasier, who showed up in 1986 and would eventually marry and divorce him through the course of the series.

When Long left in 1987, her shoes as Sam's beleaguered and much hit-upon foil were filled by Rebecca Howe (Kirstie Alley). Rebecca became the bar manager after Sam sold the place to a big corporation and decided to buy a boat and sail around the world. The boat sank, Sam's fortunes going down with it, and he was forced to return to Cheers as a bartender. Until the series' 1993 finale,

Top 3 Moments

- Never jumped.
- When Rebecca replaced Diane.
- When Sam and Rebecca did it.

For more, visit www.jumptheshark.com.

Rebecca matched wits and quips with Sam, who was determined to make her one of his romantic conquests.

This was one of the all-time great ensembles, but what's sometimes forgotten is that NBC almost pulled the plug on the show in its first season because of low ratings. But NBC president Brandon Tartikoff championed it and kept it on the schedule. Gradually, viewers began to take notice of the top-shelf writing, the intoxicating cast chemistry, the quirky and colorful assortment of peripheral characters, and the flat-out hilarious plots. Soon it became an anchor of the network's Thursday Must-See lineup. Celebrities who dropped by included Johnny Carson, Alex Trebek, Dick Cavett, and Righteous Brothers Bill Medley and Bobby Hatfield.

Created by Glen Charles, Les Charles and James Burrows, who cut their comic teeth on *The Mary Tyler Moore Show*, *The Bob Newhart Show*, *Phyllis* and *Taxi*, the series went on to become a ratings monster. It finished in the Top 10 for 7 of its 11 seasons. Nominated for an astonishing 111 Emmys, it won 26 times, and all 10 of the regulars were nominated, with wins going to Perlman (four times), Danson (twice), Neuwirth (twice), Alley, Long and Harrelson. *Cheers* also won four times for Outstanding Comedy Series. The final episode, which featured the return of Diane, was seen by 80.4 million people, one of the highest-rated programs ever. It was a fitting toast to one of the classiest sitcoms in TV history.

TV and Film Connections

Spin-offs:

Frasier
The Tortellis

Cast:

Ted Danson *Sam Malone*, **Shelley Long** *Diane Chambers (1982–87)*, **Rhea Perlman** *Carla Tortelli LeBec*, **Nicholas Colasanto** *Ernie 'Coach' Pantusso (1982–85)*, **George Wendt** *Norm Peterson*, **John Ratzenberger** *Cliff Clavin*, **Kelsey Grammer** *Dr. Frasier Crane (1984–93)*, **Woody Harrelson** *Woody Boyd (1985–93)*, **Bebe Neuwirth** *Dr. Lilith Sternin-Crane (1986–93)*, **Kirstie Alley** *Rebecca Howe (1987–93)*

The Cosby Show

By Ali Gazan

Broadcast History: NBC, 9/20/1984–9/17/1992
Runtime: 30 minutes
Genre: Sitcom

I was 6 when *The Cosby Show* debuted in 1984. Every Thursday night, I'd settle down with my older sister and my parents to watch the lives of the Huxtables. Sure, nothing dramatic ever really happened on the show. No one died (excluding Rudy's goldfish), huge fights never erupted and people weren't doing pratfalls. Yet every week, I couldn't wait to watch *The Cosby Show* because I knew it would make me laugh and to be honest, I wanted to be part of their family.

And really, what kid didn't? Dr. Cliff Huxtable (Bill Cosby) was always making funny faces, giving his youngest daughter, Rudy (Keisha Knight Pulliam), "zerberts" or trying to sneak a forbidden hoagie or piece of cake. Mom Clair (Phylicia Rashad) was so pretty and truly seemed to understand her kids. She only wanted the best from—and for—them and would have done anything to help them succeed. Even though both parents worked—Cliff was a doctor and Clair a lawyer—they were always around for their children and never missed an important event. As far as siblings go, Sondra (Sabrina Le Beauf), Denise (Lisa Bonet), Theo (Malcolm-Jamal Warner), Vanessa (Tempestt Bledsoe) and Rudy didn't seem too bad either. Everyone pretty much got along and even when there was a fight or one of the kids messed up, the situation never really got out of hand. Instead, Cliff and Clair, with patience, understanding and loving firmness, would teach them a lesson.

One of the most memorable was when they decided to show Theo just how hard it is to be an adult. Theo, who had annoyed the family by constantly borrowing cash and mooching, swears he'll survive the real world because he's going to be a model and will never have to worry about money. To prove just how

> ## Classic Episode Close-Up
>
> "Happy Anniversary"
>
> *(Original telecast: October 10, 1985)*
>
> Cliff Huxtable's parents (Earle Hyman, Clarice Taylor) celebrate their 49th wedding anniversary in a classic episode. Cliff and Clair surprise them with a dinner party, after which Sondra, Denise, Theo, Vanessa and Rudy join their parents and entertain Grandma and Grandpa by lip-synching favorite tunes such as Ray Charles's "Night Time Is the Right Time." By showing the three generations together, "Happy Anniversary" helped define the series' underlying message: Strong, positive children are a parent's greatest legacy.

hard the real world is, the Huxtables turn their home into "The Real World Apartment Building" where each member of the family poses as different characters—Rudy's the landlord, Clair runs the furniture store and the local restaurant, Cliff plays the handyman—and Theo has to rent an apartment, buy furniture and eat on a salary. In the end, the Huxtable parents bring Theo dinner and he admits that it's not as easy out there as he thought. In this home, life lessons were fun, not a chore.

> ### Did You Know?
>
> Real-life husband and wife John Ritter and Amy Yasbeck guest-starred in one episode as a couple preparing for their first child.

The Cosby Show was an uncommonly smart and funny show (it was No. 1 from 1985 through 1989), winning six Emmy Awards, a Peabody and 14 NAACP Image Awards. This was sitcom entertainment of the highest order, but there were educational and cultural lessons to be learned, too. Cosby, a huge fan of jazz, introduced a generation of 10-year-olds to music legends. Lena Horne sang on the show in 1985 when the family went to see her perform for Cliff's birthday. The kids and Clair got to meet Stevie Wonder and record a track with him. And though Ray Charles was never a guest, his music made a very memorable appearance when the Huxtables lip-synched to Charles's "Night Time Is the Right Time" as part of their anniversary gift to Cliff's parents. Artwork of prominent African-Americans hung throughout the home and, in honor of the Mandelas, Sondra and her husband, Elvin, named their twins Winnie and Nelson.

When I was young and watched *The Cosby Show*, the Huxtables were just another family on a TV show. I didn't think about them in terms of race or income. But that was one of the most defining points of the series. It presented a black family that was unlike any we had seen before. They were upper-middle class with two professional parents. While they didn't avoid racial issues and questions, it was never really the focus. In many ways, *The Cosby Show* became a common ground for people from different backgrounds. Everyone could watch the show and identify with the characters in some way. The sitcom was seen as such a unifying force that in April 1992 when Los Angeles was in the midst of race riots, the L.A. mayor successfully lobbied the local NBC station to air *The Cosby Show* finale instead of continuing coverage of the events.

There was just something calming and reassuring about this series that couldn't—and still can't—be denied. Over the eight seasons, the main cast only changed slightly. Denise left for

> ### TV and Film Connections
>
> Spin-off: *A Different World*

Hillman College in 1986, which resulted in the spin-off *A Different World*, only to return two years later to announce she was dropping out of college to travel to Africa as a photographer's assistant. When she again came back to the Huxtable nest, she had a husband, Martin (Joseph C. Phillips), and his daughter from a previous marriage, Olivia (Raven-Symone), in tow. With the Huxtable kids into their teenage years, Olivia gave Cliff another tot to bond with and ultimately helped the show continue its success. As much as the cast stayed the same, the show remained true to its initial formula: a comedy about a regular family, facing normal issues. You were never surprised by the Huxtables, just comforted by them—just as you would be by your own family.

Cast:

Bill Cosby *Dr. Heathcliff Huxtable*, **Phylicia Rashad** *Clair Huxtable*, **Malcolm-Jamal Warner** *Theo Huxtable*, **Lisa Bonet** *Denise Huxtable Kendall (1984–87; 1989–91)*, **Tempestt Bledsoe** *Vanessa Huxtable*, **Keshia Knight Pulliam** *Rudy Huxtable*, **Sabrina Le Beauf** *Sondra Huxtable Tibideaux*, **Geoffrey Owens** *Elvin Tibideaux (1986–92)*, **Raven-Symone** *Olivia Kendall (1989–92)*, **Joseph C. Phillips** *Lt. Martin Kendall (1989–92)*, **Erika Alexander** *Pam Tucker (1990–92)*

CSI: Crime Scene Investigation

By Tim Holland

Broadcast History: CBS, 10/6/2000–
Runtime: 60 minutes
Genre: Crime drama

Gory crime scenes. Graphic autopsies. Grave-yard-shift investigators. Doesn't sound too promising. That's just what CBS thought back in 2000 when it picked *CSI* up at the last minute and launched it with little fanfare on Friday nights.

But as CBS executives learned, there's considerable ratings life in dead bodies.

CSI is a bona fide juggernaut and is responsible for the proliferation of cop-show "procedurals" that dominate network lineups, including two CBS spin-offs, *CSI: Miami* and *CSI: NY*. Not bad for a show that's the brainchild of a former Las Vegas tram operator (working the graveyard shift, of course). Anthony E. Zuiker created the innovative drama after his wife convinced him to watch an episode of *The New Detectives*, a documentary series about forensics. And get this: *CSI* was the first TV script Zuiker had ever written.

After watching the documentary, Zuiker visited the Las Vegas criminology department and asked if he could ride along with CSIs on cases. "I did it for five weeks," he said, "and saw the most horrific, exciting, exuberating, crazy world and said to myself, 'There's probably a series here.'" Indeed.

Watching *CSI* for the first time is like getting injected with a pure shot of adrenaline. Its expert mix of gritty subject matter, painstaking deduction, and compelling characters with grisly special-effects shots that wind their way through dead bodies like a plumber's snake twisting through a clogged drain seizes your senses and rattles your nerves. It's TV's equivalent of a drug-induced rush. What else would you expect from a series executive produced by action-oriented film mogul Jerry Bruckheimer.

> ### Did You Know?
>
> All of *CSI*'s lab equipment is authentic, according to co-producer and technical consultant Elizabeth Devine, who often tests prototypes sent by manufacturers.

For the uninitiated, the series focuses on Las Vegas criminologists who use scientific methods to solve crimes, mostly murders. Methodical Gil Grissom (William Petersen), a leading entomologist who possesses a Sherlock Holmes–like devotion to detail, heads the forensics team and is aided by a stellar group that includes Catherine Willows (Marg Helgenberger), a single mom and former stripper who is the daughter of a wealthy casino owner; Warrick Brown (Gary Dourdan), a Las Vegas native and recovering gambler;

Sara Sidle (Jorja Fox), a feminist intellectual who is in love with Grissom; Nick Stokes (George Eads), a Texas native and son of a state supreme-court judge; and Greg Sanders (Eric Szmanda), a wildly enthusiastic lab technician who was quickly promoted to field work. Capt. Jim Brass (Paul Guilfoyle), a tenacious detective and former crime-lab supervisor, investigates many of the cases along with the CSIs, and Dr. Albert Robbins (Robert David Hall), a double leg amputee, serves as the city's chief medical examiner.

"Sin never sleeps," says a sleek ad campaign for the series. It certainly is alive and well in Las Vegas, especially after the sun goes down, and *CSI* uses its lurid Sin City backdrop to full advantage. Few of the cases the CSIs work on could be called typical. The series revels in bizarre behavior. In fact, the more disorienting the story, the better. Viewers are more likely to find cases revolving around infantilism, masochism or human werewolf syndrome than they are domestic disputes. On *CSI*, a severed head might have a rattlesnake stuffed down its throat or a dead scuba diver might be found lodged in a tree. The over-the-top stories, along with the aforementioned computer-generated body shots, are, of course, series staples.

When *CSI* premiered on Friday, October 6, 2000, it drew more than 17 million viewers and averaged more than 14 million in that time slot. CBS smelled a hit and quickly moved the show to a lucrative Thursday time period in February where it exploded in the ratings, at times pulling in more than 30 million viewers. By the end of its second season, *CSI* was the No. 1 drama and it dominated Thursday nights for the next five years. But when ABC moved its breakout hit *Grey's Anatomy* from Sundays to Thursdays in a head-to-head competition in the fall of 2006, the once indomitable *CSI* took a slight ratings hit. In an effort to regain its supremacy, the series resorted to some gimmicky stunts (Cirque du Soleil, talking corpses, the addition of Liev Schreiber to the cast), but it appears the two megahits are destined to duke it out for some time to come.

Preview Review
September 30, 2000

Premise: It's the evidence, stupid. This slick drama focuses on "crime scene investigation," the specialty of the forensic team in the Las Vegas police department's Criminalistics Bureau. By relentlessly analyzing every detail at the scene of the crime, no matter how seemingly irrelevant or grotesque in nature, these sleuths have science and experience on their side to solve the case.

We Say: If only the characters were as animated as the evidence. The detective work is often gripping, but the detectives are mired in cliché, including the always terrific Marg Helgenberger (*China Beach*) as a conflicted single mom. Wasting actors like her and William Petersen would be a crime. (Jorja Fox, last seen protecting the first daughter on *The West Wing*, joins *CSI* in the second episode.)

It's said that what happens in Vegas stays in Vegas, but when it comes to TV that certainly isn't true. The Las Vegas version of *CSI* has altered network television's landscape more than any other series over the past decade. Its influence can't be overstated. *CSI* isn't just successful. It's the first crime drama in the history of television to be ranked No. 1 for the season. (*Dragnet* finished second in 1953–54, back when everyone was in love with *Lucy*.) Reruns of the show on CBS and cable rate higher than many first-run network programs. It's also been the top-rated foreign program in Germany, France, Italy, Spain, Australia, the United Kingdom and Canada. It has affected network schedules, from what shows get made to how they are made. *CSI* upped the ante when it comes to network violence, gore and explicit story lines.

> ## TV and Film Connections
>
> Spin-offs:
>
> *CSI: Miami*
> *CSI: NY*

"Vegas is 24 hours. Vegas is seven days a week. Vegas is edgy . . . and anything can happen," Zuiker told TV critics in 2000 just before the show debuted. "It's totally insane!"

Seven years later, Zuiker's comments still ring true, not only for the city of Las Vegas, but for the insanely successful procedural the tram operator created after his wife persuaded him to watch a documentary on forensics.

Thank you, Mrs. Zuiker!

Cast:

William Petersen *Gil Grissom*, **Marg Helgenberger** *Catherine Willows*, **Gary Dourdan** *Warrick Brown*, **George Eads** *Nick Stokes*, **Paul Guilfoyle** *Capt. Jim Brass*, **Jorja Fox** *Sara Sidle*, **Eric Szmanda** *Greg Sanders*, **Robert David Hall** *Dr. Albert Robbins*

Curb Your Enthusiasm

By Joe Friedrich

Broadcast History: HBO, 10/15/2000–
Runtime: 30 minutes
Genre: Sitcom

At the height of its popularity, *Seinfeld* **soared** in such rarefied air that fans and critics alike hailed it as the mother of all sitcoms. It redefined NBC's Must-See TV on Thursday nights, raised the property value of neighboring shows on the schedule, and contributed numerous catch phrases, such as "yada, yada, yada" and "master of my domain," to the pop-culture lexicon. It made household names of its characters, and occupied the No. 1 ranking among TV GUIDE's 50 Greatest Shows of All Time. So it came as a bit of a surprise that there developed something of a *"Seinfeld* curse," which seemed to have doomed, apart from its eponymous star, subsequent outings by Michael Richards (*The Michael Richards Show*), Jason Alexander (*Bob Patterson* and *Listen Up*) and, until her 2006 Emmy award for *The New Adventures of Old Christine*, Julia Louis-Dreyfus (*Watching Ellie*).

However, one of the series' unseen alums (but not unheard—he voiced New York Yankees owner George Steinbrenner in various episodes) fared far better in the post-*Seinfeld*ian universe. Larry David, *Seinfeld*'s co-creator, principal writer and the inspiration for Alexander's selfish, tactless George Costanza, found a perfect niche at HBO with *Curb Your Enthusiasm*, an off-puttingly hilarious, semi-real look at the life of the even more selfish, tactless Larry David. In a refreshing change of pace, the show, which was based on a 1999 HBO special of the same name, is a product not of scripts churned out by stables of writers, but rather improvisations by its actors from story lines conceived by David, and these everyday, cringe-inducing situations benefit from the lack of predictable, laugh-track-driven punch lines that make much of television practically unwatchable.

Almost from the beginning, *Curb* fell into the realm of love-it or hate-it entertainment. Devotees reveled in the uncommonly gauche, oh-no-he-didn't kind of predicaments in which David manages to find himself, whether it's being blamed for an obscene typo in a relative's obituary (from the first season's "The Beloved Aunt"), convincing a little girl to chop off her doll's hair ("The Doll," from Season 2), or appalling guests by inviting a sex offender to a Passover Seder (Season 5's "The Seder"). Its list of Emmy nominations include four for Outstanding Comedy Series and three for David as Lead Actor, and it won the Golden Globe for Best TV Comedy in 2003. On the flip side, by glorifying the faux pas, the show also fueled its detractors, who might have dismissed it as crude, rudderless, pointless or simply vulgar, and probably considered David the kind of loathsome jerk not even a mother could love. But comedy, like beauty, is in the eye of the beholder.

After a number of dead-end jobs in his native New York City during the 1970s and 1980s, David endured the stand-up comedy scene amid decidedly mixed reviews. He was a favorite of other comics, including a promising new-comer named Jerry Seinfeld, but audiences weren't sure what to make of his caustic temperament and unconventional material. A single sentence from a 2004 article in *The New Yorker* epitomizes his enigmatic manner: "One night at Catch a Rising Star, a comedy club on Manhattan's Upper East Side, David stepped onto the stage, scanned the room from side to side, said, 'Never mind,' and walked off." But David eventually joined his pal Seinfeld in the unforget-table series pitch to NBC executives, a near-disaster encounter re-enacted in the show's fourth season, and the rest, as they say, is history.

In *Curb*, with the jaunty, carnival-like theme of Luciano Michelini's "Frolic" camouflaging an onslaught of impending discourtesies, David has the free-dom to be as inappropriate as he deems appropriate, and every episode has the potential to out-Costanza his erstwhile alter ego. His wife, Cheryl (two-time Emmy nominee Cheryl Hines), frequently calls him on the carpet for his behavior, while his manager, Jeff (Jeff Garlin), tacitly approves of it, and a ros-ter of celebrity friends and associates, including Richard Lewis, Ted Danson, Wanda Sykes, Mel Brooks and Ben Stiller, are consistently left shaking their heads at his effrontery. Virtually no one is safe from the far-reaching tentacles of his thoughtlessness, and an endless list of his sparring partners, foils and antagonists would have to start with Jeff's wife, Susie (Susie Essman), but also includes sales clerks, meteorologists, golfers, relatives, interior decora-tors, Hugh Hefner, nursing-home residents, Shaquille O'Neal, lesbians, porn stars, in-laws, doctors and, in many a spirited exchange, children. Scenarios usually start someplace innocent, but quickly spiral out of control once David ratchets up the tension by turning flattery into insult, gallantry into gracelessness, or generosity into self-indulgence. An equal-opportu-nity offender, his incivility crosses

> ### Did You Know?
>
> In the first episode, Larry and Cheryl men-tion their kids, even though they were never shown—and never spoken of again.

racial, religious, social, age, physical and gender boundaries, and his penchant for putting out fires with gasoline makes him appear genetically predisposed to rudeness. Quite simply, even when he's right, he *sounds* wrong.

In the summer of 2000, before *Curb* debuted, David was asked by a reporter, who referenced *Seinfeld* as the oft-repeated "show about nothing," to summarize his new project. "I would describe it as a show about Larry David," said David, "which is as pretty close to 'nothing' as it gets." *Curb* may not last nine years (the sixth season is scheduled for 2007), yield a respectable shelf life in reruns or attract more than 70 million viewers for its farewell, but with its brazen, off-the-cuff delivery, cinema-vérité insouciance and uncanny knack for eliciting winces of laughter, it may just outdo *Seinfeld* as far as "nothing" goes. And as we've all found out by now, that kind of nothing is uniquely something.

Cast:

Larry David *Himself*, **Cheryl Hines** *Cheryl David*, **Jeff Garlin** *Jeff Greene*

The Daily Show

By Jeff Gemmill

Broadcast History: Comedy Central, 7/22/1996–
Runtime: 30 minutes
Genre: Newsmagazine/comedy

When you get right down to it, it occurs to me, many of the news anchors who have broken from the pack of teleprompter-reading wannabes and established their names in the cultural ethos of our time can be summed up in two syllables. That is to say, their last names possess not one, not three or four, but *two* distinct speech sounds. Think about it: Murrow. Cronkite. Rather. Jennings. Brokaw. Stewart. Stewart? Jon Stewart?! Yes.

Since signing on as *The Daily Show* anchor in January 1999, replacing Craig Kilborn (OK, OK, so *his* two syllables didn't exactly add up to much), the venerable Jon Stewart has, like his esteemed counterparts, offered a succinct summary of the day's news, spicing the fair-and-balanced recitations with reports from a select group of grizzled correspondents. He's grilled presidential candidates (John Kerry, John Edwards), former presidents (Jimmy Carter, Bill Clinton), and an almost-president (Al Gore); talked policy with heavyweight politicos (Sens. Joe Biden, Hillary Clinton, Ted Kennedy, John McCain and Barack Obama, among others); and elicited insights from a long list of former administration officials, commentators and authors. In short, when the news matters most, and even when it doesn't, the nation's eyes and ears turn to him.

In the words of President Bush (as channeled by Stewart): *"Heh, heh, heh, heh, heh!"*

The multi-Emmy-winning *Daily Show* is—as we all know by now and Stewart readily admits—"fake news." The concept itself is essentially *Saturday Night Live*'s "Weekend Update" juiced up on steroids. It satirizes the issues of the day, mocks our elected and unelected leaders, and skewers a news media that too often acts like movie critics delivering thumbs-up/thumbs-down reviews (that is to say, dumbing down most stories). I hesitate to use the word "gravitas," yet in an emotional monologue following 9/11, Stewart revealed a deeper understanding of America's greatness than most in the public sphere. "The show in general, we feel, is a privilege. Even the idea that we can sit in the back of the country and make wisecracks, which is really what we do—we sit in the back and we throw spitballs—but never forgetting the fact that it is a luxury in this country that allows us to do that. That is, a country that allows for open satire . . . that's really what this whole situation is about. It's the difference between closed and open, it's the difference between free and burdened."

In addition to Stewart, the show features a ready supply of "correspondents" and "experts" guaranteed to raise smirks, if not smiles and out-and-out laughs. For example, when the Bush administration readjusted the formula for dispersing antiterrorism funds in 2006, reducing New York City's budget by 40 percent while upping the amounts given to places like Indiana (which improbably claimed the most terrorist targets in the nation at 8,591), the always dry Dan Bakkedahl visited the state to investigate and ended up skating the day away in one of the alleged targets, a roller rink. Likewise, correspondent Jason Jones, who has yet to meet a story he can't regurgitate as a guffaw, offered a provocative piece on the military's "don't ask, don't tell" policy. While an expelled homosexual military linguist translated Arabic text, Jones stripped down to his skivvies in order to gauge if, as the theory goes, the man's gayness interfered with his job. And, shortly before the 2004 presidential election, Samantha Bee ventured to Pennsylvania to learn why some voters remained undecided. After bringing together a focus group of unfocused citizens, she harangued them in hilarious fashion. "What the [bleep] are you waiting for?! Why can you not decide?! [Bleep] or get off the pot!"

> ### TV and Film Connections
> Spin-offs:
> *The Colbert Report*
> *The Red State Diaries*

In fact, from longtime cranky commentator Lewis Black (who reminds me, in a good way, of John Belushi's "but, nooooo!" character on the original "Update"), to former reporter Mo Rocca, who's since found a home on many VH1 *I Love Whatever* retrospectives, the supporting cast is almost, but not quite, as important as Stewart. A few have actually become, if not stars, then comets zooming through the fractured universe that is today's pop culture—Steve Carell (NBC's *The Office*), Stephen Colbert (Comedy Central's *The Colbert Report*) and Rob Corddry (Fox's *The Winner*). Colbert is arguably the most notable of that bunch, forever rocking the free world with his fact-free zone. There aren't many Americans who can claim victory in a contest to have a Hungarian bridge named after him—with more votes (17,231,724) than Hungary has citizens (10,076,581). While he didn't receive quite that much love as a mere *Daily Show* correspondent, he did engender plenty of hysterics. On a set reminiscent of the old *Joker's Wild* game show, for instance, his regular "This Week in God" spot lampooned every sacred cow and elephant—and not just in India.

> ### Did You Know?
> In 2004, Sen. John Edwards announced his intention to run for president on *The Daily Show*.

The Daily Show also pokes fun at celebrities and, as "This Week in God" suggests, the so-called "culture wars," including the Left's annual "attack" on Christmas. However, it does not, as clueless Geraldo Rivera once claimed to Bill O'Reilly, feature "videos of old ladies slipping on ice." (Maybe Bakkedahl and Jones, but never old ladies—unless Geraldo knows something about those

The Daily Show

two the rest of us don't. *Heh, heh, heh, heh, heh.*) It is liberal with a lowercase "l," not Democratic but democratic, filled with bleeped curses and ribald jokes, gleefully taking potshots at anyone and everyone who wanders into the public eye. It's satire—what a grand two-syllable word—of and for the people.

Cast:

Craig Kilborn *Host (1996–98)*, **Jon Stewart** *Host (1999–)*

Dallas

By Stuart Michaelson

Broadcast History: CBS, 4/2/1978–5/3/1991
Runtime: 60 minutes
Genre: Drama

J. R. Ewing wasn't one to gild the lily: As indelibly played by Larry Hagman on the slick nighttime soap *Dallas*, the iconic oil honcho always dished out his vitriol as tersely as possible.

So it's no surprise that when Hagman, interviewed in 2005 on *Showbiz Tonight*, looked back at the classic series, he minced no words in summing up the show's setup: two millionaires, J. R. and his good brother Bobby (Patrick Duffy), living with their wives and the elder Ewings under the same dysfunctional Southfork roof.

"That seems a little far-fetched to me."

And, he might have added, far-reaching: The series was truly addictive—the top-rated program for three seasons in the early 1980s—and a pleasure as guilty as J. R. was in countless slimy schemes.

I still savor the tension-filled meals that were frequently punctuated with Bobby's often fruitless attacks on J. R. and his misdeeds. One breakfast, for instance, was interrupted by a cop asking questions about a skeleton found on the ranch; between bites, Bobby casually asked if J. R. had killed someone as a kid and forgotten to tell the family.

The Michaelsons weren't quite as contentious as the Ewings, but our house was small, our voices loud, and sometimes, as a kid, I escaped the cacophony by burying myself in the latest Superman comic. The Man of Steel's arch-nemesis, the brilliantly twisted Lex Luthor, wasn't too different—minus the booze and women—from J. R., the charming high-octane villain with a devilishly malicious grin. You loved to hate J. R. and he was unquestionably the centerpiece of a serial you hated to miss. As an adult, I didn't, any more than I

> **TV and Film Connections**
>
> Spin-off: *Knots Landing*

missed my comics as a kid. That was largely because *Dallas* was a lot more than J. R.'s beddings, back-stabbings, betrayals and bourbon; or the big hair, shoulder pads, seductive charms and sordid secrets of wives Pam (Victoria Principal) and Sue Ellen (Linda Gray).

There was a lot more, too, than the celebrated "Who Shot J. R.?" cliffhanger resolution that attracted 83 million viewers on November 21, 1980. (The issue of who, among the many wanting J. R. dead, actually pulled the trigger was so vital that Israeli Prime Minister Menachem Begin, for one, successfully pried the shooter's identity from actress Susan Howard; Begin kept the name quiet, explaining, "Since my days in the underground fighting the British, I have been able to keep a secret." Israeli viewers saw the episode nearly two years after Americans.)

Amid all the duplicity, rampant passions and sordid machinations that are requisite for the soap genre, *Dallas* was also smart enough to deal with some issues that, for the time, were fairly touchy. There was, for instance, "Royal Marriage," a sensitive take on homosexuality in which Lucy (Charlene Tilton) is nearly forced to marry a gay suitor; "Election," offering a nuanced examination of legalized abortion in the midst of political intrigue involving J. R.'s rival Cliff Barnes; and a wrenching two-part episode about mastectomy, in which J. R.'s mother, Ellie (Barbara Bel Geddes), fears that husband Jock (crusty Jim Davis) will leave her after her surgery.

But it was the icy angst between J. R. and Sue Ellen (often driven to alcohol and lovers by her husband's infidelities and cruelties) that was most stunning: they made great sport out of hating each other's guts. A pouty Sue Ellen's angry eyes would glare from her bedroom mirror to J. R. as she castigated and accused, while he glibly inquired about which tie to wear for a business trip that more often than not included adultery, even with his wife's sister, Kristin (Mary Crosby). Sue Ellen would ask what slut J. R. was headed for, and he'd answer that whoever she was, she'd be better than the one he was looking at. Delicious!

I also relished J. R.'s rivalry with Ken Kercheval's forever-frustrated Cliff Barnes. Barnes's father, Digger, believed that J. R.'s father, Jock, had cheated him of his fortune and his woman (Digger had dated Ellie). Bad apples fell close to the tree, as Cliff and J. R. upped the ante with all manner of schemes financial, romantic (Cliff bedded Sue Ellen) and political (J. R. secretly financed Cliff's run for Congress so he would quit the Office of Land Management, which Cliff wielded against Ewing Oil interests.)

Top 3 Moments

- When Bobby Ewing's death turned out to be a dream.
- When Bobby Ewing died.
- When Jock Ewing died.

For more, visit www.jumptheshark.com.

Bobby's clashes with his older brother were nearly as vicious, though leavened a bit by blood: The younger, handsomer brother was forever trying to undo J. R.'s heartless business dealings, which even included betting the sacred Southfork mortgage on an overseas oil deal. J. R's take on white knight Bobby was that he saw things too much in black and white, good and evil. J. R. never burdened himself with messy questions of morality. What mattered was power and money. And, of course, some adultery on the side. Without Hagman, whom Duffy called TV's most underrated actor, the series would simply not have been the same show. The villainy, of course, was never ending, but check out J. R.'s anguish and tender emotions following the death of Jock (a plot development necessitated by the real-life passing of Jim Davis). This was acting of the highest order. Incredibly, Hagman never won an Emmy and the series itself never really got its critical due. It amassed an impressive list of nominations, but only one acting win, for Bel Geddes.

Along the way, of course, there were some egregiously famous story-line missteps and odd casting changes. So what if embittered drunk Digger Barnes went from a befuddled David Wayne to a more stoic Keenan Wynn? That weak-kneed brother Gary went from David Ackroyd to Ted Shackelford? And that, most ridiculously, Miss Ellie, for a year, went from Barbara Bel Geddes to Donna Reed and then, mercifully, back to Bel Geddes? Fans were incredulous, but, like myself, forgiving—even overlooking the preposterous return of "dead" Bobby, whose season as one of the departed was dismissed with the ruse, cooked up by Patrick Duffy's wife, that the previous year had been one l-o-n-g dream of Pam's.

Dallas wound up its long run with its own take on *It's a Wonderful Life*, in which an apprentice angel (Joel Grey) lets J. R. know what life for those around him would have been like had there never been a J. R. The finale even ends with a mysterious gunshot.

You can draw a straight line from *Peyton Place*, TV's first hit prime-time soap, to more recent ones, like *The O.C.*, and, certainly, in between, there have been a plethora of rich-folks-behaving-rotten clones, some good (notably spin-off *Knots Landing* and *Dynasty*), more of them bad (remember *Flamingo Road*?) that all owe a debt to *Dallas*.

This remains the best of the breed precisely because it is dramatically—in a word that J. R. would appreciate—richer.

Cast:

Larry Hagman *John Ross "J. R." Ewing Jr.*, **Barbara Bel Geddes** *Eleanor Ewing (1978–84; 1985–90)*, **Donna Reed** *Eleanor Ewing (1984–85)*, **Jim Davis** *John Ross "Jock" Ewing (1978–81)*, **Patrick Duffy** *Bobby Ewing (1978–85; 1986–91)*, **Victoria Principal** *Pamela Barnes Ewing (1978–87)*, **Charlene Tilton** *Lucy Ewing Cooper (1978–85; 1988–90)*, **Linda Gray** *Sue Ellen Ewing (1978–89)*, **Steve Kanaly** *Ray Krebbs (1978–89)*, **Ken Kercheval** *Cliff Barnes*, **David Ackroyd** *Gary Ewing (1978)*, **Ted Shackelford** *Gary Ewing (1979–81)*, **Joan Van Ark** *Valene Ewing (1978–81)*, **Susan Howard** *Donna Culver Krebbs (1979–87)*, **Mary Crosby** *Kristin Shepard (1979–81)*, **Howard Keel** *Clayton Farlow (1981–91)*, **Priscilla Presley** *Jenna Wade (1983–88)*, **Dack Rambo** *Jack Ewing (1985–87)*, **Sheree J. Wilson** *April Stevens (1986–91)*, **George Kennedy** *Carter McKay (1988–91)*, **Sasha Mitchell** *James Richard Beaumont (1989–91)*, **Lesley-Anne Down** *Stephanie Rogers (1990)*

Deadwood

By Joe Friedrich
Broadcast History: HBO, 3/21/2004–8/27/2006
Runtime: 60 minutes
Genre: Western

You couldn't blame Gene Autry, Roy Rogers, Tex Ritter and their clean-cut brethren for riding past *this* town. Because if these singing cowpokes had accidentally wandered in, they likely wouldn't have lasted 10 minutes. As *Gunsmoke* redefined the genre for TV in the 1950s, *Deadwood*, an unusually brutal (and expletive-laden) oater about a late 1870s South Dakota settlement, similarly—though certainly more graphically—changed the rules. In the series' very first scene, a marshal stoically hangs a repentant horse thief in front of an angry mob itching to do the same. What follows is a grimy and vulgar but ostensibly more accurately drawn portrait of frontier life.

The series was conceived by David Milch, Emmy-winning writer for *Hill Street Blues* and *NYPD Blue*, the latter of which he co-created with Steven Bochco. Milch had originally pitched a series to HBO brass about the nascent police force during Emperor Nero's reign, but the network already had *Rome* in the works, so he turned to the American West for his fact-based tale of lawlessness and disorder. Milch did more than a year of research on Deadwood and its environs, and presented, in footnoted, term-paper fashion, a meticulous examination of the era's attitudes, customs, violence and language. His series uses actual names or composites of real people, but in the end—and to his and *Deadwood*'s credit—historical accuracy often cedes just enough fertile ground to let bloom a stirring narrative. His dramatic license might be summed up best by a line in an article in *The New Yorker* that says Milch "learned as much as he could and then threw out most of what he knew when he began writing the show."

The series begins in July 1876, a short time after the Battle of Little Big Horn. At the time, Deadwood wasn't even part of the United States: it sprung to life on land deeded to the Lakota-Sioux in the Treaty of Fort Laramie in 1868. But as stories of gold discoveries in the mid-1870s spread and could no longer be suppressed by the government, not even federal troops could keep out all the prospectors, con artists, businesspeople and adventure-seekers who flocked to it. Rather than being discouraged by Custer's resounding defeat, a new wave of settlers eagerly sought to snatch as much real estate as possible from the Indian population.

Although Deadwood has no law to speak of, what passes for it at the outset fits firmly in the Machiavellian grip of Al Swearengen (Emmy-nominated and

Golden Globe–winning Ian McShane). A foul-mouthed, mustachioed Brit with a hair-trigger temper, Swearengen runs a profitable saloon and brothel, and shrewdly dangles money, liquor, women and drugs to persuade a small army of assassins, ne'er-do-wells and sycophants to do his bidding. Another enterprising, though far more scrupulous soul is Seth Bullock (Timothy Olyphant), who migrated from Montana to open a hardware store with his European-born, Jewish business partner, Sol Star (John Hawkes). Not surprisingly, the morally bankrupt Swearengen occasionally locks horns with the marginally righteous Bullock, though both men are wise enough to know when to bury the hatchet in pursuit of a common goal (such as the inevitable annexation) or against a common foe. The most prominent rival is ruthless mining magnate George Hearst (Gerald McRaney), the father of media tycoon William Randolph Hearst, who, in the show's third season, wielded a heavy influence in his quest for what he called the "color"—gold.

Like Hearst, Swearengen and Bullock were real people (Swearengen's business interests took in, by some accounts, thousands of dollars a week; Bullock became a close friend of Theodore Roosevelt), and the roster of those who visited Deadwood is populated by some of the era's better-known personalities. They include Wild Bill Hickok (Keith Carradine), the legendary gunslinger whose already storied reputation was only enhanced after he was slain playing poker just a few days after his arrival. Calamity Jane (Emmy-nominated scene-stealer Robin Weigert) is Hickok's boozy sidekick, who remains after he's killed and pitches in during a smallpox outbreak; and the third season witnessed a brief tour by brothers Wyatt and Morgan Earp (Gale Harold, Austin Nichols), several years before the Gunfight at the OK Corral.

But *Deadwood* is much more than a Who's Who of the Old West, and its ensemble cast of entertaining characters, real and imagined, runs the gamut from the more-spice-than-sugar Trixie (Paula Malcomson), Swearengen's lover, to Alma Garret (Molly Parker), a refined New Yorker who, between bouts of opium addiction, becomes the wealthiest woman in town after inheriting her late husband's lucrative gold claim. There is also E. B. Farnum (William Sanderson), a spineless toady who runs a hotel as well as interference for Swearengen; A. W. Merrick (Jeffrey Jones), publisher of Deadwood's first newspaper; stooping, shuffling Doc Cochran

Top 3 Moments

- Never jumped.
- When Al's swearing became too much.
- Bad from Day 1.

For more, visit www.jumptheshark.com.

(Emmy nominee Brad Dourif), who practices primitive medicine while battling the demons of his horrifying days as a Civil War surgeon; and Mr. Wu (Keone Young), the de facto mayor of the Chinese contingent, overseer of opium and prostitution rings, and whose pigs are fed with a steady diet of murdered corpses.

Now, about that language. It is raw and relentless. But if Milch's exhaustive probe of this unruly fringe of society taught him anything, it was that this brand of frontier life was no place for shrinking violets. It was survival of the fittest, writ large, every single day, and if that called for a supremely coarse vernacular, then so be it. While the substitution of 21st-century swearing may sound somewhat anachronistic, it has a more dramatic impact than the archaic 19th-century oaths, and, anyway, his point is to show that obscenities were as natural as breathing.

As for the violence, Milch also found that, in its infancy, the settlement averaged about one murder every 24 hours, which is why there always seems to be a corpse chilling in the creek (and why Wu's pigs stay fat). The streams of profanity are often shrouded in lilting soliloquies, but there's nothing subtle about the rampant beatings, shootings and throat-cuttings. One of the most unforgettable scenes contained nary a word of dialogue. It was a third-season confrontation between Swearengen's chief enforcer, Dan Dority (W. Earl Brown), and Hearst's henchman, Captain Turner (Allan Graf). Spoiling for a fight ever since they met, these two mighty rivals clashed in an ursine street ballet for the ages, teeth bared, backs up and claws out, trading one punishing blow after another and tumbling breathlessly down the muddy thoroughfare. After nearly five excruciating minutes of sputtering, bloodthirsty brawling, Dority, at the point of no return, turned the tables by gouging one of the Captain's eyeballs clean out of its socket, staggering to his feet and, with a glance at Swearengen for approval, forever silencing his adversary's screams with a log to the back of the head, the life gone out of him. It was a ferocious spasm of hand-to-hand combat, absurdly poetic in its brutality, and it even *sounds* disturbing. But if that was Milch's desired effect, it certainly worked its magic on me.

> ## Did You Know?
>
> *Picky, picky:* In one memorable episode, Starr told Bullock: "Your fly is down." However, in 1876 trousers had buttons not zippers, so his fly would have been "open" not "down."

Contractual obligations put an end to the show after three seasons. It was far too short a run, though Milch has agreed to produce an epilogue of sorts, likely in the manner of a pair of two-hour films in 2007. The real Deadwood suffered a terrible fire in 1879, forcing the community to almost completely rebuild itself, so it's understandable that the series could not go on in perpetuity. But thanks to TV's *Deadwood*, we are afforded a graphic tutorial on the seven deadly sins and a plunge into the depths of human nature. It boasts a dazzling array of Emmy-winning direction, cinematography, sets and costumes; nominations for acting, casting, writing, theme music and drama series; and, in Swearengen, certainly one of TV's all-time villains. In the TV landscape, the Western may be largely dead, but *Deadwood*, for a few short years at least, gave it a distinctively powerful and profane new life.

Cast:

Timothy Olyphant *Seth Bullock*, **Ian McShane** *Al Swearengen*, **Molly Parker** *Alma Garret*, **Keith Carradine** *Wild Bill Hickok (2004)*, **John Hawkes** *Sol Star*, **Brad Dourif** *Doc Cochran*, **William Sanderson** *E. B. Farnum*, **Paula Malcomson** *Trixie*, **Powers Boothe** *Cy Tolliver*, **Robin Weigert** *Calamity Jane*, **W. Earl Brown** *Dan Dority*, **Dayton Callie** *Charlie Utter*, **Ricky Jay** *Eddie Sawyer (2004)*, **Sean Bridgers** *Johnny Burns*, **Kim Dickens** *Joanie Stubbs*, **Ray McKinnon** *Rev. H. W. Smith (2004)*, **Tim Omundson** *Brom Garret (2004)*, **Garret Dillahunt** *Jack McCall (2004)/Francis Wolcott (2005–06)*, **Leon Rippy** *Tom Nuttall*, **Jeffrey Jones** *A. W. Merrick*, **Jim Beaver** *Ellsworth*, **Titus Welliver** *Silas Adams*, **Bree Seanna Wall** *Sophia Metz*, **Anna Gunn** *Martha Bullock (2005–06)*, **Josh Eriksson** *William Bullock (2005–06)*

Degrassi: The Franchise

By Daniel Manu

Degrassi Junior High and *Degrassi High*
Broadcast History: PBS, 1987–1991
Runtime: 30 minutes
Genre: Drama

Degrassi: The Next Generation
Broadcast History: CTV, 10/14/2001;
    Noggin (The N), 4/1/2002–
Runtime: 30 minutes
Genre: Drama

For 20 years, the most realistic adolescents anywhere in American pop culture have spoken with distinctly Canadian accents. Created by a former Toronto schoolteacher turned producer, the fictional students of *Degrassi* have spawned several television series, numerous spin-off specials, countless Web sites and at least two generations of devoted fans on both sides of the border—all thanks to the deceptively simple concept of portraying teen life from the singular perspective of the teenagers themselves.

The seeds were planted in 1980 with a 30-minute film, *Ida Makes a Movie*, from Playing With Time, an independent production company founded by middle school instructor Linda Schuyler and her partner, Kit Hood. After the short was aired on television by the Canadian Broadcasting Corporation (CBC), additional stories were commissioned, leading to the 26 episodes that made up *The Kids of Degrassi Street*. After that series ended in 1985, Playing With Time created a groundbreaking repertory company that not only discovered and trained young actors through a series of workshops, but also allowed them to offer input on the scripts for a new show that would become the cornerstone of a franchise: *Degrassi Junior High*.

Produced by the CBC in association with Boston's WGBH, a flagship PBS station, *Degrassi* debuted in 1987, an era in which prime-time American television marginalized young characters in family sitcoms like *Family Ties*, *The Cosby Show* and *Growing Pains*—where problems were always solved within 22 minutes with a reassuring hug and a final laugh-track burst. In sharp contrast, Schulyer decreed that on her show, adults would rarely solve problems for the kids—they'd have to deal with issues on their own or with the help of their peers.

In addition, according to Kathryn Ellis's book *Degrassi Generations*, the series insisted on casting age-appropriate actors, many of them with little or no training other than their rep workshops. This meant that the kids actually looked like regular kids in all of their multiethnic, awkward, acne-ridden glory (no 25-year-old "teens" with receding hairlines here) and that the writers had to create characters around the teens' actual personalities. At the same time, the relatively low-budget production had to film in a real school without the sophisticated cameras, lights and sound of major network shows. The result was a compelling, then-unique naturalism on the part of both the actors and the visual aesthetic of the show—an unsuspecting viewer could be forgiven for thinking they'd stumbled across a documentary—that was only bolstered by *Degrassi*'s incredibly bold approach to issues that most adult programming still considered taboo.

Unlike the now parodied "very special episodes" of U.S. shows of that day, *Degrassi* and its 1989 successor, *Degrassi High*, didn't bring in guest stars to suffer the affliction du jour, teach a valuable life-lesson to the series regulars and then disappear forever by episode's end. Instead, every major *Degrassi* student faced problems that were truly organic to their situations and characters. A full inventory of the issues covered by *Degrassi Junior High* and *Degrassi High* could fill pages, but they included teen pregnancy, HIV infection, abortion, illegal drugs, suicide, coming out gay, sexual abuse, alcoholic parents and interracial dating. In each case, the series distinguished itself with its refreshing lack of didacticism, moral judgment or pat resolutions. Just like in life, problems had consequences that were felt across episodes and even seasons, with right and wrong consistently up for thought-provoking debate.

But as Schuyler later emphasized in an interview with TVGUIDE.com, although enlightening her young audience was her ultimate goal, entertaining them was always the show's first priority. Characters like irrepressible Joey Jeremiah (Pat Mastroianni), idealistic Caitlin Ryan (Stacie Mistysyn), punked-out Spike (Amanda Stepto), boy crazy twins Erica and Heather (Angela and Maureen Deiseach), insecure rocker Snake (Stefan Brogren) and the rest of the large ensemble provided plenty of comedy and romance to balance out the dark drama.

An award-winning, mainstream sensation during its original 1989–92 run in Canada, where it attracted millions of viewers and later became a staple of afterschool reruns, *Degrassi Junior High* and *Degrassi High* were a true cult phenomenon in the United States thanks to the vagaries of local PBS scheduling (not to mention public broadcasting's decidedly uncool reputation among teens). Few of the series' original American fans were lucky enough to know other *Degrassi* devotees—for many of them, writer-director Kevin Smith's hilarious reference to the show in his 1997 film *Chasing Amy* was the first sign that others out there had also grown up with a thing for boys and girls who say "aboot."

Kept alive in memory during the mid-'90s by überfans like Smith and hundreds of Internet sites and message boards, *Degrassi*'s return was sparked by a highly rated cast reunion on a Canadian afternoon talk show called *Jonovision* in 1999, which led one of the original series' writers to realize that if teen mom

Spike had been real, her daughter Emma would be old enough to attend junior high, according to author Kathryn Ellis.

With that scenario as a starting point, Schuyler and her new production company, Epitome Pictures, launched *Degrassi: The Next Generation* in 2001, featuring a new set of teens (including Miriam McDonald as Emma) as well as several returning *Degrassi Junior High* characters (Joey, Snake, Spike and Caitlin) in supporting roles—brilliantly bridging the gap between new and older viewers. This time around, the series was slicker in all respects: though workshops were still used to develop scripts, the young cast came to the show with professional credits and real acting chops. And instead of filming at a school, a bigger budget meant a studio soundstage—the naturalism of the '80s was gone, replaced by a professional polish and financial backing and distribution courtesy of two commercial networks, CTV in Canada and fledgling cable channel The N in the United States.

Did You Know?

J. T.'s full name, James Tiberius, is a reference to Capt. James Tiberius Kirk from *Star Trek*.

But what hadn't changed was the *Degrassi* team's commitment to teen-centric storytelling and an unflinching approach to the most relevant hard-hitting issues, beginning in the first *Next Generation* episode with Internet predators and moving on to date rape, gay-bashing, school shootings, bisexuality and more. A two-parter in the third season in which a main character (Manny, played by Cassie Steele) had an abortion was even held back from broadcast by The N for two years, while other controversial episodes were edited for U.S. audiences, prompting complaints from fans and an eager audience for director's cut DVDs. Even in the new millennium, it seemed, *Degrassi* still maintained its edge.

More popular and heavily publicized than ever, the franchise continued to break new ground with the sixth season of *The Next Generation* in 2006, following several characters to college for the first time while also bringing in new cast members to replenish the high school ranks. It's a creative strategy that could potentially allow *Degrassi* to continue another 20 years, if not more. As creator Linda Schulyer told TVGUIDE.com at the beginning of that new season, "As long as they'll have us, we'll be there."

Cast for *Degrassi Junior High* and *Degrassi High*:

Pat Mastroianni *Joey Jeremiah*, **Maureen McKay** *Michelle Accethe*, **Stefan Brogren** *Archie "Snake" Simpson*, **Maureen Deiseach** *Heather Farrell*, **Angela Deiseach** *Erica Farrell*, **Darrin Brown** *Dwayne Myers*, **Duncan Waugh** *Arthur Kobalausky*, **Amanda Stepto** *Christine "Spike" Nelson*, **Anais Granofsky** *Lucy Fernandez*, **Neil Hope** *Derek "Wheels" Wheeler*, **Michael Carry** *Simon Dexter*, **Irene Courakos** *Alexa Pappadopoulos*, **Sara Ballingall** *Melanie Brodie*, **Rebecca Haines** *Kathleen Mead*, **Jacey Hunter** *Amy Holmes*, **Siluck Saysanasy** *Yick Yu*, **Nicole Stoffman** *Stephanie Kaye*

Cast for *Degrassi: The Next Generation*:

Daniel Clark *Sean Cameron (2001–04; 2006–)*, **Lauren Collins** *Paige Michalchuk*, **Aubrey Graham** *James "Jimmy" Brooks*, **Shane Kippel** *Gavin "Spinner" Mason*, **Miriam McDonald** *Emma Nelson*, **Melissa McIntyre** *Ashley Kerwin (2001–05; 2006–)*, **Cassie Steele** *Manuella "Manny" Santos*, **Ryan Cooley** *James Tiberius "J. T." Yorke*, **Jake Goldsbie** *Toby W. Isaacs*, **Stefan Brogren** *Archie "Snake" Simpson*, **Amanda Stepto** *Christine "Spike" Nelson*, **Christina Schmidt** *Terri McGreggor (2001–04)*, **Dan Woods** *Principal Daniel Raditch (2001–05)*, **Stacey Farber** *Eleanor "Ellie" Nash (2002–)*, **Adamo Ruggiero** *Marco Del Rossi (2002–)*, **Jake Epstein** *Craig Manning (2002–)*, **Andrea Lewis** *Hazel Aden (2002–06)*, **Pat Mastroianni** *Joey Jeremiah (2002–06)*, **Stacie Mistysyn** *Caitlin Ryan (2003–06)*, **Shenae Grimes** *Darcy Edwards (2004–)*, **Jamie Johnston** *Peter Stone (2005–)*, **Deanna Casaluce** *Alex Nunez (2005–)*, **Mike Lobel** *Jay Hogart (2005–)*, **Melissa DiMarco** *Ms. Daphne Hatzilakos (2005–)*

Desperate Housewives

By Paul Droesch

Broadcast History: ABC, 10/3/2004–
Runtime: 60 minutes
Genre: Comedy-drama

Wisteria Lane's first skeleton wasn't in any-body's closet. It was under the pool behind Mary Alice and Paul Young's house in that posh and seemingly peaceful cul-de-sac in suburban Fairview. It was bound to surface, and when it did (on October 3, 2004) Wisteria Lane's housewives began acting strangely. Desperately, even.

Mary Alice shot herself in the pilot episode because she didn't want to be blackmailed by the neighbor who knew about that skeleton. Viewers weren't let in on the mystery's resolution until the first-season finale the following May, and if you need a refresher (or if you're not a *Desperate Housewives* fan), here goes: the bones were those of Deirdre, a onetime drug addict and the lover of plumber Mike Delfino. Mary Alice had killed her 15 years before in a fight over her (and Mike's) son, Todd, whom the Youngs abducted as an infant and renamed Zach. Later, Paul murdered Mrs. Huber, the blackmailer.

Those, and other less lethal but no less sordid doings, have made *Housewives* one of ABC's biggest hits in recent years. And they earned the show an Emmy nomination in 2005 for Outstanding Series—in the comedy division, because who says murder can't be funny?

Well, not exactly funny (although George Williams's Season 2 overdose and Nora Warren's Season 3 shooting came close), but at least absurd. Plus the mayhem is mixed in with so much stuff that really is funny—Gaby (Eva Longoria) brawling with the nun who had designs on Carlos (Ricardo Antonio Chavira). Lynette (Felicity Huffman) dancing on a bar. Bree (Marcia Cross) having her first orgasm (and not knowing what it was). Come to think of it, when Edie (Nicollette Sheridan) burned down Susan's house in the second season, that was funny, too. Nobody got hurt, and the sight of plucky Susan (Teri Hatcher) living in a trailer was delicious. Creator Marc Cherry and his writers also give us moments of real pathos here and there (more so for Gabrielle when she lost the baby she never knew she wanted in Season 3). But what they're usually trying to do is elicit the satisfied chuckle that comes from knowing that the mock melodrama you've just seen is very clever indeed. It's the chuckle that comes with knowing you're in on the joke. It's a send up of *Knots Landing*, with a little *Twin Peaks* thrown in.

The *Twin Peaks* connection shouldn't be overemphasized, although Brenda Strong, who played Mary Alice and continues to keep tabs on Wisteria Lane doings from beyond the grave as the series' unseen narrator, has *Peaks* among her career credits (she was in four 1991 episodes). And then there's Agent Cooper himself, Kyle MacLachlan (more about his *DH* character, Orson, later). But David Lynch's cult favorite was surreal and *Housewives* isn't. *Peaks* wasn't nearly as funny as *Housewives* is, either, and it burned itself out in a year while *Housewives* clearly didn't. What they do have in common, though, is that tweaking of the dark side. Then there's the fact that Cherry once told the Associated Press that *Peaks* inspired him to do the show.

Cherry had cut his TV eyeteeth several years earlier as Dixie Carter's personal assistant on *Designing Women*, a female-ensemble show. Then he got a job writing for *The Golden Girls*. And then he was a co-creator of the 1994 CBS sitcom *The Five Mrs. Buchanans*. Is a trend emerging here? (Not only that, *Buchanans* was set in the suburbs and had a character named Bree.)

Rounding out Cherry's resume are two more forgotten sitcoms (*The Crew* and *Some of My Best Friends*) that *weren't* female-ensemble comedies, so he wasn't exactly a watercooler name when he pitched *Housewives* in 2004. In fact, at age 42, Cherry was getting a bit desperate for a hit. So it was back to what had worked best—suburbs and Bree (plus Gaby, Lynette, Susan and Edie).

But this is a comedy most of the time, remember, and the murder's only part of the mix. For that matter, the Youngs' problem was placed on the back burner after Season 1, although Zach's machinations with his grandfather, Noah, got some Season 2 airtime. The Applewhite murder mystery, which also played out over the second season, remained mostly on the back burner as well, since Alfre Woodard, who played Applewhite matriarch Betty, didn't have as much time to devote to the series as the producers would have liked. The story line (which involved Betty's mentally challenged son and his involvement in a young woman's murder) never really captured fans' imaginations, anyhow. (Maybe more Woodard would have added more oomph to it.)

Bree, the Martha Stewart-on-steroids housewife (and, after the first season, the only actual housewife of the bunch), had murder woes as well. First, husband No. 1, Rex (Steven Culp), was killed—by Bree's second-season fiancé, wacko-pharmacist George (Peter Bart), who tampered with Rex's heart medications. Then George took an overdose of sleeping pills. He did it on purpose, but only so Bree could save him, and she pointedly didn't, so that's almost murder, isn't it? Next there was husband No. 2, Orson (MacLachlan) and the business with his mistress, Monique, who turned up dead on the night he married Bree. And, don't forget, it was Orson who ran over poor Mike (James Denton) at the end of the second season, putting him

Did You Know?

Among the actresses considered for the role of Susan Mayer were Calista Flockhart, Mary-Louise Parker and Heather Locklear. The part went to Teri Hatcher.

into a six-month coma. But through it all, Bree remained the perfect wife and mother. Okay, she drank too much in Season 2, her nasty gay son, Andrew (Shawn Pyfrom), turned to hustling after she threw him out of the house, and daughter Danielle (Joy Lauren) had an affair with her history teacher. But the ever-proper Bree ("I don't do *that*. I'm a Republican.") is certainly the doyenne of the domestic arts. Wasn't that first orgasm precipitated in part by Orson's uncanny ability to remove stains from wineglasses? It's no surprise that when Wisterians learned the Season 3 hostage crisis in which Nora died was being covered live on local TV they immediately headed to Bree's house. They knew that she'd be serving canapés.

Lynette was wounded in that crisis, but that didn't slow her down much. A mother of four and a successful advertising executive, Lynette's the superachiever of the group. So it's a good thing that she and her hus-

> ## Preview Review
> ### September 12, 2004
>
> **The Setup**: It's a beautiful day in the neighborhood, until seemingly perfect suburbanite Mary Alice Young shockingly ends her life. Her tragedy threatens to unravel the secretly turbulent existence of the friends and family she left behind.
>
> **The Twist**: Mary Alice, observing the melodrama from the afterlife, acts as our narrator.
>
> **We Say**: Wow. A little *Knots Landing*, a little *American Beauty*, this sexy and satirical twist on the prime-time soap is TV bliss, with a perfect blend of humor and intrigue and a delightful eclectic cast (including Felicity Huffman as a career woman turned frazzled mom and Marcia Cross as a tightly wound control freak).

band, Tom (Doug Savant), who's not quite as accomplished as she is, have Wisteria Lane's best marriage. That bond helped them weather his disastrous attempt at house-husbandry, her stint as his superior at the ad agency, and the arrival of his love child who had been conceived with the conniving Nora before he met Lynette.

Not so happily married were the fiery Solises: former runway model Gaby and shady businessman Carlos. (He went to jail in Season 2.) In fact, they split up in Season 3, and no wonder, after Gaby's first-season fling with lawn boy John Rowland (Jesse Metcalfe); Carlos's second-season affair of the soul with Sister Mary Bernard (Melinda Page Hamilton), the nun who had befriended him in prison; and his third-season dalliance with Xaio-Mei (Gwendolyne Yeo), the illegal-immigrant housekeeper who was carrying their baby. Isn't it delectable that it's the Mexican couple who hired the illegal-immigrant housekeeper?

That leaves sweet, clumsy Susan, a children's book illustrator who's prone to being caught, literally (and innocently) with her pants down, and real-estate saleswoman Edie, a vixen for whom *deshabille* is always strategic. These two, divorcées at the outset of the series, are not friends. After all, friends don't burn down friends' houses. The arson was rooted in their competition for Susan's ex, Karl (Richard Burgi), but Edie also stole Mike away from her after he awoke from his Orson-induced coma with amnesia and was thus unable to remember Susan, who had been keeping vigil by his bedside.

Edie dumped Mike immediately after his third-season arrest for the murder of Monique (remember her?), and Susan came to his rescue because she's both sweet and sweet on Mike. But, for Susan, things are never simple: by then, she had a new boyfriend, Ian (Dougray Scott), a very rich British ex-pat who had been keeping a bedside vigil for his wife, who also happened to be in a coma.

Wait a second, parallel comas? Isn't that romantic? It's just silly enough to work on *Desperate Housewives*, and Cherry has plans to keep Wisteria Lane percolating through the 2010–11 season. Or until those chuckles turn to groans.

Cast:

Felicity Huffman *Lynette Scavo*, **Teri Hatcher** *Susan Mayer*, **Marcia Cross** *Bree Van De Kamp*, **Eva Longoria** *Gabrielle Solis*, **Nicollette Sheridan** *Edie Britt*, **Mark Moses** *Paul Young*, **Cody Kasch** *Zack Young*, **Richard Burgi** *Karl Mayer*, **Andrea Brown** *Julie Mayer*, **Steven Culp** *Rex Van De Kamp (2004–05)*, **Ricardo Antonio Chavira** *Carlos Solis*, **James Denton** *Mike Delfino*, **Doug Savant** *Tom Scavo*, **Jesse Metcalfe** *John Rowland*, **Shawn Pyfrom** *Andrew Van De Kamp*, **Joy Lauren** *Danielle Van De Kamp*, **Brenda Strong** *Mary Alice Young (Narrator)*, **Alfre Woodard** *Betty Applewhite (2005–06)*, **Mehcad Brooks** *Matthew Applewhite (2005–06)*, **Kyle MacLachlan** *Orson Hodge (2006–)*

The Dick Van Dyke Show

By Ileane Rudolph

Broadcast History: CBS, 10/3/1961–9/7/1966
Runtime: 30 minutes
Genre: Sitcom
Black and White

Rob and Laurie Petrie (aka Dick Van Dyke and Mary Tyler Moore) made it OK for married people to have sex. Oh sure, the series was exquisitely funny, had indelible characters and was wonderfully acted, but to viewers who were young back in 1961, *The Dick Van Dyke Show* is fondly remembered as the first sitcom to have real sex appeal. Rob and Laura made marital whoopee, we kids were *sure* of it. How could we not be when Laura, played by the adorable 24-year-old Moore in her first major role, sighed "Ohhhh, Rob!" All the teenage boys—and some of their fathers—in my Philadelphia neighborhood wanted to date the lithe actress in her capri pants. And it goes without saying that females of all ages wanted to look and dress like her. No one ever said that about Donna Reed. Oh, how I suffered trying to torture my hair into a semblance of her perfectly upturned flip!

This was Carl Reiner's second attempt at a series based on both his home life in New Rochelle, New York, and his experiences as a cast member and writer on Sid Caesar's variety shows. (We all thought the show's rarely seen fictional comic tyrant Alan Brady, played from time to time by Reiner, was based on the volcanic Caesar, but Reiner said that Milton Berle and Jackie Gleason were more in his mind.) CBS passed on his first pilot, *Head of the Family*, with himself and Barbara Britton as the lead couple. Reiner wasn't considered "the right type" to play himself.

Two years later, the retitled and retooled show's casting was impeccable, with the rubber-limbed Van Dyke (fresh off a success on Broadway in *Bye Bye Birdie*) as the young husband and *Alan Brady Show* head writer; comic veterans Rose Marie and Morey Amsterdam as fellow writers Sally and Buddy; and Richard Deacon as bald, haughty producer Mel Cooley, the long-suffering butt of Buddy's barbs.

Sublimely funny as they were, the unknown or semi-known actors were no shoo-ins for success. Amsterdam's quip when Rose Marie told him about the show—"What's a Dick Van Dyke?" could have been asked by many at the time. Moore, whose main claim to fame were her legs, the only part of her seen on *Richard Diamond, Private Detective*, was the last regular cast and was almost nixed by Van Dyke because she was so young. Others worried about her lack of comedy credentials. She may have been a comic neophyte, but she learned quickly and well. The show, she later told me, "was among the first situation comedies that made truth in comedy as important as the laugh."

The result was a cornucopia of pleasure; a witty and sometimes silly look at real people with real foibles ("We never tried to be caricatures of human beings," Van Dyke said). It was the perfect reflection of that transitional period after the benign innocence of the 1950s and just before the coming maelstrom of civil rights, the women's movement, hippies and the Vietnam War brought with it more daring sitcoms like *All in the Family*. In the early 1960s, TV was still a place where the connubial bed was a twin set and CBS could chastise Moore because her pants "cupped" her behind.

Not that Reiner and crew didn't occasionally sneak a bit in that would shake up the censors. Perhaps the series' single funniest moment was the look on Rob Petrie's face in a flashback episode called "That's My Boy???" (September 25, 1963). After son Richie's birth, the new dad became convinced that the hospital switched his child with another family's baby. The denouement came when that couple—played by Greg Morris and Mimi Dillard—showed up on the Petrie doorstep and both the audience and Rob realized they were black. The sponsor, Procter & Gamble, and then CBS were worried that viewers might think they were making fun of the black family. The producers made a deal: if the live audience was offended, the ending would be reshot. Hardly. Rob's embarrassed double take drew the show's longest laugh ever. And with their first script, young writers Sam Denoff and Bill Persky began their ascent to comedy writer stardom.

Preview Review
September 16, 1961

The Dick Van Dyke Show comes at you two ways: (1) Its principal character Rob Petrie is a gag writer (for a show Richard Deacon produces), so he and his two colleagues (Morey Amsterdam and Rose Marie) zing lines at you all show long. (2) Petrie has a pretty wife and cute child, which provide all sorts of family palpitations.

Sample episode: Dick's wife is afraid to go out because she thinks their son is sick—the boy refuses to eat his chocolate cupcake. Dick persuades her to go anyway. When they return home his wife goes into shock because the doctor is there, spatterings of blood dot the kitchen, and the neighbors are fluttering around and about. Turns out the baby sitter, who's the neighbors' kid, bumped her head on the refrigerator. Nothing serious—and the laughs keep coming. *Debut: October 3.*

Incredibly, *The Dick Van Dyke Show* was almost a mere blip in our cultural history. In its first season, it died against NBC's *Perry Como Show*. Moore's soon-to-be husband Grant Tinker saved the day when he helped producer Sheldon Leonard land Kent cigarettes—it was the '60s, folks—as a sponsor for the struggling show. Great summer rerun ratings ensured its pickup and, luckily for viewers then and now, the laughter continued.

All fans of the show have their own favorites, episodes that remain gem-like in the memory. I'll pick three. "The Blonde-Haired Brunette" (October 10, 1961), in which Laura dyes her hair blonde to rekindle what she believes is Rob's fading interest, marks Moore coming into her own as a comedienne. And it initiates her trademark tragi-comic crying jags (which, she admits, she stole from Nanette Fabray).

For pure silliness, to my mind nothing beats "It May Look Like a Walnut!" (February 6, 1963), a surreal *Twilight Zone* spoof in which Rob dreams that an alien (played by Danny Thomas, a producer of the show) sets out to conquer the world with the help of marauding walnuts. And in devout appreciation of Van Dyke's brilliant physical comedy, I have to go with "October Eve" (April 8, 1964). The vision of an anguished Rob grabbing—and holding on to—the burning-hot coils of a stove in reaction to Laura's tortured explanation of why there's a nude painting of her in an art exhibition, is vivid decades after it first made me laugh until the tears came.

> ## Did You Know?
>
> Johnny Carson was a runner-up for the role of Rob Petrie.

Despite its still-strong ratings, this classic show only lasted five seasons. After 15 Emmys and landing in the Top 10 three times, Reiner (who, some 30 years later, won a Guest Actor Emmy when he revived the role of Alan Brady in an episode of *Mad About You*) pulled the plug. "The network offered quite a bit of money," he said years later, "but five years seems like a nice package. We went out with a bang." There would be no more of Rob tripping over the iconic sofa, but four decades later, Earl Hagen's delightful syncopated theme still plays in our heads. Tah-dah-da-da-da-da-da-da . . . And we smile.

Cast:

Dick Van Dyke *Rob Petrie*, **Mary Tyler Moore** *Laura Petrie*, **Rose Marie** *Sally Rogers*, **Morey Amsterdam** *Buddy Sorrell*, **Richard Deacon** *Mel Cooley*, **Carl Reiner** *Alan Brady*, **Jerry Paris** *Jerry Helper*, **Ann Morgan Guilbert** *Millie Helper*, **Larry Matthews** *Ritchie Petrie*

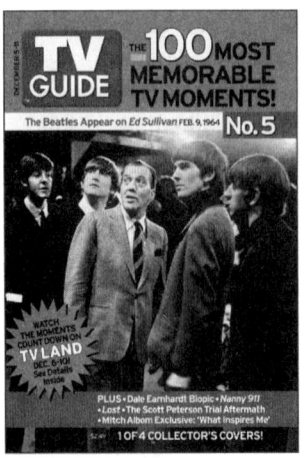

The Ed Sullivan Show

By Michael Davis

Broadcast History: CBS, 6/20/1948–6/6/1971
Runtime: 60 minutes
Genre: Variety show

Everyone's a critic in New York. It's a town without pity.

Once, back in 1948, a professional heckler named Patsy Flick tormented Ed Sullivan from the audience of his nascent CBS variety show, *Toast of the Town*. "Did you look dat vay vhen you vere alive?" razzed the Yiddish provocateur.

That Sullivan actually had a *paid* Patsy to mock him is a telling historical note, given that a host of others would make great sport of him through the decades. For even in the primordial days of television, Ed Sullivan, the emcee, knew he was a dead man walking, a stiff of the highest order, a sportswriter turned gossip columnist turned broadcaster whose rigor mortis manner just begged to be belittled. By the 1960s, the CBS schedule had *Mr. Ed* and Ed. One was a talking horse, the other was a variety host saddled with no discernible stage presence.

Sullivan was made for ridicule and an entire generation of impressionists, starting with the incomparable Will Jordan and carried on by John Byner, Rich Little, Jackie Mason and others, carved out careers by mimicking him. Even small children could do Ed. They'd fold their arms and hollow their cheeks, pretending they were sucking lemons. "Tonight we have a rilly big shew," they'd say, spinning on their heels.

Watching *The Ed Sullivan Show* on Sunday nights at 8 o'clock provided America a weekly opportunity to feel superior. Who among us didn't secretly believe that we could do a better job hosting than the guy who mangled and mispronounced the names of the very performers he had *hand-picked* for the show?

Sullivan was the easiest target on television, and that was fine with him, just as long as viewers tuned in each week to his little entertainment cavalcade. He was its creator, producer, talent coordinator and master of ceremonies; he shaped nearly every aspect of the program and goosed it into becoming a TV colossus. Ed Sullivan's variety extravaganza provided the republic with a shared experience each Sunday, something to talk about the next morning at work or school or in the prison yard. Damn near everyone watched Ed, cardinals and convicts alike.

His aim was to provide something for everyone, and to him, audience reactions constituted "the word of God." If a comic bombed in afternoon dress rehearsal, the funnyman would get bounced from that evening's actual broadcast. Ed didn't need a focus group; he had his gut and his notes from dress to fine-tune the final lineup. Every show had his imprint, every act his preapproval.

As dictators go, Ed Sullivan the producer was neither benign nor especially benevolent. But the same could be said for some of the most revered and feared moguls in stage, screen and television lore. Certainly, during a ripe period of the 1950s and '60s, Sullivan was one among them. After failing in radio and the movies, he found his niche in TV, just as America was getting used to the idea that a box of wires and tubes in the corner of the living room could provide enough visual and audio entertainment to justify an expenditure of a few hundred dollars.

Sullivan gave the new medium something new by resuscitating something old. *Toast of the Town*, later renamed the *The Ed Sullivan Show*, was vaudeville's last gasp, and for 22 seasons, he was the cathode-ray tube's answer to Florenz Ziegfeld. His variety hour was both highbrow and lowbrow, cultured and cornpone, an entertainment crazy quilt that featured opera stars and elephants, both of whom, at times, worked for peanuts. Every performer worth their salt lusted for three minutes on Sullivan's showcase. That they sometimes received a substandard performance fee was beside the point.

There were jugglers and ventriloquists, Borsht Belt comics and Tuscan tenors, Bolshevik bears and Lipizzaner stallions, bobby-socks crooners and soft-shoe shufflers. And, of course, let's not forget the little Italian mouse puppet named Topo Gigio. The range of musical styles stretched from Sophie Tucker to Ike and Tina Turner, from Bill Haley and His Comets to the Doors, from Mahalia Jackson to the Jackson 5, from Benny Goodman to Blood, Sweat & Tears. (If you care about such things, the show's all-time appearance champ was the Canadian comedy duo Wayne and Shuster, with nearly 80 guest shots.)

Did You Know?

Ed Sullivan would fly anywhere in the world to check out an act.

Sullivan became America's unofficial taste-master general. An appearance on his stage provided a kind of certification to performers, a prize that was awarded nowhere else. That was true as well for newsmakers who might be asked to take a bow from their seats in the audience. It meant you had fully arrived in the zeitgeist, even before anyone knew there was one.

Elvis Presley made a few scattered television appearances before he played the Sullivan show, including one humiliating spot with a condescending Steve Allen, who arranged to have Elvis sing "Hound Dog" to a disinterested floppy-eared fleabag. It was no way to treat a future king.

But Presley's shots on *Sullivan* were stunning. Anyone inhaling oxygen in the late '50s remembers Elvis widening the CBS eye—and making it blink—

during his hip-swiveling, swelter-inducing sessions. Sullivan deemed the lip-curled sensation "a fine young man," even as Bible-thumpers were melting Presley records into bubbling black pools of vinyl.

Pop historians note that the Beatles first appeared on American television on tape during a segment on Jack Paar's wry Friday night prime-time show on NBC. Paar looked upon the group as a curiosity. Sullivan saw more, much more. In his greatest impresario moment, he turned the Beatles into the Eighth Wonder of the World. Electrifying is the only word to describe their performance on the night of February 9, 1964 (73 million viewers watched), the first of 10 appearances on the show. It became a television touchstone, the Zenith's zenith, but it was also the beginning of the end of *The Ed Sullivan Show*. Nothing that followed on the program over the next seven years could ever top the Beatles for pure exhilaration and impact.

When *The Ed Sullivan Show* was mercifully euthanized as a weekly show in 1971, its host had withered into a forgetful, easily confused shadow of himself. Like vaudeville itself, Sullivan seemed an anachronism. Impersonations of him were no longer funny, and, besides, we had a new shrug-shouldered stiff, Richard Nixon, to mock.

It ended, like so many institutions, during a period of seismic cultural change in America. The Beatles split, the nation fractured over an unjust war, and the juggler's spinning plates finally crashed to the floor. But thoughts of *The Ed Sullivan Show* in its prime evoke happy memories in the minds of millions. They take us back to Sunday nights when family members young and old gathered around the set to enjoy an iconic variety hour presided over in memorable fashion by a rilly big shewman.

Cast:

Ed Sullivan *Host*

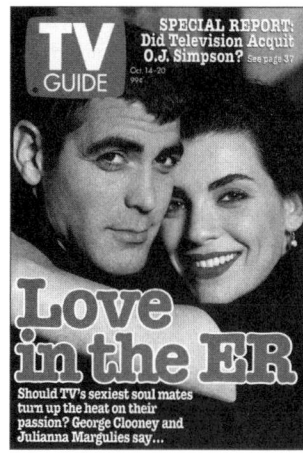

ER

By Trish Wethman
Broadcast History: NBC, 9/19/1994–
Runtime: 60 minutes
Genre: Medical drama

Back in September of 1994, two Chicago-set hospital dramas premiered on two different networks in the same time slot on the same night. One was created by TV wunderkind David E. Kelly; the other by novelist Michael Crichton. I remember this not only because it was one of those strange coincidences that happens from time to time in the competitive world of television programming, but also because my mom was absolutely livid. As an RN with many years of patient-care experience in a variety of medical-care facilities, she absolutely loved dramas revolving around hospitals and was excited by the prospect of two top-notch medical shows. Of course in the pre-DVR era, two shows airing at the same time proved to be a logistical nightmare. It required two TVs, a VCR, and the patience and compliance of three teenage children. For about a month, my mom made a valiant effort—she would diligently tape one (*Chicago Hope*) and watch the other (*ER*) as it aired. But as the weeks passed and the videotapes ran out, it became increasingly evident that one of these shows was winning the battle—at least in our household. And 13 years, numerous cast changes, and countless Emmy nominations and wins later, *ER* has also won the war.

Before his unlikely creation debuted to killer ratings and critical acclaim, Michael Crichton was best known as the author of enormously popular sci-fi thrillers such as *The Andromeda Strain*, *Congo*, *Sphere* and *Jurassic Park*. But the Chicago-born writer was also a Harvard-educated physician, so his affinity for medicine was really not all that surprising. What did come as a surprise was that this man who had crafted outlandish, far-flung tales of science gone horribly wrong was able to produce an engrossing and utterly realistic drama about the lives of ER doctors and nurses in an underfunded county hospital. This was gut-wrenching, character-driven, in-your-face storytelling that seemed to appeal to audiences and television critics alike.

People talk a lot about chemistry on television shows but it's a difficult concept to define. The original *ER* ensemble consisted of a hodgepodge of lesser-known actors and actresses with unremarkable résumés who came together and quite simply clicked in a believable, relatable way. To me, that's a hallmark of chemistry—natural interactions between characters that feel unforced and credible. From the first moments of the high-octane pilot, I felt like I had been dropped into the middle of something authentic and vital. The normal exposition that you expect from a new show was jettisoned by hyper-realistic medical jargon, frenetically paced narratives and vertigo-inducing camera work. The viewers were like interns ourselves, weaving through the crowded, unfamiliar hallways and sometimes mundane, sometimes stomach-churning cases. My mom probably summed it up best toward the middle of the first season as we viewed the seminal, Emmy-winning episode "Love's Labor Lost." She said, "Wow, they've really nailed the stress of working in an emergency room." In 1997, TV GUIDE voted this TV's greatest dramatic episode of all time.

The highest profile actor in the original cast was Anthony Edwards. Best known for his role as Tom Cruise's doomed buddy in *Top Gun*, his Mark Greene was the exhausted, slightly aloof center around which the ER swirled. Mark's comrades included his fellow resident Susan Lewis (Sherry Stringfield), ambitious surgeon Peter Benton (Eriq LaSalle), nurse Carol Hathaway (Julianna Margulies), naïve intern John Carter (Noah Wyle) and philandering pediatrician Doug Ross (George Clooney). Off-screen, the reported camaraderie that they shared was well documented. Whether or not that played into the aforementioned chemistry is probably anyone's guess, but there was something about the interplay between these medical cohorts that struck a chord with the viewers.

As the years wore on, the core ensemble thinned and new characters were phased in and out at a sometimes maddening pace. However, each departure seemed to open the door to new possibilities that, in a sense, helped to continually rejuvenate the series. When George Clooney's fame skyrocketed, many thought his departure after Season 5 would signal the beginning of the end for the series. But surprisingly, the ratings remained strong as NBC's powerhouse unceasingly adapted to every curveball. It became evident that the premise of the show—the day-to-day workings of the ER itself—was the real star. Both the strength of that

Classic Episode Close-Up
"Love's Labor Lost"
(Original telecast: March 9, 1995)

The explosive, almost-too-painful-to-watch "Love's Labor Lost" is the most riveting, harrowing and visceral hour of medical drama ever aired. What seems like a routine day in the ER turns sour for Dr. Mark Greene. Distracted by personal and professional problems, he misdiagnoses a pregnant woman and begins a downward spiral of missteps and questionable procedures that continues until all present are in over their heads, panic is thick in the air and, just as in real life, bad things happen to good people—with shocking speed.

premise and the subsequent actors and actresses who have come through the doors of County General have helped to sustain the successful formula. Goran Visnjic, Laura Innes, Maura Tierney, Mekhi Phifer and Parminder Nagra have all stepped up with dense, engrossing stories that have kept viewers riveted. However, much of the viewer loyalty can also be traced to the continuity that has been provided by the peripheral characters. The nurses (Yvette Freeman as Haleh), clerks (Abraham Benrubi as Jerry) and various doctors who have seamlessly floated in and out of the action (John Aylward's Dr. Anspaugh and Amy Aquino's Dr. Coburn, to name a few) consistently remind us that the more things change, the more they stay the same. Even actors who have left their roles, such as Paul McCrane, whose indomitable, petulant and ultimately tragic Dr. Romano remains one of the most vilified characters to ever roam the familiar halls, have returned to direct episodes, bringing a sense of the show's deep history with them.

During its 13th season, *ER* enjoyed a resurgence that is almost unprecedented in network television. It is once again thriving creatively, winning its time slot, and surpassing the expectations of a network and viewers who had assumed the show would probably limp through its final season before expiring as a series whose time had passed. Revitalized writing has breathed new life into the characters we know, and dynamic newcomers like John Stamos are adding texture and intrigue to the mix. As a loyal viewer, I feel like my role has changed as well. I am no longer that novice from the first season, watching in awe as the action unfolds around me. Today I am a little more experienced, a little more critical, but still passionate and engaged, sometimes expecting the worst but always hoping for the best outcome.

Did You Know?

During the live 1997 telecast, George Clooney's Dr. Ross watched the Cubs-Astros game in the break room. That actual baseball game was also aired live that night on WGN.

I am thrilled to see that *ER* continues to reinvent itself successfully, but I think I will always be drawn to the show's early seasons and its original cast, still relatively unencumbered by the trappings of hit-show status and still hungry for our validation. I also remember those episodes fondly because they are the ones I got to watch with my mom. The self-described "No. 1 *ER* fan" passed away in June 2001 just after the seventh season ended. For a little while, it was tough for me to watch this show, which she loved so much, without wondering what she would have thought or how she would have reacted to certain plot developments, but in an odd way, I think it provided me with some unique perspective. *ER* served to remind me of the fact that life goes on and the best way to honor our history is to remember it while we continue to evolve and grow.

Ironically in the midst of the renewed success that the show is enjoying, I recently had a chance to watch one of my favorite episodes again—the Season 1 finale rather aptly entitled "Everything Old Is New Again." As each of the main characters faced some sort of crossroads in their life, they gathered at Carol's ill-fated wedding to support their friend. There was nothing terribly remarkable about this episode except that it demonstrated the bond that had developed between these characters. We had yet to see them experience the full gamut of redemption, love and loss that awaited them, but at that point, it was clear that we were invested deeply in their lives. It's 13 years later and, as *ER* goes on, we still are.

I ♥ TV

This essay is dedicated to Carol D. Connaughton, RN.

Cast:

Anthony Edwards *Mark Greene (1994–2002)*, **Eriq La Salle** *Peter Benton (1994–2001)*, **George Clooney** *Douglas Ross (1994–99)*, **Julianna Margulies** *Carol Hathaway (1994–2000)*, **Sherry Stringfield** *Susan Lewis (1994–96, 2001–05)*, **Noah Wyle** *John Carter (1994–2005)*, **Laura Innes** *Kerry Weaver (1995–2007)*, **Gloria Reuben** *Jeanie Boulet (1995–99)*, **Ming-Na** *Deb Chen (1995, 2000–04)*, **Alex Kingston** *Elizabeth Corday (1997–2004)*, **Maria Bello** *Anna DelAmico (1997–98)*, **Kellie Martin** *Lucy Knight (1998–2000)*, **Goran Visnjic** *Luka Kovac (1999–)*, **Michael Michele** *Cleo Finch (2000–01)*, **Paul McCrane** *Robert Romano (1997–2003)*, **Erik Palladino** *Dave Malucci (1999–2001)*, **Maura Tierney** *Abby Lockhart (2000–)*, **Sharif Atkins** *Michael Gallant (2002–)*, **Mekhi Phifer** *Gregory Pratt (2002–)*, **Linda Cardellini** *Samantha Taggart (2003–)*, **Parminder Nagra** *Neela Rasgotra (2003–)*, **Shane West** *Dr. Ray Barnett (2004–)*, **Scott Grimes** *Archie Morris (2005–)*, **John Stamos** *Tony Gates (2006–)*

Everybody Loves Raymond

By Matt Roush

Broadcast History: CBS, 9/13/1996–5/16/2005
Runtime: 30 minutes
Genre: Sitcom

It didn't take long for me to discover that I wasn't the only one who loved *Everybody Loves Raymond*—though in the early days, it often seemed that way.

Struggling in the ratings, buried in a deadly Friday time period on CBS in the fall of 1996, *Raymond* was a dark-horse favorite of certain TV columnists (including myself), who saw great comic promise in the show's fractiously hilarious family dynamic. Then, out of the blue a few months into its run, I opened a personal letter from none other than Mary Tyler Moore, thanking me for my critical support of this quirky little underdog. She had no connection to the show other than that she loved it, too.

In the crackling chemistry between Ray Romano and Patricia Heaton, who played Ray and Debra Barone, the believably sexy couple at the heart of the show, this legendary TV star saw traces of Rob and Laura Petrie. And, as she reminded me when I talked to her about this afterward, neither of her two enduring CBS landmarks (*The Dick Van Dyke Show* and *The Mary Tyler Moore Show*) had been blockbusters out of the gate, either.

With friends like Mary, how could *Raymond* go wrong?

Not that it wasn't an uphill climb. Beyond the terrible time period (it moved to Monday night by the end of the first season, boosting its fortunes), the show had a goofy title, no stars to speak of, and it looked like scores of domestic sitcoms that had come and gone over the years. Besides, who *was* this Raymond everybody was supposed to be loving?

Ray Romano was David Letterman's contribution to the new wave of stand-up comic discoveries the networks put to work in the wake of megahits like *Roseanne* and *Seinfeld*. An unassuming, nasal-voiced New York comedian and family man whose act revolved around his eccentric family life (including raising twin sons), Romano became the unlikely star of an unheralded sitcom (produced by Letterman's company) that would go on to become one of the all-time greats.

> ### Did You Know?
>
> The three Barone children (Ally, Geoffrey and Michael) were played by real-life siblings Madylin, Sawyer and Sullivan Sweeten.

When *Everybody Loves Raymond* went off the air in 2005, still at the peak of its popularity and creativity, many considered it the end of an era. TV comedy styles and tastes had changed, and there was understandable speculation about whether a "traditional" sitcom about family life could ever reach such heights again.

No one would ever have predicted Top 10 ratings and multiple Emmy Awards in *Raymond*'s future when it first came on the scene. Reviews were generally kind, but the closest thing to hype was the occasional description of *Raymond* as "*Seinfeld* with kids."

The parallels were obvious. Like Jerry Seinfeld, Romano was an observational comic with a distinct New Yawk sensibility (though Italian in origin, not Jewish). Like Seinfeld, Romano was an untested, at times awkward actor (he had earlier been fired from *NewsRadio* in the part that later went to Joe Rogan), and he surrounded himself with seasoned pros in the supporting roles. They made him look good, and he helped them shine. Ultimately, like *Seinfeld*, *Raymond* would also voluntarily call it quits after nine seasons, leaving everyone including their networks desperately wanting more.

Still, loving *Everybody Loves Raymond* was never the hip thing to do—not like being a fan of contemporaries like *Seinfeld*, *Friends* or those trendy HBO comedies. It was acclaimed, immensely popular and reaped a bushel of Emmys over the years. But cool? Not quite.

It only looked old-fashioned because most of the action took place on the familiar domestic stage of a kitchen or living room or bedroom. But no TV comedy in ages, probably not since the glory days of *Roseanne*, had hit as close to home or felt as authentic as *Raymond*, which found endless variety in the universal aggravations of American family life.

A timeless classic was born within the walls of the neighboring Barone households—the gimmick, such as it was, involved sportswriter Ray and housewife Debra and their three kids living across the street from Ray's meddling, bickering parents, Frank and Marie, in whose house Ray's older brother, Robert, a divorced cop with a sad-sack demeanor, miserably lived. *Everybody Loves Raymond* was a multigenerational masterpiece about the inescapable family ties that bind, and often threaten to strangle, parent and child, husband and wife, brother and brother.

Can't live with 'em, can't survive without 'em. And you can't imagine them being played by anyone else.

Romano, who would eventually earn a 2002 Emmy for best comedy actor (something Jerry Seinfeld never achieved), was a lucky apprentice, sharing the stage with major talents in career-defining roles: the mercurial Patricia Heaton as the easily exasperated Debra (her breakthrough was an Emmy-winning performance in an uproarious episode about PMS); the towering comic Brad Garrett as the long-suffering, resentful Robert; the lovably cantankerous Peter Boyle as Frank and, most unforgettably, crafty scene-stealer Doris Roberts as Marie, the ultimate Mommie Nearest, a monstrous manipulator who never missed a chance to insult Debra's cooking and housekeeping while smothering her favorite, Ray, with unwanted affections.

Together, they concocted big laughs from small, mundane situations. Like *Seinfeld* (again!), many of the best episodes often seemed to be about "nothing." But there was something special about *Raymond*, something anyone could relate to who's ever been related to someone. The humor of *Raymond* came from real life: Romano's life, of course, and that of executive producer Phil Rosenthal— his own parents inspired Marie's show-stopping "fruit-of-the-month-club" tirade in the pilot episode—as well as the lives of the show's writers.

The staff was famous for coming to work with painfully acute anecdotes that evolved into brilliant set pieces. One of the best came late in the run: 2003's Emmy-winning "Baggage" episode (by Tucker Cawley), in which a suitcase that both Ray and Debra refuse to put away becomes a metaphor for, as Frank puts it, "who wears the pants in the family."

A suitcase, an engraved toaster, a misplaced canister, a meatball recipe, a ruined wedding video (Ray taped a football game over it): all achieved mythic proportions in the never ending war of the Barones. The comical combat was part battle of the sexes, part power struggle for domestic dominance, especially as Debra and Marie squared off to claim the heart—and, more often than not, the stomach—of passive-aggressive golden boy Raymond.

The show's title, which Romano initially hated and begged to change, is of course ironic. No one on *Raymond*, least of all Ray, was entirely lovable. It wouldn't have been as funny if they were. But we loved them for their faults, for surviving their fights, for remaining consistently and reliably amusing to the end.

Even in the show's final episode, *Raymond* resisted succumbing to hype or self-importance. It wasn't "supersized." Nobody died, or announced a pregnancy or divorce, or any of those other life-changing events that typifies so many contrived grand finales. What happened in Raymond's memorable swan song was a small but powerfully resonant moment—Ray

---

Preview Review
September 14, 1996

The Concept: Call it the anti-*Seinfeld*—an old-fashioned sitcom about something, and that something is husband, wife, kids and in-laws.

The Premise: Stand-up comedian Ray Romano plays a harried sportswriter with a wife and three young children whose suburban Long Island household is under siege by his nosy mother, meddlesome father and oddball brother.

They Say: "We're going out of our way to make a traditional sitcom," says executive producer Phil Rosenthal. "It's very much in the style of *The Dick Van Dyke Show*, *The Mary Tyler Moore Show*, *The Odd Couple*—a character-driven show where believable things happen and the humor is in identifiable things."

We Say: Romano is a very funny guy. And the supporting cast is first-rate. Plunk them down in situations that most people can relate to—which is just what the pilot does—and you have a winner.

has a medical scare during routine surgery (to have his adenoids removed, finally)—triggering reactions that veer from heartrending emotion to rollicking comedy with breathtaking agility and impact.

When Marie later learns that Ray momentarily had trouble waking up from anesthesia, she frantically rushes to her boy's side, scrambling into bed with him and crawling over Debra to pummel an aghast Ray with kisses. "I knew one day this would happen," Debra sighs from her side of the bed. So did we all, but that didn't make it any prettier, or any less hilarious.

The last scene takes place the morning after, with three generations of Barones crowded around the breakfast table, about to be fed Marie's chocolate-chip pancakes (she has commandeered, one last time, Debra's kitchen). As the camera pulls away for the final fade, I was reminded of the closing shot of *Moonstruck*, another grand comic fable about an unforgettable Italian family.

I never wanted that movie to end. I never wanted this series to end. But all good things must, though rarely with such class and confident grace.

I still love Raymond, and I imagine I always will.

Cast:

Ray Romano *Ray Barone*, **Patricia Heaton** *Debra Barone*, **Doris Roberts** *Marie Barone*, **Peter Boyle** *Frank Barone*, **Brad Garrett** *Robert Barone*, **Madylin Sweeten** *Ally Barone*, **Sullivan Sweeten** *Michael Barone*, **Sawyer Sweeten** *Geoffrey Barone*, **Monica Horan** *Amy McDougal Barone (1997–2005)*

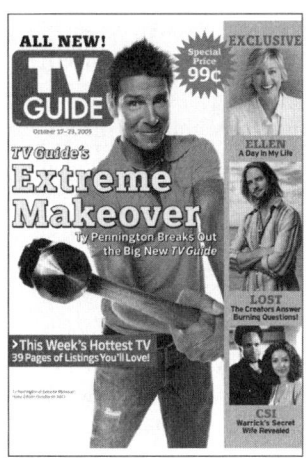

Extreme Makeover: Home Edition

By Trish Wethman

Broadcast History: ABC, 2/15/2004–
Runtime: 60 minutes
Genre: Reality program

Once upon a time, in a land not so far away, there lived families who had suffered unbearable tragedies and overcome unbelievable obstacles—challenges that would make most people run screaming from the castle. To make matters worse, their castles were literally falling down around them or infested with asbestos or termites, or seemed smaller than a breadbox and filled to capacity, or just woefully ill-equipped to deal with their daily realities. Sometimes the families had to split up just to survive, their difficult situations further exacerbated by their inability to even suffer together.

As we know, all good fables need a hero. Enter Ty Pennington, the resident Prince Charming of ABC's weekly fairy tale known as *Extreme Makeover: Home Edition*. Otherwise known as the luckiest carpenter on the planet, this onetime supporting player from the TLC series *Trading Spaces* leveraged his affable personality and good looks into a book deal, a line of home products and a job as a pitchman for Sears. It also landed him a hosting gig on a little spin-off that would emerge as a cornerstone of ABC's ratings resurrection. This all sounds too good to be true, but it should, since ABC is owned by Disney—a company that knows a thing or two about fairy tales.

The original *Extreme Makeover* debuted on ABC in April 2003, igniting some passionate watercooler conversations if not stellar ratings. Viewers have often responded to the concept of taking self-described ugly ducklings and making them into, at the very least, cuter ducklings. *Extreme Makeover* upped the ante by employing some of the country's best plastic surgeons, dentists, fitness trainers and stylists to facilitate the metamorphoses. The results were dramatic . . . and somewhat unsettling for the skittish. Later that year, in the wake of a string of breakout cable shows cen-

> **TV and Film Connections**
> Spun off from *Extreme Makeover*
> Spin-off: *Extreme Makeover: Home Edition: How'd They Do That?*

tered around home improvement, ABC smartly extended the Extreme Makeover brand to a special entitled *Extreme Makeover: Home Edition*. This time, a chord was struck—viewers responded much more positively to the idea of helping deserving families change their lives by fixing the deficiencies of their homes instead of their bodies. Some prescient programming executive recognized that the "Touched by a Carpenter" angle had Sunday night written all over it and thus, a ratings juggernaut was born.

The premise was simple. Pennington and his rowdy assemblage of architects, designers and construction specialists swooped into the hometown of the lucky family aboard their ubiquitous bus. They then set out to generate as much local goodwill as they could to facilitate the reconstruction, and, in a sense, re-imagining, of the homes of families who had suffered heart-breaking blows—parents lost to war, disease or tragic accidents; children living with autism, blindness, deafness or other rare afflictions; single-parent or foster families just trying to make ends meet. These makeovers were not merely cosmetic. The particular medical and emotional needs of each family were meticulously researched and accommodated while the family enjoyed a once-in-a-lifetime vacation, sporadically taunted by the manic Pennington with videotaped images of their old dwellings in ruin. Meanwhile, no detail was overlooked—mementos or items of particular importance to the family were integrated into the final home design in subtle, heartfelt ways—a father's favorite pair of boots by the fireplace, a mother's photo—so that the underlying reason for the makeover was never overlooked.

As the show's success grew, so too did the scope and ambition of the ventures. However, no matter how elaborate the projects became—from a camp for disabled children to an entire Native American reservation—the heart and simplicity of this show remained intact, embodied by the cast and crew who worked tirelessly to complete these projects within their appointed seven-day work cycle. What viewers seem to relate to on a visceral level is the unabashed emotion on display—the carpenters and designers shamelessly jockeying for additional resources, waxing nostalgic about the families as if they've known them forever; the humor and enthusiasm of Pennington; or the family members themselves tearfully chronicling the road that has led them to the "big reveal." Once the family has reconvened to see their new home and Ty leads the gathered crowd in shouting, "Move that bus!" you share the joy, relief and gratitude of the family because you've been along for the ride.

Did You Know?

First Lady Laura Bush appeared on an episode in which the team was helping victims of storm-ravaged Biloxi, Mississippi.

As is often the case with fairy tales, the show has had its share of detractors. Some have complained that the good works are overshadowed by relentless product placement. True, sponsoring companies play a huge role in the show, but when you get right down to it, the great tradition of advertising partnerships has been around as long as television itself—one need only look to shows like *Queen for a Day* and *The Price Is Right* to see how reality entertainment and product sponsorships have peacefully (and profitably) coexisted for a long time. And frankly, where's the harm in sharing the wealth when large corporate entities such as Sears and Kenmore are helping to foot the bill? What resonates with fans of the show and keeps us coming back for more week after week are the deserving families who are being given a chance at a new, better life. It's hard to argue with that kind of happily ever after.

Cyndy Teas, the owner of Camp Barnabas, the haven for disabled children that received a revamp, probably summed it up best to TV GUIDE when she explained the real meaning behind the renovations: "It's a hard thing for people to understand. It's not just that they gave us a new home. It's like someone said, 'Here's the world and a whole new beginning.' And there's no better opportunity than a new beginning."

Cast:

Ty Pennington *Host*, **Paul DiMeo** *Home Improvement Specialist*, **Paige Hemmis** *Home Improvement Specialist*, **Tracy Hutson** *Home Improvement Specialist*, **Michael Moloney** *Home Improvement Specialist*, **Constance Ramos** *Home Improvement Specialist*, **Ed Sanders** *Home Improvement Specialist*, **Preston Sharp** *Home Improvement Specialist*, **Eduardo Xol** *Home Improvement Specialist*, **Tanya McQueen** *Home Improvement Specialist (2005–06)*, **Daniel Kucan** *Home Improvement Specialist (2005–06)*

Family Ties

By Rebecca Paley

Broadcast History: NBC, 9/22/1982–9/17/1989
Runtime: 30 minutes
Genre: Sitcom

I was 9 years old when *Family Ties* first came on in 1982. My parents were far from hippies— my mother was more into Prada than the Peace Corps—but there was something about seeing former 1960s radicals Steven and Elyse Keaton (Michael Gross and Meredith Baxter-Birney) bumble through parenthood and all its authoritarian trappings that resonated. For everyone with baby boomer parents—the kind who like to tell you what you're listening to isn't *really* rock 'n' roll—the ambivalence toward old-fashioned discipline and turning into, well, their parents hit close to home.

The political never got more personal than in this family comedy, which aired on NBC until 1989. The crux of the conflict came with Alex P. Keaton, the right-wing eldest son who constantly shocked his folks with his reading material (*The Wall Street Journal*), ambition (to make a lot of money), his idea of role models (William F. Buckley Jr.) and extracurricular activities (Young Republicans Club, of course). The energetic (but then largely unknown) Michael J. Fox brought a compassionate side to conservatism before George W. Bush's presidential bid was a glimmer in his father's eye. And he made neckties look cool again. Alex's cynical attitude towards his parents' liberalism and his disdain for his younger siblings—ditzy shopaholic Mallory (Justine Bateman) and wisecracking Jennifer (Tina Yothers)—got such a laugh with studio audiences during the early tapings that producers revamped the series to make him the focus instead of his folks. Ironically, Fox had to fight for the role, which was originally offered to, and turned down by, Matthew Broderick. NBC executive Brandon Tartikoff initially thought that Fox had a face "you'll never see on a lunch box." (Tartikoff later kept such a box, with Fox's face on it, in his office.)

Family Ties allowed viewers to laugh at what for many in real life was a painful truth: that the idealism and radicalism of the '60s

> **Did You Know?**
>
> Geena Davis appeared in two 1984 episodes as the Keatons' trial housekeeper.

had given way to a generation that was not only conservative but also highly consumeristic. With the Reagan era in full swing, the Keaton family provided a warm and fuzzy microcosm in Columbus, Ohio, for what was happening across the country. "When else could a boy with a briefcase become a national hero?" said *Family Ties* creator Gary David Goldberg. President Ronald Reagan himself said *Family Ties* was his favorite show and, in fact, offered to do a guest appearance. The producers didn't take him up on it.

Its cultural pertinence and humor lasted. *Family Ties* was the second-highest rated show on television in 1983 and 1984, and it landed in the Top 20 for six out of its seven years (following *The Cosby Show* for several years certainly didn't hurt). Fox was rewarded not only with three Emmy awards and a big-time movie career (particularly in the *Back to the Future* franchise), but also a wife. Tracy Pollan joined the cast in 1985 as Alex's girlfriend Ellen Reed. The on-screen sweethearts were married for real three years later. Alex's string of love interests also included Lauren Miller, played by Courteney Cox of later *Friends* fame.

In 1985, Elyse and Michael had another son, Andrew, and the child actor Brian Bonsall was brought on to play the part of the youngest Keaton. It made for some interesting plotlines as Alex worked hard to shape Andrew into a kind of mini-Alex. The preschooler needed to be toughened and competitive, Alex believed, because, after all, "the dog-eat-dog world of kindergarten is just around the corner." The show moved from Thursdays to Sundays in 1987 and ratings were slipping, but Goldberg didn't wait for his creation to run into the ground before calling it quits. He ended *Family Ties* a year later and in the final episode set Alex free to pursue his dream: making the big bucks on Wall Street as passionately as his parents once waved peace signs.

Preview Review

September 11, 1982

(NBC, Editors Choice) We also liked NBC's *Family Ties*, a comedy graced by Meredith Baxter-Birney. It's a humorous look at the generation gap in reverse: the parents are former '60s radicals who can't understand how their kids turned out so right, as in -wing.

Elyse and Steven Keaton are showing their three children slides of those long-ago, faraway, good ol'days— the 1960s. The scene is a peace rally, and the person on screen has long, dark hair, a headband and a buckskin jacket. "Oh mommy, you look so pretty. Like an Indian princess," says Jennifer, 9. Elyse: "That's your father, dear." This is 1982, and the Keaton kids can't quite relate to flower children and activism. Alex, 17, dresses for success and has a poster of William F. Buckley Jr. over his bed. His sister Mallory, 15, is into designer jeans, boys and junk food. Jennifer gets off on Pac-man. They're a loving bunch—with a chronic conflict. These ex-radical parents will never stop trying to convert their children to the joys of bean sprouts and Bob Dylan. And these conservative kids will stoutly defend their right not to be Left.

Cast:

Meredith Baxter-Birney *Elyse Keaton*, **Michael Gross** *Steve Keaton*, **Michael J. Fox** *Alex P. Keaton*, **Justine Bateman** *Mallory Keaton*, **Tina Yothers** *Jennifer Keaton*, **Marc Price** *Irwin "Skippy" Handelman*, **Tracy Pollan** *Ellen Reed (1985–86)*, **Scott Valentine** *Nick Moore (1985–89)*, **Brian Bonsall** *Andrew Keaton (1986–89)*, **Courteney Cox** *Lauren Miller (1987–89)*

Special Preview: Returning Shows

What's New On Your Favorite Series
Surprises at:
Frasier
Murphy Brown
90210
Roseanne
...and Lots More

Frasier

By Karina Reeves
Broadcast History: NBC, 9/16/1993–5/13/2004
Runtime: 30 minutes
Genre: Sitcom

Frasier Crane is one of my favorite television characters of all time, although there was little evidence that he would become that when he first pulled up a bar stool on *Cheers* in 1984. Kelsey Grammer played him brilliantly for a remarkable 20 years (nine on *Cheers*, another 11 in this spin-off—matching James Arness's run as Matt Dillon on *Gunsmoke*), but he was hardly the easiest guy in the world to like. First of all, Frasier was a know-it-all. OK, shrinks are supposed to know it all, but he was snobbish, too. He had lots of money, so by society's standards he was quite successful, but to the *Cheers* regulars he just seemed too full of himself. And that's what made him so interesting to watch: He constantly doled out advice (often unsolicited), while being laughably unable to recognize that he needed help in navigating the tides of his own life. When watching *Frasier* I found myself thinking about *One Flew Over the Cuckoo's Nest*: Who's crazier, the patients or the people who care for them?

But this insight would come later. My relationship with Frasier began when I was 14. I wondered how a pompous ass like him could get anybody to go out with him, never mind marry him. How could any woman stand to listen to him droning on about *everything*? Twenty years later I'm a single businesswoman looking at Frasier through very different eyes. Pompous? Arrogant? Can't see his own flaws? Sure, but who's perfect? He was single and straight, not to mention well-meaning and very smart, and came with minimal baggage (except for his brother and father, but more about that later). All this made me very interested.

When *Frasier* premiered on NBC on September 16, 1993, Frasier was newly divorced from Lilith (Bebe Neuwirth) and had moved back to Seattle, where he grew up, to host a radio call-in show. The first episode found him barely unpacked and adjusting to his new job when he faced a dilemma: Should he ask his dad, Martin (John Mahoney), to move in with him or should he put him in an assisted-living facility? A few years back, policeman Martin had been shot in the line of duty and forced to retire, and he could no longer live on his own following a recent fall. He couldn't move in with his other son, Niles (David Hyde Pierce), because his wife, Maris, would never allow it.

> **Did You Know?**
>
> Lisa Kudrow was originally cast as Roz but was replaced by Peri Gilpin before filming got underway.

Frasier took him in and the rest, as they say, is history. It really is—*Frasier* won 37 Emmys, the most ever for a prime-time series, including Best Comedy Series five years in a row (1994–98). The reason for its success is that the humor is organic—it comes from the characters' lives. Frasier is "relentlessly human [and] relentlessly flawed," Grammer said, "but he's still trying and hasn't lost heart." And, unlike the one-dimensional character we knew from *Cheers*, we were privy here to all sides of Frasier's character, and Grammer was able to parlay them (especially his monumental ego, which was always getting him into sitcom trouble) into four Emmys for Best Actor in a Comedy.

But Frasier wasn't all there was to *Frasier*: it quickly evolved into a wonderfully sophisticated, impeccably performed ensemble comedy that also featured Peri Gilpin as Frasier's lovelorn, promiscuous producer, Roz Doyle; and Jane Leeves as Daphne Moon, a self-proclaimed psychic who was Martin's live-in home health aide and the object of Niles's constant pinings. And we can't forget Maris, Niles's unloved (and unseen) wife.

The interplay among the Crane men certainly reinforced the adage that you can choose your career, your lovers and your friends, but you can't choose your family. Who'd choose prissy Niles? As snobbish as Frasier, Niles was a fellow shrink, as well as an overly analytical ninny with massive insecurities. A lesser actor would have turned him into a ridiculous cartoon character, but Hyde Pierce (who won four Supporting Actor Emmys himself in the role) played him as a Felix Unger–like fussbudget, only a bit smarter and a lot wittier. He was a lot like Frasier, and both had to coexist with gruff Martin, their polar opposite. It was not only father vs. sons but also book smarts vs. street smarts, and the intricacies of these natural conflicts made for a steady stream of comic situations.

So did brother vs. brother, and anybody with a sibling can relate to that. Both were intelligent, successful adults and, on the surface, were responsible. But put them together and it was like they were kids. They could be discussing the merits of *Don Giovanni*, and in no time they'd be bickering like 10-year-olds arguing about which one got the bigger piece of cake. Actually, in this case, it would be whose bottle of sherry was better, but you get the point. One puzzling question about the two was: How could these apples have fallen so far from the tree? Martin was a working-class man of simple pleasures: his well-worn recliner, a bottle of beer usually in hand and his (scene-stealing) Jack Russell terrier, Eddie. He had what he wanted and couldn't understand why

TV and Film Connections
Spun off from *Cheers*

his sons, with all *they* had, weren't happy. The sight of Mahoney (who earned two Emmy nominations playing Martin) audibly sighing and withholding comment at his boys' nonsense is etched in my memory, and I have come to realize that in many ways Martin was the wisest of the Cranes. Frasier and Niles thought that they were taking care of Martin, but actually it was the other way around.

Since the series stopped production in 2004, I have truly missed looking forward to the Crane banter each week. The excellent writing (which earned four more Emmys) created conversations that flowed like well-choreographed dances, seemingly effortless and perfectly timed. There were frequent big-name guests to give the writers many different directions to take. (The list of guest actors who won or were nominated for Emmys includes John Glover, JoBeth Williams, Nathan Lane, Harris Yulin, Griffin Dunne, Marsha Mason, James Earl Jones, Patti LuPone, Piper Laurie, Jean Smart, Victor Garber, Derek Jacobi, Brian Cox, Adam Arkin, Anthony LaPaglia and Laura Linney, as well as *Cheers* alums Shelley Long, Woody Harrelson and Neuwirth.)

But in the end it was Frasier who got to me, and it stuck. I hope that he would take this tribute to him as it's intended, and not as the dithering of a TV groupie. I also wonder how things turned out with Charlotte (Linney) in Chicago. Of course I hope they're happy together. I really do, I guess. But if they're not, who knows, maybe he might thank me for my kind words and ask me if I am single. I'd say yes. Then he'd ask if I enjoy relaxing evenings in front of my TV. Yes, again. But with my luck, he'd probably be asking so he could set me up with his dad because he's a TV lover, too! No thanks.

On second thought, since I'm a pushover for all the Crane men, is John Mahoney single?

Classic Episode Close-Up

"The Match Maker"
(Original telecast: October 4, 1994)

Deftly using assumptions about sexuality as grist for farce, this episode details a mixed-up first date. Hoping to fix up Daphne, Frasier invites his station manager, Tom (Eric Lutes), to dinner, unaware he's gay. During the meal, delicately used pronouns fuel Tom's misconception that he's dating Frasier, who misreads Tom's interest for an attraction to Daphne. When Frasier learns the truth, he's stunned: "All I did was ask him if he was attached, and then we talked about the theater and men's fashions . . . Oh, my God!"

Cast:

Kelsey Grammer *Frasier Crane*, **David Hyde Pierce** *Niles Crane*, **John Mahoney** *Martin Crane*, **Jane Leeves** *Daphne Moon Crane*, **Peri Gilpin** *Roz Doyle*, **Dan Butler** *Bulldog* (1993–99)

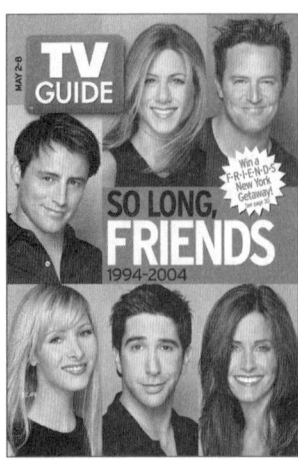

Friends

By Ali Gazan

Broadcast History: NBC, 9/22/1994–5/6/2004
Runtime: 30 minutes
Genre: Sitcom

My friend e-mailed the other day to announce that he and his wife were expecting another child. He wrote, "Now we have a new dream: Three kids and no money!" OK, he messed up the quote a little bit but I still knew immediately that he was referring to something Phoebe's younger brother, Frank Jr., said when he found out he'd be the father of triplets. At the time, it didn't strike me that he had used a *Friends* quote to announce such momentous news. It wasn't until I sat down to write this essay that I realized how often in daily life my friends and I think back to the sitcom. When a situation needs an explanation, we return to our *Friends*.

From the moment the show debuted in 1994, viewers formed a special bond with Monica (Courteney Cox Arquette), Ross (David Schwimmer), Rachel (Jennifer Aniston), Joey (Matt LeBlanc), Chandler (Matthew Perry) and Phoebe (Lisa Kudrow). We anxiously tuned in to see if Rachel was making it as a single independent woman or how Ross was handling his pregnant wife—and the fact that she had a lesbian lover. The issues were never weighty or over the top. Friday watercooler conversations soon became about not only what we had done at Thursday happy hour but also what was brewing at Central Perk.

The more we got to know the crew, the more we liked them and wanted to *be* like them. They had a loyal group of friends who never left them in a lurch, dressed better than we did and on some level were always having fun. So in no time, we were out purchasing picture frames to hang around our peepholes. We women cut our hair in shaggy layers appropriately titled "The Rachel" and we even made the show's theme song, the Rembrandts' "I'll Be There for You," the theme song to our daily lives. We used their phrases, too. Joey's classic pick-up line, "How you doin'?" became a staple at bars everywhere. Even though it was more of a joke than a genuine line, it certainly broke the ice. Whenever two people seemed

> ### Did You Know?
>
> Jennifer Aniston is also an artist; at age 11, she had a painting displayed in the New York Metropolitan Museum of Art.

destined to be together, we'd say, "He's your lobster," which is how Phoebe explained to Rachel why she and Ross would inevitably end up together.

Actors were fans of the show, too. How else can you describe the slew of Hollywood A-listers who guest starred over the years? There was Reese Witherspoon as Rachel's younger sister, Susan Sarandon as Joey's *Days of Our Lives* co-star, Bruce Willis as Rachel's crazy boyfriend, Brad Pitt (aka Mr. Jennifer Aniston at the time) as a high school classmate who hated Rachel, and, of course, Tom Selleck as Monica's older boyfriend, Richard. Stars even signed on to play themselves. Isabella Rossellini walked into Central Perk in Season 2 after Ross took her off his list of the five famous women he could sleep with while in a relationship. Chandler got stuck in an ATM vestibule with Jill Goodacre and Rachel secured a date with Jean-Claude Van Damme after visiting Ross's monkey, Marcel, on a movie set. Still, even with so much star power, the focus of the show was always the six friends, which in the end is what made it a success.

> **TV and Film Connections**
>
> Spin-off: *Joey*

Before we continue to sing the show's praises, we'd be remiss if we didn't point out that along the way we did have a few issues. We still want to know how single twentysomethings whose jobs included a coffee-shop waitress and a struggling actor were able to afford ridiculously large apartments in Manhattan. We hated the monkey Marcel despite the occasional laugh he provided. And as Jon Stewart said, *"Friends* follows the adventures of six attractive New Yorkers who drink coffee, dream life's dreams and expertly avoid the city's minority population." It was true. There wasn't a lot of diversity on *Friends* despite where they lived. Still, aside from some quibbles, these wonderfully defined characters drew us in season after season. The story lines, too, were witty and warmly relatable, and one in particular stood out among the rest—Ross and Rachel.

No matter how you break down the series, *they* were always the focal point. From Season 1, we knew his feelings for her. We all felt like the wind had been knocked out of us when we saw the videotape about the

> **Classic Episode Close-Up**
>
> "The One with the Prom Video"
>
> *(Original telecast: February 1, 1996)*
>
> "The One with the Prom Video" shows the landmark series in peak form. While watching video footage from high school, Rachel finally recognizes Ross's long-suffering devotion to her. The fateful tape also reveals a chunky teenage Monica. When she insists that the camera adds 10 pounds, Chandler asks, "So how many cameras are actually on you?"

prom when Ross gets ready to take Rachel, only to be left behind when her date shows up. We all cheered when they finally kissed outside of Central Perk. And we all understood each of their positions when Ross slept with the copy-store girl when the two were on a break. We never picked sides in their fights. We just wanted them to work it out so they could be together.

In the end, they were. Despite all of Ross's marriages and their mutual missteps, the finale found the two together. It also had Monica and Chandler, who got together at the end of Season 5, adopting twins from a single mom. Phoebe found true love with Mike and he even admitted to wanting kids. Though Joey never said he was moving to L.A., we all knew about the *Joey* spin-off and that he'd be heading west to pursue his acting career. Each of their stories ended happily—and really that's all we ever want for our true *Friends*.

Cast:

Courteney Cox Arquette *Monica Geller*, **Jennifer Aniston** *Rachel Green*, **Lisa Kudrow** *Phoebe Buffay*, **Matt LeBlanc** *Joey Tribbiani*, **David Schwimmer** *Ross Geller*, **Matthew Perry** *Chandler Bing*

The Fugitive

By Stuart Michaelson

Broadcast History: ABC, 9/17/1963–8/29/1967
Runtime: 60 minutes
Genre: Drama

"If enough people tell you you're blind, you better get yourself a dog."

That's how Roy Huggins, creator of *The Fugitive*, recalled initial reaction to his series concept of a wrongly convicted man racing desperately through small-town America, one step ahead of an obsessed lawman determined to return his quarry to be executed for murder. Huggins's colleagues (not to mention his dentist and his lawyer) were repulsed by the idea; one ABC programming honcho called the notion "a slap in the face of the American judicial system."

It may have played that way to some when *The Fugitive* debuted in 1963, and even by the time the drama concluded to record ratings in 1967 Americans were less likely to distrust authority than they are today. *The Fugitive* was a different breed of prime-time drama, but it was surely no dog.

William Conrad's basso profundo narration set the scene on a train carrying Richard Kimble to his date with the executioner before it derails: "Richard Kimble ponders his fate as he looks at the world for the last time and sees only darkness. But in that darkness fate moves its huge hand."

Kimble, hauntingly portrayed by three-time Emmy nominee David Janssen, flees the train wreck, hiding his medical skills to avoid being recognized as a doctor. He stayed under the radar by working at such blue-collar jobs as janitor, truck driver, lifeguard and bartender while hunting the real killer: one-armed Fred Johnson (played with brutal precision by Bill Raisch, who lost an arm in World War II and was Burt Lancaster's stunt double).

Preview Review

September 14, 1963

The Fugitive is a tale of hunter and hunted, *Les Misérables* in modern dress. As such, the suspense is built in. Richard Kimble is the Jean Valjean of the tale; police lieutenant Gerard his Javert. Kimble is a doctor convicted of killing his wife. He is innocent. On the way to his execution he escapes after a train wreck. Shifting his identity as he drifts from place to place, he sets out to find his wife's killer, a one-armed man he had seen clearly on the night of the murder. At the same time, he is pursued relentlessly by Gerard, who catches up only now and then, and not long enough to stop the series in mid-track. Thus there are plots within plots. Gerard is in for a merry chase—26 episodes! *Debut: September 17.*

By the time that hunt was done and *The Fugitive* ended on August 29, 1967, with a then-record 25.7 million households watching as Kimble went free, it had become a classic; what Stephen King called "groundbreaking television" in the sense that "it featured a hero who was totally powerless." TV GUIDE named the Emmy-winning show the best dramatic series of the '60s in 1993, the same year that a thrilling Harrison Ford film took on the story and copped an Oscar for Tommy Lee Jones as Ford's pursuer. (Samuel Gerard in the film; Philip Gerard on TV.)

Did You Know?

Originally, Richard Kimble's hometown was intended to be in Wisconsin, but when producers discovered that Wisconsin did not execute murderers, they changed the location to Indiana.

But those who only know Gerard as the strong-willed Jones character don't know the TV Gerard—a far more complex and divided individual than his movie counterpart. British-born stage actor and director Barry Morse—brought to *The Fugitive* by producer Quinn Martin, who worked with Morse on *The Untouchables*—didn't want to play a typical TV lawman, so he turned to Victor Hugo's Javert from *Les Misérables* for inspiration for his recurring role. And while it is not entirely coincidental that the name Gerard sounds a bit like Javert, Huggins claimed it *was* a coincidence that the premise of a doctor accused of slaying his wife was similar to that of the real-life Sam Shepard case. In any event, Morse was brilliant as the relentless and obsessed Gerard.

Janssen, who had previously played the title role of *Richard Diamond, Private Detective*, was the moody, rootless loner who drifted, like a Western hero, from town to town, winning friends, making a few enemies and attracting countless beautiful women as he wriggled out of one near-capture after another. He brought palpable paranoia to the wonderfully written, tautly directed show, which benefited from the work of such directors as Sydney Pollack, Ida Lupino, Mark Rydell and Richard Donner, and the acting of top-line guest stars like Bruce Dern, Tuesday Weld, Suzanne Pleshette, Brenda Vaccaro, Mickey Rooney, Jack Klugman, Angie Dickinson, Melvyn Douglas and Telly Savalas.

Janssen's trademark wince, demonstrated while confronting mortality on a weekly basis, was so famous that it was spoofed in a *MAD* magazine parody, as "Richard Thimble" pondered, "Here's where the tension really mounts . . . as I confront the police early in the show . . . Will I get caught? Will this be the first six-minute show in television history?"

Given the show's success, there was understandable resistance at ABC to the notion of ending Kimble's run, but Janssen, worn out by the grueling work, refused to sign on for a fifth season. And while the finale, "The Judgment, Conclusion," is the one casual TV buffs most recall, and was terrific television, it was not the best episode. In fact, the final season suffered from the fact that filming went from wonderfully noirish black and white to color, costing it some of the unforgettable moodiness that so enhanced its human drama.

Among my other favorite episodes:

- "Home Is the Hunted," in which Kimble risks his life to return home for a visit. The episode features the wrenching scene in which Richard's sister, Donna (Jacqueline Scott), collapses emotionally at the sound of her brother's voice on the phone. Scott's insistence that Janssen be on the set during the scene (he had not been scheduled until later) added poignancy to Scott's performance.

- "The Iron Maiden," in which Kimble is trapped in an underground shaft by an explosion.

- "Angels Travel on Lonely Roads," a two-part episode that finds Kimble, on the run from Nevada State Police, assisting a nun (Eileen Heckart) who plans to renounce her vows—and who learns her helper's secret.

- "Landscape with Running Figures," another two-parter, in which an exhausted Kimble accidentally signs his real name to a work sheet. This mistake draws Gerard, whose obsession to catch Kimble finally spurs Marie Gerard (Barbara Rush) to leave her husband. She travels under her maiden name, by bus . . . which also has as a passenger the very fugitive who has caused such harm to her marriage. Morse, as always, imbues Gerard with enormous pathos as the lawman's quest hits home with devastating power.

- "Ill Wind," again featuring Gerard in an outing good enough for a time capsule: The lieutenant catches up with Kimble in a barn, where a roof falls and injures him so badly that Kimble, to the astonishment of his fellow farm workers, works to save his pursuer's life.

> ## TV and Film Connections
> Inspired two feature films:
> *The Fugitive* (1993)
> *U.S. Marshals* (1998)
> Remade as a new television series with the same name in 2000

In the end, though, the series' ratings and plaudits arose not from its plotlines—surely no one expected Kimble to be put to death, any more than fans of *24* figure on the demise of Kiefer Sutherland's Jack Bauer anytime soon—but from its atmosphere, acting, directing, attention to human feelings, and most of all, to Janssen's riveting, charismatic portrayal. There were some nondescript movie roles and other TV series (including the underrated *Harry O*) to come, but *The Fugitive* was the unquestioned role of his too-brief career. He died at age 49 in 1980, among the greatest stars in one of the greatest series of all time.

Cast:

David Janssen *Dr. Richard Kimble,* **Barry Morse** *Lt. Philip Gerard,* **William Conrad** *Narrator*

General Hospital

By Damian J. Holbrook

Broadcast History: ABC, 4/1/1963–
Runtime: 60 minutes
Genre: Soap opera

Fine. Roll your eyes. I know what you're thinking. "Oh *please* . . . a soap opera? Nobody cares about those."

And if you weren't one of the folks who tuned in for the November 16, 1981, wedding of *GH* super-couple Luke and Laura, I could see your point. Of course, 30 million people attended the nups—including Liz Taylor—so it goes without saying that a lot of "nobodies" cared an awful lot at one time or another. Call them closet soapies. Just don't call them during their "stories."

Growing up in the '80s, it was a given that you either were or knew a *General Hospital* fan. It was the heyday of daytime dramas and not just because of the taboo romance between wide-eyed ingenue Laura Vining Webber Baldwin and her permed, petulant rapist Lucas Lorenzo Spencer. NBC's *Days of Our Lives* was knee-deep in its spectacular "Salem Strangler" mystery and CBS's *The Young and the Restless* had Kay Chancellor's heartbreaking battle with alcoholism. But it was *GH* that was having the most fun changing the way the world saw serialized dramas.

Which is fitting, given that the show launched on April Fool's Day, 1963 (the same day as the equally physician-centric *The Doctors*). Created by Frank and Doris Hursley, it was all sturm and drang at the eponymous medical center of fictitious Port Charles, New York. Accompanied by background organ strains and a barebones set, the action revolved mostly around platonic pals Nurse Jesse Brewer and Dr. Steve Hardy as they endured rocky romances and riotously bad dialogue.

Over the next two decades, *GH* rose and fell in the ratings on a wave of what would now be considered clichéd yarns of infidelities, back-from-the-dead spouses and botched kidnappings. In 1978, then executive producer Gloria Monty pulled the show out of the ratings gutter (and spared it from cancellation) by introducing a crew of younger characters who would wind up in the Luke and Laura phenomenon that remains unsurpassed in the pop-culture annals.

Ah, Luke and Laura. All the rage *and* enraging. Fans were torn between rooting for them and rejecting the idea of a married woman barely out of her teens being defiled by an older predator on the floor of his disco while Herb Alpert's "Rise" drowned out Laura's cries of "No!" No matter how you felt about it, it was clear that the days of those canned organ strains and tired tales of woe officially ended on October 5, 1979.

Even non-*GH* viewers couldn't escape what followed. Thanks to my mother's loving influence, I had developed a severe addiction to NBC's *Another World* and only cared about Rachel Cory stopping that wench Janice from sinking her claws into poor Mac. The antics of a bunch of scrub-wearing surgeons with really big hair meant nothing to me. Until, suddenly, all over the news and the neighborhood, people were becoming obsessed with what ABC was defending as "a seduction." Call me a bandwagoneer, but the controversy took hold and I was hooked.

How could Laura forgive such a scuzz? Why didn't we trust her wisecracking husband, Scotty Baldwin? How could Genie Francis cry so well? And more importantly, how did Anthony Geary ever get a job in daytime? He was so *not* the typical soap stud, yet there he was, a little cheesy and totally charming. And Francis? Well let's just say that a bulk of the sparks these two threw off generated from her mix of Kewpie-doll innocence and quick-witted insolence.

Noticing the pairing's incendiary heat—and the accompanying leap in the Nielsens—the writers immediately sent Luke and Laura on the run from the mob for almost a year and we followed hot on their heels. There were romantic dances in empty department stores, assumed identities, and unprecedented attention from the media and beyond. By the time these two finally tied the knot (for the first time) in '81, TV GUIDE,*ETime*, *Newsweek* and *People* had splashed them across their covers, college students were hosting viewing parties and certain sixth-graders were racing home to see what sort of adventure the couple and their growing band of action-courting cohorts would get into next.

And a lot of us are *still* planning around ABC's daytime schedule. So much has gone on since these two walked down the aisle—the ventures into sci-fi with the Ice Princess madness and the often-shirtless alien Casey, the harrowing transplant of hit-and-run victim B. J. Jones's heart into her dying cousin's chest, the ISA spy games, Stone's death from AIDS—that things have almost come full circle. The show revisited its sordid history after the Spencers' son, Lucky, learned of Luke's long-denied assault on Laura and in the last year has harkened back to its

> ## Did You Know?
>
> *General Hospital* is the longest-running dramatic serial on ABC (having aired more than 11,000 episodes) and is the longest-running daytime drama produced on the West Coast.

golden age with the returns of fan favorites Finola Hughes, Tristan Rogers, Rick Springfield, Emma Samms and Kimberly McCullough. In October of 2006, Genie Francis returned as Laura—following her institutionalization for killing her father, Rick (don't ask)—to mark the 25th anniversary of the vows heard 'round the world.

That's not to say that everything old is new again. Yes, Geary's Luke is still the *man* in Port Charles, but for almost a decade, the goings-on in town have revolved around manic-depressive mobster Sonny Corinthos (Maurice Benard), his on-again, off-again (and four-times recast) soul mate Carly Benson and their various friends, foes and bedmates. It's *The Soap-ranos* and it works, having garnered the series three Daytime Emmys for Outstanding Drama since 2000, along with awards for Geary, Benard and a handful of others.

So say what you will about soaps. They *are* silly and sexy and over the top. They also happen to churn out new episodes five days a week, 52 weeks a year without repeats or summer hiatuses or respect from the mainstream media. They win major awards, tackle social issues and train top-notch talents like former Port Charles residents Demi Moore, Ricky Martin, Vanessa Marcil and Richard Dean Anderson. They have been around since folks turned away from their radios and plugged in their TVs. And as long as they come even close to the addictive storytelling and compelling characters of *General Hospital*, millions of viewers will have something to love in the afternoon.

> **TV and Film Connections**
>
> Spin-off: *Port Charles*

Cast:

John Beradino Dr. Steve Hardy (1963–96), **Emily McLaughlin** Jessie Brewer (1963–90), **Roy Thinnes** Dr. Phil Brewer (1963–66), **Martin West** Dr. Phil Brewer (1967–75), **Rachel Ames** Audrey March (1964–2003), **Denise Alexander** Dr. Lesley Williams (1972–84), **Genie Francis** Laura Vining (1976–82; 1993–2002), **Richard Dean Anderson** Dr. Jeff Webber (1976–81), **Brooke Bundy** Diana Taylor (1977–81), **Susan Brown** Dr. Gail Adamson (1977–85), **Stuart Damon** Dr. Alan Quartermaine (1977–), **Leslie Charleson** Dr. Monica Quartermaine (1977–), **Chris Robinson** Dr. Rick Webber (1978–86), **Anna Lee** Lila Quartermaine (1978–2004), **David Lewis** Edward Quartermaine (1978–89, 1991–93), **Anthony Geary** Lucas Lorenzo Spencer (1978–83; 1984; 1991–), **John Ingle** Edward Quartermaine (1993–2004; 2006–), **Jane Elliott** Tracy Quartermaine (1978–80, 1989–93; 1996; 2003–), **Shell Kepler** Amy Vining (1979–2001), **Robin Mattson** Heather Grant (1980–83; 2004–05), **Tristan Rogers** Robert Scorpio (1981–85; 1987–92), **Sharon Wyatt** Tiffany Hill (1981–83; 1986–95), **Rick Springfield** Dr. Noah Drake (1981–83), **Demi Moore** Jackie Templeton (1982–83), **Janine Turner** Laura Templeton (1982–83), **John Stamos** Blackie Parrish (1982–84), **Emma Samms** Holly Sutton (1982–85; 1992–93), **Jack Wagner** Frisco Jones (1983–87; 1989–91), **Brad Maule** Dr. Tony Jones (1984–90), **John Reilly** Sean Donely (1984–94), **Finola Hughes** Anna Devane (1985–91), **Kimberly McCullough** Robin Scorpio (1985–87; 2005–), **Steve Burton** Jason Morgan (1990–2000; 2002–), **Wally Kurth** Ned Ashton (1991–2004), **John J. York** Mac Scorpio (1991–), **Vanessa Marcil** Brenda Barrett (1992–98; 2001–03), **Antonio Sabato Jr.** Jagger Cates (1992–94), **Jonathan Jackson** Lucas Lorenzo "Lucky" Spencer Jr. (1993–99), **Jacob Young** Lucas Lorenzo "Lucky" Spencer Jr. (2000–03), **Greg Vaughan** Lucas Lorenzo "Lucky" Spencer Jr. (2003–), **Maurice Benard** Sonny Corinthos Jr. (1993–97; 1998–), **Rena Sofer** Lois Cerullo (1993–96), **Lesli Kay** Lois Cerullo (2004–05), **Tyler Christopher** Nikolas Cassadine (1996–99), **Ingo Rademacher** Jasper "Jax" Jacks (1996–2000; 2001–), **Sarah Brown** Carly Benson (1996–2001), **Tamara Braun** Carly Benson (2001–

05), **Laura Wright** *Carly Benson (2005–)*, **Rebecca Herbst** *Elizabeth Webber (1997–)*, **Amber Tamblyn** *Emily Bowen Quartermaine (1997–2001)*, **Natalia Livingston** *Emily Bowen Quartermaine (2003–)*, **Constance Towers** *Helena Cassadine (1997–)*, **Nancy Lee Grahn** *Alexis Davis (1997–)*, **Jacklyn Zeman** *Bobbie Spencer (1977–)*, **Stephen Martines** *Nikolas Cassadine (1999–2003)*, **Robin Christopher** *Skye Chandler (2001–)*, **Rick Hearst** *Ric Lansing (2002–)*, **Alicia Leigh Willis** *Courtney Matthews (2001–06)*, **Ted King** *Lorenzo Alcazar (2002–)*, **Cynthia Preston** *Faith Rosco (2002–05)*, **Lindze Letherman** *Georgie Jones (2002–)*, **Kelly Monaco** *Samantha McCall (2003–)*, **Scott Clifton** *Dillon Hornsby (2003–)*, **Katie Stuart** *Sage Alcazar (2003–04)*, **Adrianne Leon** *Brook Lynn Ashton (2004–06)*, **Shaun Benson** *Steven Lars Webber (2004–05)*, **Ignacio Serricchio** *Diego Alcazar (2004–06)*, **Kari Wuhrer** *Reese Marshall (2005)*, **Dylan Cash** *Michael Corinthos (2005–)*, **Kent King** *Dr. Lainey Winters (2005–)*, **Kirsten Storms** *Maxie Jones (2005–)*, **Jason Thompson** *Dr. Patrick Drake (2005–)*

TV, MOVIES CREATE A HUSKY HYBRID

TV GUIDE

15c · Local Programs · June 11-17

TINA LOUISE, ALAN HALE, BOB DENVER OF 'GILLIGAN'S ISLAND'

Gilligan's Island

By Joseph Hudak

Broadcast History: CBS, 9/26/1964–9/4/1967
Runtime: 30 minutes
Genre: Sitcom

"Just sit right back and you'll hear a tale ..."
It's a fair argument that more Americans can sing the entire *Gilligan's Island* theme song than "The Star-Spangled Banner." And why not—it *is* much catchier and easier to sing. But when the sitcom about seven castaways on an "uncharted desert isle" debuted on CBS back in 1964, few would have thought the series, much less its opening ditty, would be remembered. Created by Sherwood Schwartz (who also wrote the theme and would go on to create another TV gem, *The Brady Bunch*, in 1969), *Gilligan* hit rough seas with television critics, who labeled it "inept," "moronic" and "preposterous." We *are* talking about people who couldn't figure out how to patch a boat's hull, after all.

And what a disparate group of castaways they were. Alan Hale Jr. played the "brave and sure" Skipper (his real name, Jonas Grumby, was heard only in the first episode) of the imperiled SS *Minnow*, infusing him with all the bluster of Oliver Hardy and Ralph Kramden. And if the Skipper was equal parts Hardy and Kramden, then good ol' Gilligan was his Stan Laurel and Ed Norton. Played by Bob Denver, the "little buddy" watched sheepishly as his attempts to help his fellow islanders frequently went awry, landing him in hot water with the Skipper. Not even newbie Army recruits are yelled at as much as Gilligan was! Ultimately, of course, the red-shirted, good-hearted first mate and his father figure would reconcile and focus on the task of taking care of their fellow castaways: sultry starlet Ginger Grant (Tina Louise); small-town sweetheart Mary Ann Summers (Dawn Wells); the out-of-touch millionaire couple the Howells (Jim Backus and Natalie Schafer); and the scientifically adept Professor (Russell Johnson), who could make everything from radios to telephones using only coconuts and bamboo, but couldn't come up with the know-how to make a seaworthy raft. Go figure.

> **Did You Know?**
> Jayne Mansfield turned down the role of Ginger Grant.

Many viewers pondered exactly why that was, but others—specifically coming-of-age boys—had a different question in mind: Who was hotter, Ginger or Mary Ann? Seemingly always in her evening gown, Ginger was an expert in come-hither glances and coos (even when she didn't actually *want* anyone to come hither). Mary Ann, meanwhile, was the quintessential cutie in her farmer's daughter clothes and pigtails. The girls' merits are still debated today by TV fans in watering holes around the country. (For the record, I was a Mary Ann guy.)

While a select set of viewers was introduced to the series during its initial three-year run from 1964 to '67, the majority of admitted *Gilligan* fans (and, yes, they are out there) discovered and fell in love with the show while it was in syndication. That was true for this writer, who whiled away lazy summer afternoons in the '80s watching Gilligan and his mates make the most of being marooned. But let's face it. While the gang was supposedly on a deserted island, they were hardly alone. Island natives, cosmonauts, gangsters, a surfer and a deposed dictator (the episode "The Little Dictator" was Schwartz's favorite) all popped up, and Don Rickles, Phil Silvers and a very young Kurt Russell (as a jungle boy) guest starred. Even the Harlem Globetrotters somehow found themselves on the island, in one of three TV movies spun off from the series.

> ## Preview Review
> ### September 19, 1964
>
> *Gilligan's Island* deals with the misadventures of a vacationing fishing party that becomes marooned when its charter boat, the *Minnow*, is wrecked on an uninhabited island. Gilligan, lovable but incompetent "mate and crew," and the captain lead an improbable expedition or two, like putting together a raft and finding some surprising headhunters who aren't head-hunters at all. Curvy movie-star Ginger is romantically interested in "The Professor," an unworldly (his specialty is dull metals) high-school science teacher who had been at work on a book called *Rust: The Real Red Menace.* Jim Backus and Natalie Schafer insist on maintaining their high-society way of life. From a seemingly bottomless suitcase they can produce anything from polo clothes to a dress suit.

All of this made the sitcom something of a pop-culture phenomenon, and one whose influence is still making waves on the television landscape. Mark Burnett's reality series *Survivor*, the Tom Hanks film *Cast Away* and ABC's *Lost* all owe at least some debt to *Gilligan*'s premise, and in 2004 TBS premiered a reality show based on the series called *The Real Gilligan's Island*. Eventually, the gang of seven was rescued, albeit in a 1978 TV movie—and then only for a short while until they were stranded yet again—but the actors who played them never fully sailed away from their alter egos. Denver in particular will always be remembered as Gilligan. When the actor died in 2005, obituaries around the country lamented the loss of "TV's favorite 'little buddy'."

Cast:

Bob Denver Gilligan, **Alan Hale** Jonas Grumby (The Skipper), **Jim Backus** Thurston Howell III , **Natalie Schafer** Lovey Howell, **Tina Louise** Ginger Grant, **Russell Johnson** Roy Hinkley (The Professor), **Dawn Wells** Mary Ann Summers

Gilmore Girls

By Robin Honig

Broadcast History: WB, 10/5/2000–9/12/2006;
 CW, 9/19/2006–5/15/2007
Runtime: 60 minutes
Genre: Comedy-drama

I'm not a high school teenager. Or a young single mother. And I've never lived in a rural town. But the moment I was introduced to quick-witted 16-year-old Rory Gilmore (Alexis Bledel) and her free-spirited mother, Lorelai (Lauren Graham), at Luke's Diner in quirky Stars Hollow, Connecticut, I was drawn right into their world.

Lorelai was Rory's age when she left behind her blue-blooded parents to raise her daughter alone. Their relationship is an unusual one: They gossip over bottomless cups of coffee at the diner, trade clothes, share makeup and borrow each other's CDs. There are movie nights (*Willy Wonka* is a favorite, complete with pizza, jelly beans and chocolate kisses, cookie dough and marshmallows), double dates (Lorelai and Luke join Rory and Dean at a local screening of *Pippi Longstocking*) and hangover support (Lorelai lays with Rory on the bathroom floor after the kid had drowned her heartbreak in too much spiked punch).

So are these two friends, or mother and daughter? I was skeptical at first. Shouldn't a parent act like, well, a parent? With curfews and lectures and some nutrition involved? Is this really the best way to raise a child? And can I come over sometime?

But I was also intrigued. Here's an independent, smart, thirtysomething woman who walked away from a life of privilege to support a child on her own; a woman who worked her way up from maid to manager to owner of the Dragonfly Inn; who raised a smart, incredibly responsible daughter. So why *did* she give up the money, the mansion, the Mercedes? Because staying with her snobby parents meant living with their elitist, oppressive and manipulative rules. And because leaving meant she could raise her kid her way, not their way. I admire that kind of strength and courage.

The more I watched, the more I understood Lorelai's unconventional parenting skills, and it all started to make sense. She knew that stifling her child and refusing to give her independence would drive her away. Lorelai wanted a better life for her daughter. So she straddled a difficult line between best friend and best mother. It was tricky but she pulled it off by allowing Rory to make some big mistakes and fix them on her own. Yet she was still deeply involved in Rory's life. "I have to know where you are at all times," she once told her, "*especially* when you have my shoes on." When Rory dropped out of college and moved in with her grandparents, Lorelai painfully stepped aside and waited for Rory to make it through this huge crisis. It took time but eventually she found her way back. Fans criticized Lorelai for refusing to get involved but I commended her for it. She had complete faith in her daughter and their bond. It's a reciprocal love every mother surely hopes for, and every daughter likely wants to have.

But just like real life, Lorelai's relationship with her parents couldn't be hidden away in a Tiffany box and tied up with a neat little bow. Emily and Richard Gilmore (Kelly Bishop, Edward Herrmann) never had a good relationship with Lorelai, which only got worse when she left home with infant Rory. The family dynamic finally shifted when Lorelai asked her parents for money. But she wasn't asking for herself: she needed tuition money so Rory could attend Chilton, a prestigious private school. This selfless act meant getting dragged back into a very difficult, demanding, dysfunctional relationship—and mandatory fancy-schmantzy Friday night dinners with Em and Dick. What torture! Sure there have been other struggling single moms on TV. But I can't think of one who is forced to deal with familial complexities with such dignity, grace and humor.

> ## Preview Review
> ### September 30, 2000
>
> **Premise**: Like mother, like daughter. The Gilmore Girls, single mom Lorelai and precocious daughter Rory, are just 16 years apart and act like best friends. They could almost pass for sisters. Rory is that grown-up (or maybe Lorelai is that immature). When Rory is accepted into a ritzy prep school, cash-strapped Lorelai must swallow her independent pride, act her age and make peace with her estranged blue-blood parents.
>
> **We Say**: A rare achievement in family drama, this thoroughly endearing series is sweet and smart: touching without being schmaltzy, sardonic without being nasty. After false starts (*Townies, Conrad Bloom* and *M.Y.O.B.*) the engaging Graham finally has a role that could gain her recognition.

There's a lot to like about Lorelai. Maybe what I love most is her razor-sharp wit. She's a master at the perfect comeback:

> Lorelai: *(Answering the desk phone) Independence Inn!*
> Emily: *(Snapping) You really should identify yourself when you answer the phone at work.*
> Lorelai: *(All chipper) Sorry! Independence Inn!*
> *Major Disappointment speaking. Better?*

She's even faster with pop culture. "Enjoy Wisteria Lane you major drama queen," she shouted at boyfriend Luke (Scott Patterson) during a fight. "Wrap yourself in a towel and trip over a hedge on your way out!" she yelled after him as he stormed away. Show creator and writer Amy Sherman-Palladino—who described the series, when it premiered in 2000, as "a family drama, and I include the town as part of the family"—was a genius at crafting knowing

dialogue that had heart as well as heartache, and loved to slip into conversations all sorts of lowbrow wacky references (Milli Vanilli, Señor Wences and Anna Nicole Smith) and even highbrow ones (Tolstoy, Kierkegaard and Noam Chomsky). But my favorites always were lines from *Desperate Housewives*, *The O.C.*, *Lost in Space* and many, many others. (TV characters who watch TV? Brilliant.) When I'm watching *Gilmore Girls*, I better pay close attention. These shout-outs come fast and often. If I reach for the bowl of low-fat chips, I'll probably miss two or three great ones. I love trading lines with colleagues the next day.

It should come as no surprise that Rory is equally witty, especially when she banters with her mother.

> *Rory:* *Did you talk to your parents yet?*
> *Lorelai:* *No.*
> *Rory:* *Have you tried talking to your parents yet?*
> *Lorelai:* *No.*
> *Rory:* *That's my little Kofi Annan!*

Like mother, like daughter. Rory is just as hilarious but also smart as hell. Her nose always buried in a book (she had devoured most of the classics before entering high school), she was valedictorian at Chilton and was accepted at three Ivy League schools before deciding on Yale. Not only is she brainy, she's gorgeous too, and completely unaware of her fresh-faced, doe-eyed beauty. This is a girl who could stop traffic and not know it because she's too busy reading Dostoevsky, for fun. I love Rory's intricacies because she's a TV rarity. Smart girls are often plain-Jane, lonely geeks who sit at home alone on Saturday nights. Rory not only breaks that mold, she grinds it to dust.

No wonder there are lots of cute boys surrounding these *Girls*. Rory went through the typical teenage experience: trying on different guys to see who fit best. She first dated innocent, good guy Dean (Jared Padalecki), who was sweet but hardly a match intellectually. I wasn't surprised when she moved on to bad boy Jess (Milo Ventimiglia), who'd dropped out of school but read Kerouac in his spare time. (I readily confess he was my favorite—the bright, brooding type.) In college, she fell for a wild, partying, trust-fund baby with whom she had seemingly little in common. She's deeply drawn to all of them, some at the same time. Who hasn't been a teenager utterly confused over matters of the heart? When she falls in love and her heart is broken, so is yours.

Lorelai's had a similar track record, dating wildly different men. She has a long-standing friendship-bordering-on-more relationship with Rory's unpredictable, unreliable father, Christopher (David Sutcliffe). And then there's Luke, the scruffy-faced, backwards-baseball-cap-wearing, tells-it-like-it-is diner owner who's pined away for Lorelai for close to 10 years. I was a little uneasy when they first started dating because they'd always acted more like brother and sister, constantly pushing each other's buttons. ("Red meat kills. Enjoy," deadpanned Luke, after dropping off a freshly grilled hamburger in front of Lorelai.) But as their relationship moved forward, it was clear that Luke can match Lorelai quip for quip, and loves Rory like she was his own daughter. So I quickly came around. When Lorelai got on one knee and asked Luke to marry *her*, I was surprised to find myself all choked up. In true fashion, Lorelai planned the entire wedding in one day. When I was engaged it took me an entire day to choose the stamps for the invitations.

But disaster ensued when Luke discovered a long-lost daughter. The wedding was put on hold; Luke kept Lorelai away from his child and practically pushed her out of his life. And the fans went nuts. I'm hardly shocked—people are seriously invested in these characters. My TV GUIDE e-mail box quickly filled with letters from fans who desperately wanted to see these two tie the knot. I was surprised how badly their relationship had fallen apart. Matters only got worse when creator Sherman-Palladino announced she was leaving the show and ended the sixth season with Luke and Lorelai splitting up and a heartbroken Lorelai sleeping with ex Christopher. Fans were devastated. Even I was teary eyed, and I'd read all the spoilers before the episode aired. The minute the show ended, the e-mails came pouring in, and the TV GUIDE message boards filled with diatribes from diehards who hated the finale. ("How could Luke be so stupid?" "How could Lorelai be so reckless?" "Will they ever get back together?")

> ### Did You Know?
> Because of the characters' fast-paced speech, an average script runs 75–80 pages, compared with the normal 45–50 for a standard hour-long show.

Then again, *Gilmore Girls* has never offered simple solutions. In the seventh and last season, Lorelai hastily elopes with Chris, then slowly discovers she might've made a huge mistake. Quite typical from a show that unfolds at its own pace and does not rush to solve life's inevitable conflicts. Each character's motives, needs and desires are revealed in thoughtful, smart, deliberate ways. From quirky Kirk (Sean Gunn) to annoying Taylor (Michael Winters), everyone in Stars Hollow serves a meaningful purpose. There are no throwaway lines, there are no padded scenes. All of these things make *Gilmore Girls* one of the best TV shows of all time.

It is hard for me to leave the Gilmores' world. But *Gilmore Girls* finished the way it started: strong characters with solid foundations who finally find the true happiness they deserve. And the perfect pair of shoes.

Cast:

Lauren Graham *Lorelai Gilmore*, **Alexis Bledel** *Rory Gilmore*, **Kelly Bishop** *Emily Gilmore*, **Edward Herrmann** *Richard Gilmore*, **Melissa McCarthy** *Sookie St. James*, **Yanic Truesdale** *Michel Gerard*, **Keiko Agena** *Lane Kim*, **Scott Patterson** *Luke Danes*, **Liza Weil** *Paris Geller*, **Sean Gunn** *Kirk*, **Jared Padalecki** *Dean Forester (2000–05)*, **Milo Ventimiglia** *Jess Mariano (2001–03)*

The Golden Girls

By Raven Snook

Broadcast History: NBC, 9/14/1985–9/14/1992
Runtime: 30 minutes
Genre: Sitcom

Back in the 1980s when I was a rebellious teen and my mom was a fiftysomething corporate professional, the two of us rarely agreed on anything. But on Saturday nights (the ones I stayed home, anyway), we concurred on *The Golden Girls*. Of course the Emmy-winning sitcom appealed to us for different reasons. She enjoyed watching mature women (i.e., those her age) leading vibrant, full lives while I adored the unbridled raunchiness. In the end, we both agreed that this sly (if unhip) sitcom had something on its mind and, better yet, lots of belly laughs.

Despite its familiar premise—a quartet of antithetical roommates bicker and bond over the years—the series transcended its formulaic roots due to superlative writing and brilliant performances by four post-menopausal funny ladies who all won Emmys for their work: TV series veterans Bea Arthur, Betty White and Rue McClanahan, as well as newcomer Estelle Getty, tackling her first regular sitcom role. Over the years, the show also employed many other senior thespians as guests, including Jerry Orbach, Jack Gilbert, Nancy Walker, Cesar Romero and Hal Linden; and, in one of the odder guest appearances, Quentin Tarantino appeared as an Elvis impersonator in the episode "Sophie's Wedding."

McClanahan played widowed Blanche Devereaux, a sexy Southern belle who rented out rooms to a trio of other single women of a certain age: scatterbrained storyteller Rose Nylund (White), wry substitute schoolteacher Dorothy Zbornak (Arthur), and Dorothy's wise-cracking octogenarian mother, Sophia Petrillo (Getty, who in real life was a few months younger than Arthur and who got the lion's share of outrageous punch lines). In a medium, then as now, obsessed with youth, it's interesting that the idea for *The Golden Girls* originated with a network suit. Brandon Tartikoff, president of NBC Entertainment in the '80s, asked producing partners Paul Junger Witt and Tony Thomas to come up with a series about sassy seniors. Witt brought the challenge to his wife, *Soap* creator Susan Harris, and in September 1985 *The Golden Girls* premiered.

> ### Did You Know?
>
> Initially, Betty White was to play Blanche and Rue McClanahan was to be Rose. However, White didn't want to play another "sexpot" (reminiscent of Sue Ann Nivens from *The Mary Tyler Moore Show*).

The Golden Girls

The show wasn't only for the AARP crowd. It wasn't cool to admit, but many of my contemporaries watched the sitcom, just as I did, with parents and grandparents who howled at the risqué punch lines. At the same time, while the protagonists dealt with aspects of friendship and the difficulties of aging—loss of looks, change of life, the threat of mortality—they remained filled with youthful vigor and gave one another emotional support. There was little time for whining or self-pity. There were some hard knocks and disappointments, but they persevered. They partied. And, positively *shocking* for TV characters over 60, they still had sex. They did, in short, pretty much everything that people half their age did on other shows—just with much wittier scripts (*Arrested Development* creator Mitchell Hurwitz and *Desperate Housewives* creator Marc Cherry were among the series' writers).

Unlike its short-lived spin-off, *The Golden Palace*, which deservedly died a quick death, there was genuine poignancy on *The Golden Girls* and the laughs were rarely cheap. The humor stemmed from the characters' credible reactions to various personal struggles: Dorothy's love-hate relationship with her toupee-wearing ex-husband, Stan; Sophia's brushes with senility and sickness; Blanche's lack of self-esteem in any area besides her looks; Rose's first long-term romance since the death of her husband with a mild-mannered teacher named Miles (though the storyline that revealed Miles was actually an accountant in the witness protection program was one of the show's few gimmicky missteps that sacrificed logic for laughs).

Plus, *The Golden Girls* wasn't afraid to tackle edgy social and political issues. Dorothy openly criticized the first President Bush (although she was too shocked to give him a piece of her mind when he showed up at their house for a photo op). Blanche endorsed safe and frequent sex, and took the gals on

Preview Review

September 14, 1985

(NBC, Editors' Choice) This year, once again, the best new series, in our view, is a half-hour sitcom, NBC's *The Golden Girls*. So comedy is hardly moribund. But it may be getting a little long in the tooth: *The Golden Girls* is a geriatric giggle that manages to wring laughs out of dentures and decrepitude, thanks to the writing of Susan Harris and the comic talents of Bea Arthur and Co.

Three older women share a house in Miami. That may not strike you as a premise with promise, but creator Susan Harris, who was also responsible for *Soap* and *Benson*, can turn "old" into gold. The regulars in this half-hour comedy are wry-witted Dorothy, a substitute teacher; Rose, a dingbat who works as a grief counselor; Blanche, the widow who owns the house; and Sophia, Dorothy's 80-year-old mother—at the moment, she's "visiting" because her old-age home just burned down—who's still sharp as a tack. In the premiere episode, Blanche has a date with Harry, who sounds like quite a catch. "He doesn't talk loud at the movies and doesn't take his pulse. He's a great dancer," says Blanche, "and he doesn't make noises when he chews." Dorothy: "Chewing. That's way up there on my list. Comes right after intelligent."

a hilariously embarrassing drug store outing to buy condoms. Rose was tested for HIV, fielded advances from a lesbian admirer and dated a little person (who broke up with her because she wasn't Jewish). Blanche's brother came out on the show and Dorothy's cross-dressing but heterosexual brother was the butt of many jokes. The series also addressed generational gaps, as the girls came to terms with their grown children's decisions and attitudes: Blanche's daughter becoming a single mom via artificial insemination; Dorothy's son marrying a black woman twice his age; and, of course, Sophia goofing on pretty much every single thing Dorothy did.

TV and Film Connections

Spin-offs:

Empty Nest (which spun off *Nurses*)

The Golden Palace

Somehow, 15 years after its last first-run episode, *The Golden Girls* remains fresh (and relevant), which explains why it had a resurgent popularity among younger viewers and college students when Lifetime began airing repeats in 1997. Although the ladies have become camp icons—particularly the acid-tongued Sophia and deadpan diva Dorothy, whose appearance and shtick resembled a drag queen's—they still resonate as real people. And in a world in which people are living longer (and struggling with a host of new age-related problems), the plight of these characters feels distressingly timely. People over 60 (particularly women) have long been pretty much exiled from pop culture. For seven seasons, *The Golden Girls* changed that. It engaged and entertained us, and gave us some wisdom to go with its wit. Among fondly remembered shows *The Golden Girls* may not be the absolute gold standard, but its characters and stories stay priceless.

Cast:

Bea Arthur *Dorothy Zbornak*, **Betty White** *Rose Nylund*, **Rue McClanahan** *Blanche Devereaux*, **Estelle Getty** *Sophia Petrillo*

Grey's Anatomy

By Tracy Phillips

Broadcast History: ABC, 3/27/2005–
Runtime: 60 minutes
Genre: Medical drama

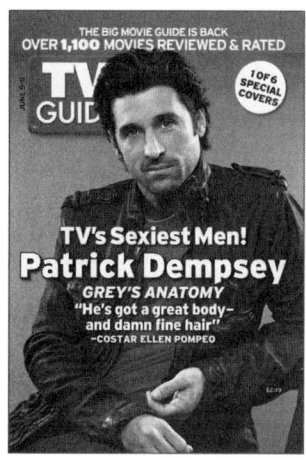

Seriously? Seriously. That's a favorite exchange often heard on one of my favorite shows. I use it here to shamefully admit that I sometimes have a case of Schadenfreude. There's this little devil in me that loves it when an overhyped show crashes and burns—like, say, *Joey*. But to keep my universe balanced, I also genuinely love it when an underdog scores—like the movie *Rudy*. Or a little midseason show called *Grey's Anatomy*. The title didn't inspire much hope, I must say. But when ABC launched the one-hour drama (booting *Boston Legal* from its prestigious Sundays-at-10 spot) on March 27, 2005, I was immediately hooked on this confection of five overworked, oversexed surgical interns at Seattle Grace Hospital.

Timing, it seems, *is* everything, a statement sounding much like one of Meredith Grey's life lessons that's not-so-subtly introduced in her voice-overs at the opening and closing of every episode. It's usually a lazy writer's device to introduce each episode's "theme," but here it works. There are hints of *ER*, *Sex and the City* and *Friends*, all meshed beautifully into one dynamite series.

It's all about saving lives—and saving their own sanity, a form of self-medication that often involves everyone sleeping with each other *and* their bosses. The action centers on doctor-to-be Meredith Grey (played to whiny, frail and pale perfection by relative newcomer Ellen Pompeo)—and her love life. The supporting cast is equally compelling: there's aggressive alpha-female Cristina Yang (Sandra Oh); warm-and-fuzzy Izzie Stevens (Katherine Heigl); smart aleck Alex (Justin Chambers); puppyish George O'Malley (T. R. Knight), who, for a time, was smitten with Meredith; Chandra Wilson's Miranda Bailey, affectionately known as "The Nazi"; and Isaiah Washington as genius surgeon Preston Burke. Then there's "Dr. McDreamy." Sensitive, smart and sexy, Patrick Dempsey has the role of his career as Derek Shepherd, Meredith's on-again, off-again love interest (really, does anyone doubt that these two *won't* end up together?). When they aren't hooking up, they're making eyes at each other in their many elevator encounters (the most happening spot in this hospital isn't an operating table, it's the elevator).

Hot new additions to the gang in Seasons 2 and 3 included Kate Walsh, whose portrayal as Dr. Shepherd's ex-wife quickly won over fans; Derek's rival Eric "McSteamy" Dane; heart patient with a heart of gold Jeffrey Dean Morgan; and sassy Callie (Sara Ramirez). Meanwhile, patients and relatives provided guest-star opportunities for Kate Burton, Chris O'Donnell, Natalie Cole, Rosanna Arquette, Abigail Breslin, Kyle Chandler, Christina Ricci, Mare Winningham, Diahann Carroll and Fred Ward.

Executive producer Shonda Rhimes has created real, flawed, smart and funny characters, and is credited for bringing a respectable, well-rounded ethnic diversity to the show. It's a terrific cast, and one of the reasons *Grey's* has become such an obsession is that these are people you want to be friends with.

Intrigue and cause for occasional snickering is supplied by the absurd patient of the week, from the patient who swallowed a bunch of doll heads, to the woman who spontaneously orgasms, to the guy who hurt himself because he liked scars, and the one who ate his book because it sucked. Then there's the crying. Anyone in need of a weekly purge can usually find something touching to make them weep. Cristina and the baby loss. The impaled victims. The coma patient who woke up years later to find his family moved on without him. The little girl with superpowers. New mommy Bailey. Denny's demise. For story lines like these, tissues come in handy.

Meanwhile, there's always someone in Hollywood looking to take credit for success, and at first, those *Desperate Housewives* were cited for supplying the hefty lead-in audience to *Grey's*. True, but soon enough, the interns were pulling highly competitive ratings—occasionally beating the loony ladies of Hysteria Lane. *Grey's* further proved itself when it skated over to Thursday nights in the fall of 2006, where it was set against juggernaut *CSI*.

> **Did You Know?**
>
> The show was originally supposed to be called *Complications*.

There was much ado about the timeslot showdown, and once again, *Grey's* was reverted to underdog status when critics presumed the hot docs would take a hit from the intimidating investigators. The winner? *Grey's* came out with the edge. It was one of the most significant (and risky) scheduling moves since CBS propped up *Survivor* against NBC's *Friends*, and the gamble paid off, reinventing Thursdays yet again.

While it has occasionally taken a dip in jump-the-shark waters (a post–Super Bowl episode about a bomb exploding in the hospital, for example), the series is infinitely watchable, and its formulaic, frothy fun tempered with poignancy should lend the show some serious longevity. Not many shows can be alternately heartwarming and heartbreaking—*Grey's Anatomy* is, and that's why it's captured this loyal fan's heart.

Cast:

Ellen Pompeo *Meredith Grey*, **Patrick Dempsey** *Derek Shepherd*, **Sandra Oh** *Cristina Yang*, **Katherine Heigl** *Izzie Stevens*, **T. R. Knight** *George O'Malley*, **Justin Chambers** *Alex Karev*, **Chandra Wilson** *Miranda Bailey*, **Isaiah Washington** *Preston Burke*, **James Pickens Jr.** *Richard Webber*, **Kate Walsh** *Addison Shepherd*, **Sara Ramirez** *Callie Torres (2006–)*, **Eric Dane** *Mark Sloan (2006–)*

Gunsmoke

By Paul Droesch

Broadcast History: CBS, 9/10/1955–9/1/1975
Runtime: 30 minutes (1955–61);
 60 minutes (1961–75)
Genre: Western

It's indisputable that after gorging on West-erns in the 1950s and early '60s, viewers lost their taste for them. Oh, every now and then one will turn up and catch our attention briefly, as AMC's *Broken Trail* did in 2005, but over the last three decades or so Westerns have been about as common as a teetotaler in the Long Branch. Let's see: there's *Lonesome Dove* and *Deadwood* . . . and then what? If you can come up any others, memorable ones anyway, you're probably the sort of hard-core TV fan who'd pick up this book. And as you leaf through it, you'll notice that there are only two others, *Deadwood* and *Maverick*, in it. Even *Bonanza* didn't make our cut.

So why did *Gunsmoke*?

First, it would be hard to ignore the longest-running prime-time dramatic series in network history even if you wanted to. Twenty seasons (1955–75) and 635 episodes (almost 32 per season) is a remarkable accomplishment.

It's also worth remembering that in September 1955, when Marshal Matt Dillon (James Arness) first rode into Dodge City, TV's Old West was a pretty simpleminded place: good guys wore white hats, the bad guys wore black and the U.S. Cavalry could be counted on to save the settlers just in time. OK, nobody arrived at the Alamo in time to save Davy Crockett, 1955's biggest Western hero, but you get the picture.

Gunsmoke was a trailblazing Western for grown-ups. True, there were thundering hooves, bank robberies and plenty of gunplay, but that wasn't all there was. This was the first of the character-driven "adult" Westerns, and the charge it led (by 1959 there were more than

Preview Review

November 26, 1955

Unlike other new TV Westerns this season, *Gunsmoke* furnishes its hero with a girl. But the writers don't let her interfere much with the show's taut, action-packed stories. The series relates the exploits of Marshal Matt Dillon, and the program's writers have given him plenty of opportunity to display his quick-on-the-draw technique. So far, he's killed a psychotic gunslinger who had wounded him in an earlier gun battle; he's saved another gunman from being lynched by an angry mob; and he's amputated the leg of a wounded rancher. Arness is backstopped each week by a fine supporting cast: Dennis Weaver as his buddy, Chester, and Amanda Blake as his saloon hostess girlfriend.

25 Westerns on the air) was marked by thoughtful dramas about people whose bad deeds came with explanations, many of them involving family ties: a young man out to kill the uncle who killed his father, say, or a cattle baron who insists that his sons are above the law.

> ## TV and Film Connections
> Spin-off: *Dirty Sally*

There were also social issues. *Gunsmoke* might have been set in the 1870s, '80s and '90s, but Marshal Dillon's racial attitudes were right at home in the civil-rights era. As for Dodge City, it was kind of an oasis—as close to a civilized place as you'd find on TV's lawless frontier. Marshal Dillon's job was to keep it that way.

He was just the guy to do it. As portrayed by the 6-foot-7 Arness, the intimidating, laconic Dillon was fair-minded, slow to anger and always looking to keep the peace. Heck, he didn't even allow guns in Dodge City. In one episode he turned in his badge after shooting a horse thief who had once been his friend. And in another he agonized over hanging a murderer. But he knew what his duty was, and he was decisive and deadly when he had to be.

Kind of like John Wayne, and in fact—or maybe it's legend (stories differ)—Wayne was originally offered the role of Dillon. He definitely did introduce the opening episode ("I think it's the best thing of its kind to come along . . . It's honest, it's adult, it's realistic."). And Arness, the brother of Peter Graves and a WWII Purple Heart recipient, had a tie to the Duke—he had appeared in four Wayne movies in the early '50s.

Joining Arness in the ensemble cast were Milburn Stone as kindly "Doc" Adams; Dennis Weaver as good-natured Dep. Chester Goode, who walked with a limp ("Wait for me, Mister Dillon"); and Amanda Blake as businesslike Long Branch owner Kitty Russell. There was definite chemistry between Kitty and Matt, but it was never acted upon—the most physical contact their characters had, Blake once quipped, was "when I fainted and Matt picked me up."

Arness, a sturdy series centerpiece if ever there was one, stayed all 20 seasons (also a record, although Kelsey Grammer played Frasier for that long on *Cheers* and *Frasier*). So did Stone, and Blake stayed for 19. But Weaver left in 1964, replaced by Ken Curtis as Dep. Festus Haggen, and a number of semiregulars appeared from time to

> ## Did You Know?
> *Gunsmoke* began as a radio show that aired from 1952 to 1961, overlapping the TV version for the last six years of its run.

time, most notably Burt Reynolds as blacksmith Quint Asper from 1962 to '65; and Pat Hingle, who took over medical duties for several months in 1971 when Stone was recovering from a heart attack.

There were guest stars, too, particularly in the later years. Bette Davis, Lee J. Cobb, Carroll O'Connor and Martin Landau were among the biggest names, and Davis's 1966 star turn as a crazed widow poisoned by revenge fantasies made TV GUIDE's 1997 roster of The 100 Greatest Episodes of All Time. Also in the mid-'60s, the producers took an anthology approach, emphasizing outsiders and giving major guest roles to familiar character actors, William Schallert, James Broderick, Victor French and a young Tom Skerritt among them.

The outsiders gave Dodge a sprucing up just when it needed one. *Gunsmoke* hadn't been an immediate hit, but it did crack the Top 10 (at No. 7) in its second season. The following year (when it also became the first Western to win a major Emmy) it hit No. 1, where it stayed for four years. But in 1961, when episodes were expanded from 30 minutes to an hour, ratings began to dip—to No. 3 (behind *Wagon Train* and *Bonanza*) in '62, and then so precipitously that the series was canceled in 1965, only to be saved by a fan in a high place: CBS chairman William Paley.

Paley must have known what he was doing because by 1967 *Gunsmoke* was back in the Top 10, where it stayed for another six years. Marshal Dillon finally got out of Dodge for good (not counting the five reunion movies) on March 31, 1975, and when he did, he rode off into the sunset alone: there were no Westerns at all on the networks' 1975–76 schedules. Talk about the last of a dying breed.

Cast:

James Arness *Marshal Matt Dillon*, **Milburn Stone** *Dr. Galen "Doc" Adams*, **Amanda Blake** *Kitty Russell (1955–74)*, **Dennis Weaver** *Chester Goode (1955–64)*, **Burt Reynolds** *Quint Asper (1962–65)*, **Glenn Strange** *Sam (1962–74)*, **Ken Curtis** *Festus Haggen (1964–75)*, **Roger Ewing** *Clayton Thaddeus "Thad" Greenwood (1965–67)*, **Buck Taylor** *Newly O'Brien (1967–75)*

Happy Days

By Matt Webb Mitovich

Broadcast History: ABC, 1/15/1974–7/12/1984
Runtime: 30 minutes
Genre: Sitcom

In the venerable Smithsonian Institution hangs a leather jacket. That in and of itself speaks volumes about the lasting impact *Happy Days* had on television audiences and the American landscape. And to think that the Fonz's trademark togs almost never made it to air. That's right—in one of my favorite anecdotes from Garry Marshall's *Wake Me When It's Funny*, the *Happy Days* creator relates how stuffy network suits put their foot down at the prospect of a motorcycle jacket–wearing hoodlum fronting ABC's 8 o'clock hour. Ever crafty, Marshall—who later carved out a considerable career as a movie director (*Pretty Woman*)—coerced the execs into letting Fonzie (Henry Winkler) be leather-clad only when his bike was in the scene, then proceeded to ensure that the motorcycle was omnipresent. Thus an antihero was born and welcomed into living rooms nationwide.

In the same way that TV viewers of the '90s cottoned to flashing back to the days of disco via *That '70s Show*, the audience of the '70s thought that the idea of revisiting the '50s was, well, "the bee's knees." Initially dismissed as a series idea (the pilot was burned off as a *Love, American Style* segment) but rushed onto ABC's lineup in the wake of the big-screen success of *American Graffiti* and the Broadway hit *Grease, Happy Days* filled a growing need for nostalgia, a desire to travel back to when life was all about sock hops, necking and being cool. Richie (Ron Howard), Potsie (Anson Williams), Ralph Malph (Donny Most) and the gang made you want to find thrills on Blueberry Hill, tell a pal to "Sit on it," jolt a jukebox into action with the thump of a fist or summon a harem of cuties with a snap of your fingers. And, make no mistake, the Fonzie influence was *huge*,

TV and Film Connections

Spun off from *Love, American Style*
Spin-offs:
Laverne & Shirley
Blansky's Beauties
Mork & Mindy (which spun off
Out of the Blue)
Joanie Loves Chachi

sometimes in ways that had nothing to do with television. Take the 1977 episode titled "Hard Cover," for example, having to do with Richie at college. The Fonz suggested to him that the library is a good place to meet girls, and when Fonzie got his first library card and proclaimed that reading was cool,

Happy Days

there was, Winkler later said, a surge inlibrary card registration among school children.

Happy Days would not be remembered solely for the 11 years of laughs it brought us. No, it proved to be a rather fertile show, birthing not one (*Laverne & Shirley*), not two (*Mork & Mindy*), but *three* spin-offs (the so-so and justifiably short-lived *Joanie Loves Chachi*). To this day, the show resonates not only in the repeats still running rampant on syndication, but in the later-in-life products of its primary players—Academy Award–winning director Ron Howard (*A Beautiful Mind*) being but one example.

Make no mistake, *Happy Days* wasn't perfect. At the series' very start, it gave us the clumsy, never-explained disappearance of Chuck Cunningham. (Marshall's book explains that the sibling was snipped once it became clear that Fonzie would be Richie's big brother figure.) Far worse, toward the end of *Happy Days*' run the core characters and set pieces became almost unrecognizable as the show watered down that which made it memorable—the Fonz as a high school teacher? Arnold's a country-western diner? And most infamously, it *is* the show that gave us the derogatory term "jump the shark," born of the episode where Milwaukee's toughest trades his trashcan-leaping motorcycle for (ugh, it pains me to recall it) *water skis*. Yet to this day the series remains a touchstone for many of us, where but a channel-surfing glimpse of an early episode can, in the blink of an eye, take you back a half century.

Top 3 Moments

- When Fonzie jumped over a shark while waterskiing.
- When the show started taping in front of a live audience.
- When Richie left.

For more, visit www.jumptheshark.com.

Having given us (spin-offs included) more than 20 years of entertainment, these *Happy Days will* continue to be yours and mine.

Cast:

Ron Howard *Richie Cunningham (1974–80)*, **Henry Winkler** *Arthur "Fonzie" Fonzarelli*, **Tom Bosley** *Howard Cunningham*, **Marion Ross** *Marion Cunningham*, **Anson Williams** *Warren "Potsie" Weber (1974–83)*, **Donny Most** *Ralph Malph (1974–80)*, **Erin Moran** *Joanie Cunningham*, **Gavan O'Herlihy** *Chuck Cunningham (1974)*, **Randolph Roberts** *Chuck Cunningham (1974–75)*, **Linda Purl** *Gloria (1974–75)/Ashley Pfister (1982–83)*, **Pat Morita** *Arnold (1975–76, 1982–83)*, **Al Molinaro** *Alfred Delvecchio (1976–82)*, **Scott Baio** *Charles "Chachi" Arcola (1977–84)*, **Lynda Goodfriend** *Lori Beth Allen Cunningham (1977–82)*, **Cathy Silvers** *Jenny Piccalo (1980–83)*, **Ted McGinley** *Roger Phillips (1980–84)*

Heroes

By G. J. Donnelly

Broadcast History: NBC, 9/25/2006–
Runtime: 60 minutes
Genre: Sci-fi/fantasy

In 2006, the phrase "Save the cheerleader, save the world!" became a mantra for millions of TV viewers who tuned in to this series about ordinary people endowed with superhuman abilities. It's not a new concept—it's been explored in everything from the *X-Men* to *The 4400*—but the rationale for their existence is quite novel: it seems these individuals are part of a natural evolution to deal with stressors facing Mother Earth.

It is interesting to compare *Heroes* to the *X-Men* in that both groups consist of mutants who are beset with personal problems. Although *Heroes'* protagonists don't wear spandex—at least not yet—their formidable gifts are often hampered by crises of conscience.

Isaac (Santiago Cabrera) can paint portraits depicting future events, provided he's on heroin. Niki (Ali Larter) is a single mom who pays the bills by stripping on the Internet. She also has a violent split personality called Jessica (who has the same name and personality as Niki's dead sister). Niki's estranged husband, D. L. (Leonard Roberts), has demonstrated an ability to walk through solid objects. Their son, Micah (Noah Gray-Cabey), is a genius who can fix anything. Hiro (Masi Oka), one of the 2006–07 TV season's breakout characters, is an idealistic comic-book fanatic who can teleport across time and space—though it took some doing to convince his best friend Ando (James Kyson Lee) of his ability. Matt (Greg Grunberg) is an LAPD officer who reads minds—and learns that his wife is having an affair with a fellow cop. Peter Petrelli (Milo Ventimiglia) is a hospice nurse capable of emulating the powers of those he comes in contact with, such as his brother, Nathan (Adrian Pasdar), a slimy politician who can fly. Finally, there's Claire (Hayden Panettiere), the aforementioned cheerleader, who heals almost instantly from any wound, no matter how mortal. Many others come and go, but they are the core.

Generally these characters keep their powers under wraps, though it's not long before several "normal" figures learn their secrets. Skeptical genetics professor Mohinder Suresh (Sendhil Ramamurthy) is dragged into the mystery while investigating the murder of his father, who was seeking proof of the mutants' existence. Simone Deveaux (Tawny Cypress) is an art dealer who sells Isaac's works; she becomes romantically involved with Peter. Claire's father (Jack Coleman)—known as "Horn-Rimmed Glasses" (or H. R. G.) for his distinctive specs—is a shadowy operative who has been tracking the development of mutants for years, and protects his adopted daughter with ruthless zeal.

In this show's first season, he had good reason to. A serial killer—Sylar (Zachary Quinto)—was on the loose and targeting mutants. A former watchmaker, Sylar had a particularly gruesome modus operandi—removing the brains from his victims' skulls to obtain their gifts.

The interaction of these diverse characters form a complex tapestry of interweaving subplots, all of which are tied to an impending catastrophe. In the wrong hands, *Heroes* could have come off as self-indulgent and ponderous, but under the direction of creator–executive producer Tim Kring, the results proved crisp and hypnotic. As if inexorably drawn together by fate, the individual mutants slowly cross paths.

Admittedly, even die-hard fans could sometimes need a scorecard to keep up with all the action. In a diner, Hiro and Ando met Nathan, who literally flew the coop after being confronted by some roughs in a Las Vegas hotel room. It was there he had a one-night stand with Niki's alter ego, Jessica. An escaped con, D. L. reenters Niki's life looking for a briefcase of money and after a confrontation with Jessica, escaped with Micah. A future version of Hiro—speaking perfect English and brandishing a sword—traveled in time to urge Peter to save Claire ("Save the cheerleader, save the world!"), which he did when Sylar showed up during her school's homecoming celebration. His attempt on Claire foiled, Sylar was soon kidnapped by two of H. R. G.'s metahuman associates: Eden (Nora Zehetner), who had awesome powers of persuasion, and the Haitian (Jimmy Jean-Louis), who can remove memories. (Eden later killed herself to prevent an escaping Sylar from obtaining her power.) Sylar is also on the mind of Matt, who is recruited by FBI agent Audrey Hanson (Clea DuVall) to help track the killer down. Are you with me?

Somehow, it all works. These examples only scratch the convoluted surface of this most captivating adventure. But as mind-bending as some of the mutants' exploits can be, *Heroes* is at its best when it aims for the heart. For example, Hiro's star-crossed romance with a young waitress suffering from a brain aneurysm provided moving moments.

> ### Did You Know?
>
> Greg Grunberg had the role of the doomed pilot in the first episode of *Lost*.

The magic of *Heroes* doesn't lie in its characters' tremendous abilities—though, let's face it, they are pretty cool. Rather, it posits how ordinary people would behave if they were suddenly given extraordinary gifts. The answer: they'd be very human.

In the 2006–07 TV season, which was largely devoid of freshman successes, we—and hit-starved NBC—needed something new that was original, provocative and engaging. *Heroes* performed, well, heroically for the network, so it's not surprising that it was renewed for a second year.

Cast:

Santiago Cabrera *Isaac Mendez*, **Tawny Cypress** *Simone Deveaux*, **Noah Gray-Cabey** *Micah Sanders*, **Greg Grunberg** *Matt Parkman*, **Ali Larter** *Niki Sanders*, **Masi Oka** *Hiro Nakamura*, **Hayden Panettiere** *Claire Bennet*, **Adrian Pasdar** *Nathan Petrelli*, **Sendhil Ramamurthy** *Mohinder Suresh*, **Leonard Roberts** *D. L. Hawkins*, **Milo Ventimiglia** *Peter Petrelli*, **Jack Coleman** *Horn-Rimmed Glasses*, **James Kyson Lee** *Ando Masahashi*

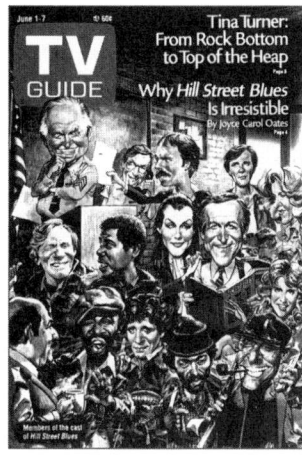

Hill Street Blues

By Roger Leister

Broadcast History: NBC, 1/15/1981–5/19/1987
Runtime: 60 minutes
Genre: Crime drama

To call composer Mike Post an unsung figure in TV history isn't a stretch. Decades after we first heard his classic themes, those unforgettable notes still lurk in our subconscious. There is perhaps no better example than the achingly sweet melody that—following morning roll call, of course—dropped us off on the cold, gloomy streets of the Hill district and introduced us to a baker's dozen of richly developed characters inhabiting the grimy Hill Street police station. At show's end, the melancholic music eased us out of an emotionally charged final frame.

The instrumental won Post two of his five Grammy Awards and charted in the Top 10 (in the days when TV actually produced pop hits). But that's just a small corner of the sparkling trophy case for *Hill Street Blues*, a series that revitalized the cop genre. Co-creators Steven Bochco and Michael Kozoll brought a new realism to the small screen. Life around the station house was a more chaotic and vivid version of *Barney Miller*, shot documentary-style, with hand-held cameras and overlapping dialogue. *Hill Street* was where men's room scenes, scatological references and posteriors made their way into prime time (a precursor to Bochco's butt-filled days ahead with *L.A. Law* and *NYPD Blue*). Much more than cardboard cops, these characters were complex, flawed people with problems: rotten salaries, messy love lives and stressful ethical dilemmas. A workplace, in short, most average people can relate to.

The multiple story lines would shift radically in tone, from violent encounters to stationhouse slapstick (windows shattered almost weekly) to soap opera–like sexual situations, sometimes within the same segment. Refreshingly, plot details carried over from one week to the next, even ridiculous stuff like crusty undercover ace Mick Belker (Bruce Weitz) taking on an orangutan as his desk mate for three episodes.

> ### Did You Know?
> When actor Michael Conrad passed away from cancer, the show had his character, Sgt. Phil Esterhaus, die as well—he had a heart attack during sex.

In a 1985 TV GUIDE cover story, Joyce Carol Oates praised *Hill Street* for "developing characters much like in a novel, they really grew, developed and changed over time."

Thus, we grew intimately familiar with everyone in the precinct, no one more so than Capt. Frank Furillo (Daniel J. Travanti). He soldiered through his daily—and rather unrealistic—volume of corruption, drugs and violent crime, while having every facet of law-enforcement politics thrown on his desk. We eventually learn that the unblinking (literally) Furillo is a recovering alcoholic, and we understand why every time his flaky ex-wife, Fay (Barbara Bosson, Bochco's wife at the time), shows up.

The romantic spark in Furillo's life was ignited by sassy Joyce Davenport (Veronica Hamel). Not quite an adolescent, I didn't fully appreciate Joyce when the series began. But upon further examination, she supplied more good exposure for defense attorneys than the rest of television's DAs put together. Joyce was to *Hill Street* what Marilyn was to the *Munsters*. Or as Belker put it, she's "as far from a dirt bag as you can get." Too bad Hamel became Susan Lucci at Emmy time, going winless after five straight nominations.

Though he may not have the name recognition of Klinger or Kramer, Belker is as identifiable an icon of '80s TV as the *M*A*S*H* and *Seinfeld* funnymen were in the surrounding decades. An ever-present cigar only left Belker's mouth to make room for some bizarre snack (an onion; a head-cheese and ox-tongue sandwich) when he dealt with his mother's daily phone call. While characters like Sgt. Esterhaus (Michael Conrad) and pipe-smoking Lt. Howard Hunter (James B. Sikking) spoke with a professorial wisdom and grace, Belker rarely ended a sentence without combining slime- dirt- scum- or dog- with -bag, -ball or -breath.

Despite the strong cast, ratings were slow to materialize for *Hill Street*, but Emmys were a different story. The show was so dominant for four years, they could've held the Emmy ceremony right there on The Hill. (And, by the way, just where was the show set? While shot in L.A., it was based on The Hill neighborhood in Bochco's college town of Pittsburgh and used Chicago-styled police cars, but the creators took pains never to establish it as one particular locale. One script misdirection in Season 2 had Sgt. Esterhaus' buddy Mike (soon to be ex-buddy, following his coming out of the closet during lunch) offering up hockey tickets for a Sabres game. So, now we're in *Buffalo*?)

After reeling in eight Emmys out of a record 21 nominations in its rookie season, *Hill Street* piled up the statues the way the Yankees collect World Series rings—a total of 26 (from 98 nominations). Most impressive was winning all five nominations for best supporting actor in 1982, by Taurean Blacque, Michael Conrad, Charles Haid,

Classic Episode Close-Up
"Grace Under Pressure"
(Original telecast: February 2, 1984)

It's in this touching episode Capt. Furillo announces that Sgt. Phil Esterhaus has died of a heart attack at age 55. "This is going to be a difficult day," he says. "I know the caution Phil would urge you: Be careful out there." It would be a terrible day for the grieving officers, especially Joe Coffey, whose girlfriend (guest star Linda Hamilton) is raped. Esterhaus's death was no ratings stunt—Michael Conrad, who played him, died of cancer just two months before. But "Grace Under Pressure" gives Phil a droll exit: His last act was making love. It's the kind of offbeat and human touch that made *Hill Street* one of TV's most inventive cop series.

Michael Warren and Bruce Weitz. Warren hadn't been part of such an accomplished quintet since captaining two national-champion UCLA basketball squads.

The Emmy gold rush dried up, coincidentally or not, shortly after Conrad's death midway through the show's seven-year run (Betty Thomas won the show's final Emmy, in 1985). Sgt. Stan Jablonski (Robert Prosky) had the unenviable task of replacing the avuncular Esterhaus, eloquent speaker of *Hill Street*'s most famous five words: "Let's be careful out there." Making matters worse, Jablonski was saddled with the catchphrase "Let's get them before they get us." The transition was not nearly as seamless as, say, *Cheers* shifting from Coach to Woody, but the superb cast and writing were more than good enough to keep the show at a high level. If *Hill Street* did weather a jump-the-shark watch in its last two seasons (the post-Bochco years—he was fired by MTM for going over budget), Dennis Franz was a major reason why. As no-nonsense Lt. Norman Buntz, the future *NYPD Blue* star truly stood out, and not just because he had already been on the show briefly as slimy Det. Sal Benedetto.

> **TV and Film Connections**
>
> Spin-off: *Beverly Hills Buntz*

Maybe one reason the cast clicked like it did was the writers not forgetting *Paris*, one of a handful of cop shows Bochco and Kozoll created in the '70s. *Paris* was the forceful but short-lived L.A. police drama centered on Capt. Woody Paris (a precursor to Frank Furillo played by James Earl Jones) that included no fewer than six of the eventual *Hill Street* regulars. Not only was it like a *Hill Street* farm team, it proved to be a conceptual petri dish for Bochco and Kozoll's eventual masterpiece.

If *Cheers* and *The Cosby Show* were the heart of NBC's turnaround in the '80s, *Hill Street Blues* was its groundbreaking soul. It created an oft-copied template for ensemble dramas and pioneered a new era of "quality" television. And above all, by artfully breaking from traditional boundaries, its success announced to network programmers a message that the medium would do well to remember today: hey, let's *not* be so creatively careful out there.

Cast:

Daniel J. Travanti *Capt. Frank Furillo*, **Michael Conrad** *Sgt. Phil Esterhaus (1981–84)*, **Bruce Weitz** *Det. Mick Belker*, **Michael Warren** *Off. Bobby Hill*, **Veronica Hamel** *Joyce Davenport*, **Charles Haid** *Off. Andy Renko*, **Rene Enriquez** *Lt. Ray Calletano*, **Kiel Martin** *Det. Johnny "J. D." LaRue*, **James B. Sikking** *Lt. Howard Hunter*, **Joe Spano** *Sgt./Lt. Henry Goldblume*, **Taurean Blacque** *Det. Neal Washington*, **Betty Thomas** *Off./Sgt. Lucy Bates*, **Ed Marinaro** *Off. Joe Coffey (1981–86)*, **Barbara Bosson** *Fay Furillo (1981–86)*, **Barbara Babcock** *Grace Gardner (1981–82; 1986)*, **Robert Hirschfeld** *Off. Leo Schnitz (1981–85)*, **Jon Cypher** *Chief Fletcher Daniels*, **George Wyner** *ADA Irwin Bernstein (1982–87)*, **Dennis Franz** *Det. Sal Benedetto (1982–83)/Lt. Norman Buntz (1985–87)*, **Lisa Sutton** *Off. Robin Tataglia (1983–87)*, **Ken Olin** *Det. Harry Garibaldi (1984–85)*, **Mimi Kuzyk** *Det. Patsy Mayo (1984–85)*, **Robert Prosky** *Sgt. Stan Jablonski (1984–87)*, **Peter Jurasik** *Sid Thurston (1985–87)*, **Robert Clohessy** *Off. Pat Flaherty (1986–87)*, **Megan Gallagher** *Off. Tina Russo (1986–87)*

Homicide:
Life on the Street

By Roger Leister

Broadcast History: NBC, 1/31/1993–5/21/1999
Runtime: 60 minutes
Genre: Crime drama

The best cop show not enough people watched began its way-too-short run promisingly enough, with a captive audience in the cushy hour following the 1993 Super Bowl. Shortly after the Dallas Cowboys dealt the Buffalo Bills the third of four consecutive losses in the big game, we were introduced to an intriguing squad of Baltimore homicide detectives. What followed was considerable critical acclaim (including three Peabody Awards) and disappointing ratings. It certainly didn't help that NBC never showed any real enthusiasm for this uncommonly gritty drama or knew quite what to do with it, ultimately exiling it to low-viewership Friday nights and once ordering only *four* episodes for an entire season. Maybe co-executive producer Barry Levinson was right: "We're like an outsider who's been accepted, but still feels like an outsider."

The drama's signature prop was an office grease board that neatly listed each detective's work log of corpses: red marker for unsolved cases, black marker for closed cases. After six-plus seasons, it was time for *Homicide* itself to go on the board, a victim of TV's killer numbers game. Throughout its run, there seemed always to be a well-publicized threat of imminent cancellation, and maybe that's what made fans like myself savor each episode like a stay of execution and who knows, perhaps also freed the creators to throw caution to the wind and boldly experiment in whatever creative ways they wanted. Whatever, this was one cop show definitely *not* about car chases and shoot-outs. An array of socially relevant issues (including race relations, poverty, religion and police corruption) were dealt with deftly, using trenchant dialogue, hand-held cameras and jump cuts to give the stories a feel of documentary-like authenticity. The material was a lot more jarring than, say, *Law & Order*, and even more visceral than the similarly superb *NYPD Blue*. *Homicide* was uncompromising in its lacerating intensity, and above all, seemed electrifyingly real. Plus it could serve up jolting surprises.

In just its fifth episode, for example, an out-of-the-box tone was set with nearly an entire hour spent *in* "the box," where Dets. Frank Pembleton (Andre Braugher) and Tim Bayliss (Kyle Secor) had 12 hours to get a confession from a suspected child killer. More than just good cop–bad cop boilerplate, this was an interrogatory heavyweight fight, with Bayliss keeping the suspect upright just enough for Pembleton to pummel the felon's psyche like a speed bag. The cop-show bible says the suspect had to spill the beans, right? Not here. The effort proved fruitless and the case haunted the department. That's where *Homicide* was different.

The first season yielded Emmys for Levinson (directing) and co-executive producer Tom Fontana (writing), and established Braugher as first among equals in an extraordinary ensemble cast. His Pembleton was a volatile loner who seemed to exist in a different space. He spoke like a professor, yet possessed—and showed—an explosive rage, and was the show's forceful anchor.

For all its sordid and violent content, *Homicide* made great use of gallows humor and often showed a tender side in developing its characters. A highlight came in the first season when a waitress played by Julianna Margulies connects with the twice-divorced Stanley Bolander (Ned Beatty) through their mutual love of stringed instruments. When they finally play together, the music accompanies a wild scene of a suspected trigger-happy cop being arrested.

Bolander left after three seasons, though four of his cohorts lasted for the show's run: Bayliss, the intuitive if strait-laced idealist; John Munch (Richard Belzer), the deadpan office jokester; Meldrick Lewis (Clark Johnson), a streetwise team player; and Al Giardello (Yaphet Kotto), aka "Gee," the firm-but-fair lieutenant.

For the imposing Kotto, a journeyman actor perhaps best known as a Bond villain in *Live and Let Die*, *Homicide* was a career-maker. As Giardello, he provided a generous supply of the show's considerable heart, bear-hugging squad members with one arm while using the other to whip them through their day-to-day paces. A Baltimore native of black and Italian heritage, Giardello was also the department historian, lamenting the transformation of once-proud ethnic neighborhoods into drug-riddled streets. Bayliss and Lewis had their fair share of quirks, but it's Munch and his cynical musings—often linking the day's events with some arcane bit of history—that became most identifiable (along with that ever-present ringing phone at headquarters).

It didn't help enough, but in an effort to get better ratings, the show also made great use of guest stars. In Emmy-nominated appearances, Robin Williams was a tourist grieving the death of his wife in a mugging; Lily Tomlin was a housewife suspected of killing her philandering husband; Alfre Woodard (reprising the character of Roxanne Turner, played by her

Did You Know?

The series is based on a book by *Baltimore Sun* reporter David Simon (*The Wire*); Simon served as a civilian assistant in the Baltimore Police Homicide Unit in order to research the goings-on in a metropolitan homicide squad.

on *St. Elsewhere* from 1985 to 1987) was a doctor who defended a patient's right to die; Charles Durning was a retired detective returning to work an old case; and, most memorably, Vincent D'Onofrio turned in a gut-wrenching portrayal as a man wedged between a subway station platform and a train, sharing his last hours of life with Pembleton. (The 1997 episode was also the subject of a telling, must-see two-hour documentary titled *Anatomy of a 'Homicide: Life on the Street.'*)

Apart from the regulars (and there were numerous and seamless cast changes along the way), as well as impeccable writing and direction, *Homicide* worked because, as Johnson said, "Baltimore was such a big part of the show." For his part, Braugher dedicated his 1998 Emmy win to "all the people in Baltimore. This is a town that I love. We have finally made it." In what amounted to a postmortem, a 2000 TV movie had Giardello shot while delivering a mayoral campaign speech, prompting the return of every detective from the series to assist in hunting the shooter. Die-hard fans may argue that the show hasn't really ended; it's just living on intermittently through John Munch. Yes, that was Richard Belzer appearing in his record ninth different show as the same character in a May 2006 episode of *Arrested Development*. You can be sure Munch told the guys all about it back at the bar in Baltimore.

Cast:

Ned Beatty *Det. Stanley Bolander (1993–95)*, **Richard Belzer** *Det. John Munch*, **Daniel Baldwin** *Det. Beau Felton (1993–95)*, **Melissa Leo** *Det./Sgt. Kay Howard (1993–97)*, **Clark Johnson** *Det. Meldrick Lewis*, **Jon Polito** *Det. Steve Crosetti (1993–94)*, **Andre Braugher** *Det. Frank Pembleton (1993–98)*, **Kyle Secor** *Det. Tim Bayliss*, **Yaphet Kotto** *Lt. Al Giardello*, **Isabella Hofman** *Lt./Capt. Megan Russert (1994–96)*, **Reed Diamond** *Det. Mike Kellerman (1995–98)*, **Max Perlich** *J. H. James Brodie (1995–97)*, **Michelle Forbes** *Dr. Julianna Cox (1996–98)*, **Jon Seda** *Det. Paul Falsone (1997–99)*, **Callie Thorne** *Det. Laura Ballard (1997–99)*, **Peter Gerety** *Det. Stuart Gharty (1997–99)*, **Toni Lewis** *Det. Terri Stivers (1997–99)*, **Giancarlo Esposito** *Agent Mike Giardello (1998–99)*, **Michael Michele** *Det. Rene Sheppard (1998–99)*

The Honeymooners

By Alan Appel

Broadcast History: CBS, 10/1/1955–9/22/1956
Runtime: 30 minutes
Genre: Sitcom
Black and White

How sweet the night was.

His gray hair and mustache were not at all familiar to me, but the girth and outsized personality were, and the raspy laugh was unmistakable. Balancing a cigarette in one hand and a drink in the other, Jackie Gleason was holding court at Manhattan's 21 Club during a fall night in, if memory serves, 1984. He and Art Carney were ostensibly in town to publicize a TV movie for CBS titled *Izzy & Moe*, but that's not really what members of the press—nor, for that matter, Gleason—wanted to talk about. The subject at hand was *The Honeymooners*, and the Great One (as Orson Welles dubbed Gleason), an unusually articulate and insightful performer, was telling us all to, please, not overcomplicate the artistry of this classic blue-collar sitcom about the Kramdens and the Nortons, and why it continued to endure. "The audience likes us," he said, "because we're them." And, oh yes, Carney added, it happens to be "a very, very funny show. Period."

Indeed it is. *The Honeymooners*, Gleason's crowning career achievement—voted by TV GUIDE in 2002 the third-best show of all time, behind No. 2 *I Love Lucy* and top-ranked *Seinfeld*—began as a sketch on the DuMont network's barely remembered variety show *Cavalcade of Stars*, but after Gleason moved to CBS in the fall of 1952 he took his comedy creations with him. Among them were besotted playboy Reginald Van Gleason III, the Poor Soul, Joe the Bartender, loudmouth Charlie Bratton and, of course, bus driver Ralph Kramden. Ralph lived in a sparsely furnished Brooklyn flat with his sweet-natured wife, Alice (Audrey Meadows), and they—along with their upstairs friends, sewer worker Ed Norton and his wife, Trixie (Carney, Joyce Randolph)—were breakout characters. They were so popular, in fact, that Gleason decided to spin them off into their own self-contained series. What emerged from that single memorable TV year—the fall of 1955 to the fall of '56—were the so-called "Classic 39" episodes, whose timeless influence can be seen in shows ranging from *The Flintstones* right down to *The King of Queens*.

> ## Did You Know?
>
> If you ever notice Jackie Gleason patting himself on the stomach, it was a sign that he had forgotten his line.

On its surface, *The Honeymooners* was kitchen-sink comedy at its purest. Certainly it was a more benign television landscape during the innocent '50s. Unlike much of what we see in today's sitcoms, the humor in *The Honeymooners* wasn't coarse, whiny or mean-spirited; the sentiments here were honest, the laughs *huge* and there was a fascinating improvisational feel to the series. Gleason filmed two episodes a week before an audience at New York's Adelphi Theatre and was not a big believer in too much rehearsal. As a consequence, lines are sometimes flubbed (as they are in real life) and there's a wonderful spontaneity about the show. Check out, for example, the inspired (and ad-lib laden) episode "Better Living Through TV," in which Ralph talks Norton into buying TV time so that the two of them can go on the air and sell 2,000 of their kitchen gadgets, the Handy Housewife Helper. Before the telecast, Ralph is the picture of calm, but as they prepare to go on the air, panic sets in, he goes into one of his trademark "hummina-hummina" meltdowns and he warns a worrisome Ed: "Stop it, nervous, you're going to get yourself all Norton." It's a quintessential *Honeymooners* moment, but the true series nuts—including those who were card-carrying members of RALPH (Royal Association for the Longevity and Preservation of *The Honeymooners*)—still talk about the celebrated ad-lib in which a part of the kitchen gizmo accidentally flies off. Gleason, without losing a beat, walks off his mark and directly in front of the camera, eyes the spare part, and says: "Maybe we ought to say something about spear fishing."

"These two guys just understood each other," series writer A. J. Russell is quoted as saying in *The Official Honeymooners Treasury*, by Peter Crescenti and Bob Columbe. "If anything ever went wrong, they would keep going until they found themselves, and they would be right on track again. The cues would be right, and the jokes would be right. There was no throwing them." The jokes seemed somehow or other always to be about either a) Ralph's weight or b) Ralph's get-rich-quick schemes (like the episode in which he was a contestant on a quiz show, or the time he tried to market a new appetizer that was actually dog food). But as series fan Ray Romano (*Everybody Loves Raymond*) has said, *The Honeymooners* is a character-driven series that "doesn't live joke to joke." There may be plenty of insults from Alice and bluster from Ralph ("One of these days, Alice, POW! right in the kisser"), but there is never a doubt that there is genuine love and respect in this marriage, no matter their threadbare possessions or uncertain financial prospects. So, whatever the arguments, frustrations or disappointments, we know that at the end of each half hour there'll be a reassuring embrace, with Ralph exclaiming, "Baby, you're the greatest." The most

Top 3 Moments
- Never jumped.
- When lost episodes were found.
- Bad from Day 1.

For more, visit www.jumptheshark.com.

important things that beloved underdogs like the Kramdens have—and all they really need—are each other.

In the wiry, rubber-limbed Carney, the show has perhaps the medium's most accomplished second banana ever, and Gleason credited him with most of the show's success. I mean, could *anybody* but Carney provide one of TV's true iconic moments when he uttered two simple words, "Hello, ball!" in an episode titled "The Golfer," in which he shows Ralph the proper way to address the ball. But the contributions of the appealing Audrey Meadows (who replaced Pert Kelton early on in the role of Alice), with her superb timing, and Joyce Randolph, nicely underplaying as Trixie, should not be underestimated. This was a small but superlative ensemble. In the years after the "Classic 39" first aired, *Honeymooners* sketches continued for years in various Gleason shows and specials, later with different actresses as Alice and Trixie; and in the '80s, there were *Honeymooners* so-called "lost episodes" that Gleason released to cable. But these were really variety-show sketches that first aired in the early '50s, and apart from their historical value, are a mixed bag.

When we think of *The Honeymooners*, it's mostly the 39 shows from the 1955–56 season that still make us smile. Meadows won an Emmy as Alice, and Carney won five of them as Norton. Gleason never won, and how ridiculous is *that*? It hardly seems to matter. This peerless sitcom lives on forever, in glorious black and white, in syndication, in my consciousness.

Baby, it's the greatest.

Cast:

Jackie Gleason *Ralph Kramden*, **Art Carney** *Ed Norton*, **Audrey Meadows** *Alice Kramden*, **Joyce Randolph** *Trixie Norton*

House

By Paul Droesch
Broadcast History: FOX, 11/16/2004–
Runtime: 60 minutes
Genre: Medical drama

Throughout my life, I have been healthy. In fact, one of my bosses once called me "the Cal Ripken of TV GUIDE." (Too bad he didn't put it on my performance evaluation.) But over the last 20 years or so I have been laid low seven or eight times by a mysterious illness that knocks me for a loop. I get feverish, achy and feel like I'm dying, with symptoms that are sort of flu-like, but worse. I just lie in bed in a fetal position and moan. I might even hallucinate. Then, after a day or so, the fever breaks and I'm fine. I don't think I have ever missed more than a day or two of work from this mystery malady, and whenever I have gotten around to telling a doctor about it, usually months later during a checkup, when it was no longer fresh in my mind, he or she has always shrugged it off with some benign diagnosis. "You look OK to me," I'm told.

But I can't escape the feeling that something awful is lurking in my body. What if—the next time it hits or the time after that—it doesn't go away but rears up with more intensity than in the past and threatens my life?

Then I could be a patient on *House*. I think I'd like an actor known for wise-cracking—Alan Alda would be perfect if he were 10 years younger—to play me.

Chances are, Dr. Gregory House (Hugh Laurie), the head of diagnostic medicine at New Jersey's Princeton/Plainsboro Teaching Hospital, would figure out what's wrong just in time to save my life, which would be just before the end of my episode. But before he did, I'd have to put up with a thoroughly unpleasant man. Marcus Welby this guy isn't.

First of all, I wouldn't expect anything approaching TLC: To House, I'd be a puzzle, not a person, and he'd treat me with as much emotional intensity as I treat a crossword puzzle, except that I don't assume that the puzzle is lying to me. Or that the cause of my illness is my own fault. House, as has been said, has little patience for patients. This description might be somewhat glib, but it does get to the nub of House's irascible, antisocial essence. His good side, of course, is that he's as brilliant as diagnosticians get, and he'd stop at nothing—medical ethics, what are *those*?—to find what's killing the patient.

OK, just about all TV doctors are brilliant, and most will tiptoe over fuzzy ethical lines, but without a second thought House will leap headlong over crystal clear ones, breaking laws as he goes. He routinely has his associates break into patients' houses. He performs tests without permission. You name it.

And sure, TV medics can be moody (older viewers will remember *Ben Casey*), but House is almost *always* in a bad mood. He's also misanthropic, manipulative, cynical, rude and selfish. Not to mention vindictive. In a Season 2 episode, for instance, he even went to the trouble of learning Farsi so he could read medical journals that substantiated his suspicion that a med-school classmate was pushing a bogus but profitable breakthrough.

House can be lazy, too, and that's in a profession known for workaholics. True, he spends a lot of time thinking, but he does have three "flunkies" (immunologist Allison Cameron, intensive-care specialist Robert Chase and neurologist Eric Foreman)—all esteemed in their own right—to do the scut work. "[The] patient is also having unexplained, intense abdominal pain," Cameron told House in a Season 3 episode. "So explain them," he barks. "Wake me when they've done an exploratory laparotomy."

And when he's awake, House is likely to be watching soap operas (sometimes in a comatose patient's room), whiling away afternoons at OTB parlors (although that can come in handy, as in the Season 2 episode when a woman played by Cynthia Nixon conveniently collapsed at his feet) or evenings at monster-truck rallies (his idea of a Season 1 date with Cameron). He also likes to tool around central New Jersey on his Honda motorcycle. (Laurie, incidentally, is also a motorcycle buff.)

So it's no wonder that a former patient's husband shot him in the second-season finale, and he did it because House's behavior toward him had been so typical: After House told the guy to be totally honest, he admitted to an affair. House then told his wife about it *even though it had nothing to do with her medical case*, and she killed herself.

So, we're agreed. House isn't a nice guy—a combination of brilliant and not nice that makes for a compelling character. And a runaway hit, which *House* became midway in its first season on Fox (2004–05), when *Rebel Billionaire*, the forgettable Richard Branson reality flop that preceded it on Tuesdays, was canceled, and our dour doc got to follow *American Idol*. But just what is it that keeps House's boss, always-exasperated hospital administrator Lisa Cuddy (Lisa Edelstein), from firing him? Or keeps underlings Cameron (Jennifer Morrison), Chase (Jesse Spencer) and Foreman (Omar Epps) from taking the better-paying jobs they all could easily get? Or drove his married erstwhile girlfriend, hospital lawyer Stacy Warner (Sela Ward), back to him? (In the end,

Preview Review
September 12, 2004

The Setup: "Humanity is overrated," growls Gregory House, a doctor with a bedside manner so abrasive it could give you bedsores. Leading a team of young specialists in solving bizarre medical mysteries, House defies authority and insults patients but is too brilliant to be fired. Yet.

We Say: Laurie is terrific as the prickly focus of a refreshingly unsentimental medical drama. The cast is strong, the writing sharp and the visuals often startling, including *CSI*-style close-ups inside the body.

he spurned her.) Or keeps his oncologist pal James Wilson (Robert Sean Leonard) in his corner no matter how much he abuses their friendship? House even stole Wilson's prescription pad, and got him into trouble with that vengeful cop (David Morse) House slighted in Season 3.

Surely drugs are part of the reason. They all know that he's addicted to the Vicodin he takes practically by the handful to relieve the almost constant, apparently agonizing pain caused by a misdiagnosed infarction he suffered before the series premiered (on November 16, 2004), which has rotted away the muscle tissue in his right leg. That wasn't his fault; he's a victim. Anybody can sympathize with that.

Did You Know?

In the Season 2 episode where Wilson moves in with House, viewers can see that one of the shows House TiVos is *Blackadder* (which featured Hugh Laurie).

House *does* relate to some people. He just does it in odd ways, and for reasons you'd never think of. He's unpredictable, and that's always interesting. Take the time, in the third season, when the patient was a 10-year-old autistic boy. Now there's somebody whose pain he felt. But he didn't feel sorry for him. "Why would you feel sorry for someone who's allowed to opt out of the inane courteous formalities that are utterly meaningless, insincere and therefore degrading?" he asked Cameron. "I don't pity the kid, I envy him."

Could you imagine *Grey's Anatomy*'s Derek Shepherd (Patrick Dempsey), TV's other hot healer, saying *that*?

You can't. McDreamy's a terrific matinee-idol soap character, and *Grey's* an extraordinarily well-crafted medical soap, but House is a complex contrarian who usually manages to do the right thing, whatever his reasons might be. He might have learned Farsi partly, maybe mostly, to settle a score (and one that wasn't justified), but he also stopped a useless procedure in its tracks.

And, unlike *Grey's*, *House* is a medical drama with lots of serious medicine (and *CSI*-style graphics to show they mean business). True, each week's patient is plugged into a pretty rigid formula (initial crisis, followed by a rally, followed by crises before each commercial break until House solves the case in the nick of time). But it's something of an intellectual challenge just to follow it.

It has to be a challenge for Laurie (an English doctor's son who made his name as a comedian in *Jeeves and Wooster*, the hit adaptation of P. G. Wodehouse stories) to act the part. But he limps, grimaces, sneers, yells, grins like a Cheshire cat, and still manages to make House sympathetic in the way that the Roadrunner is when he's dropping anvils on people's heads. And, being British, Laurie has to do it while faking an American accent.

So what does the future hold? Continued success for a while, no doubt, and more accolades to go along with the Emmy, Peabody and Humanitas Awards already earned by series creator David Shore (a Canadian-born lawyer whose previous writing and producing credits include *Law & Order* and *Hack*). But most hit medical dramas don't last all that long (*ER* being a glaring exception), especially those that focus on one doc who gets hot and stays that way until the Next Big Thing comes along. So that could happen. Or Laurie might tire of being an expatriate in L.A. Then again, somebody could take another shot at House. After tracking the guy for as long as the show has been on, I might be tempted to try it myself, but then he wouldn't be around to save my life if I needed him.

Cast:

Hugh Laurie *Dr. Greg House*, **Linda Edelstein** *Lisa Cuddy*, **Robert Sean Leonard** *James Wilson*, **Jennifer Morrison** *Allison Cameron*, **Omar Epps** *Eric Foreman*, **Jesse Spencer** *Robert Chase*

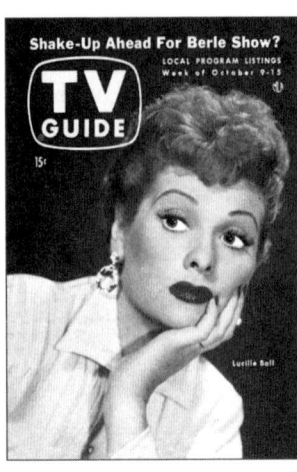

I Love Lucy

By N. F. Mendoza

Broadcast History: CBS, 10/15/1951–5/6/1957
Runtime: 30 minutes
Genre: Sitcom
Black and White

Let's be honest, it's impossible not to love Lucy.

Before *The Powerpuff Girls*, before *Buffy* and before Grace Adler, Lucy was empowered. Sort of. Actually, she *wanted* to be, in a way that women almost never were in 1951. True, she was usually thwarted, if not by her Cuban bandleader husband, Ricky Ricardo (Desi Arnaz), then by her best friends and upstairs neighbors (and landlords), Fred and Ethel Mertz (William Frawley and Vivian Vance). But at her core she was independent, strong and determined, if ditzy. And, man, was she ever ambitious.

Mix Lucille Ball's talent, charisma and incredible knack for physical comedy into this redheaded dynamo and you have one of the most iconic characters in entertainment history. Ball either won or was nominated for Emmys as the Best Comedienne every year the series ran (1951–57), and there's a little bit of Lucy in stars from Carol Burnett and Goldie Hawn (during her *Laugh-In* days) to *Will & Grace*'s Debra Messing. You say "Lucy," and everybody knows whom you're talking about, five and a half decades later. It's no surprise that, in 1996, TV GUIDE selected Ball as the Greatest TV Star of All Time. *I Love Lucy* was our first great sitcom.

Lucy wanted to be a glamorous star—basically what Ball was off-screen and had been since her feature-film debut in the 1930s. But she was stuck in that apartment at 623 East 68th Street in Manhattan (623? Wouldn't that put the building in the East River?), always scheming to get into one of Ricky's shows at the Tropicana nightclub. Ricky was an indulgent husband to a point, but that point passed as soon as Lucy came up with one of her harebrained ideas. Or when she started to sing,

Classic Episode Close-Up

"Lucy Goes to the Hospital"
(Original telecast: January 19, 1953)

In May 1952, Desi Arnaz told producer Jess Oppenheimer that his wife and co-star Lucille Ball was pregnant. "Wonderful," Oppenheimer replied. "It's just what we needed to give us excitement in our second season. Lucy Ricardo will have a baby, too." Thus, episodes about Lucy's pregnancy built up to this classic show, in which the funniest moments stem from chaotic efforts to get Lucy to the hospital. It delivered a phenomenal 71.7 rating that topped the viewership of Eisenhower's Inauguration. Three months after the broadcast, Lucy and infant Desi Jr. had their own inauguration: they turned up on the first cover of TV GUIDE.

or tried to. She couldn't carry a tune to save her life. I remember being really surprised when, years later, I saw Ball in *Fancy Pants* with Bob Hope, singing the title tune beautifully.

I Love Lucy began in 1948 as a radio show on CBS titled *My Favorite Husband*, with Richard Denning playing the husband opposite Ball. It was so popular that the network decided to transfer it to the rapidly burgeoning medium of television. But Ball, who had married Arnaz in 1940, refused to make the move without her real-life husband. CBS countered that audiences wouldn't accept the Hispanic Arnaz and the clearly non-Hispanic Ball as a married couple (this was the early '50s, remember), so to prove the network wrong Lucy and Desi dusted off their old vaudeville act and took it on the road. Audiences loved it. They followed that up with a kinescoped pilot (with Ball hiding her first pregnancy) and CBS loved it—hence the *I Love Lucy* title.

TV and Film Connections

Spin-off: *The Lucy-Desi Comedy Hour*

America loved *Lucy*, too, of course, not only because Ball and Arnaz were dead-on funny, but because they (along with producer Jess Oppenheimer) were technical innovators as well, filming *Lucy* like a movie with multiple cameras before a studio audience. That hadn't been done before. In fact, many TV shows aired live. They also hired cinematographer Karl Freund, whose credits had included Fritz Lang's *Metropolis* and Tod Browning's *Dracula*, and Freund gave the show a lustrous look you didn't often see on TV in those days. Plus, they filmed not in New York, where just about everything else on TV was produced, but in L.A., where they lived (on a San Fernando Valley ranch with their baby daughter, Lucie). CBS balked at much of this because the Arnazes were going over the allotted $25,000-per-episode budget. So they each took a $1,000 pay cut—and ended up with complete control of the series. Not a bad bargain when you consider that the show has been on the air someplace (often most places) ever since, and the reason is not just that it's so funny but that it looks as fresh as shows that are not nearly as old.

Among the show's highlights: Ball's real-life pregnancy was incorporated into the series, culminating in the January 19, 1953, birth of Little Ricky, the same night Desi Arnaz Jr. was born (a little guy cute enough and famous enough to be TV GUIDE's first cover boy). That season, *Lucy* averaged a 67.3 *rating* (not share)—the highest in TV history by six points (Uncle Miltie was second, in 1950–51). Sure, there weren't many channels, or all that many TV sets then, but still, this was a really big deal.

The following season the Ricardos received a visitor from Tennessee, Lucy's "cousin" Ernest (Tennessee Ernie Ford). He soon overstayed his welcome and Lucy (in a black wig and sequined dress) had to "vamp" him back home to Bent Fork. In 1955, the Ricardos and Mertzes returned the visit—and ended up in jail. Ever gallant, Ernest volunteered to marry one of the sheriff's hilarious man-hungry daughters, Teensy or Weensy, in return for the visitors' freedom.

That Tennessee pit stop (where the gas-station attendant was played by Aaron Spelling) was one leg in a zany cross-country journey that ended (where else?) in Hollywood, where Lucy set about stargazing. It was a full-on celebrity hunt that any of today's paparazzi could go to school on. In those L.A. episodes it was stunt casting galore, with visits from A-listers like John Wayne, Richard Widmark, Rock Hudson, Van Johnson, William Holden and, most unforgettably for me, Harpo Marx. His guest shot (May 9, 1955) is the episode in which Lucy, decked out in top hat, blonde wig and bike horn, transforms herself into Harpo, then actually encounters him and mirrors his movements, just as the Marx brothers did themselves in 1933's *Duck Soup*.

In 1956, it was off to Europe, with predictably catastrophic results and more guest stars. Lucy missed Queen Elizabeth (lucky for her) but "met" (OK, stalked) Charles Boyer in Paris and got purple feet in Italy. Slapstick doesn't get any better than "Lucy's Italian Movie." Except, maybe, for Lucy and Ethel singing Cole Porter's "Friendship" while taking apart their inadvertently matching dresses. Or working on that candy production line. Or tangoing while wearing a jacket filled with eggs. Or trying to play "Glow Worm" on the saxophone. And how do you spell uproarious? V-I-T-A-M-E-A-T-A-V-E-G-A-M-I-N.

They got back to New York just in time to hook up with Bob Hope and, later, Orson Welles. Then they visited Ricky's family in Cuba (pre-Castro). "After what I did," Lucy moaned, "Cuba might cut off America's sugar supply."

> ### Did You Know?
> Series sponsor Phillip Morris forbade the use of the word "lucky" on the show, as it could suggest their rival's product, Lucky Strike cigarettes.

Finally, the Ricardos and Mertzes settled in a country home in Westport, Connecticut. The show was still No. 1 when it wrapped, with the May 6, 1957, episode (although occasional *Lucy-Desi Comedy Hour* specials continued until 1960), and in it, the Ricardos dedicated a statue, a Revolutionary War memorial. Of course, for all they brought to the new medium of television (and to American popular culture), few would argue that Lucy and Desi rated their own statue.

Cast:

Lucille Ball *Lucy Ricardo*, **Desi Arnaz** *Ricky Ricardo*, **William Frawley** *Fred Mertz*, **Vivian Vance** *Ethel Mertz*, **Richard Keith** *Little Ricky Ricardo (1956–57)*

Jeopardy!

By Sue Tiedeck

Broadcast History: NBC, 3/30/1964–1/3/1975,
    10/2/1978–3/2/1979; ABC, 6/16/1990–9/8/1990;
    Syndicated, 1974–1975, 1984–
Runtime: 30 minutes
Genre: Game show

The category is Quiz Shows, and the answer for $100 is: This long-running series was recently inducted into *The Guinness Book of World Records* for the most awards won by a game show. The reason the dollar value is so low is that this one is so easy to anyone who's watched TV in the past four decades: What is *Jeopardy!*? This honor was bestowed after the 2006 Daytime Emmy Awards when the show picked up yet another pair of statuettes, taking its total to 27.

Jeopardy! is my all-time favorite game show, and I admit that I've watched them all, and have since I was a child, from *Truth or Consequences* to *Press Your Luck* (sometimes I think that GSN was designed just for me). But I've always preferred the games that require at least a little brain power, like *Password* or *Pyramid*. And in that regard, *Jeopardy!* is in a class by itself.

I love *Jeopardy!* so much that I was indignant with my own employer back in 2001 when it was ranked second after *The Price Is Right* on TV GUIDE's list of the 50 Greatest Game Shows of All Time. Then, much to my dismay, GSN did the same thing, declaring *Jeopardy!* the runner-up to its top-ranked *Match Game*. Now, *The Price Is Right* and *Match Game* are both fun shows, but they're guilty pleasures. Half of the entertainment value of the former comes from marveling at the seemingly ageless Bob Barker and watching the excited contestants jump up and down, while the latter was a showcase for clever celebrities hosted by the charming Gene Rayburn. But did contestants have to bone up on their Shakespeare before daring to go on?

To succeed at *Jeopardy!*, on the other hand, a player must have instant recall of facts in a wide variety of subjects, ranging

> ### Did You Know?
>
> More than 300 game shows have come and gone since the 1984 syndicated premiere of *Jeopardy!*

from the commonplace to the arcane, plus good reflexes with the signaling button. There isn't time for silliness since the contestants have to stay on the ball. Even playing along at home is challenging. And while you don't actually win money by getting the answers right, it's still pretty satisfying (not to mention how smug I get to feel if I get one right when the contestants all miss). It's also a daily competition in my family, where we all try to blurt out the questions first, and I imagine my house isn't the only one where that goes on.

The show was the brainchild of Merv Griffin, a self-professed puzzle aficionado who developed it from an idea given to him by his then wife, Julann. Back in the early '60s, he was trying to come up with a new game show that the networks would accept in the wake of the quiz-show scandals of 1958 that resulted from the discovery that producers were supplying contestants with the answers. Julann, Griffin said in a June 2006 interview in the *Miami Herald*, asked, "Why don't you do a show where you give the contestants the answers?" He first replied, "How do you think all those people just got sent to jail?" Then he realized her suggestion just might work.

It took him a year to iron out the format: the contestants would be given the answers and have to provide the question, earning money for each correct one. He introduced the idea of penalizing an incorrect response by taking away money, the first show to do so. He even came up with the theme song, aptly named "Think," which he wrote in less than half an hour at the piano in his apartment. Griffin says that familiar piece of music (come on, hum along: lah de dah dah, lah de dah) is "the most famous short tune in America, even compared to 'Happy Birthday,' which is three seconds longer." It's earned him some $80 million in royalties, a figure that's sure to increase now that it's also being sold as a ring tone.

Griffin began pitching the show to network executives as *What's the Question?* but changed the name after one producer complained that the show didn't have enough "jeopardizes." That's also when he came up with the Daily Double, in which a player has to wager all or part of his earnings on getting it right, as a way to increase the risk. The revamped concept was picked up by NBC for its daily daytime lineup.

Top 3 Moments

- Never jumped.
- When Ken Jennings became a contestant.
- When it got dumbed down.

For more, visit www.jumptheshark.com.

Art Fleming, who'd previously worked as an actor and on *Pantomime Quiz* and *Doctor I.Q.*, was the host and Don Pardo (now known as the voice of *Saturday Night Live*) was the announcer when it premiered on March 30, 1964. The format was the same as it is today, although the amounts of money won were much lower. There were three contestants and six categories with five questions each. In the first round, correct questions earned $10 to $50 and there was one hidden Daily Double. In the second round, dollar values were double and there were two Daily Doubles. The winner (who took home $345 that first day) was determined in the Final Jeopardy round, in which all of the players were given the same answer and made bets based on their earnings to that point.

The syndicated version we watch now first began airing on September 17, 1984, with Alex Trebek as the host and Johnny Gilbert as the announcer.

Jeopardy!

Trebek, a Canadian whose previous work included hosting *High Rollers*, even produced the show briefly. The original format returned, with the first-round dollar values increased to $100–$500 and twice that in the second. Those amounts were doubled again in 2001, partly to compete with the greater earnings potential of *Who Wants to Be a Millionaire?*

For the first 19 seasons, contestants were limited to five appearances and there were caps on the total winnings ($75,000 in Seasons 1–6; $100,000 in 7–13; $200,000 in 14–19). In the 20th season, those limits were all eliminated, and players were allowed to stay on as long as they could keep winning.

That new ruling allowed Ken Jennings of Salt Lake City to start setting records. Jennings was on 75 episodes, winning 74 of them. He holds the record for appearances, the largest one-day total ($75,000) and is in *The Guinness Book of World Records* for the largest cash prize won on a TV game show ($2,520,700). He is not, however, the show's top earner. That title belongs to Brad Rutter of Lancaster, Pennsylvania. Rutter picked up $55,102 in his initial five-day run in 2000, and then returned to win the $100,000 Tournament of Champions in 2001, the Million Dollar Masters Tournament in 2002 and the Ultimate Tournament of Champions in 2005. That last event was devised to see how former champions could have competed against Jennings, who came in second. Rutter's triumph earned him an additional $2 million, bringing his total up to $3,255,102.

There have been some changes over the years, like an updated set and theme; the addition of a Clue Crew who provide on-location footage for some questions; and tournaments added for celebrities, college students, teens and even kids. Basically, though, it's the same *Jeopardy!* I first loved 40-some years ago. And there are enough fans like me to have made it the second-most successful game show in history, right behind the other show Griffin created, *Wheel of Fortune*. We look forward to testing our memories each day. Evenings just wouldn't be the same without it.

Cast:

Art Fleming *Host (1964–75; 1978–79)*, **Alex Trebek** *Host (1984–)*

L.A. Law

By Ileane Rudolph

Broadcast History: NBC, 9/15/1986–5/19/1994
Runtime: 60 minutes
Genre: Legal drama

On September 15, 1986, one of TV's most venerable genres changed forever. From the premiere-episode shot of a law-firm partner face-down dead in a plate of franks and beans still clutching tax documents, while womanizing divorce lawyer Arnold Becker (Corbin Bernsen) calls dibs on the deceased's office, we knew *L.A. Law* was going to be a different kind of legal show.

And how! Who can forget the Venus Butterfly, the exotic sexual technique that won pudgy tax guy Stuart Markowitz the heart of his sleek colleague Ann Kelsey (the real-life couple Michael Tucker and Jill Eikenberry) and in those pre-Google days sent many of us begging the show's producers for the secret. (It was a figment of a writer's imagination, alas.) Then there was hunky Michael Kusak (Harry Hamlin) in a gorilla suit breaking up the wedding of his love Grace Van Owen (onetime *Partridge Family* teen star Susan Dey), and the first girl-girl kiss on network TV, between a surprised Abby Perkins (Michele Greene) and the sensual bisexual Brit C. J. Lamb (Amanda Donohoe). Not that Abby—who changed, as we put it in a profile, from a "meek nerd to a tigress" during her stint—gave guys short shrift. She had the show's most explicit heterosexual sex scene as well. And most iconic of all, the nasty litigator Rosalind Shays's (Diana Muldaur) jaw-dropping—and well-deserved—fatal fall down an elevator shaft. (It was in the episode "Good to the Last Drop," telecast on March 21, 1991.)

Every Thursday night, as the sax wailed in Mike Post's addictive opening theme, millions of us would settle on our couches with a frisson of expectation. Indeed, every Friday morning for nearly a decade my colleagues and I would repeat the mantra, "Do you believe what happened at Mackenzie, Brackman, Chaney & Kuzak & Becker & Kelsey, Markowitz & Morales last night?" (The firm had more name changes than Elizabeth Taylor.)

A million law briefs and laughs away from the earnest upstanding attorneys of *Perry Mason* and *The Defenders*, *L.A. Law*'s legal eagles

> ## Did You Know?
>
> The *L.A. Law* cast re-created the 1987 cover of *MAD* magazine that spoofed their series as *L.A. Lewd*, and they sent a picture to the magazine.

were—usually—accomplished, if a bit theatrical in the courtroom, and equally selfish, greedy, morally ambiguous and dysfunctional outside of it. And yet, much like *thirtysomething*, that other show reflecting the zeitgeist of the era, *Law* tackled such issues as AIDS, feminism, homosexuality and the right to die, and despite its general air of cynicism, offered a sensitive, well-rounded developmentally disabled character, Benny, brilliantly embodied by the Emmy-winning Larry Drake.

Preview Review

September 13, 1986

The standout is *L.A. Law*, a one-hour NBC drama from Steven Bochco, co-creator of *Hill Street Blues*. Because it's set in a high-powered Los Angeles law firm, *L.A. Law* has a more polished look than *Hill Street* but the characters—attorneys and clients—are pure Bochco. That is to say they're warm, cold, funny, sad, devious, caring, imperfect, sharply drawn, fascinating to watch. Harry Hamlin, Richard Dysart and Jill Eikenberry are among the regulars.

A senior partner in the law firm of McKenzie, Brackman, Chaney & Kuzak is found dead at his desk, apparently of a heart attack. Arnie Becker, one of the two people to find Chaney, has a heartfelt reaction to this event: "I got dibs on his office." Welcome to *L.A. Law*, a new series from Steven Bochco, co-creator of *Hill Street Blues*. (Richard Dysart, Jill Eikenberry and Jimmy Smits are in the large cast.) This high-powered law firm has its share of opportunistic rats, but even the good guys aren't perfect. Take Michael Kuzak, for instance. He's a partner in the firm and a good person. Alice Ratakowski, a stunning and very strict judge, discovers that Kuzak has managed to accumulate $4200 worth of traffic tickets and orders the bailiff to take him into custody. Kuzak thinks she's overreacting: "Who's got forty-two hundred dollars?" Ratakowski: "You've got one phone call. I suggest you use it to find out."

Sometimes outré, sure, but its depiction of the legal system was real enough that cast members spoke at American Bar Association conventions and law school applications soared (no doubt a lot of young men were tempted by lawyer Becker's astounding number of nubile bed partners). The result of the show's skillfully blended disparate elements produced a show riveting enough to earn 15 Emmys and win a large—though never Top 10—audience. Indeed, *Law* represented the culture enough to merit a parody on a *Mad* magazine cover in 1987.

You could say the genesis of *L.A. Law* was a mistake. After an erroneous report in *Variety* noted that producer Steven Bochco, who created the cop-show masterpiece *Hill Street Blues* and the baseball-themed fiasco *Bay City Blues*, was doing a legal show for NBC, then network president Grant Tinker called him to say it wasn't a bad idea. As Bochco later recalled to TV GUIDE, "I said, I'd been thinking for some time about doing a show on the law. [It's] always interested me. It has everything—good and bad, right and wrong. The law is human behavior in the crucible of stress—emotional, financial, moral, sometimes even physical stress."

With a green light from NBC, he chose Terry Louise Fisher, a former L.A. deputy DA who had produced *Cagney & Lacey*, as his co-producer, and gathered immensely talented writers like David E. Kelley (who, with *Picket Fences, Ally McBeal, The Practice* and *Boston Legal*, later created his own quirky law-show universe) and *Hill Street Blues'* Jacob Epstein, who admitted he hated lawyers and enjoyed writing "the bad things" they do. Then he assembled a strong, racially integrated ensemble cast. Canny veterans like Richard Dysart, who played the wise, bemused senior partner Leland McKenzie, and Alan Rachins, who amusingly portrayed the crass and greedy Douglas Brackman, were mixed with young (or at least, youngish) hotties, many of whose careers got huge jump starts from their roles on *Law*, Jimmy Smits and Blair Underwood among them. In its very first season, the rookie show received an astonishing 20 Emmy nominations.

It's true Bocho sometimes ventured into *Dynasty* territory. If the firm's lawyers (especially the females) weren't beaten, kidnapped, shot, stalked or forced to kill in self-defense, they were having lots and lots of sex. While some real-life attorneys liked the show, finding some evidence of verisimilitude, others likened it to *Peyton Place*. And to be fair, as the years progressed, the writing got a little sloppy and outlandish, though it rebounded toward the end. When that finale came at the end of its eighth season, with McKenzie announcing his retirement at a surprise 65th birthday party, it was the right time to take down the shingle.

But all in all, the writing was witty, the characters sympathetic, the legal cases intriguing and the plots involving. A truly memorable show has to be both of its time and beyond it. Emblematic of its "greed is good" yuppie era and timeless in its tackling of the noble, ignoble and often ethically thorny issues encountered in the legal process, *L.A. Law* passes that test with flying colors.

Cast:

Richard Dysart *Leland McKenzie,* **Corbin Bernsen** *Arnie Becker,* **Jill Eikenberry** *Ann Kelsey,* **Alan Rachins** *Douglas Brackman Jr.,* **Michael Tucker** *Stuart Markowitz,* **Jimmy Smits** *Victor Sifuentes (1986–91),* **Harry Hamlin** *Michael Kuzak (1986–91),* **Susan Dey** *Grace Van Owen (1986–92),* **Michele Greene** *Abby Perkins (1986–91),* **Susan Ruttan** *Roxanne Melman (1986–93),* **Larry Drake** *Benny Stulwicz (1987–94),* **Blair Underwood** *Jonathan Rollins (1987–94),* **Diana Muldaur** *Rosalind Shays (1989–91),* **John Spencer** *Tommy Mullaney (1990–94),* **Cecil Hoffman** *Zoey Clemmons (1991–92),* **A Martinez** *Daniel Morales (1992–94),* **Debi Mazar** *Denise Ianello (1993–94),* **Alan Rosenberg** *Eli Levinson (1993–94),* **Alexandra Powers** *Jane Halliday (1993–94)*

The Larry Sanders Show

By Craig Tomashoff
Broadcast History: HBO, 8/15/1992–5/31/1998
Runtime: 30 minutes
Genre: Sitcom

If you haven't spent any time in the past decade living and working in the Southern California area, you might well consider *The Larry Sanders Show* to be one of the funniest half-hour comedies in the history of television. To some of us who make our living in Hollywood, however, this show about a late-night talk show—whose host alternates between being petty and paranoid—seems more like reality fare that strikes *very* close to home.

A few years ago I worked as a producer on Martin Short's short-lived talk show. About three months into the series, one of our executive producers called the entire staff to the stage for a quick meeting to reassure everyone that the rumors of our imminent cancellation were untrue. We'd be around for a long time to come.

My first thought upon hearing this was, "What rumors? I hadn't heard any rumors." My second thought was about the *Larry Sanders* episode where Larry's head writer, Jerry (Jeremy Piven), was reassured the rumors of his firing were untrue. Shortly thereafter, naturally, he was canned.

I honestly never figured there was a connection between the thoughts. Until a few weeks after our pep talk, when the same guy who'd told us we were going to survive told us we were canceled. Now my first thought was, "I don't have a job." And my second thought was that I should have listened to *Larry*. The moment I heard our jobs were safe, I should have started getting the resume out.

In fact, I probably should have re-watched all six seasons of the series to remind myself that life in show biz is not unlike working in the crocodile exhibit at the zoo. Sure you might make it through a day or two safely, but sooner or later, somebody is going to take a bite out of you.

If anybody would know about the jungle out here, it was the star and creative mind behind the series, Garry Shandling. He had plenty of experience in the talk-show world, having been a regular guest host on *The Tonight Show* and a contender for the permanent job when Johnny Carson retired. Rather than fight for the job that eventually went to Jay Leno, Shandling—two years after his ahead-of-its-time Showtime sitcom *It's Garry Shandling's Show*, in which he occasionally spoke directly to the camera—went to HBO with this idea of turning his experiences as Garry into the life of Larry, a smooth and charming host on-camera and a neurotic mess just about any other time.

Which, based on my Martin Short experience (and later talk-show gigs with Craig Kilborn and Jesse Ventura), was not too far from reality. I was also amazed at the behavior of people behind the scenes, massaging some considerable egos and doing *whatever* was required to prop up the host. On *The Larry Sanders Show*, for example, producer Artie (Rip Torn) was more like a caretaker, keeping the host from having nightly nervous breakdowns (and reassuring him in the process that his ass *didn't* look fat in those pants). And there was the buffoon of a sidekick, the obsequious Hank Kingsley (Jeffrey Tambor). It was always hard to say which Hank enjoyed more, praising himself or putting down everyone else.

Anyone who's ever worked on a talk show could also appreciate the level of detail that went into Larry's fictional staff. From Beverly (Penny Johnson—who later got a breakout role as venal Sherry Palmer on *24*), the assistant who knew more about Larry's life than he did, to booker/producer Paula (Janeane Garofalo), who was constantly stuck between an emotionally unstable host and self-absorbed celebrities.

As a former booker/producer, I could very much identify with her awkward position. There were constantly situations that we staffers would refer to as "a Larry Sanders moment." When a host has his assistant write his autograph on photos for the fans, *that's* a Sanders moment. When a big star won't come on your show unless you buy her a very expensive bottle of champagne, *that's* a Sanders moment. When a guest notorious for his love of marijuana gets all the production assistants high half an hour before the show, *that's* a Sanders moment.

To every booker/producer

> ### Did You Know?
>
> In one episode, a talk show was pitched to follow Larry's, and Tom Snyder appeared as himself as a hopeful for the hosting job. Because of that appearance on *Larry Sanders*, David Letterman's Worldwide Pants production company hired Snyder to host *The Late Late Show with Tom Snyder*, a talk show developed to follow *The Late Show with David Letterman*.

in the world, these situations were no laughing matter. For the movie and TV stars of Hollywood, however, they were apparently a riot. Nearly every episode of the series had a brilliantly telling moment when the glib fake talk-show chit-chat with celebrities like Billy Crystal, Vince Vaughn and Jim Carrey cut to a backstage shot of those same celebs behaving like the spoiled, self-indulgent types many figure they must be when the cameras stop rolling.

And they all seemed to enjoy the chance to play against type. Carol Burnett played herself as a crabby, impatient guest. David Duchovny didn't mind pretending to have a guy crush on Larry. Sharon Stone was hysterical when she dated Larry, eventually breaking up with him because neither could stand that the other might be more famous.

The Larry Sanders Show

On most shows about Hollywood that are written by people in Hollywood, these story lines would come across as inside jokes nobody living between New York and Los Angeles would get. Instead, the behind-the-scenes bad manners and desperation at *The Larry Sanders Show* could just as easily have taken place behind the counter at a bank or in the cubicles of an insurance company.

There was one episode in which Larry reluctantly invites his staff to a party at his house, then sweats out the entire evening because he's forced to actually socialize with his underlings. I saw this shortly after my boss at the magazine I was working for at the time got talked into hosting a party at his home, then followed us around all night making sure we used coasters and didn't break anything (which we did anyway, accidentally shattering a glass table with a pool ball). I wasn't even working in television at the time, yet there I was having yet another Larry Sanders moment.

Which provided some wonderful irony. At every talk show I worked on, they drilled into us that every chat on the stage should seem like a casual conversation and not an interview (despite the fact that guests and hosts both review their questions and answers before going on-camera). That way, they would all come across as real human beings and not self-absorbed jerks to the viewers.

It's what made me want to get into the talk-show business in the first place, and writing about *The Larry Sanders Show* brings back a lot of memories. I recently re-screened some episodes on DVD, and seeing all the eggshell-thin egos and backstage backstabbing made me kind of miss my old talk-show days. At least until I remember, for example, the actor who changed his shirt three times before going on the set or the TV star who smoked so much pot before his appearance that his dressing room looked like a smokehouse.

It's not that I didn't enjoy my talk-show experiences. There were moments that are never to be forgotten, like sitting in a room with Tom Hanks and Martin Short and having them ask *me* to think of something funny for them. However, I'm realizing now that perhaps I could have saved myself lots of headaches by just learning the lessons of *The Larry Sanders Show*. It was perhaps the funniest show in TV history. It was the smartest on the air in its time and still ranks at the top even a decade later. Just as importantly, it's the best reason ever for not working in Hollywood.

Cast:

Garry Shandling *Larry Sanders*, **Rip Torn** *Artie*, **Jeffrey Tambor** *Hank*, **Wallace Langham** *Phil*, **Janeane Garofalo** *Paula (1992–97)*, **Penny Johnson** *Beverly*, **Jeremy Piven** *Jerry (1992–93)*, **Megan Gallagher** *Jeannie Sanders (1992–95)*, **Kathryn Harrold** *Francine (1993)*, **Scott Thompson** *Brian (1995–98)*, **Mary Lynn Rajskub** *Mary Lou (1996–98)*

The Late Show with David Letterman

By Bruce Fretts

Broadcast History: CBS, 8/30/1993–
Runtime: 60 minutes
Genre: Talk show

From New York—the greatest city in the world—we present the Top 10 Reasons Why We Love *The Late Show with David Letterman* ...

10. **Dave loves his mom.** Back when he hosted NBC's *Late Night* from 1982 to 1993, Dave had a reputation for being cranky and mean-spirited (Cher notoriously called him an "asshole" in '86.) But with his move to CBS in '93, Dave started to show a softer side—especially in his segments with his endearingly homespun mom, Dorothy. He sent her to cover the 1994 Winter Olympics, and she instantly won America's heart, too.

9. **Dave ♥ NY.** He could've gone Hollywood long ago, but Dave's stayed put in the Big Apple. His affection for the city was never more evident than in his first show back after 9/11. He skipped the traditional monologue and delivered a moving speech from behind his desk: "If you didn't believe it before, you can believe it now: New York City is absolutely the greatest city on earth."

8. **Dave's the new Johnny.** He may have lagged in the ratings behind Jay Leno's *Tonight Show*, but creatively speaking, Dave is the true heir to Johnny Carson as the King of Late Night. After Dave paid a posthumous tribute to Johnny at the 2005 Emmys, Jon Stewart put it best: "The way [Letterman] feels about Johnny Carson is the way all of us— the comedians of our era—feel about him."

7. **Dave's the new Ed Sullivan.** Dave's decision to broadcast *Late Show* from the Ed Sullivan Theater wasn't coincidental. With hellzapoppin' bits like "Stupid Pet Tricks," "Will it Float?" and "Kid Inventors," Dave has kept the spirit of TV variety alive.

6. **Dave's a good neighbor.** Everybody's part of the act on *Late Show*, including the shopkeepers near the Ed Sullivan Theater. Dave struck comic gold with souvenir salesmen Mujibur and Sirajul, and he's enjoyed a delicious partnership with unassuming Hello Deli proprietor Rupert Jee. To thank Rupert for his many years of comic service, Dave bought a Times Square billboard for the Hello Deli. What a guy!

5. **Dave's a good dad.** He became a first-time father at 56 in 2003 when longtime girlfriend Regina Lasko gave birth to their son, Harry Joseph Letterman (named after Dave's dad). He's proudly shown off baby pictures—as well as his gag "World's Oldest Dad" mug.

4. **Dave's not afraid to show his heart.** After undergoing quintuple bypass surgery in 2000, Dave invited the doctors and nurses who'd saved his life onto the *Late Show* stage so he could personally thank them. He even got a little choked up—no joke.

3. **Dave's not afraid to be political.** His point of view isn't predictable— he's hammered President Bush over the war in Iraq, even as he's flown to the Middle East to entertain the troops at the holidays. But Dave doesn't shy away from calling 'em as he sees 'em: He boldly told Bill O'Reilly, "I have a feeling about 60 percent of what you say is crap."

2. **Dave does great TV.** Night in and night out, Dave has an unerring instinct for what makes must-see viewing. Take his 16-years-in-the-making reunion with Oprah Winfrey, with whom he'd allegedly had a feud. When Dave escorted her arm-in-arm to the opening of her Broadway musical *The Color Purple*, it was brilliantly staged television.

> **Did You Know?**
>
> One of Dave's early jobs, in the 1970s, was as a weatherman for a local Indiana station.

1. **Dave does great Top 10 lists.** NBC threatened to sue Dave for taking "intellectual property" like his trademark Top 10 lists with him to CBS. Dave got his revenge with *Late Show*'s opening-night list of "Top 10 Things We Like About CBS." Among them: "Doesn't have foul-smelling, disease-carrying bird mascot," "The strong, understanding hands of Mr. Charles Kuralt" and "Executives are much more advanced form of weasel."

No wonder we love this guy.

Cast:

David Letterman *Host*, **Paul Shaffer** *Bandleader*

Law & Order

By Megan Walsh-Boyle

Broadcast History: NBC, 9/13/1990–
Runtime: 60 minutes
Genre: Crime drama/legal drama

A critics' favorite, a ratings hit, at last, that Emmy. The inside story on 'Law & Order,' one of TV's most surprising success stories

Hello, my name is Megan, and I'm a *Law & Order* addict. I got hooked at 17, as a freshman in college. Today, more than 15 years later, I watch the original and its spin-offs. Repeats in syndication have helped feed my habit. I watch the *L&O* brand five to six times a week (at least). Can I break my addiction? Probably, but I won't, because *Law & Order* is just too damn good to give up. It is TV comfort food: simple and satisfying, if somewhat predictable.

"In the criminal justice system, the people are represented by two separate yet equally important groups—the police who investigate the crime, and the district attorneys who prosecute the offenders. These are their stories." Thus begins each episode of the longest-running crime series and the second-longest-running scripted program (*Gunsmoke* holds the record at 20 years) on television, not to mention my favorite TV show of all time. The brilliantly conceived procedural meshes two durable genres (cops and lawyers), and splits the drama into two distinct halves: the investigation of the crime, followed by the prosecution of the case in court. Dick Wolf, a former ad man who wrote for the gritty *Hill Street Blues* and co-produced the glitzy *Miami Vice* before he went on to create and executive produce the award-winning *Law & Order* franchise, perhaps summed it up best: "The first half is a murder mystery. The second half is a moral mystery."

> ### Did You Know?
>
> In 1996, when Jill Hennessy was shooting an appearance on *Homicide: Life on the Street*, her twin sister, Jacqueline Hennessy, played Claire Kincaid during her *Law & Order* courtroom scenes.

It's a winning formula that has enthralled viewers since it debuted on September 13, 1990, when the late, legendary Brandon Tartikoff, then head of NBC, put *Law & Order* on the air (after Fox and CBS had turned it down). However, it wasn't an immediate hit. While critics praised it, *L&O* suffered through mediocre ratings its first season and turned off advertisers with its controversial plots. *L&O* didn't crack the Nielsen Top 20 until the 1997–98 season and the Top 10 until 2000–01. *L&O* has proven itself durable, with both the original and its spin-offs airing nearly every day of the week on NBC, TNT, USA or Bravo.

First and foremost, *Law & Order* is a plot-driven series. It's a throwback to Jack Webb's original, "just the facts, ma'am" *Dragnet*. Story lines are thinly disguised dramatizations of high-profile cases drawn from newspaper head-lines. Events move at a quick pace, with that familiar "cha-chung" sound effect signaling a change of scene. The series regulars' back stories and personal lives are only mentioned in passing, if at all. The audience, instead, connects to the different personalities. Anyone, however, is replaceable—and pretty much everyone has been, which only goes to prove that compelling storytelling can be as big a draw for viewers as stars. Not to say that *L&O* doesn't feature some first-rate acting. Filmed in New York City (where all of the *L&O* shows are set), the series draws on accomplished stage actors for guest starring roles, as well as more recognizable stars like Christine Baranski, Candice Bergen, Chevy Chase, Claire Danes, Edie Falco, Lauren Graham, Edward Herrmann, Philip Seymour Hoffman, Felicity Huffman, Samuel L. Jackson, Allison Janney, James Earl Jones, Laura Linney, William H. Macy, Camryn Manheim, Amanda Peet, Julia Roberts, Elaine Stritch, Kathleen Turner, and the list goes on.

Classic Episode Close-Up
"DWB"
(Original telecast: October 7, 1998)

A vicious hate crime—the murder of a black man who was dragged behind a car—is the focus of a powerful 1998 episode involving a nervous eyewitness, racial profiling and the "blue wall of silence" of the police. The staggering realization that the killers may be cops leads McCoy to grant immunity to a policeman (John Ventimiglia) who says the victim "was in the wrong neighborhood, [at the] wrong time [and had the] wrong skin tone." When McCoy later tries to revoke the immunity, Schiff is outraged and tells him that if the plan fails, he expects McCoy's letter of resignation.

The show is a superbly acted ensemble, which has flourished despite its many cast changes over the years. *L&O*'s detectives have included Chris Noth (who, in 2005, brought his character of Det. Mike Logan over to *Law & Order: Criminal Intent*), George Dzundza, Paul Sorvino, Benjamin Bratt, Jesse L. Martin and, most memorably, Jerry Orbach.

I never would have thought *L&O* could have survived the May 19, 2004, departure of Orbach as quintessential New York cop Lennie Briscoe, a role that made the former Broadway star a household name after he joined the cast in 1992, its third season. The wry-with-a-caustic-edge Briscoe has been missed, and it's hard to understand why Orbach's considerable contribution to the show has seldom gotten its proper due (not one Emmy and only a single nomination in 2000). I had looked forward to Orbach bringing back Briscoe on *Law & Order: Trial by Jury*, but sadly the actor had filmed only two episodes before he died of prostate cancer December 28, 2004, at the age of 69.

Another character whom I consider irreplaceable is Sam Waterston's veteran prosecutor Jack McCoy, who took over for Michael Moriarty's Ben Stone at the start of Season 5, in 1994. "It was the furious, aggressive, un-Hamlet-like character that attracted me," said Waterston, an accomplished stage and film actor, about his decision to join the *Law & Order* cast. "And then to have him forge through these problems that are very morally difficult. It's an end-lessly interesting place to live." Waterston, who plays McCoy as a thoughtful, eloquent, justice-seeking man, has earned three Emmy nominations for the role.

For Season 17, NBC moved *L&O* for the first time in 14 years from Wednes-days to Fridays at 10 p.m., the time slot where two other Wolf series (*Law & Order: Trial by Jury* and *Conviction*) both failed. The season also saw the intro-duction of *L&O*'s first female detective, Nina Cassady, portrayed by Milena Govich, who co-starred on *Conviction*. In addition, Alana De La Garza (*CSI: Miami*) joined the show as prosecutor Connie Rubirosa, the latest in a succes-sion of young—and attractive—female sidekicks for McCoy (the others were played by actresses Jill Hennessy, Carey Lowell, Angie Harmon, Elizabeth Rohm and Annie Parisse, who was killed off on the finale for the show's 16th season). Being Hispanic makes De La Garza the first non-white playing an assistant district attorney since Richard Brooks as Paul Robinette starred in the show's first three seasons.

For the record, Steven Hill, Dianne Wiest and Fred Dalton Thompson have played the top DAs; and Dann Florek (now with *Special Victims Unit)* and S. Epatha Merkerson have played the two precinct lieutenants. Interesting fact: Merkerson and Hennessy were brought on by Wolf in 1993 when, under threat of cancellation, he agreed to add more estrogen to the show.

Curiously, none of the series' outstanding regulars have ever won an Emmy for the show despite more than a dozen nominations, though the show itself won in 1997 for Outstanding Drama Series.

Over the past several years, NBC has relied heavily (perhaps too much so) on the *L&O* franchise to prop up its ailing schedule. It has spun off two popular incarnations (*Law & Order: Special Victims Unit*; *Law & Order: Criminal Intent*), and two flops (*Law & Order: Trial by Jury* and *Conviction*).

> ## TV and Film Connections
> Spin-offs:
> *Law & Order: SVU*
> (which spun off *Conviction*)
> *Law & Order: Criminal Intent*
> *Law & Order: Trial by Jury*

The formula has been embraced by others, most notably Jerry Bruckheimer, whose top-rated CBS show about crime-scene investigators, *CSI*, has also spawned two spin-offs, *CSI: Miami* and *CSI: New York*.

Dick Wolf's goal to keep *Law & Order* on the air for at least 21 years, and beat the long-running record set by *Gunsmoke*, seems within reach, as long as it doesn't stray from the rock-solid formula that has made it a success: a good mix of mystery mixed with ethical dilemmas. Headline-based plots keep the show relevant, and cast turnovers keep it fresh, which should keep me and millions of other fans still feeding our *L&O* habit.

Cast:

George Dzundza *Det. Max Greevey (1990–91)*, **Chris Noth** *Det. Mike Logan (1990–95)*, **Michael Moriarty** *ADA Ben Stone (1990–94)*, **Richard Brooks** *ADA Paul Robinette (1990–93)*, **Steven Hill** *DA Adam Schiff (1990–2000)*, **Dann Florek** *Capt. John Cragen (1990–93)*, **Paul Sorvino** *Det. Phil Cerreta (1991–92)*, **Carolyn McCormick** *Dr. Elizabeth Olivet (1991–94)*, **Jerry Orbach** *Det. Lennie Briscoe (1992–2004)*, **S. Epatha Merkerson** *Lt. Anita Van Buren (1993–)*, **Jill Hennessy** *ADA Claire Kincaid (1993–96)*, **Sam Waterston** *ADA Jack McCoy (1994–)*, **Benjamin Bratt** *Det. Reynaldo Curtis (1995–99)*, **Carey Lowell** *ADA Jamie Ross (1996–98)*, **Angie Harmon** *ADA Abbie Carmichael (1998–2001)*, **Jesse L. Martin** *Det. Edward Green (1999–)*, **Dianne Wiest** *DA Nora Lewin (2000–02)*, **Elisabeth Rohm** *ADA Serena Southerlyn (2001–05)*, **Fred Dalton Thompson** *DA Arthur Branch (2002–)*, **Dennis Farina** *Det. Joe Fontana (2004–06)*, **Annie Parisse** *ADA Alexandra Borgia (2005–06)*, **Milena Govich** *Det. Nina Cassady (2006–)*, **Alana De La Garza** *ADA Consuela "Connie" Rubirosa (2006–)*

Lost

By Shawna Malcom

Broadcast History: ABC, 9/22/2004–
Runtime: 60 minutes
Genre: Drama

It's hard to imagine now, but when *Lost* premiered in September 2004, it didn't seem destined to find an audience, let alone become the most fanatically worshipped and dissected television drama since *The X-Files*. ABC, its network home, was then firmly entrenched in fourth place, and its concept—"*Survivor*, the drama," as then network president Lloyd Braun proposed it during a brainstorming session at an executive retreat—had more than a slight whiff of desperation. To flesh out the premise, Braun recruited J. J. Abrams, a whipsmart producer who'd created ABC's cult darling *Alias*, who in turn partnered with fellow sci-fi fan Damon Lindelof (*Crossing Jordan*). The duo's resulting pilot—in which Oceanic Airlines Flight 815 crashes, stranding its survivors on a mysteriously dangerous island somewhere in the South Pacific—was an adrenaline-fueled thrill ride that captured the attention of 18 million view-

ers. Yet it still begged the question: How could its gimmicky B-movie premise generate sufficient juice for a weekly series?

The answer lay, in part, with its characters. Each week's episode highlighted one survivor from the refreshingly diverse cast and used flashbacks to their pre-crash lives in order to shed light on their post-crash decisions. And as the flashbacks revealed, the survivors were lost not only physically but emotionally. Among them: Jack (Matthew Fox), a spinal surgeon with major daddy issues and the island's de facto leader; Kate (Evangeline Lilly), a freckled fugitive who went on the run after blowing up her abu-

> ## Preview Review
> *September 12, 2004*
>
> **The Setup**: In this game of *Survivor*, everyone wants off the island. After a terrifying plane crash onto a remote Pacific isle, 48 bewildered castaways scramble for safety while seeking answers. Where are they? What's that fearsome creature stalking them from the woods? Are they truly alone?
>
> **We Say**: *Alias* creator J. J. Abrams has done it again, bringing a thrilling, sensational urgency to the hokiest of premises. Relentlessly suspenseful, lavishly produced and terrifically cast with a large ensemble, *Lost* is a good showcase for *Party of Five*'s Matthew Fox—a standout as a doctor who takes charge.

sive stepdad's house . . . while he was in it; Sawyer (Josh Holloway), a con man seeking revenge on the man responsible for the death of his parents; Locke (Terry O'Quinn), a former paraplegic office drone who mysteriously regained the use of his legs post-crash; Charlie (Dominic Monaghan), a washed-up rock star and junkie struggling to overcome a heroin addiction; and Hurley (Jorge Garcia), a hefty lottery winner haunted by his use of a set of "cursed" numbers.

With seemingly no chance of rescue, the survivors were left to fend for themselves on the island against intimidating inhabitants, a lethal black smoky monster and the odd polar bear—all of which were part of an increasingly elaborate show mythology. What was the significance of Hurley's winning numbers (4, 8, 15, 16, 23, 42) and why did the survivors have to input them into a computer every 108 minutes? Who are the people behind the Dharma Initiative, and why have they created a series of underground (and, in at least one case, underwater) hatches on the island? Could they be using the survivors to test experiments? And might they have chosen the survivors, some of whose paths crossed pre-crash, deliberately? Who exactly are the child-napping Others, and how long have they lived in a suburban enclave on the island? Are they resistance fighters rising up against the Dharma Initiative or the puppet masters behind it?

Did You Know?

Creator J. J. Abrams originally wanted Michael Keaton to play Jack, and the character was going to be killed off in the pilot episode.

Season after season, *Lost* posed more questions and fans formed endless theories in an effort to explain them. The most popular—that the survivors were caught in purgatory—was quickly debunked by producers. Mostly, though, the forces behind *Lost* chose to let the theories run rampant and to feed into them by creating faux Web sites, like the ones for Charlie's rock band, Drive Shaft, and the Dharma Initiative.

While the result was a wildly addictive series that was widely respected—the show won a Best Drama Emmy after its first season—even the show's diehard fans were often left bewildered. Some vocal viewers worried that producers didn't have answers to the show's increasing number of questions. Others, like me, were content to just go along for the ever-twisty ride.

Having covered the show for TV GUIDE since it began, I've seen firsthand that producers more often than not know exactly where the show is going far in advance. They meticulously—and with great respect for the fans—plan and plot each detail. Including this one: In a flashback in the second-season episode "Collision," troubled L.A. cop Ana Lucia is called to the scene of a domestic dispute between a young couple. The guy is named Travis, and the girl is named . . . Shawna. According to executive producer Carlton Cuse, she was, indeed, named after yours truly.

Consider that one (albeit small) mystery solved.

I ❤ TV

Cast:

Matthew Fox *Jack*, **Evangeline Lilly** *Kate*, **Josh Holloway** *Sawyer*, **Ian Somerhalder** *Boone (2004–05)*, **Maggie Grace** *Shannon (2004–05)*, **Dominic Monaghan** *Charlie*, **Jorge Garcia** *Hurley*, **Malcolm David Kelley** *Walt*, **Naveen Andrews** *Sayid*, **Harold Perrineau** *Michael*, **Terry O'Quinn** *Locke*, **Daniel Dae Kim** *Jin*, **Yunjin Kim** *Sun*, **Emilie de Ravin** *Claire*, **Michelle Rodriguez** *Ana Lucia (2005–06)*, **Adewale Akinnuoye-Agbaje** *Mr. Eko (2005–06)*, **Cynthia Watros** *Libby (2005–06)*, **Henry Ian Cusick** *Desmond (2005–)*, **Michael Emerson** *Henry Gale (2006–)*, **Elizabeth Mitchell** *Juliet (2006–)*

Did TV Victimize the Loud Family?

TV GUIDE

Local Programs May 19-25
15¢

-AMSEL-

Mary Tyler Moore

The Mary Tyler Moore Show

By Angel Cohn

Broadcast History: CBS, 9/19/1970–9/3/1977
Runtime: 30 minutes
Genre: Sitcom

Who can take a nothing day and suddenly make it all seem worthwhile? The answer to that question has always been Mary Richards. While I was too young to catch *The Mary Tyler Moore Show* during its original CBS run, I found myself addicted to this stylish and sophisticated series when Nick at Nite began airing it in 1992. I was in college and found the show more entertaining than much of what was on TV, and soon the WJM gang became friends to me while I was far away from my family. I became a faithful watcher and rarely missed an episode. My GPA may have suffered a tad, but when Nick at Nite offered a quiz a few years later I took it and earned a "Mary Merit Badge," a sleek little pin with a retro look, which I happily consider among my prized possessions. When I returned to my parents' home my mother would get annoyed at the loud guffaws coming from my bedroom until she realized the program that had me cracking up so loudly was one that *she* had related to at the same age. Sure, the show earned an impressive 29 Emmys over the course of its run, but few series can be watched two decades later and still have the same relevance and ability to inspire young women on the verge of adulthood. I now look forward to playing the DVDs for my own daughter in a few years to see if the show gives her the same compelling urge to toss her hat in the air in the middle of a busy street.

At the forefront there was always Mary Richards (Mary Tyler Moore), the thirtysomething woman who bravely decides not to marry a doctor who took her for granted, moves to Minneapolis and finds a new job. (I wonder if the *Friends* creators had Mary in mind when they thought up Rachel?) Mary is a big softie at heart who even apologizes to furniture when she errantly bumps into it, but while she can blubber with the best of them, she's also got great warmth, spirit

> ### Did You Know?
> The name of Ted and Georgette's baby is Marylou in honor of Mary and Lou Grant, who helped to deliver her.

and, yes, spunk. Those qualities come in handy because Mary might otherwise have few friends, based on her famously disastrous dinner parties. Her dating dilemmas and staunch ability not to settle for something less than perfection was and still is something to be admired. Not many female TV characters at the time were content with living on their own and working instead of trying desperately to change themselves in order to catch the perfect man. She was *the* single girl and her charming apartment (with its ever-present M on the wall) clearly showed that she wasn't afraid to be independent. Over the course of the show she had many beaus with various issues; they were either height-challenged, married, Murray's father, or just plain obnoxious. While she maintained her single status on the show, behind the scenes Moore was divorced and remarried to future network exec Grant Tinker, with whom she co-founded MTM Enterprises. In addition to *The Mary Tyler Moore Show*, MTM was the production company behind *The Bob Newhart Show*, *Hill Street Blues*, *St. Elsewhere* and *WKRP in Cincinnati*, to name a few.

Classic Episode Close-Up

"Chuckles Bites the Dust"

(Original telecast: October 25, 1975)

There's no guest star, no cliffhanger, no birth (although there is a death)—yet "Chuckles Bites the Dust" is one of the best-loved shows in TV history, and earned the No. 1 ranking in TV GUIDE's 100 Greatest Episodes of All Time. Chuckles the Clown showed up at a parade dressed as Peter Peanut and, as Lou puts it, "a rogue elephant tried to shell him." Death is death, and it shouldn't be funny, but this one is—to all but Mary. She's aghast at her colleagues' insensitivity . . . until she gets her own case of the giggles during the funeral. Moore gives a bravura bipolar performance in an episode that punctuates a social taboo with wit and impeccably good taste.

The series itself kept a light balance between Mary's life at work and at home. At the WJM newsroom, there was the wonderfully irascible Lou Grant (the brilliant Edward Asner), who ran his nightly news program with an iron fist, but who cared deeply for his staff; Murray Slaughter (Gavin MacLeod), the cynical, sharp-tongued news writer who simmered as pompous silver-haired newscaster Ted Baxter (Ted Knight) botched his carefully scripted lines night after night; Georgette Franklin (Georgia Engel), a sweet innocent who inexplicably fell for (and later married) the clueless Baxter; and Sue Ann Nivens (Betty White), the spicy host of "The Happy Homemaker" who often seemed peeved that the younger and attractive Mary got the lion's share of male attention.

At home Mary had to cope with her loving yet flaky landlady, Phyllis (Cloris Leachman), who was envious of Mary's single status and tried to overcompensate by constantly mentioning her husband, Lars, and daughter, Bess. Then there was Rhoda (Valerie Harper), Mary's upstairs neighbor and best friend. Rhoda considered herself to be plain compared to her thin and beautiful gal pal, but she had a sense of style all her own and made lengthy head wraps look cool. (Note: Few can pull off this look like Harper did. If you try it, be prepared for ridicule. Trust someone who knows from experience.)

Thanks to my job at TV GUIDE, I've actually gotten to meet Moore and Asner (twice!) and once Asner even kissed me on the cheek when I expressed my love of the show. For a young journalist just starting out, that was a highlight and confirmed that the nights I watched reruns instead of studying were actually well spent.

Since its seven-year run on CBS, *The Mary Tyler Moore Show* spawned three spin-offs (*Phyllis*, *Rhoda* and *Lou Grant*) and has become a permanent part of our pop culture. The title characters in *Romy & Michelle's High School Reunion* have a fight over which of them is the Mary and which is more like Rhoda. Joan Jett did a cover version of Sonny Curtis's infectious "Love Is All Around" theme song. Even those who aren't dedicated fans are familiar with "Chuckles Bites the Dust"—ranked the Greatest Episode of All Time in a 1997 TV GUIDE survey—in which Mary's giggling gets out of control during the funeral for WJM's kiddie-show host, who was trampled to death by an elephant while dressed like a peanut. Sitcoms like *Murphy Brown*, *Friends* and *Sex and the City* have roots that can clearly be traced to the sharp humor, expertly written dialogue and frank talk about relationships that *The Mary Tyler Moore Show* excelled at. Mary and Co. may have turned off that light switch while singing "It's a Long, Long Way to Tipperary" in the '70s but the effects of this beloved series can still be happily felt today. She truly did make it after all.

> ### TV and Film Connections
> Spin-offs:
> *Rhoda*
> *Lou Grant*
> *Phyllis*

Cast:

Mary Tyler Moore *Mary Richards*, **Edward Asner** *Lou Grant*, **Ted Knight** *Ted Baxter*, **Gavin MacLeod** *Murray Slaughter*, **Valerie Harper** *Rhoda Morgenstern (1970–74)*, **Cloris Leachman** *Phyllis Lindstrom (1970–75)*, **John Amos** *Gordy Howard (1970–73)*, **Georgia Engel** *Georgette Franklin Baxter (1973–77)*, **Betty White** *Sue Ann Nivens (1973–77)*

M*A*S*H

By Jon McDaid

Broadcast History: CBS, 9/17/1972–2/28/1983
Runtime: 30 minutes
Genre: Sitcom

The draftees and enlisted personnel of the 4077th Mobile Army Surgical Hospital, serving during the Korean War, were dedicated Army doctors and nurses trying desperately to save lives while clinging precariously to their own sanity.

Not exactly your standard setup for a sitcom, but in some ways a military camp is a useful series backdrop. New cast members can be easily explained (or shipped out in a jeep), costumes (with the exception possibly of frocks worn by the cross-dressing Klinger) never change and little from the outside world (i.e., the wives and kids back home) influences the action. However, unlike more conventional service sitcoms (*The Phil Silvers Show*, *Hogan's Heroes*, *McHale's Navy*), *M*A*S*H* never divorced itself from the more harrowing aspects of its subject matter.

That subject matter, in this case, was handed to Larry Gelbart, who superbly developed the series from director Robert Altman's 1970 movie. The original source material was the semiautobiographical 1968 novel *MASH* (Hollywood added the asterisks) by Richard Hooker (a pseudonym of former Army doctor Richard Hornberger). Premiering in September 1972, the early episodes aped Altman's look and feel, including an opening montage of helicopters bearing wounded over the theme song "Suicide Is Painless." The TV version eliminated the lyrics, but harder to excise was the CBS-dictated laugh track, which disappeared only during the show's operating-room scenes. Over 11 seasons, guided by Gelbart and producers Gene Reynolds and Burt Metcalfe among others, it developed its own voice, a smart balance of broad comedy and thoughtful dissections of the insanities and inanities of war.

The cast was led by Alan Alda as Capt. Benjamin Franklin "Hawkeye" Pierce. Part besotted playboy, part self-righteous

> ### Did You Know?
>
> The character Spearchucker Jones (played by Timothy Brown) was deleted from the cast when creators discovered there were no black surgeons in the Korean War.

surgical whiz, Alda played Hawkeye as a cross between Groucho Marx and Albert Schweitzer. It was a terrific part, which garnered Alda two Emmys for the performance. It didn't hurt that he was often giving himself some very good lines and direction (Alda also took home Emmys for writing and directing). All told, the series collected 14 Emmy awards and more than 100 nominations.

From the homespun Cpl. Radar O'Reilly (Gary Burghoff) to the boorish Maj. Charles Emerson Winchester III (David Ogden Stiers), each character was given moments of humor and humanity. Maj. Margaret Houlihan, played by Loretta Swit, morphed from the oversexed harridan known as "Hot Lips" to a conflicted and complicated woman over the show's run. Even Jamie Farr's Section 8 hopeful, Cpl. Max Klinger, a one-joke character if there ever was one, got his moments of pathos. Special note, however, must be made of Larry Linville's inspired character, Maj. Frank Burns. "Old Ferret Face" is the gold standard for TV buffoonery. I believe every sniveling, obnoxious TV character of the past 35 years owes a major debt to both Burns and Linville.

With the possible exception of *Cheers*, no other sitcom successfully negotiated as many cast changes as *M*A*S*H*. The transitions from Col. Henry Blake to Col. Sherman Potter (McLean Stevenson to Harry Morgan), from Trapper to B. J. (Wayne Rogers to Mike Farrell), and from Frank Burns to Charles Winchester all made sense within the show's conceit and created new comic and dramatic possibilities. Hell, the creators of *M*A*S*H* weren't even afraid to kill off a lovable lead. Who can forget the pregnant pause following Radar's announcement that Henry's plane had crashed into the Sea of Japan? The only thing sadder was the sight of McLean Stevenson's career crashing into *Hello, Larry*.

> ## TV and Film Connections
>
> Based on a 1970 movie by the same name
>
> Spin-offs:
>
> *Trapper John, M.D.*
> *After MASH*

The kind of reference-heavy and literate writing that was a hallmark of the series is exemplified for me in a favorite 1974 scene in which Hawkeye refuses to carry a weapon. He rants, "I'll carry your books, I'll carry a torch, I'll carry a tune, I'll carry on, carry over, carry forward, Cary Grant, cash and carry, carry me back to Old Virginia, I'll even hari-kari if you show me how, but I will not carry a gun!" Rarely has television comedy been so defiantly smart and inspired, while still remaining true to character and just plain funny.

Setting a series in such a specific time and place, however, does create certain problems. Most obviously, *M*A*S*H* ran nearly four times as long as the actual Korean conflict, which lasted from 1950 to 1953. If nothing else, this generates a surplus of Christmas episodes. Also, over the years actors age while characters do not. By the time of his exit in Season 8, Burghoff bore little resemblance to the young Radar O'Reilly he created for Altman's film 10 years before. Also, certain plot devices tend to repeat over time. The touching home movie, the impressed general who can't punish the Swampmates and the sound of incoming choppers leap to mind. In the world of episodic TV, however, good characters and big Nielsen ratings trump logic and verisimilitude every time. And *M*A*S*H* had both.

As if combat and death weren't weighty enough, the series touched on other serious topics such as racism, alcoholism, sexism, psychological disorders and

McCarthyism. Sometimes, it seemed, all in the same episode. Certainly by the show's final season, jokes often took a back jeep seat to liberal humanism and dime-store Freudianism. (How many neuroses did Dr. Sidney Friedman [Allan Arbus] cure in Korea?) To the show's enduring credit, however, almost every later episode of *M*A*S*H* has at least a couple hearty laughs.

The run of *M*A*S*H* was also peppered with "stunt" shows. Starting with the pilot, the "letter home" was a favorite. Almost every character got a chance to write to a loved one, as well as missives to President Harry Truman and Sigmund Freud. Many other episodes were, as they say in Hollywood, "high concept." There was the episode in real time (complete with running clock); there was the dream episode (talk about your dime-store Freudianism); there was the point-of-view episode seen through the eyes of a wounded GI; there was even a ghost episode featuring a dead soldier. One of the most memorable was the faux documentary "The Interview" from the show's fourth season. Shot in black and white and largely ad-libbed, it was a stellar half hour of TV and a moving look at a cast of characters fans had come to love. It was such a good idea, they did it again in Season 7.

Perhaps the biggest stunt was the show's final episode, if you can call a two-and-a-half-hour movie an episode. "Goodbye, Farewell and Amen," co-written and directed by Alda, was overwrought, overly sentimental and . . . touching as hell. On February 28, 1983, I was among the more than 100 million viewers who watched the 4077th bug out for the final time. It remains the medium's highest-rated program ever.

War is hell, but then again, Gelbart quipped, "so is TV." But, as *M*A*S*H* demonstrated, who knew it could also be so hilarious and heartwarming?

Classic Episode Close-Up

"Abyssinia, Henry"

(Original telecast: March 18, 1975)

McLean Stevenson's last appearance as the 4077th's beloved commander, Lt. Col. Henry Blake, occurred at the end of the third season. Henry's going home to his family in Illinois. After a night of wine, wontons and song, and a touching good-bye with his surrogate son, Radar, Henry takes off on a plane . . . which is shot down over the Sea of Japan. When Radar stumbles into the operating theater with the news, it is a shattering moment—a measure of just how precious these characters had become to us.

Cast:

Alan Alda *Capt. Benjamin Franklin "Hawkeye" Pierce,* **Wayne Rogers** *Capt. John "Trapper John" McIntyre (1972–75),* **Loretta Swit** *Maj. Margaret "Hot Lips" Houlihan,* **McLean Stevenson** *Lt. Col. Henry Blake (1972–75),* **Larry Linville** *Maj. Frank Burns (1972–77),* **Gary Burghoff** *Cpl. Walter "Radar" O'Reilly (1972–79),* **William Christopher** *Father Francis Mulcahy,* **Timothy Brown** *Spearchucker Jones (1972),* **Jamie Farr** *Cpl. Maxwell Klinger (1973–83),* **Harry Morgan** *Col. Sherman Potter (1975–83),* **Mike Farrell** *Capt. B. J. Hunnicut (1975–83),* **David Ogden Stiers** *Maj. Charles Emerson Winchester III (1977–83)*

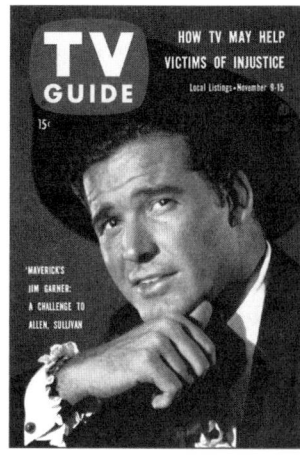

Maverick

By Maitland McDonagh

Broadcast History: ABC, 9/22/1957–7/8/1962
Runtime: 60 minutes
Genre: Western
Black and White

Bret Maverick wouldn't have cottoned to Al Swearingen's profane way with the mother tongue—his pappy didn't raise potty mouths—but TV Westerns started down the road to *Deadwood* when the likes of *Have Gun, Will Travel, Wagon Train, Gunsmoke, Cheyenne* and *Maverick* drove the Lone Rangers and Cisco Kids out of town.

I came to *Maverick*, which originally ran on ABC from 1957 to 1962 in haphazard reruns, so it took me a while to figure out that there were two wily, itinerant cardsharps named Maverick plying their shady trade in Old West towns with names like Apocalypse, Hallelujah and Oblivion. Natural-born charmer James Garner was Bret, and his brother, Bart, was played by Jack Kelly—who brought significantly less roguish sparkle to his repartee. Bret was the original and Bart was the afterthought—the only way to keep the show on schedule was to shoot more than one episode at once, which required another main character—and they rarely appeared together. I venture to say that I'm not the only person for whom *Maverick*'s appeal is entirely bound up with Garner's: He's such good company, gliding through life on a pair of aces and the promise of larky adventure. Who wouldn't want to hang with Bret Maverick, basking in the glow of his shifty joie de vivre, even if you inevitably wound up footing the bill?

Looking at *Maverick* through the prism of *Deadwood*, it's hard to imagine how utterly subversive it was for series creator Roy Huggins to build a wry Western around a dapper dude who'd rather grift than fight. When Hollywood started mining the mythology of the Old West, Wyatt Earp was alive to cross paths with John Ford. Forty years of reworking the rugged clichés of the untamed frontier later, even Ford was venturing into dark and morally ambiguous territory with movies like *The Searchers* (1953), while TV Westerns went back to square one. Their audience was the kids who packed movie matinees for simplistic black-hat/white-hat horse operas, and their first generation of stars were scout masters in ten-gallon hats: Gene Autry (of the squeaky clean "Cowboy Code"), Roy Rogers and "Hopalong" Cassidy, strong, uncomplicated fellows who upheld the law, respected good women

> ### Did You Know?
>
> James Garner has appeared on three networks playing the character of Bret Maverick: on the original series (ABC), in 1979 in the premiere episode of *Young Maverick* (CBS) and in the 1981 series *Bret Maverick* (NBC).

and were kind to bad ones, kept their guns holstered until a fair fight found them, and never drew first or shot a man in the back. And then in moseyed Bret Maverick, the kind of guy who wouldn't recognize an honest day's work if it crawled out of his boot and bit him. Smooth-talking dandies schooled at their sainted pappy's knee in the arts of winning ladies and talking their way out of trouble, the brothers Maverick weren't cowards; they just didn't see why a man should come out swinging when he could quote one of pappy's homespun aphorisms and slither out of a potentially ugly dustup. Nor could they see the point in punching cattle when there were poker games to play and suckers to fleece. As Bret said, "You can fool all of the people some of the time, and some of the people all of the time, and those are very good odds."

> ## TV and Film Connections
>
> Inspired a 1994 feature film of the same name
>
> Spin-off:
> *Bret Maverick*
> *Young Maverick*

Huggins famously went in intending to have some fun with Western clichés while playing *Maverick* straight enough for more tradition-minded fans. But Bret Maverick's sly-fox smirk was there from the first episode, in which he advises a poker table full of hard-faced robber barons that his business is grass inspection. "You inspect grass?" "The kind that's always greener in the other fellow's yard," he drawls. Garner's trickster charisma preceded the fabled bit of snide stage direction—"Maverick looks at him with his beady little eyes"—that signaled the show's definitive transition to dark comedy. *Maverick* cheerfully twitted the straight-faced likes of *Gunsmoke* ("Gun-Shy") and *Bonanza* ("Three Queens Full") on the one hand and made hay with genre conventions on the other. How many wronged high plains drifters spent an entire episode in a rocking chair, whittling from a block of wood and deflecting the scorn of townsfolk expecting fireworks with a mild-mannered "I'm working on it," while his partners in crime executed the elaborate stock swindle that evened the score with a corrupt banker (the classic episode "Shady Deal at Sunny Acres")?

Huggins left after the second season to create *The Fugitive* and in 1974 reunited with Garner for *The Rockford Files*. When Garner left *Maverick* after the third season, its sparkle was gone. The series limped on a bit, adding yet another brother, Brent Maverick (Robert Colbert, later of *The Time Tunnel*) and Bond-to-be Roger Moore as suave English cousin Beauregard Maverick. Garner, who briefly reprised the character in *Bret Maverick* (1981–82) and appeared more than a decade later in the Mel Gibson–Jodie Foster big-screen *Maverick*, was always the ace in *Maverick*'s deck, so be warned: If it's a Bret episode, it's a winning hand. If not, there's always another game—like *The Rockford Files*.

Cast:

James Garner *Bret Maverick (1957–60)*, **Jack Kelly** *Bart Maverick*, **Roger Moore** *Beauregard Maverick (1960–61)*, **Robert Colbert** *Brent Maverick (1961)*

Melrose Place

By Rich Sands

Broadcast History: FOX, 7/8/1992–5/24/1999
Runtime: 60 minutes
Genre: Drama

Mondays are a bitch.

That simple tagline on posters promoting the third season of *Melrose Place* pretty much said it all. With the addition of Heather Locklear to the cast of the campy Fox soap (spun off from *Beverly Hills, 90210*), *Melrose*'s impact on the pop-culture landscape went from mediocre to meteoric. Initially the slow-moving look at the lives of a group of residents at a stylish complex at 4616 Melrose Avenue in Los Angeles failed to get any Nielsen traction. Enter Amanda Woodward, the ambitious, cut-throat, sexually voracious advertising executive played by Locklear—famously billed as a "special guest star" throughout her run—who joined the cast in January 1993. There was no looking back. "What we had in the beginning was a very interesting, but very passive group," legendary producer Aaron Spelling told TV GUIDE. "We needed Heather to stir the pot." Love triangles, catfights, baby snatching, murder and mayhem quickly ensued.

The two main principals—Alison Parker (Courtney Thorne-Smith) and Amanda Woodward (Locklear)—had too many lovers to count, but they set the tone for the revamped *Melrose* with their spirited tug-of-war over simpleton Billy Campbell, a cab driver and aspiring screenwriter played by Andrew Shue.

And it wasn't just the ladies who slept around. Doctors Michael Mancini (Thomas Calabro) and Peter Burns (Jack Wagner) made the rounds, so to speak. Bitchiness was contagious. Even sweet Jane Mancini (Josie Bissett) got in touch with her dark side. Having been cheated on by her cad of a husband, Michael, Jane finally started to stand up for herself, bedding complex himbo Jake (Grant Show), brawling with her slutty sister Sydney (Laura Leighton) and delivering a nasty right hook to long-suffering photographer Jo (Daphne Zuniga).

> ### Did You Know?
>
> When the series ended, bottles of the swimming pool water were sold on eBay by people who worked on the show.

Over seven seasons cast members came and went, but a seemingly infinite wave of new vixens was always waiting in the wings, most notably Lisa Rinna as conniving Taylor McBride; Alyssa Milano as Michael's bratty sister, Jennifer; and Jamie Luner as scheming Lexi Sterling, who, in the show's final episode, found herself bound and gagged, wearing nothing but a bra and panties. (Not surprising since slinky lingerie was a vital part of the *Melrose* aesthetic.)

While Locklear was the heartless soul of *Melrose Place*, it's not hard to argue that the show's most explosive character was, quite literally, Dr. Kimberly Shaw Mancini. Marcia Cross played the role with a menacing intensity she would later demonstrate as Bree Van De Camp on *Desperate Housewives*. Cross made the psychotic physician TV's most unpredictable whack job, a needy, manipulative time bomb. Her mania reached its defining moment when she detonated a bomb that totaled the complex. And in perhaps the most iconic *Melrose* moment, in the appropriately titled episode "The Bitch Is Back," Kimberly—returning, in true soap fashion, from the dead—removes a wig to reveal a hideously monstrous scar running across the side of her head. Even for a prime-time soap that was among the guiltiest of pleasures, you'd have to say this was one hell of a hair-raising development.

TV and Film Connections

Spun off from *Beverly Hills, 90210*
Spin-off: *Models Inc.*

Cast:

Thomas Calabro *Michael Mancini*, **Josie Bissett** *Jane Mancini (1992–97; 1998–99)*, **Marcia Cross** *Kimberly Shaw (1992–97)*, **Doug Savant** *Matt Fielding (1992–97)*, **Grant Show** *Jake Hanson (1992–97)*, **Courtney Thorne-Smith** *Alison Parker (1992–97)*, **Andrew Shue** *Billy Campbell (1992–98)*, **Daphne Zuniga** *Jo Reynolds (1992–96)*, **Jack Wagner** *Peter Burns (1992–96)*, **Laura Leighton** *Sydney Andrews (1993–97)*, **Vanessa Williams** *Rhonda Blair (1992–93)*, **Amy Locane** *Sandy Louise Harling (1992)*, **Heather Locklear** *Amanda Woodward (1993–99)*, **Kristin Davis** *Brooke Armstrong (1995–96)*, **Kelly Rutherford** *Megan Lewis Mancini McBride (1996–99)*, **Rob Estes** *Kyle McBride (1996–99)*, **Lisa Rinna** *Taylor McBride (1996–98)*, **David Charvet** *Craig Field (1996–98)*, **Brooke Langton** *Samantha Reilly (1996–98)*, **Jamie Luner** *Lexi Sterling (1997–99)*, **Alyssa Milano** *Jennifer Mancini (1997–98)*, **Linden Ashby** *Dr. Brett Cooper (1997–98)*, **John Haymes Newton** *Ryan McBride (1998–99)*

Miami Vice

By Joseph Hudak

Broadcast History: NBC, 9/16/1984–7/26/1989
Runtime: 60 minutes
Genre: Crime drama

There were few more stylish (or flashy) cop-series pilots than the one that aired on September 16, 1984. With its distinctive neon look, a throbbing soundtrack (The Rolling Stones's "Miss You" opened the episode) and two relatively unknown yet extremely charismatic leads, *Miami Vice* seemed to fulfill what NBC entertainment president Brandon Tartikoff had in mind when he scribbled the words "MTV Cops" on a pad. And while "groundbreaking" is tossed around a lot these days, *Vice* truly was. The series was executive produced by Michael Mann (whose later credits include *Heat* and *Collateral*, and who *very* loosely adapted the series in 2006 for the big screen), and it played out like an expensive movie, both in look and story. It was even shot primarily on location in Miami, a big deal for a mere TV show. And looking back, it's clear that the series had to be, as no Hollywood soundstage could hardly do the city justice. Its sun-soaked streets and shimmering waterways either made you want to relocate to Miami to become a cop or consider running contraband as a smuggler.

Airing from 1984 to '89, *Vice* starred Don Johnson as undercover detective Sonny Crockett, a rough and tumble character with a sleek Ferrari convertible (shouldn't every detective have one?), a pet alligator named Elvis, a penchant for pastels in his wardrobe and perpetual stubble. Philip Michael Thomas perfectly inhabited Sonny's more urbane partner, Ricardo Tubbs, a former New York City cop who favored silk shirts and a more classic, double-breasted look. Together, the hipper-than-words pair reported to the stoic, brooding Lt. Castillo, played with Emmy-winning appeal by Edward James Olmos. With attitude to burn and an effortless command of the dialect of the street, Crockett and Tubbs were the epitome of cool, and soon their fashions, mannerisms and even personal hygiene were influencing young men across 1980s America. These cops were definitely dressed for crime-fighting success. Just try to think of a guy who wore socks or shaved regularly during *Vice*'s heyday.

But perhaps even more influential than the series' high fashion was its use of pop music. First and foremost was Jan Hammer's driving theme song,

> ### Did You Know?
>
> Because of Don Johnson's poor track record (he was a part of four failed pilots), NBC executives were reluctant to cast him for the show.

which kicked off each week's episode over a montage of tanned bodies and fast boats, resulting in the kind of publicity most cities' chambers of commerce can only dream of. An accompanying soundtrack album, which included Hammer's theme, hit No. 1 on the Billboard charts in 1985. The series also employed contemporary songs already on the radio. Cyndi Lauper, Glenn Frey and, most memorably, Phil Collins all had their music used to great effect. In fact, many of the show's guest stars were musicians. Collins, Frey, Frankie Valli and Sheena Easton all popped up, with Frey's turn as a maverick cargo pilot arguably the most fun. (His episode was actually inspired by one of his solo hits, "Smuggler's Blues.") But not all the guest stars were of the music variety. Melanie Griffith (Johnson's ex-wife), Bruce Willis and, for whatever reason, Lee Iacocca also appeared. And let's not forget Jimmy Smits, who got blown to smithereens in the first 10 minutes of the pilot.

Ah, there's that pilot again. If that's all that existed of *Miami Vice*, it'd still be worthy of inclusion in this book. At two hours, the series' first episode unspools like a movie, with an intricate story line and enough gunplay and tension to rival anything released in theaters by Michael Bay. The scene where Crockett and Tubbs cruise along the Miami streets to meet the drug dealer Calderone in Crockett's Ferrari Spyder may be the coolest sequence of the entire series. Set to Phil Collins's thumping "In the Air Tonight," the scene culminates with Sonny, recently betrayed by his former partner, pulling the car over to use a pay phone (it was the 1980s, remember) to call his ex-wife. "The way we used to be together," he says, "it was real, wasn't it?" It was brave emotional territory for a tough-guy TV cop, not to mention a remarkable synergy between soundtrack and scene—and we instantly felt what was coming on the air that night.

Preview Review

September 8, 1984

(*NBC, Editors Choice*) *Miami Vice* is an unusual crime drama that's sure to be controversial. Indeed, critics of TV violence are already taking aim—or is that the wrong metaphor? The show is wry and savvy and tough yet handsomely filmed, with entire sequences done in a combination of music and videos. The creator of *Miami Vice* is Anthony Yerkovich, who wrote frequently for *Hill Street Blues*.

Sonny Crockett lives in Miami, drives a hopped-up sports car and sleeps on a 40-foot sloop in a marina. He has a pet on board—a 10-foot alligator named Elvis. Known to the locals as an ocean guide, Sonny seems to live the good life. But do not be deceived: in this offbeat crime drama, things are seamier than they seem. Crockett is an undercover vice detective. His pursuit of a Colombian drug kingpin will lead Sonny to team up with Ricardo Tubbs, a cop from New York who is also not quite what he seems. Nor, for that matter, is Elvis just any old alligator: he was once the official mascot of the University of Florida football Gators. And compared to the pushers, racketeers, hired killers and assorted scuzzballs we'll meet in this gritty but visually lyrical series, Elvis is a pussycat.

Miami Vice

Of course you could get only so much dramatic mileage out of music and a fashion statement, and *Vice* saw its popularity diminish when it became darker and more convoluted. At its peak, however, it did leave an indelible mark on the culture, and how many series can say that?

Cast:

Don Johnson *Det. Sonny Crockett*, **Philip Michael Thomas** *Det. Ricardo Tubbs*, **Edward James Olmos** *Lt. Martin Castillo*, **Saundra Santiago** *Det. Gina Navarro Calabrese*, **Olivia Brown** *Det. Trudy Joplin*, **Michael Talbott** *Det. Stan Switek*, **John Diehl** *Det. Larry Zito* *(1984–87)*

Mister Rogers' Neighborhood

By Michael Davis

Broadcast History: PBS, 2/19/1968–8/31/2001
Runtime: 30 minutes
Genre: Children's educational

Did you ever wish that you could somehow pass through the television screen and arrive in that place where the shows came from?

It happened to me once, sort of, not that many years ago, when I met Mister Rogers. The experience was both surreal and sublime, a through-the-looking-glass day that was so unlike any other, it has taken on dreamlike qualities as the years pass.

I must admit, without exaggeration, that the encounter represents my worst-ever performance as a reporter. For reasons I will never be able to explain, two tape recorders failed me that day, a primary and a backup, both loaded with fresh batteries. Pens ran dry, pencil leads snapped and what observations remained in my notebook at day's end were the random jottings of one who had taken a deep dive off the shallow end of the pool. One page simply read: Fred = Holy man.

So now, as I take the measure of that summer afternoon, I rely completely on what lingers in the folds of gray beneath my aging skull and, more to the point, in my heart.

The first thing I recall upon coming face-to-face with Fred Rogers is that he leaned forward, ever so slightly, and offered an outstretched hand. "So pleased to meet you," he said in a voice that was unmistakable and calmingly therapeutic. "Welcome to Pittsburgh."

It was like meeting an old friend for the first time, familiar yet new, which might explain why the first words out of my mouth to him were "Great place to be if you're in the mood for a polka."

He smiled away the non sequitur in a manner that suggested many people didn't quite know what to say to him upon first meeting. Through the years, in airport waiting rooms and museum galleries and church vestibules, viewers of his PBS program, *Mister Rogers' Neighborhood*, would rush up to him and be suddenly rendered incapable of intelligent speech. Many would simply embrace him. Some would cry so hard their shoulders would tremble. People of color, most notably black women, would touch his face and offer up stories of childhood abuse and neglect. "You were the only one who ever listened to me," they'd say, and Fred Rogers, the ordained Presbyterian minister, would gently say, "Bless your heart."

Mister Rogers' Neighborhood

As my hand shook his that afternoon, I was transported back not to my childhood but to those of my two daughters. When they were 2 and 4, they used to insist that Mister Rogers lived inside the TV. "Impossible," I'd say. "If that were true, you could run around to the other side of the TV and see the back of Fred's head." But they believed what they would believe, like tens of millions of other children who thought that the man in the cardigan and canvas lace-ups came to visit only them each day. Such was the enduring charm of that beloved program, in which Mister Rogers told each child (though it was addressed to mostly 2- to 5-year-olds), "I like you just the way you are." It was the closest television has ever come to providing emotional outreach to children.

Fred Rogers brilliantly used puppetry, songs, storytelling and make-believe in some 900 episodes of *Mister Rogers*, each one as worthy as the next. (Original episodes were produced for 33 years, until his retirement in 2000.) In aggregate, they constitute a video handbook for talking to—and listening to—preschoolers. For inasmuch as Fred spoke directly to children about their questions and fears (and how to better deal with them), discussing everything from what to expect on the first day of school to why moms and dads divorce, he inserted pauses in his remarks to allow his audience to think and respond. "Did you ever worry you might swirl down the drain with the bath water?" he'd ask, and, after a beat, the little voice within the child would answer yes.

For most of the medium's history, children's television has chattered incessantly. Fred Rogers respected his audience to such a degree, he provided the necessary silence. "The space between the television and the child is a holy one," he told me during our day together.

In the 1950s and '60s, a look behind the curtain at the hosts of children's shows would disclose some hideous phonies, opportunists who made little effort to hide their disdain for kids once the red light blinked off. Fred Rogers was the antithesis, the antidote, the television personality who wore street clothes, not a clown costume or cowboy chaps. His puppets were primitive and hand-manipulated, and his Neighborhood of Make Believe sets so static, they brought to mind elementary school pageants. But the props made little matter; what did were the spoken words.

> ### Did You Know?
>
> For many years, Mister Rogers' mother knitted the sweaters he wore on the show.

To some adults, Fred's television manner could seem effeminate and his singsong voice condescending. He was an easy target for parodies, some created good-naturedly by high-powered fans like Johnny Carson, Robin Williams and, most famously, Eddie Murphy in his *SNL* skits titled "Mister Robinson's Neighborhood."

Along the way, Fred accumulated countless honors, including the Presidential Medal of Freedom, two Peabody Awards and four Emmys, and one of his sweaters is on display at the Smithsonian Institution. That was all nice, of course, but what always mattered most to this gentle, deeply caring man was hearing that children found him calmly reassuring, patient and kind. Certainly, his actual neighbors in Pittsburgh recognized that there was no separating the Mister Rogers kids adored from the Mr. Rogers who made that town his home for most of his adult life.

It is significant, I think, that his program emanated from the studios of WQED in that western Pennsylvania town. That Fred Rogers was Mr. Pittsburgh is one of the reasons his series always rang so true. It came from a very real place, not Hollywood. Pittsburgh was where Fred raised two sons, prayed daily, composed music, wrote piles of personal letters, and made friends all over town.

It is where I made his acquaintance, during his final summer of life. (He died in 2003 at age 74.)

Nothing went as expected that day, and as I look back on it, Fred Rogers interviewed *me* more than I interviewed *him*.

He cleared his calendar that afternoon, with the intention of listening to me.

He probed my fears and asked opened-ended questions that made me think and disclose truths.

Nothing tangible remains of my visit, only memories of feeling safe, protected, appreciated and respected.

Viewers liked and admired Mister Rogers just the way he was.

That's what everyone took from his Neighborhood.

Cast:

Fred Rogers *Host*

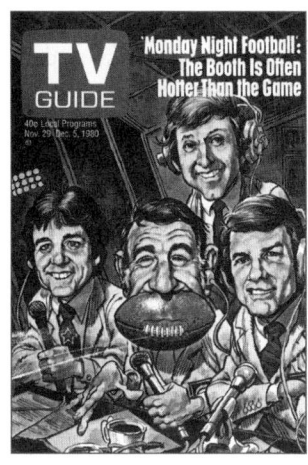

Monday Night Football

By Jon McDaid

Broadcast History: ABC, 9/21/1970–12/26/2005;
    ESPN, 8/14/2006–
Runtime: Varied
Genre: Sports program

In an era of *SportsCenter*, **fantasy football** and the 10-minute ticker, it's well to recall just how important *Monday Night Football* has been to NFL fans. In the dark ages of the 1970s and '80s, there was simply no other way to regularly see pro football teams from other parts of the country. For a Philadelphia-based Seattle Seahawks fan living 3,000 miles from the Kingdome, *Monday Night* was a godsend. I still remember with some glee that night in 1988 when Seattle QB Dave Krieg hoisted TD passes to five different players in a sloppy 35–27 squeaker over the Raiders with the AFC West title on the line. Granted, I had to jump around and high-five myself, but still. Until their 2006 trip to Super Bowl XL, watching that *Monday Night* game was the emotional high-water mark of my long-distance Seahawks love affair. Of course, just the year before I had endured Bo Jackson's *Monday Night* coming-out party, a record-setting 221-yard rushing performance in Oakland's 37–14 rout of Seattle. (At times, living a continent away from a favorite team isn't so bad.)

A world without *Monday Night Football* is now difficult to imagine. I was born just a year before the show debuted, so I have lived my entire sports-fan existence with a Monday night NFL fix. The series kicked off with a New York Jets–Cleveland Browns game on September 21, 1970. At the time, a union between pro football and ABC's prime-time schedule seemed a shotgun wedding at best. Of course, that was before Super Bowls had Roman numerals and achieved through-the-roof Nielsen ratings. The series was the brainchild of then ABC Sports president Roone Arledge, who understood the nature—and potential—of the NFL; that the sport could be packaged and covered like an *entertainment* event unfolding on a new and grander stage, with more cameras, more snazzy graphics, more visual excitement.

Arledge also innately understood the necessary ingredients of "up close and personal" sports drama. You need simple story lines, easily identified heroes and villains (no wonder the Oakland Raiders have appeared on more Monday nights than any other team), failure and redemption, dynamic visuals and good theme music. Of course, leggy cheerleaders also help. And great announcers.

If *Monday Night Football* is a modern-day athletic circus, the announcing booth has frequently been its indispensable sideshow. And its first and greatest barker was Howard Cosell, "telling it like it is." Brashly opinionated, abrasive and razor-sharp (and looking somewhat uncomfortable in oversized headphones and a yellow blazer), Cosell was an oddly compelling and nasal-sounding spectacle unto himself. You had to not only watch, but also listen. He was right and journalistically courageous a good deal of the time (and narrated, at halftime, a virtuoso fast-paced highlights package), but he could also be unapologetically provocative, arrogant and annoying. I sometimes felt it was like slowing down for a car wreck and having the guy inside the flaming car give you the finger. Ironically, one of my more vivid memories of Cosell on *Monday Night* was one of his most controversial. I was watching the night Howard referred to Redskins wideout Alvin Garrett as a "little monkey." Even in a pre-PC 1983, this 14-year-old knew *that* was trouble.

Apart from the play on the field, what lives in *Monday Night* lore are other (well-publicized) moments of high drama and low comedy. There was embarrassment (Cosell, in the booth, throwing up on himself in 1970), minor scandal (Nicollette Sheridan's 2004 towel-dropping *Monday Night* promotion skit with Terrell Owens), tragedy (many Americans learned of John Lennon's murder in 1980 from Cosell during a *Monday Night* broadcast) and plenty of self-serving visits to the booth from a who's who of celebrities, including three U.S. presidents. Arledge's stroke of genius in the early going was pairing Cosell with "Dandy" Don Meredith. He was the folksy Southerner parrying with Cosell's New York smart aleck. It's really hard not to like a guy with Dandy right there in his name. Along with Keith Jackson (and later Frank Gifford) the *Monday Night* broadcast team became, as Cosell famously said, "bigger than the game."

After Cosell and "Dandy" came a parade of announcers of every ilk and ability. Some were good, some were bad and some were, well, Dan Dierdorf.

Did You Know?

The *Monday Night Football* theme music is titled "Heavy Action," and was originally composed by Johnny Pearson for the BBC sports show, *Superstars*.

The *Monday Night* logo has adorned the lapels of such luminaries and lowlights as Fred Williamson, Alex Karras, Fran Tarkenton, O. J. Simpson (when he was still just the future Hall of Famer from the Hertz commercials), Joe Namath, Boomer Esiason and the woefully underrated Dan Fouts. A two-year experiment with comedian Dennis Miller proved a fiasco. Critics derided ABC for taking a shot with Miller, but it speaks volumes about how far removed *Monday Night* is from your average TV sports. Think about it: is there any other sports broadcast which would have considered, even for a nanosecond, putting a comedian who references former British Prime Minister Neville Chamberlain behind the mic during games?

More recently, the teaming of John Madden and Al Michaels proved that the show's tradition of three voices isn't necessary to make Monday nights memorable. Michaels was the gold standard in play-by-play and there's never been anyone quite like Madden. Over his run of Mondays from 2002 to 2005, the former Oakland coach became a slightly doddering parody of himself. However, no color commentator was ever better at offering information and insight for both casual viewers and hardcore fans at the same time. It says something that both my mom and I like Madden.

Monday Night Football's move to ESPN was probably inevitable, and NBC began its own prime-time Sunday-night slate of NFL games (with Michaels and Madden in the booth) in 2006. Sure, after nearly four decades, the brand is not what it once was, but sentimental attachments count for something, and since *Monday Night* got there first, when Hank Williams Jr. shouts out the rousing (if cheesy) musical question, "Are You Ready for Some Football?" you'll understand why I continue to answer with a resounding "Yes!"

Cast:

Howard Cosell *Analyst (1970–83)*, **Don Meredith** *Analyst (1970–73; 1977–84)*, **Keith Jackson** *Play-By-Play (1970)*, **Frank Gifford** *Analyst (1971–98)*, **Alex Karras** *Analyst (1974–76)*, **Al Michaels** *Play-By-Play (1986–2005)*, **Dan Dierdorf** *Analyst (1987–98)*, **Boomer Esiason** *Analyst (1998–2000)*, **Dan Fouts** *Analyst (2000–02)*, **Dennis Miller** *Analyst (2000–02)*, **Melissa Stark** *Reporter (2000–02)*, **John Madden** *Analyst (2002–05)*

Monty Python's Flying Circus

By G. J. Donnelly

Broadcast History: BBC, 10/1/1969–12/1/1974
Runtime: 30 minutes
Genre: Sketch comedy

I vividly remember the first time I saw *Monty Python's Flying Circus*. I was 11, and the title alone had me intrigued—what could this *be*? A trapeze act, maybe? And who was this Monty Python guy anyway?

I tuned in and saw a grubby little man flash various old ladies, who turned away in disgust. Then he flashed the camera, with a sign hanging around his neck that read "Boo!"

I was hooked.

From then on I was a rabid *Python* fan. I collected the records and the books, and watched the TV show avidly, memorizing lines from great sketches. When Graham Chapman, John Cleese, Terry Gilliam, Eric Idle, Terry Jones and Michael Palin formed what Palin called their "mutual admiration society" back in 1969, little did they know that the fruits of their comic inspiration would be parroted (in more ways than one) by millions. However bemused they might be by the fanaticism of their converts, it's their fault for being so funny. These guys have virtually defined British humor for nearly four decades.

They melded absurdity, media satire, wordplay, warped interpretations of history, weird science, cross-dressing, sex, cartoons, violence, penguins and just plain madness into a wonderful stream-of-consciousness tapestry that was as unpredictable as it was hilarious.

It took a kind of wonderfully demented intelligence to crank out such silliness. Part of *Python*'s appeal was that it didn't underestimate its audience. On the Cambridge side was Chapman, a certified medical doctor; Cleese, a law student; and Idle, an English scholar. Representing Oxford were Palin and Jones—historians both. (Animator Gilliam emigrated from America.) Collectively, the Oxbridge lot honed their skills writing for David Frost—a frequent target of their barbs—before starring in vehicles like *At Last the 1948 Show* and *Do Not Adjust Your Set*.

Once they joined forces, they fused the eloquent sting of the satirical revue *Beyond the Fringe* with the whimsical lunacy of radio's *The Goon Show*. The Cambridge side—Chapman and Cleese together, and Idle on his own—contributed logical lunacy in the form of highly verbal sketches such as "Nudge, Nudge," "The Argument Clinic," "The Cheese Shop," "Upper Class Twit of the Year" and the legendary "Dead Parrot"—in which a frustrated

Cleese pounds a lifeless bird on the counter in a futile attempt to get a refund from Palin, who insists the creature is only "stunned."

The Palin-Jones team was more visually oriented and specialized in wild juxtapositions. Their sketches included such gems as "The Spanish Inquisition," "The Summarize Proust Competition," "Blackmail," "Working Class Playwright" and the infamous "The Ministry of Silly Walks," where the gangly Cleese (who hates the sketch to this day) plays a government official with an extraordinarily bizarre gait. Gilliam linked the skits together with his trend-setting cutout animation, which drew from art sources as varied as old Sears catalogues to Bronzino's *An Allegory of Venus and Cupid* (the source of the foot that came crashing down during the opening credits).

They also subverted the very medium of TV itself by dropping the titles anywhere in the program, or listing the credits in the form of, say, anagrams. Characters from one sketch would appear in another. Often they made references to other items in the program, or even those in other episodes. Sketches could be interrupted for a quick gag, or else abandoned without a punch line. Chapman's indignant Colonel, for example, would often barge into a vignette and end it on the grounds that it was "too silly." Because the Pythons wrote their own material, they were able to fine-tune a kind of disciplined chaos that, however manic, always served rather than obscured the jokes.

After 45 episodes (including six without Cleese) they turned their attentions to film, releasing two bona fide classics in *Monty Python and the Holy Grail* (a loopy send-up of the Arthurian legend that Idle later adapted into the musical *Spamalot*) and *Life of Brian* (a controversial parody of religious zealotry). After 1983's *The Meaning of Life* they split up, with Chapman's 1989 death from cancer ending any chances of a full-scale reunion, though the survivors did regroup for an A&E special in 1999.

They had individual successes, too. Idle scored with a riotous Beatles parody entitled *All You Need Is Cash*, a profile of the very Fab-like Rutles. Chapman wrote a surreal memoir entitled *A Liar's Autobiography*, which became a cult classic. Palin starred in the series *Ripping Yarns* and in such films as *A Private Function, American Friends* and *The Missionary*. Jones divided his time between directing films (*Personal Services, Erik the Viking*) and writing books on medieval history (*Chaucer's Knight*).

But it's Cleese and Gilliam who have maintained the highest profiles. Cleese co-created and starred in the wonderful sitcom *Fawlty Towers* and, later, had a sizeable movie hit with the 1988 farce *A Fish Called Wanda*, which also featured Palin. Gilliam abandoned animation to concentrate on film, delivering a string of wildly imaginative projects to the big screen. His directorial resume includes *Time Bandits, Brazil,*

Did You Know?

The troupe did nearly all of its own stunts, including Michael Palin's 15-foot fall into a canal in "The Fish-Slapping Dance" after being smacked in the head with a trout by John Cleese.

The Fisher King, *The Adventures of Baron Munchausen*, *12 Monkeys* and *The Brothers Grimm*.

Yet, however rewarding the Pythons were as solo artists, they were at their best as a unit, where their remarkable synergy created something completely different. That's why many—George Harrison included—likened them to "The Beatles of Comedy."

They also opened my eyes to British comedy as a whole. Through *Python*, I discovered such artists as Peter Cook, Spike Milligan, Alan Bennett, Rowan Atkinson, Billy Connolly, Ben Elton, Chris Morris, Stephen Fry, a pre-*House* Hugh Laurie, Dawn French, Jennifer Saunders, Eddie Izzard . . . the list goes on.

Then there's the matter of their influence. Everything from *Saturday Night Live* to *South Park* owes a debt to these erudite bad boys. For that matter, so do I. I probably wouldn't be a writer without their inspiration. There was something about the craziness they discovered in the commonplace that sparked my imagination. Who else could reference Hegel and then hit you with something as cockamamie as "The Fish-Slapping Dance"?

In tribute to these unique comic artists, the sign I would happily hang around my neck might simply read "Bravo!"

Cast:

Graham Chapman *Performer*, **John Cleese** *Performer*, **Eric Idle** *Performer*, **Terry Jones** *Performer*, **Michael Palin** *Performer*, **Terry Gilliam** *Performer*

Moonlighting

By Craig Tomashoff

Broadcast History: ABC, 3/3/1985–5/14/1989
Runtime: 60 minutes
Genre: Comedy/crime drama

Perhaps it's genetic. Then again, it could be simply social conditioning. Whatever the reason, this fact is indisputable. Guys do not like romantic comedies. OK, sure, there are exceptions to the rule every once and a while, courtesy of Tom Hanks. The vast majority of the time, however, those of us worth our XY chromosomes would sooner pour honey on our bodies and roll around naked atop a fire-ant nest on an August afternoon in the Mojave Desert than watch anything that pairs, say, Hugh Grant and Julia Roberts. Or Hugh Grant and Sandra Bullock. Or Hugh Grant and Andie MacDowell.

Anyway, that's probably why, more than anything else, *Moonlighting* can be fondly remembered as a singularly sly, hip series that changed television. It managed to turn the notion of romantic comedy into something guys were *happy* to watch when their girlfriends or spouses were in the room. They'd even switch over on their own from, say, a *T. J. Hooker* episode (even the ones where Heather Locklear posed as a hooker) in order to catch an episode of this legendary program.

Originally a midseason replacement, *Moonlighting* launched on March 3, 1985, as a full-length film before slipping into its Tuesday night time slot. The premise, dreamed up by an underappreciated genius named Glenn Gordon Caron, seemed pretty routine. A former fashion model named Maddie Hayes (Cybill Shepherd) discovers that her manager has cheated her out of her money. While looking into her few remaining assets, she discovers she's the owner of the world's least effective private-eye business, the low-rent Blue Moon Detective Agency—presently being run by the world's oldest juvenile delinquent, the swaggering David Addison (Bruce Willis).

It was love and hate at first sight for David and Maddie, which of course meant it'd eventually be love in the true spirit of romantic comedy. And, well, that's pretty much it. There were some other oddball elements to the concept, like the receptionist Agnes DiPesto (Allyce Beasley), who answered all calls in rhyme. However, it was David and Maddie's chemistry that carried *Moonlighting* through 66 episodes and into TV history as a series where romance and manliness could walk arm in arm.

Theirs was the classic battle-of-the-sexes setup that went back to Shakespeare and beyond (no coincidence, then, that the series' most famous episode was a twisted take on *The Taming of the Shrew*, complete with costumes and iambic pentameter dialogue). David, as exemplified by the then-unknown Willis, made it clear from his first exchange with Maddie that he was going to talk the way all guys wished they could talk. As in, he thought up the clever lines on the spot rather than coming up with them an hour later in the car on the way home.

> David: *The year's a little fuzzy for me, but I will bet the house you were a Miss March.*
>
> Maddie: *A Miss What?*
>
> David: *A Miss March. A Playmate of the Month. What? About 1976? I can see the layout in my head. You like jazz. Your favorite movie was* Jonathan Livingston Seagull. *You wanted to help underprivileged kids. Am I right or am I right?*

David was perhaps the only guy in TV history who could get away with lines like, "Women . . . can't live with 'em, can't leave 'em on the side of the curb when you're done" or "A promise is something you make very late at night to someone you'll probably never see again so you can get to the good stuff." Offensive? Sure. But Maddie usually gave as good as she got, and their bickering banter made every episode seem like an edgier, latter-day *His Girl Friday*. (Of course, this dialogue worked much better on television than it did in real life. As I quickly discovered after tossing out the "curb" line at the end of my second and unfortunately *final* date with an artist named Emily.)

It wasn't just the snappy screwball patter that made *Moonlighting* so appealing. It was also the imaginative ways Caron found to tell his tales. The aforementioned "Atomic Shakespeare" episode is by far the show's most famous, featuring the cast sporting authentic period garb and a very sardonic '80s attitude. As evidenced by the opening sequence, in which a boy and his mother debate the merits of watching the episode.

> Son: *Hey, Mom! It's* Moonlighting. *You know, that show about the two detectives, a man and a woman . . .*
>
> Mom: *. . . and they argue a lot but all they really want to do is sleep together.*
>
> Son: *Yeah!*
>
> Mom: *Sounds like trash to me.*

There were constant experimental innovations that pushed the limits of traditional television. "The Dream Sequence Always Rings Twice," complete with an Orson Welles cameo, was a black-and-white show that tweaked the usual handling of small-screen dream sequences. "Big Man on Mulberry Street" featured an elaborate dance sequence set to a Billy Joel tune. "Come Back Little Shiksa" showcased David dealing with a Claymation version of Maddie. Dr. Ruth Westheimer, sex therapist and cultural gadfly of the late '80s, popped up to offer advice.

The potent cast chemistry, irreverent tone and unusual plot devices made *Moonlighting* a true original. However, the will-they-or-won't-they foreplay could only keep up for so long before something had to give. And on March 31, 1987, in an episode called "I Am Curious . . . Maddie," they finally went to bed while 60 million voyeuristic viewers tuned in. That gave rise to the idea in some quarters—the show's Big Bang theorists, if you will—that once Maddie and David did it, the series was done. But that's not entirely true. It stayed on the air for two more seasons and, at least for a short time, was as creative as ever.

When *Moonlighting* began to fall apart, it was for a variety of reasons, not the least of which was most likely the backstage (and well-publicized) bickering going on between Willis and Shepherd. Producers decided to get Maddie pregnant with David's baby, which she would eventually lose in a miscarriage (a twist not exactly loaded with laughs). For a short time, she also was married to a dweeby guy (Dennis Dugan) she met on the train, who was to David Addison what mayonnaise is to a pastrami sandwich. By the time Caron was let go from his own show, the creative lamp at *Moonlighting* had gone dark.

Ultimately, it's only fitting that the series burned brightly for a short period of time and then left our lives for good. This series that made romantic comedy man-friendly was a lot like a manly man's dream relationship. Intense. Amusing. Attractive. And over before he has too much time to take it seriously.

Cast:

Cybill Shepherd *Maddie Hayes,* **Bruce Willis** *David Addison,* **Allyce Beasley** *Agnes Dipesto,* **Curtis Armstrong** *Herbert Viola (1986–89)*

My So-Called Life

By Jeff Gemmill
Broadcast History: ABC, 8/25/1994–1/26/1995
Runtime: 60 minutes
Genre: Drama

"When someone dies young, it's like they stay that way forever," muses 15-year-old Angela Chase (Claire Danes) in the memorable "Halloween" installment of *My So-Called Life*, which found her entranced by a student said to have died in 1963. In a weird way, the same thing applies to TV series like *My So-Called Life* and, to use two other examples, *Wonderfalls* and *Freaks & Geeks*, which were axed before their time. We're left with but a handful of episodes and the promise of what could have been if only . . . if only.

The drama, which debuted in August 1994 and lasted a scant 19 episodes, told the story of Angela (she called school "a battlefield for your heart"), her family and friends; and while it's probably best remembered for showcasing the mercurial acting talents of the Emmy-nominated Danes, it featured an equally capable supporting cast. Bess Armstrong portrayed Patty, Angela's homecoming-queen mom who struggles with the problems many working mothers face; and Tom Irwin was terrific as quixotic dad Graham. Likewise authentic were Angela's friends—her troubled pal Rayanne (A. J. Langer), gentle Ricky (Wilson Cruz), heavy-lidded crush Jordan (Jared Leto), ex-best friend Sharon (Devon Odessa) and geeky neighbor "Brain"—er, *Brian* (Devon Gummersall). Even little sister Danielle (Lisa Wilhoit) comes across as a believable kid whose bratty behavior we understand.

In many ways, largely because of the voice-over narration, the episodes play like intimate diary entries woven into the fabric of ongoing stories. Unlike a diary, however, each episode expands the viewpoint to reveal the perspectives of other characters and also tells their stories independently of Angela. The most notable plotlines are Angela's infatuation with Jordan, whose inability to articulate anything of substance proves as frustrating to him as it is for us (and leads to a wondrous season-ender in which he turns to "Brain" for help); drug and alcohol–troubled

> ### Did You Know?
>
> Among those considered for the role of Angela Chase was Alicia Silverstone.

Rayanne, who reminds Patty—and us—of kids we knew; Ricky's descent into homeless hell and slow rebound to stability; and the slow growth of Graham's restaurant ambitions, to say nothing of his possible dogging around. In the pilot, we discover that he almost stepped out on his wife; and in the finale, he again veers close with feisty restaurant partner Hallie Lowenthal (Lisa Waltz).

My So-Called Life

Of course, there's also Brian's quiet yearning for Angela. It's only when he becomes Cyrano de Bergerac to Jordan's Christian de Neuvillette in the last episode, "In Dreams Begin Responsibilities," and she learns the truth, that she begins to see him in a new light. It doesn't stop her from leaving with the hunk, mind you, but the quizzical look she gives Brian says it all. If there had been a second, third or fourth season, that would have been explored. If only.

What lifted *My So-Called Life* above a well-acted, angst-ridden sudsfest, however, was the superlative writing. Stewarded by creator/co-executive producer Winnie Holzman, who earned an Emmy nomination for the pilot's script, the show explored topics not generally associated with teen dramas of the 1990s, including body image, homosexuality and, however improbable, the world of metaphysics. In the Halloween episode, Angela interacted with a ghost; and in "Other People's Mothers," which finds Rayanne spinning out of control, there's an introduction to tarot that, in the installment's final moments, sounds suspiciously like real life: "The cards are read in sequence. Each card leads to the next. We move from terror and loss to unexpected good fortune, and out of darkness, hope is born."

As good as they are, however, it's the Christmas episode ("So-Called Angels") that sends shivers up my spine no matter how often I view—or think about—it. Alternative rock-pop genius Juliana Hatfield guest stars as a seemingly homeless girl who appears to Angela and, on Christmas Eve, to Patty, and guides both of them to Ricky, who's been living on the streets since being banished from his home. In the final scene, we see Juliana turn away from the camera and, with the flap of a wing, ascend—like the guardian angel her character is—toward heaven. Of course, to single out a specific episode for praise is akin to recommending just one Juliana Hatfield album—it can't be done, as each has something special to offer and deserves to be heard.

It matters not, really, whether one believes in ghosts, the tarot, angels or dreams. What matters is that the characters are so believable that we embrace

Preview Review

September 17, 1994

Premise: Bittersweet drama about life, as seen through the eyes of a 15-year-old high school student.

Strong Point: From the producers of *thirtysomething*. Danes is eerily talented and pretty but she's no supergirl or supermodel. That's a plus: It makes her more human to kids who can identify with her, and parents who'll recognize her.

Weak Point: Thursday's an NBC night (*Mad About You*, *Seinfeld*), so this ABC show has more than its share of obstacles. But the question is, will anyone consider adolescence entertaining . . . or just an embarrassing era in our life that we're all trying to forget?

Bottom Line: One of the best of the new season. The show has just enough of a dark, gritty edge to be convincingly realistic. There's no shortage of angst, but it doesn't have that grating *thirtysomething* whine. And it could go over with junior-high and high-school kids. (They may have seen it already: It premiered early, in late August.)

them much as we do the people in our daily lives, quirks and all. Angela, Brian and the rest are no different than many a teenager, forever thinking they're seeing the full picture when, in truth, they're viewing slivers. As the season progresses, however, they gradually begin to grasp life's complexities. In "The Substitute," for example, Angela's inspirational English teacher (Roger Rees) turns out to be a deadbeat dad on the lam from the law; yet he still motivates her to hold on to her ideals and risk suspension in order to distribute the school's banned literary magazine. Likewise, Patty and Graham—though more clued in about life—are far from perfect, with each confronting the same challenges many adults face at one time or another.

In the end, though, watching *My So-Called Life* is like viewing photos of someone who passed too soon. We lose ourselves in the snapshots and episodes, laughing at every mention of Tino (the show's own Godot) while, at the same time, wishing for a different conclusion. And when Angela slides into the passenger seat of Jordan's car in the show's final moments, her eyes glued on Brian . . . sadness seeps in. In a flash, everything that could and would have been is no more—except in our hearts, where Angela and her friends live on.

Cast:

Claire Danes *Angela Chase*, **Bess Armstrong** *Patty Chase*, **Wilson Cruz** *Rickie Vasquez*, **Devon Gummersall** *Brian Krakow*, **A. J. Langer** *Rayanne Graff*, **Jared Leto** *Jordan Catalano*, **Devon Odessa** *Sharon Cherski*, **Lisa Wilhoit** *Danielle Chase*, **Tom Irwin** *Graham Chase*

NYPD Blue

By Paul Wolfe

Broadcast History: ABC, 9/21/1993–3/1/2005
Runtime: 60 minutes
Genre: Crime drama

It may have been the bare butts and coarse language that generated the initial headlines (and got the show booted off the schedule, for varying periods of time, by more than 50 ABC affiliates), but on its own raw and uncompromising terms, co-creator Steven Bochco's *NYPD Blue* redefined the cop drama, just as his *Hill Street Blues* had more than a decade earlier.

Bochco and David Milch had endured nearly a year and a half of preproduction controversy surrounding *Blue* content stemming from complaints by network execs, affiliates, conservative groups and politicians. Some nudity and profanity did punctuate the pilot, but critics and curious viewers quickly realized the drama was less about being blue and more about NYPD's officers *in* blue. The lingo that actually stood out most—skel, perp, hump, mope, laid hands on, lawyered up, reach out and, of course, The Job—largely came straight from the mouth of key series consultant and former NYC homicide detective Bill Clark. Those flavorful words, delivered with heavy accents and jumbled cop grammar, gave the series its credibility among New Yorkers, cops and fans, and each week made it clear that you had entered the *Blue* zone. It was a space brilliantly accentuated with a percussive soundtrack, frenetic camera work and editing that produced a distinctively gritty, documentary-like look.

The first episode, introducing a rich, intersecting gallery of characters, was one of those rare pilots that signified the arrival of something different and special; something that demanded you return every Tuesday night. The first 60 minutes had more "wow" moments than some series yield in an entire season: Det. Andy Sipowicz telling ADA Sylvia Costas to "Ipsa this, you pissy little bitch!" as he grabbed his crotch. Sipowicz getting set up by his hooker and taking six bullets from the gun of his nemesis, Alfonse Giardella. And the biggest shock of all, Off. Janice Licalsi, already established as a love interest for Det. John Kelly, secretly meeting with mob boss Angelo Marino. That she was in the mob's pocket was a shock of its own, but when he asked her to kill Kelly, I was stunned. And

> ### Did You Know?
>
> Originally, Det. John Kelly was going to be named Flinn and be played by Jimmy Smits, who turned down the part. Ironically, Smits's character, Det. Bobby Simone, was Det. Kelly's replacement.

addicted. That feeling was heightened moments later when a ventilated Sipowicz squeezed Kelly's hand in the hospital, signaling the bond between the two detectives and, for the first of many times, Andy's ability to cheat death. Cue the music. Cue the credits. And cue 12 seasons and 261 episodes of the life and times of New York's finest.

How good was that first season? Ratings-wise, it was in the Top 20 (and remained so for its first seven seasons). On the awards front, it garnered a staggering 27 nominations, including seven for its actors and all five writing noms.

With his red hair, blue eyes and Irish lilt, David Caruso was an instant sensation as Kelly. During location filming on the streets of New York—another element that gave *Blue* its authenticity—fans would shout their preferences as to which woman (Licalsi or estranged wife Laura) was better suited for Kelly. Caruso, however, was apparently paying more attention to what his agents were saying. With huge success came new contract demands, and Caruso left early in the second season to pursue a movie career. His exit stands as one of the all-time bonehead career decisions. Not that he cares, but I still haven't forgiven him. And I won't watch *CSI: Miami*.

> ## Preview Review
> *September 18, 1993*
>
> **Premise**: *Hill Street Blues* wises up in the nasty '90s, in nasty New York. But instead of an ensemble of cuddly cops, this series focuses on one: David Caruso as Det. John Kelly, an honest man with a burned-out partner and a wife who left him because of his work.
>
> **Strong Point**: The show has a killer cast—Caruso is right on target; you can't help rooting for the guy. And Franz is always outrageously fun to watch. Best of all, *NYPD Blue*—like Steven Bochco's previous successes, *Hill Street Blues* and *L.A. Law*—is one of those rare shows that think we, the audience members, are smart.
>
> **Weak Point**: It *is* another cop show, and TV has had so many, they do start to sound the same.
>
> **Bottom Line**: The much-discussed R-rated flashes of flesh and bad words are just convention-busting distraction compared to the series' more substantial elements. This show is a Bochco classic all around.

Caruso's departure opened up a desk for Jimmy Smits, the *L.A. Law* star Bochco originally wanted for the role of John Kelly. Instead, Smits strolled into the 15th Precinct as introverted Det. Bobby Simone and struck up an immediate chemistry with Dennis Franz's Sipowicz. The transition was seamless and set the stage for another love affair. Over the next five seasons, Bobby helped Det. Diane Russell (Kim Delaney) deal with alcoholism, her abusive past and a miscarriage, while she helped the widowed Simone find love again. They tied the knot in Season 5, but the marriage was nearly as short as their lunch-hour civil ceremony. After a failed heart transplant, Simone died the next season during an emotionally draining, dream-laced episode that touched fans far more than the traditional gunned-down-in-the-line-of-duty death. The entire precinct—and viewers—bid a slow, tearful farewell as Simone drifted off to heaven, where he held the hand of the son he and Diane had lost.

Caruso and Smits were terrific. But the anchor was always Andy Sipowicz and not just because he was with the show from start to finish. Franz transformed a bigoted, foul-mouthed, chain-smoking, alcoholic Vietnam vet into a complex, haunted and strangely likeable figure—and won four Emmys in the process. But overcoming racism and beating the booze (several times, over several seasons, not just one very special episode) was just the start. Milch and succeeding writers dealt Sipowicz more highs and lows than perhaps any TV character has ever endured or should. He rebuilt a relationship with his son Andy Jr., then learned the boy was fatally shot trying to halt a robbery just days before entering the police academy. He repaired a relationship with that pissy little ADA Costas, who slowly softened his off-the-job personality, married him and gave birth to their son, Theo. She was killed by a stray bullet during a courtroom shoot-out. Andy later served as a father figure to his third partner, Danny Sorenson (Rick Schroder, in a credible transition from child actor to adult star), but he died during an undercover operation. Only Det. John Clark Jr. (former teen idol Mark-Paul Gosselaar in another offbeat casting move that worked) lasted as Andy's partner.

Without Sipowicz, *NYPD Blue* wouldn't have survived cast defections rivaled only by *Law & Order*. A string of new faces, repetitive cases and soap-worthy plots remained tolerable only because hard-core viewers were curious to see what Sipowicz would do next. In the 11th season he got married for a third time, to fellow detective Connie McDowell (Charlotte Ross), and together they raised Theo, her niece and their newborn, Matthew. Finally, on March 3, 2005, Andy assumed lieutenant duties in the series finale, watched by 16 million viewers, about half the number that tuned in for the premiere. Considering Sipowicz's personality and past actions, that promotion might have been the most unrealistic moment in the history of the rooted-in-reality series. But that doesn't mean we didn't enjoy the hell out of seeing him succeed.

Cast:

Dennis Franz *Det. Andy Sipowicz,* **David Caruso** *Det. John Kelly (1993–94),* **James McDaniel** *Lt. Arthur Fancy (1993–2001),* **Nicholas Tuturro** *Det. James Martinez (1993–2000),* **Amy Brenneman** *Off. Janice Licalsi (1993–94),* **Sherry Stringfield** *Laura Hughes Kelly (1993–94),* **Gordon Clapp** *Det. Greg Medavoy (1994–2005),* **Jimmy Smits** *Det. Bobby Simone (1994–98),* **Kim Delaney** *Det. Diane Russell (1994–2001),* **Gail O'Grady** *Donna Abandando (1994–97),* **Sharon Lawrence** *ADA Sylvia Costas Sipowicz (1994–98),* **Andrea Thompson** *Det. Jill Kirkendall (1995–2000),* **Rick Schroder** *Det. Danny Sorenson (1998–2001),* **Bill Brochtrop** *John Irvin (1999–2005),* **Henry Simmons** *Det. Baldwin Jones (2000–05),* **Charlotte Ross** *Det. Connie McDowell (2001–04),* **Mark-Paul Gosselaar** *Det. John Clark (2001–05),* **Esai Morales** *Lt. Tony Rodriguez (2001–05),* **Garcelle Beauvais-Nilon** *ADA Valerie Haywood (2001–05),* **Jacqueline Obradors** *Det. Rita Ortiz (2001–05),* **Bonnie Sommerville** *Det. Laura Murphy (2004–05),* **Currie Graham** *Lt. Thomas Bale (2004–05)*

The Odd Couple

By Donica O'Bradovich

Broadcast History: ABC, 9/24/1970–7/4/1975
Runtime: 30 minutes
Genre: Sitcom

A classic scene: Felix and Oscar are fighting about Oscar's ulcer and are barely speaking. Still, it's dinnertime and both men are hungry. Felix is eating a gourmet meal by himself. He's sitting down with an immaculate place setting, a candle and a good bottle of wine. Oscar comes barreling into the house and throws a paper bag onto the table—his meal. To rub it in Felix's face, he takes out chili dogs, enchiladas and burritos along with his dessert, a chocolate ice pop. Felix looks on, horrified, and implores him to please use a place mat. Oscar intended to—his paper bag. He then magnanimously offers Felix some of his glop, which causes Felix to take his table setting, candle, wine and meal and scurry off to the bedroom. Oscar feels triumphant, but only for a moment—he runs for the phone and dials the hospital doubled over in pain.

So the question needs to be asked again, can two divorced men share an apartment without driving each other crazy? Well, these two couldn't anyway. How lucky for us.

When *The Odd Couple* debuted on TV in 1970, Neil Simon's story about a sloppy divorced sportswriter who shares his apartment with his fastidiously neat divorced photographer best friend had already been a hit Broadway show and movie. Walter Matthau and Art Carney originated the roles on Broadway in 1965, then, three years later, Matthau and Jack Lemmon played them in the movie. But when Garry Marshall and Jerry Belson adapted it for TV, they chose Jack Klugman and Tony Randall, two veteran actors with successful TV and movie careers, but not exactly superstars. Yet Klugman's craggy features coupled with Randall's refined manners seemed a perfect match. The first season even replicated the exact apartment

Preview Review

September 12, 1970

Tony Randall and Jack Klugman star as the mismatched apartment mates in this latest reincarnation of *The Odd Couple*. It's part of a Thursday-night double bill based on Neil Simon plays—it follows *Barefoot in the Park*. Klugman plays the slob of a sportswriter who keeps spilling ashtrays all over the place; Randall is Felix Unger, the compulsively neat photographer who keeps tidying up after him. (Felix: "Where'd you get all the dust cloths?" Oscar: "This happens to be my laundry.") Both divorced, they coexist— just barely—in a Manhattan apartment. Every once in a while the birdbrained Pigeon sisters (Monica Evans and Carol Shelly) flutter down from upstairs.

from the movie and used the same plots, but with the canned laugh track and strange lack of, well, laughs, it played like a black comedy.

According to Rip Stock's fun trivia book *Odd Couple Mania*, Randall and Klugman suggested that they play in front of a live studio audience with three cameras in the second season. The ratings didn't improve, but the show appeared fresh and funny; even the leads seemed to have a better time. By the time the show went off the air in 1975, Klugman and Randall had been nominated for Emmys for each year of the run (Klugman won twice, and Randall won his sole long-overdue prize after the show was cancelled, sighing at the ceremonies, "Now if I only had a job.") and it instantly became a syndication champion. So why is it that we can't we get enough of the irascible Oscar and his best friend Felix some 31 years later?

The Odd Couple wasn't social commentary, but it debuted in a tumultuous decade when divorce rates were skyrocketing and living arrangements were becoming more and more creative. The series proved that friendship between two heterosexual men, both tender and sweet one moment, and testy and tempestuous the next, could exist without any hint of sexual possibility; we always knew that Felix wanted Gloria back and Oscar had an active and happy single life. And though Felix's obsessive-compulsive disorders would have been probably cured by a dose of today's vast array of medications,

> ### Did You Know?
>
> Jack Klugman was married to Brett Somers, who played Blanche Madison, Oscar's ex-wife.

back then one could see that he was pretty much *right* about everything from Oscar's health to being a great parent to his two children.

Tension and conflict were Felix and Oscar's other two roommates, but you always knew that the two men would be there for each other at the end of the episode. Still, you couldn't help but wonder, was *this* going to be the episode in which Oscar was finally going to throw Felix down the dumbwaiter for good?

As a native of Manhattan, I can attest to the fact that Felix and Oscar were great New Yorkers who contributed to the city and shared in all it has to offer. When Felix tried to convince Oscar that New York was not the cold, unfeeling city he had written about in a particularly nasty column, I heartily cheered him on. Ironically, I grew up in the same building where series cast member Penny Marshall lived, but we never spoke a word to each other. Could Oscar have been right about New York after all?

Most series take a few seasons to get their groove. There was no warming up with *The Odd Couple*. Almost from the start, Klugman and Randall embodied their characters with astonishing grace, wit and charisma. Each knew the idiosyncratic quirks of his character and could do just about anything that a script called for. In two episodes, "The Odd Decathlon" and "Fat Farm," you could hear the audience gasp as Randall physically jumped onto a desk as a way to show his prowess. But Klugman could slump and stammer just as well. Nobody could enter a room with his eyes half closed, wearing a ratty bathrobe and a backwards Mets baseball cap, and open a can of beer into his orange juice with as much panache as Klugman. Because the show had such great writing, none of the other cast members got short shrift either.

Some of their memorably suffering counterparts were Marshall as Oscar's ditzy secretary, Myrna Turner; Elinor Donahue as Felix's sometime girlfriend Miriam; Al Molinaro as the world's most ineffectual cop, Murray Greshner; Janis Hansen as Felix's suffering but understanding ex-wife, Gloria; and Brett Somers as Oscar's suffering but rarely understanding ex-wife, Blanche. Even recurring guest stars such as the droll Richard Stahl or the incomparable Bill Quinn as Dr. Melnitz always stood out.

Like any classic sitcom, *The Odd Couple* had its very own vernacular and its share of memorable lines that fans can still recite or remember with absolute glee. What fan hasn't secretly wanted to taste Oscar's culinary masterpiece "goop mélange," which he fed to poor Felix. Remember when Oscar tormented poor Murray the Cop with the politically incorrect nicknames "Nosé Feliciano" and "Tokyo Nose"? And, really, who didn't want to hire Felix to be their defense attorney after he successfully defended both himself and Oscar against a ticket-scalping charge with the succinct line "When you A-S-S-U-M-E, you make an A-S-S of U and M-E!!!" in the memorable episode "My Strife in Court."

TV and Film Connections
Based on a movie
by the same name (1968)

Even the discrepancies within the show were charming. Oscar and Felix were either childhood friends or they met on jury duty; they shared an enviably huge New York City apartment on Park Avenue and then mysteriously moved to a big bright one on Central Park West. And why, for heaven's sake, were Felix's children, Edna and Leonard, played by at least three or four different actors?

Gleason and Carney; Lucy and Desi; Fred and Barney. These names each conjure up their own memorable moments, their own eras and their own delights. Add to that Klugman and Randall. When Randall passed away in 2004, Klugman appeared on several TV shows to talk about their years together on the series. He talked about Randall with such reverence you felt that Klugman had truly lost not only a co-star, but a friend. It reminded me of the series' final episode in which Felix remarried Gloria and Oscar celebrated with glee—I wondered what Oscar was going to do by himself in that huge apartment without his best pal.

Cast:

Tony Randall *Felix Unger*, **Jack Klugman** *Oscar Madison*, **Al Molinaro** *Murray Greshner*, **Larry Gelman** *Vinnie*, **Brett Somers** *Blanche Madison*, **Penny Marshall** *Myrna Turner* (1971–75)

The Office

By Daniel Manu

The Office (UK)
Broadcast History: BBC America, 1/23/2003–
11/16/2003
Runtime: 40 minutes
Genre: Sitcom

The Office (U.S.)
Broadcast History: NBC, 3/24/2005–
Runtime: 30 minutes
Genre: Sitcom

For more than 50 years, the brightest minds from Harvard to Oxford, the Catskills to the Improv, Chicago's Second City to L.A.'s Groundlings, strived to create great sitcoms. Many came close. In the early 21st century, two complete unknowns from the fringes of the British media world accomplished it, creating eight hours of precision-honed, almost agonizingly brilliant television comedy that not only set a new benchmark for the genre, but also created a template that has since been successfully exported to other countries and even different languages.

The story of *The Office* started in 1977 at London's struggling XFM Radio when Ricky Gervais, the station's "head of speech," hired Stephen Merchant as his assistant. The pair immediately bonded over a shared sense of humor and obsession with pop culture. Out of work a year later after a company merger, Merchant became an assistant producer in training at the British Broadcasting Corporation (BBC), where he was assigned to create a short demo. Remembering a lecherous, smarmy character called "Seedy Boss" that his friend would improvise at XFM, Merchant filmed Gervais in his acting debut.

Shot on a shoestring budget, the 20-minute tape established the most crucial hallmark of the later *Office* series: the faux-documentary style, heavily influenced by the cult film *This Is Spinal Tap*. In point of fact, Merchant could only afford a crew for one day, so the elaborate multi-angle setups of traditional TV would've been impossible, leaving him no choice but to simply point the camera at the actors and let them talk. But the result was serendipitous gold. Because the characters knew they were being filmed, they couldn't simply blurt out their true thoughts; rather, they were forced to adhere to the same social strictures as actual people, which only heightened the mockumentary realism of the eventual show, as did the moments of sheer monotony—workers typing, or sharpening pencils, or simply yawning—that would be interspersed between the action.

After circulating through the BBC maze for two years, the demo tape finally led to the commissioning of an *Office* script, then a pilot and then a six-episode first season, to air on the less prestigious BBC2 channel. From the beginning,

Gervais and Merchant insisted on not only writing the teleplays, but co-directing each one as well. While even the greatest minds in American comedy, from Caesar to Seinfeld, relied on the help of a large writing staff, every line and every frame of *The Office* would be the product of a singular, shared vision, leading to a remarkable consistency of voice throughout the series.

Gervais's actual voice, of course, dominated the show thanks to his lead character David Brent, the general manager of the suburban Slough branch of paper merchants Wernham Hogg. Truly a unique comic creation, Brent was at once overconfident and insecure; offensive and eager to please. He labored under the pathetic (but hilarious) self-delusion that his true calling was not middle management, but entertainment. "When people say, 'Would you rather be thought of as a funny man or a great boss?' my answer's always the same: They're not mutually exclusive. There's a weight of intellect behind my comedy," he says in one of the direct-to-camera "interviews" conducted by the unseen documentarians in each episode.

Brent's aide-de-camp was a relatively humorless (at least intentionally so) assistant named Gareth (Mackenzie Crook), a frail-looking, "fledgling-pigeon faced" (in Gervais's words) pseudo-militaristic sort with a small mind, an utterly tactless mouth and an oddly touching dedication to carrying out Brent's every whim. He was also an easy target for practical jokes played by the most endearing characters on the series: sarcastic but sweet sales clerk Tim (Martin Freeman) and his secret crush, receptionist and would-be artist Dawn (Lucy Davis), who was engaged to Lee (Joel Beckett), a loutish, unappreciative warehouse worker.

More than even Brent's misguided attempts at motivating his troops, his ridiculously leering attempt to impress a pretty job applicant (leading him to inadvertently head-butt her) and his cringe-worthy attempt at dancing, Tim and Dawn's relationship struck the deepest chord with *Office* viewers. Star-crossed romances, of course, were nothing new to sitcoms (witness Ross and Rachel's seemingly endless cycle of breakups and reconciliations on *Friends*), but what made Tim and Dawn so painfully wonderful to watch was, once again, the mock-doc construction of the show. "Because the camera's filming them, they can't show their emotions for each other. So you've got almost a Victorian seething melodrama. Just him touching her or her touching him means as much as a kiss," Merchant noted.

British audiences became heavily invested in the Tim-Dawn scenario, as well as Gervais's evolution from a boorish boss to sympathetic victim of corporate reorganization, but it took time, as Ben Walters, author of *BFI TV Classics: The Office*, wrote. Early ratings for the show's debut season in the summer of 2001 were terrible, as were the scores it received from audience focus groups. However, almost unanimous critical support and strong word of mouth made ratings inch up enough for BBC2 to commission a second six-episode season. And by the time it aired, multiple awards and strong ratings for repeats of the first six (higher, remarkably, than when they were first run) had made

The Office into a bona fide part of mainstream British culture, culminating in record-high UK DVD sales.

The second season, which followed the Slough branch of Wernham Hogg's merger with another office—and Brent's woeful, stubborn inability to adjust to his new boss, a younger, more handsome, better-liked man—ended with a doubly heartbreaking cliff-hanger: Dawn's rejection of Tim's gutsy acknowledgment of his feelings for her, on the eve of her move to Florida with Lee, and Brent, sacked and teary-eyed, pleading for his job back.

Fans would have to wait a full year for the resolution, but it was worth it. The two-part conclusion to *The Office*, billed the "Christmas Specials," aired on December 26 and 27, 2003, on the flagship BBC1, garnering the series' best ratings yet. Simply put, the final episodes were 100 minutes of what I consider to be perfect television comedy—a leap ahead three years that found Brent selling cleaning supplies, bouncing from one disastrous blind date to the next and, most of all, attempting to capitalize on the modicum of notoriety he had achieved by the airing of the documentary filmed at Wernham Hogg. Increasingly humiliated over the course of the specials, Brent finally finds redemption, payback and a healthy new outlook on life by the stirring ending, which just

> ### Did You Know?
>
> The computers on the Dunder-Mifflin office set are wired for the Internet. Cast members have admitted that when they're in the background of scenes they are often checking e-mail and surfing the Net.

as importantly, gave Tim and Dawn—and millions of viewers—exactly what they were looking for in dramatic fashion.

Fresh from this artistic triumph, Gervais, Merchant, Freeman and Davis were feted by the Hollywood Foreign Press Association a month later when *The Office*, merely a cult show in the United States thanks to airings on BBC America, shocked everyone by winning the Golden Globes for Best Comedy and Best Comedic Actor, beating such sitcom heavyweights as *Friends* and *Will & Grace* (an achievement that was trumpeted on the front pages of London newspapers for days). Shortly afterward, casting began on NBC's version of the show, developed for U.S. audiences by *King of the Hill* co-creator Greg Daniels, for airing as a midseason replacement in March 2005.

In the U.S. interpretation, Slough became Scranton, Pennsylvania; Wernham Hogg became Dunder-Mifflin; David Brent became Michael Scott (Steve Carell), Tim became Jim (John Krasinski); Dawn became Pam (Jenna Fischer); and Gareth became Dwight (Rainn Wilson). While the basic premise and cinemaverité style remained the same as the original *Office*, the American version—aside from a mediocre pilot that attempted to replicate the first UK episode scene by scene—quickly veered off into its own story lines, adding a whole new supporting cast of office workers, each with their own subtle, quirky characterizations. And though Jim still quietly pined for Pam, Michael Scott was notably different than Brent: instead of fooling himself into believing he was a "chilled-out entertainer," Michael instead proudly displayed his "World's Best Boss" mug and declared, "I'm a friend first and a boss second."

Over the course of its low-rated, short first season and its full-length second one (made possible partly by Carell's unexpected big-screen hit *The 40-Year-Old Virgin*), Michael was revealed, refreshingly, to have far more nuance and attractive qualities than his UK counterpart—while still side-splittingly egotistical, obliviously hurtful and often woefully misguided. Halfway through the second season, it became apparent—almost shockingly—that he was extremely skilled at his job, a natural with children and even something of a catch.

Following an Emmy Award for Outstanding Comedy Series in August 2006 (after having aired almost three times as many episodes as the British version), NBC's series ventured further into uncharted *Office* territory in its third season as it dealt with the fallout of Jim declaring his love for Pam, and his subsequent relocation to another Dunder-Mifflin branch. Meanwhile, the BBC also licensed the show to French television, where it gained acclaim as *Le Bureau*. And an unofficial German knock-off, *Stromberg*, similarly proved that seedy bosses and frustrated employees are a universal phenomenon.

As for Gervais and Merchant, the unequivocal success of their creation, and the complete validation of their artistic vision that it implies, has resulted in innumerable personal and professional changes, but none more important than this: They will never, ever have to work in an office again.

Cast for *The Office* (UK):

Ricky Gervais *David Brent*, **Mackenzie Crook** *Gareth Keenan*, **Martin Freeman** *Tim Canterbury*, **Lucy Davis** *Dawn Tinsley*, **Ralph Ineson** *Chris Finch*, **Ewan Macintosh** *Keith Bishop*, **Stirling Gallacher** *Jennifer Taylor Clarke*, **Oliver Chris** *Ricky Howard*, **Joel Beckett** *Lee*, **Robin Hooper** *Malcolm*, **Sally Bretton** *Donna*, **Patrick Baladi** *Neil Godwin*, **Stacey Roca** *Rachel*, **Julie Fernandez** *Brenda*, **Howard Saddler** *Oliver*

Cast for *The Office* (U.S.):

Steve Carell *Michael Scott*, **Jenna Fischer** *Pam Beesly*, **John Krasinski** *Jim Halpert*, **Rainn Wilson** *Dwight Schrute*, **B. J. Novak** *Ryan Howard*, **Leslie David Baker** *Stanley Hudson*, **Brian Baumgartner** *Kevin Malone*, **Kate Flannery** *Meredith Palmer*, **Melora Hardin** *Jan Levinson*, **Angela Kinsey** *Angela Martin*, **Oscar Nunez** *Oscar Martinez*, **Phyllis Smith** *Phyllis Lapin*, **Mindy Kaling** *Kelly Kapoor*, **Ed Helms** *Andy Bernard (2006–)*, **Rashida Jones** *Karen Filippelli (2006–)*

The Oprah Winfrey Show

By Sue Tiedeck

Broadcast History: Syndicated, 9/8/1986–
Runtime: 60 minutes
Genre: Talk show

It's impossible to write about *The Oprah Winfrey Show* without first discussing its host, the woman TV GUIDE named Performer of the Year in 1997 and *Time* dubbed Queen of All Media in 1988. Oprah is, after all, the reason that her self-named daily talkfest is the most successful talk show in TV history and why it has outlived countless others. Her triumphant show and her vast influence are in part explained by an inspiring life that has seen her surmount considerable obstacles.

Oprah Gail Winfrey was born in Kosciusko, Mississippi, on January 29, 1954. (She was originally named Orpah after a woman in the Bible's Book of Ruth, but that name proved difficult for people to pronounce and spell.) Her parents, Vernita Lee and Vernon Winfrey, weren't married, and their relationship didn't work out. She was then left in the care of her maternal grandmother, a woman well suited to nurture the intelligent, outgoing little girl who was able to read at a very early age (two-and-a-half!) and loved to speak in public.

Oprah moved to Milwaukee when she was six to live with her mother, a transition that proved difficult. Life in the city was very different from what she was used to on the farm. Her mom was busy with her work as a maid, so Oprah was frequently left on her own. During that unsupervised time she was sexually abused by several different men, and the trauma caused her to act out and misbehave. Not really knowing the cause of the problem, her frustrated mother sent her to Nashville to live with her father, who helped her turn her life around by bringing out her strengths and talents. He added structure to her routine, and encouraged her to be a good student and to love learning.

Her early skill at public speaking resurfaced, and she won a full scholarship for a speech she gave in Philadelphia to the Elks on "The Negro, the Constitution and the United States." While still in high school, she entered a pageant for Miss Fire Prevention in Nashville and won, the first black to do so. She spoke so well during the contest that its sponsor, radio station WVOL, gave her a job reading the news. She then won the titles of Miss Black Nashville and Miss Black Tennessee before starting college at Tennessee State University.

While she was a student, she was offered the chance to co-anchor the evening news on WTVF-TV, a Nashville CBS affiliate, and began her work as the first woman at that station. During her senior year, she took a similar job as a reporter and news anchor at ABC affiliate WJZ-TV and relocated to Baltimore. It was there that her battle with weight began when she sought solace in food after a disastrous permanent during a station-mandated makeover caused all of her hair to fall out. Appearing bald isn't the best confidence booster for a young on-air personality.

Her hair grew back and she began to get even more airtime as she was assigned to handle the local breaks on *Good Morning America*. In 1977 the station made a move that changed her destiny. She joined Richard Sher as the co-host of *Baltimore Is Talking*, a morning talk show. It soon became evident that she was perfectly suited for this type of work. She was able to handle a wide range of topics and could interact with all types of people, and she stayed there for seven years.

In January 1984, she relocated again to accept a job as the host of *A.M. Chicago*, which at the time was a not very successful morning talk show up against big competition, *Phil Donahue*.

> ### TV and Film Connections
> Spin-offs:
> *Dr. Phil*
> *Oprah After the Show*

That changed rapidly after her arrival. Within a month she had tied Donahue's ratings, and in two months had surpassed them. The name was changed to *The Oprah Winfrey Show* in September 1985 and the running time doubled to an hour. She formed her own production company in August 1986 (Harpo, her name spelled backward), and the show was picked up by King World Productions for national syndication.

The topic for her first national telecast on September 8, 1986, was "How to Marry the Man or Woman of Your Choice," chosen because she hadn't been able to book a high-profile guest. It was an instant success, topping the ratings in her time slot on almost all of the 138 stations on which it aired. That number has since grown to 197 stations, in addition to the 122 foreign countries where it's just as popular.

I've been watching since that first day and have seen the show evolve over the years. Early topics leaned more to the provocative and controversial. It was during a show on sexual abuse that she broke down and revealed her own childhood experience. I remember her 1987 visit to Forsyth County, Georgia, which at the time had had no black residents for more than 75 years, and her 1992 confrontation with people who had taken part in the L.A. riots following the Rodney King beating. In 1994, she decided to switch gears and focus on issues that would help viewers to improve their lives, using the theme "Remember Your Spirit." She began the "Angel Network," encouraging viewers and companies to join her in donating to charities, and she's helped to fulfill people's "Wildest Dreams." The experts she introduces become household names, most notably Dr. Phil McGraw and Rachael Ray, who've gone on to host their own shows.

She'd always been an avid reader, and launched her now-famous book club in 1996, choosing one title per month and later devoting a number of follow-up shows to the work. Publishers grew to love her, since her selections all became instant best sellers. She also encouraged people who'd never actually read a novel before to give it a try. As a big reader myself, I'll always be grateful to her for turning me on to titles that make my list of favorites, especially Wally Lamb's *She's Come Undone*, Barbara Kingsolver's *The Poisonwood Bible* and Ursula Hegi's *Stones from the River*, all of which my daughter and I read together. She stopped making monthly choices in 2002, turning to classic literature in 2003, beginning with *East of Eden* by John Steinbeck. I began to realize her real influence several summers ago when *Anna Karenina* was the summer selection, and I noticed how many others were reading Tolstoy's hefty Russian novel along with me as we sat on the beach in New Jersey. She now makes occasional picks of contemporary fiction and nonfiction.

But just what is it about Oprah that keeps viewers tuning in each day whether she's interviewing celebrities (just about every big name in politics and entertainment has visited) or ordinary people, or dealing with relationship issues, or, as she famously did to open her 19th season, giving away cars to members of her Chicago studio audience? The answer is simple. She is warm, genuine, articulate and caring. She seems to ask the questions of her guests that *we* would ask. She isn't afraid to show her flaws, and her guests (even celebrity ones, like a hyper-excited, couch-jumping Tom Cruise) aren't afraid to express themselves. We marveled when she lost 87 pounds and realized she was human just like us when she put it back on. She's shared some of her innermost personal conflicts and life experiences. Oprah comes across as though she's speaking personally to those of us watching at home, allowing us to think for a brief moment that she's confiding in us like a friend. The show is always entertaining and frequently educational and enlightening, and it deserves the nine Emmy Awards it received

Did You Know?

President Bill Clinton signed into law the U.S. National Child Protection Act of 1993, dubbed the "Oprah Bill," which establishes a national database of convicted child abusers.

for Outstanding Talk Show and the seven she won for Outstanding Host. She stopped winning only after withdrawing from the competition after being given Emmy's Lifetime Achievement Award in 1998.

It's probably obvious that I'm a fan. I find it easy to relate to her. We're not the same race, but we're of similar age and share a love for *To Kill a Mockingbird*. My weight has gone up and down along with hers, and I salute her for deciding that being healthy was a better goal than being thin. For those who aren't fans or who think she's become too full of herself because she's always on the cover of her own magazine, I challenge you to think of another celebrity who's a better role model for children, regardless of their race or gender. After all, if a poor little girl from Mississippi can overcome a difficult childhood and grow up to become a billionaire media mogul who champions education as the reason for her success while getting the masses to read great literature, the rest of us have no excuse for not trying to be the best we can be, or as she puts it, to live your best life. Thanks, Oprah.

Cast:

Oprah Winfrey *Host*

The Real World

By Sabrina Rojas Weiss

Broadcast History: MTV, 5/21/1992–
Runtime: 30 minutes
Genre: Reality program

Seven actors picked to live in a house. What would television look like today if MTV had gone with their original plan to develop an edgy soap opera in 1992? Many a reality-TV hater (and out-of-work actor) must wish it had worked. The rest of us are pretty grateful the cable channel executives realized they didn't have the budget for actors. So producers Jonathan Murray and Mary-Ellis Bunim pounced on the opportunity to pitch their clever experiment. That's when we found out what happens when ordinary people stop being polite, and start being real. And entertaining.

This influential series owes a huge debt (for good or bad, depending on your point of view about the reality genre) to PBS's groundbreaking 1973 cinemaverité series *An American Family*. And to Season 1's Julie, the virginal 19-year-old dance student from Alabama who was both the protagonist in her own coming-of-age story and the wide-eyed stand-in for those of us at home, as she drank in the experiences of living in New York City with six very different roommates. The others were already residing there, trying to make it in their respective MTV-friendly careers: Eric the model, Heather the rapper, Andre the rocker, Becky the singer-songwriter, Norman the painter and Kevin the writer. The youngest of the group and plucked directly from the home of her protective, conservative family, Julie was the one who interacted most with the rest of the cast and her new surroundings.

Though they were living in a gorgeous SoHo loft and followed by cameras for most of their waking hours, they continued about their daily business. There was, of course, plenty of time for assorted personal dramas and personality clashes. In the same year that Rodney King's beating sparked riots in Los Angeles, racial tensions often flared between politically aware African-American Kevin and his white roommates, who were more naive than racist. (In one instance, when the camera crew was unfortunately on break, Julie alleged that he physically threatened her because she interrupted his phone conversation.) Whether or not his accusations of racism were fair, the arguments in the house brought social issues to life for MTV's short-attention-span audience. Other important topics were also illustrated: Julie befriended a homeless woman; Norman was surprised to find that his roommates were tolerant of his homosexuality; some of the cast attended pro-choice and Jerry Brown rallies.

That's not to say the show was all serious business, a compendium of "very special episodes." We saw Eric using his burgeoning modeling career to further his efforts with the opposite sex, while Heather recorded her first solo album and Andre filmed a video with his band. The three women were whisked off to Jamaica, where they went on a fruitless manhunt, then Becky got involved with one of the show's producers (he was immediately fired for it). Interestingly enough, none of the cast hooked up with each other. But even without obvious sexual intrigue, young audiences were instantly addicted—and could relate—to these dynamic roommates. As a 14-year-old visiting New York that summer, I was thrilled by the possibility that I could run into the cast on the street, and I was certain my life would be like Julie's when I finally moved here. You couldn't say that about *Beverly Hills, 90210*.

Now filming its 18th season, *The Real World*'s formula has evolved quite a bit, its producers pumping up the conflict quotient. You won't catch a cast member watching TV, playing video games or sticking to their day job while they're in the house. Most distractions have been removed, and no one in the cast can hail from that season's city. The roommates are younger now (24 is the cutoff age as opposed to Kevin's mature 26). The cameras are ubiquitous, so not a minute of action is missed—even in showers and dark bedrooms, where plenty *has* taken place since Season 1. In addition to the one-on-one interviews that framed the first season, the cast is encouraged to vent their frustrations in a "confessional" room. To bring the roommates closer to each other and to stimulate some kind of action, there's always a hot tub, a group job and an exotic vacation.

But all these machinations would be nothing if we didn't have such carefully chosen, memorable characters: volatile bike messenger Puck (*San Francisco*); the sensitive Pedro, who died of AIDS soon after the S.F. season wrapped; troubled but fun-loving alcoholic Ruthie (*Hawaii*); sheltered Mormon Julie (*New Orleans*); promiscuous Trishelle (*Las Vegas*); ignorant frat boy turned open-minded kind soul Mike (*Back to New York*) and his strong yet forgiving roommate Coral, among others. While many of the cast members treat their three-month tenure as license to do nothing but drink, party, hook up and fight, these standout personalities keep bringing us back.

> **Did You Know?**
>
> In 1994, two years after *The Real World* premiered, creators Mary-Ellis Bunim and Jonathan Murray tried to sell another version of the show—this time with sixtysomethings as housemates.

Thanks to the show's spin-off of a spin-off, *Real World/Road Rules Challenge*, diehard fans get to see their favorites practically make a living from the franchise. *The Challenge* removes any pretense of serious significance, but it's a great guilty pleasure for anyone who enjoys watching scantily clad hotties bungee jump, swim with sharks and generally stab each other in the back.

RW/RR Challenge is just an example of how far this little experiment has gone. Sure, it is a direct ancestor to such evil spawn as *Paradise Hotel* and *The*

Flavor of Love, and it's partially responsible for taking the "music" out of MTV. The show's patented style of editing days of footage into a compelling episode with a clear story line is what separates surveillance footage from successful reality TV. It's hard to name a reality program that hasn't copied the "picked to live in a house" feature—put to use in everything from *Big Brother* and *Survivor* to *America's Next Top Model* and *Project Runway*. Even scripted dramas and comedies have adopted the individual confessionals as a narrative device. It seems *The Real World* might just have the staying power of a soap opera after all.

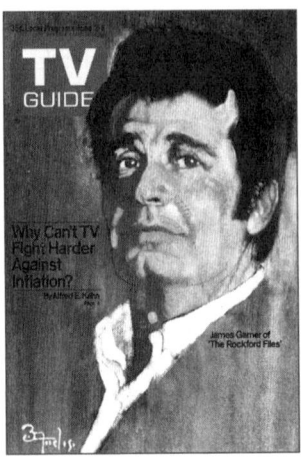

The Rockford Files

By Craig Tomashoff

Broadcast History: NBC, 9/13/1974–7/25/1980
Runtime: 60 minutes
Genre: Crime drama

Some kids grow up idolizing professional athletes, pasting posters on every spare inch of their bedroom walls. Others follow every move of their favorite actors, adopting their hair, clothing and (scarily) lifestyle choices. There are even a few student-body president types who worship, egads, politicians. But me? I spent my school days in the '70s as a private-eye geek.

I read everything I could get my eyes on that involved Phillip Marlowe, Sam Spade and Lew Archer. I begged my mom to let me stay up late enough to watch Mannix, Cannon or Simon Templar do their thing. I would look in the Yellow Pages for detective schools and then send them letters asking when I could enroll.

My future career seemed all set. Except for the fact that I was the geek in gym class who couldn't climb the rope and the dweeb who got turned down five times for the prom before finally giving up. In other words, I had zero in common with my tough-guy heroes. Until Jim Rockford came along.

From the minute *The Rockford Files* series debuted in the fall of 1974 (a *Rockford* TV movie had aired earlier that year), it was clear that this guy was unlike any previous prime-time PI. In the first moments of the opening credits, a caller on Rockford's answering machine announced: "Jim, it's Norma at the market. It bounced. You want us to tear it up, send it back or put it with the others?"

Shortly after that, when Rockford (James Garner) was grazed by a bullet, his dad, Rocky (Noah Beery Jr.), said, "Two inches to the right and you might be missing that eye." To which Rockford dryly replied, "Look at it this way. Two inches to the left and it would have missed me completely." And when he gets a fist to the face after failing to punch a bad guy, he complained, "Didn't you notice I was wearing glasses?" In those moments, I knew all I needed to about Rockford. He was a bit of a loser. He was a smart-ass. He wasn't particularly brave and certainly not anxious to trade punches ("I bruise easy," he said). He was, well, me. Or at least me if I cracked cases for $200 a day plus expenses, his going rate.

> ### Did You Know?
>
> James Garner's favorite food was tacos, and in many episodes he could be seen having them for breakfast.

As played by the wonderfully affable (and, because he always makes everything he does look so darn easy, too often underrated) Garner, Rockford was perhaps the most normal detective television had ever seen. You couldn't watch an episode of the show and not feel like you once drank beer with this guy. Sure he never met a case he couldn't solve, but he usually only did so after getting berated by angry cops, shot at by two-bit bad guys or shot down by hot women.

Tooling around L.A. in a cool Pontiac Firebird, Rockford was constantly getting mixed up in the sort of seamy, Raymond Chandler–esque drama that hooked me on the genre in the first place, whether he was tracking down the murderer of an old friend (like Season 2's "2 Into 5.56 Won't Go"), getting pushed around by mysterious mobsters (as in Season 1's "This Case Is Closed" and "Find Me If You Can"), or delving into the secret lives of the well-to-do (Season 5's "With the French Heel Back, Can the Nehru Jacket Be Far Behind?").

However, while the typical tough guy PI had an attitude only slightly less upbeat than a prison guard during a summer heat wave, Rockford was different; he was, well, a maverick. He wasn't so much hard-boiled as he was scrambled, a guy who was as interested in tracking

> ## Preview Review
> ### September 7, 1974
>
> James Garner is private eye Jim Rockford, who also happens to be an ex-con—he spent five years in the slammer on a bum rap. Now his home base is a trailer on the beach, where he gets an occasional assist from his father. Rockford is especially interested in the cases the police haven't been able to solve. This doesn't make him terribly popular at police headquarters, but he trudges onward, smiling that amiable Garner smile, tailing suspects, being tailed by other suspects, trying to talk people out of beating him up and hoping that this week, for a change, the seductive woman who has invited him to her apartment won't pull a gun on him.

down his stolen barbecue grill (Season 4's "The Queen of Peru") as he was in catching crooks. (Not surprisingly, he made it clear he did not believe in carrying a gun because "I don't want to shoot anybody.")

This mix of gumshoe shtick and smart-ass comedy wasn't surprising, considering the show's source. The co-creators were Roy Huggins, who had previously goofed his way through the Western with Garner in the series *Maverick*, and Stephen J. Cannell, the writer who would later be responsible for such breezy (none dare call them cheesy) action shows like *The A-Team* and *The Greatest American Hero*. They both knew how to be true to familiar genres while still raising the hip quotient.

Huggins and Cannell had originally created Rockford to be a guest character on the hit (and much more standard issue) ABC detective show *Toma*. However, after the network rejected the pilot script's oddball attitude, the series finally made its way to NBC. In the beginning, Rockford was given a pretty simple motivation for his career as a detective: he'd spent five years in prison for a crime he didn't commit.

This made him a prime-time Robin Hood. That is, if Robin Hood lived in a trailer on the beach and considered the local hot-dog stand to be fine dining. In the beginning, his tendency was to take on only cases closed by the police. His reasoning? Fewer encounters with cops who would yell at him, the exception being his friend, Lt. Dennis Becker (Joe Santos). But the reality? He wanted to do the right thing for the little guy.

Sure the Philip Marlowes and Travis McGees of the world were working-class heroes too, but Rockford was, well, warm and fuzzy where they were cold and hard. For instance, Rockford was always spending time with his dad. He remained true to his friends, even the ex-con buddies (most notably Stuart Margolin's con man, Angel, and Isaac Hayes's gentle giant, Gandolf Fitch) who were always stopping by for no apparent reason except to get him in trouble. He wasn't even above doing charity work. Witness his working for the "special sucker rate" of $23.74 to help a woman looking for her missing brother in Season 2's "The Reincarnation of Angie."

Because he was the kind of detective you wouldn't mind taking home to Mom, it's no wonder he was a hit with viewers as well as his clients. *The Rockford Files* landed in the Top 20 in its debut season and was still going strong right up until the last original episode aired on January 14, 1980. That was when Garner, who'd endured one medical malady after another while making the show, decided he'd had enough. And there's no Rockford without Garner, so NBC canceled the series.

Rockford was out of the private-eye business (except for some CBS TV movies in the '90s) and I decided that I was too. Maybe it was because I'd learned, thanks in part to *The Rockford Files*, that life as a PI basically meant getting beaten up regularly while dealing with other people's problems for very little money.

TV and Film Connections
Spin-off:
Richie Brockelman, Private Eye

Then again, it may have had something to do with my changing reading habits—my friend Chris sneaked a very used copy of *Everything You Always Wanted to Know About Sex* to me—and the fact that I'd seen *WKRP in Cincinnati* and discovered Loni Anderson.

Now *there's* a sight for private eyes. Suddenly, the idea of going undercover had a much different meaning.

Cast:

James Garner *Jim Rockford*, **Noah Beery Jr.** *Joseph "Rocky" Rockford*, **Joe Santos** *Det. Dennis Becker*, **Stuart Margolin** *Evelyn "Angel" Martin*, **Gretchen Corbett** *Beth Davenport (1974–78)*, **James Luisi** *Lt. Doug Chapman (1976–80)*

Roseanne

By Mary Murphy

Broadcast History: ABC, 10/18/1988–5/20/1997
Runtime: 30 minutes
Genre: Sitcom

A budding career as a stand-up comedian who focused on everyday life as a blue-collar wife had earned her the nickname of "Domestic Goddess." When she turned that act into a TV sitcom she reigned supreme. The series averaged a 40-share during its heyday, which is hard to imagine now. It is astounding to think of the number of people addicted to the show. The humor was crude and the leading lady was like no other female star on TV. She was overweight, loud and even crass. But the poignancy of her own life and the lives of her TV family members resonated with viewers. These were people who not only understood Roseanne but in many cases looked like her. Driving to Palm Springs one day when the sitcom was in its feisty prime, I stopped into a bowling alley to grab a bite to eat and was fascinated to see that everybody there looked like Roseanne. There were grandma Roseannes, mom and pop Roseannes and baby Roseannes.

Roseanne wasn't anybody who would have been on *Dynasty* or *Dallas* and if she had, she would have been the maid or the cook or the housekeeper. And that was her appeal. More people in America felt a sense of identification with Roseanne Connor than they ever did with Alexis Carrington or Sue Ellen Ewing. Roseanne was sometimes impatient ("Go play in traffic," she famously once told one of the kids) and hardly infallible. Middle-class and lower middle-class families had somebody who could speak about the pain and sorrows and fun of their lives, not the lives of characters created by TV writers sitting around their pools.

The casting on the show was brilliant. John Goodman and Laurie Metcalf, who played her husband and sister, were magnificent actors whose characters'

Classic Episode Close-Up

"A Stash from the Past"
(Original telecast: October 5, 1993)

"A Stash from the Past" is a wise, waggish and exceedingly daring episode from a sitcom renowned for its unflinching audacity. When Roseanne finds a bag of pot in one of the kids' rooms, she's angry—and worried about how Dan is going to react. Of course, he goes ballistic, until he realizes the stuff is a 20-year-old relic of his and Roseanne's youth. Inevitably, they roll a joint for old times' sake, and before you can say "like, wow," Dan, Roseanne and her sister, Jackie, are adrift in a Cheech and Chong time warp. At first, they have fun sneaking around like they did in the '70s, hoping not to get busted by their children, but then adult realities set in like a bad trip.

love for Roseanne softened her; their devotion to Roseanne allowed audiences to forgive her rough edge. Despite the histrionics in the family there was a great deal of affection. They would take a bullet for each other, they would step in front of a bus for the kids even though they were at war with them; that paradox is what made it a great show. I think it was perhaps the first situation comedy that was brutally honest while being incredibly funny. Roseanne did not sugarcoat family life. She made no effort to put on some idealized version of parenting. Personally I felt a sense of relief that at least one TV mother wasn't perfect, but simply kept trying to do her best. I am sure women could relate to her in a much more real way than they ever could to the TV role models who came before her, like Donna Reed or Harriet Nelson. When Roseanne was in the kitchen and the kids wanted a piece of pie before dinner, she didn't give loving rebukes, she just told them the pie was radioactive and if they touched it they might die. When I look back those are the moments I remember—Roseanne and the pie that glowed in the dark.

To understand Roseanne's power you had to know that she ruled over the story lines and the writers, since the comedy came out of her life. "Everybody who wrote on that show became a better writer," says Chuck Lorre, the creator and executive producer of *Two and a Half Men*, who got his start on *Roseanne*. "It brought out the best in you or it killed you." Ultimately Roseanne's antics got in the way of the show's popularity. In Hollywood, personal lives often derail professional ones. In Roseanne's case, it became clear that you couldn't spit after singing the National Anthem and get away with it. She tried to explain she was mocking baseball players but it was too late. That was the beginning of the downward spiral. There were tantrums, divorces, charges of sexual abuse against her parents and radical plastic surgery. All of that took a toll on her popularity and eventually the ratings.

> ### Did You Know?
> The show's original title was *Life and Stuff*.

But to her credit, in an era that predated *South Park*, Roseanne took on every controversial issue of the time including abortion, premarital sex, racial prejudice and homosexuality—in a hallmark episode she faced down the worst critics of homosexuality by kissing Mariel Hemingway. I am often asked these days, "What's wrong with TV comedies?" One thing that we don't have is a woman like Roseanne, who had the unique vision of someone outside of Hollywood, who had tended calves, lived in a trailer park, and survived intense physical, mental and emotional problems to bring the truth of her life to TV. Comedy plays it too safe today, and that is the one thing we can't say about Roseanne—she never played it safe.

Cast:

Roseanne *Roseanne Conner*, **John Goodman** *Dan Conner*, **Sara Gilbert** *Darlene Conner*, **Lecy Goranson** *Becky Conner Healy (1988–93; 1995–96)*, **Sarah Chalke** *Becky Conner Healy (1993–95; 1996–97)*, **Michael Fishman** *D. J. Conner*, **Laurie Metcalf** *Jackie Harris*, **Natalie West** *Crystal Anderson Conner (1988–95)*

Rowan & Martin's Laugh-In

By Ray Stackhouse

Broadcast History: NBC, 1/22/1968–5/14/1973
Runtime: 60 minutes
Genre: Sketch comedy

Rarely has a TV show been so aptly named. *Laugh-In* got you laughin' and kept you laughin'. The musical-comedy-variety series was a mishmash of sketches, sight gags, blackouts, star cameos, one-liners and knockout punch lines. It was lightning-paced and frenzied and topical and anarchic and controversial and subversively silly and politically incorrect and irreverent and giddily goofy. And it was an immediate success.

Nightclub comics Dan Rowan and Dick Martin fared well as replacement hosts for *The Dean Martin Summer Show* in 1966. In September of 1967, an NBC pilot was so well received that the network gave the go-ahead for this new prime-time "happening." It made its debut on Monday, January 22, 1968, and, within a year, was the top-ranked show (it was No. 2 the following season).

If you wanted to take the pulse of America in the late 1960s and early '70s, this was the place to be. The political satire was smart, sharp and edgy, and no topic was off limits. There were jokes about Vietnam, Nixon, drugs, homosexuality, race, scandals. You name it and it was fair game. They even took snappy potshots at their network competition. How they got everything past the network censors was a mystery. Martin once pointed out that they had seven marijuana jokes in the pilot that the network censors overlooked—or just plain didn't get. Far out.

Not many shows spawned so many national catchphrases—"Here come da judge," "You bet your sweet bippy," "Look it up in your Funk & Wagnalls," "Verrrry interesting," "The Flying Fickle Finger of Fate," "Ring My Chimes," "Beautiful downtown Burbank" and the ever-popular "Sock it to me," which was inspired by a line in Aretha Franklin's hit song "Respect." Even 1968 presidential candidate Richard M. Nixon uttered the phrase during his cameo that year on the show. (How's this for a saying having legs? The first contestant to win $1 million on the game show *Who Wants to Be a Millionaire?* did so by providing the answer "Richard Nixon" to the question, "Who was the only president to appear on *Laugh-In?*")

The ensemble cast was a gas. In addition to glib straight man Rowan and his wifty sidekick Martin, there were cockney charmer Judy Carne, bombastic Jo Anne Worley, ditzy Goldie Hawn, chameleonic Ruth Buzzi, faux artsy Henry Gibson and protean everyman Arte Johnson, the only regular to win an

Emmy. Buzzi and Hawn were nominated twice each. When she joined the cast in 1970, Lily Tomlin made a splash with her characters Edith Ann, a tiny tot who spouted her worldly views from an oversized rocking chair and liked to punctuate her observations by blowing the audience a raspberry, and Ernestine, a pinch-faced, snorting, insultingly officious telephone operator ("One ringy dingy, two ringy dingy").

With success, inevitably, came cast turnover. During the show's five-year run, it went through more than 40 regulars, and the only members of the original cast left when it went off the air were Rowan, Martin, Buzzi and announcer Gary Owens.

Regular segments included the "Cocktail Party," during which regulars and guests would boogaloo, hobnob and banter; "Hollywood News with Ruth Buzzi"; "A Poem by Henry Gibson"; "Sock It to Me," in which Carne got "socked" any number of watery or slapsticky ways; "*Laugh-In* Looks at the News"; "Mod, Mod World"; and the show's finale, the "Joke Wall," where cast members would pop out from windows on a brightly colored, Peter Max–ish backdrop and drop bawdy bons mots or engage in ribald repartee. There were also comical interludes that featured a bikini-clad, go-go-dancing nymphet (usually Goldie Hawn) whose writhing torso would be adorned with witty sayings and messages.

> ### Did You Know?
>
> *Laugh-In*'s one-liner "Sock it to me!" was ranked #10 in TV GUIDE's list of TV's 20 Top Catchphrases.

The *Laugh-In* craze resulted in seemingly every big name clamoring to make an appearance, some several times. Among those who dropped by: the Smothers Brothers, Harry Belafonte, John Wayne (14 appearances), Sammy Davis Jr., Johnny Carson, Bob Hope, Bing Crosby, Sally Field, Diana Ross, Johnny Cash, Lena Horne and Debbie Reynolds. Even sports figures wanted to get in on the action. That roster included Joe Namath, Sugar Ray Robinson, Vida Blue, Bill Russell, Willie Shoemaker and Wilt Chamberlain. Musical acts also got into the act, as popular "Age of Aquarius" rockers like the Nitty Gritty Dirt Band, Kenny Rogers and the First Edition, the Strawberry Alarm Clock, the Bee Gees and Three Dog Night popped in, along with R&B greats the Temptations.

Rowan and Martin tried to parlay *Laugh-In* mania into a movie career with 1969's big-screen *The Maltese Bippy*, a none-too-funny spoof of thrillers that had none of the show's other big-name regulars. There was also a short-lived 1977 Saturday morning cartoon called *Baggy Pants and the Nitwits*, in which Ruth Buzzi and Arte Johnson gave voice to their series roles as handbag-wielding spinster Gladys and her nemesis, amorous codger Tyrone.

Laugh-In doesn't play especially well in reruns; the material today seems dated and the show burned out fairly quickly. But during its heyday, was it must-see TV and a cultural touchstone? You bet your sweet bippy!

Rowan & Martin's Laugh-In

Cast:

Dan Rowan *Host*, **Dick Martin** *Host*, **Gary Owens** *Announcer*, **Ruth Buzzi** *Performer*, **Eileen Brennan** *Performer (1968)*, **Roddy-Maude Roxby** *Performer (1968)*, **Charlie Brill** *Performer (1968–69)*, **Chelsea Brown** *Performer (1968–69)*, **Dave Madden** *Performer (1968–69)*, **Pigmeat Markham** *Performer (1968–69)*, **Mitzi McCall** *Performer (1968–69)*, **Dick Whittington** *Performer (1968–69)*, **Judy Carne** *Performer (1968–70)*, **Goldie Hawn** *Performer (1968–70)*, **Jo Anne Worley** *Performer (1968–70)*, **Arte Johnson** *Performer (1968–71)*, **Henry Gibson** *Performer (1968–71)*, **Larry Hovis** *Performer (1968; 1971–72)*, **Alan Sues** *Performer (1968–72)*, **Teresa Graves** *Performer (1969–70)*, **Jeremy Lloyd** *Performer (1969–70)*, **Pamela Rodgers** *Performer (1969–70)*, **Byron Gilliam** *Performer (1969–70)*, **Harvey Jason** *Performer (1970–71)*, **Nancie Phillips** *Performer (1970–71)*, **Johnny Brown** *Performer (1970–72)*, **Ann Elder** *Performer (1970–72)*, **Barbara Sharma** *Performer (1970–72)*, **Lily Tomlin** *Performer (1970–73)*, **Dennis Allen** *Performer (1970–73)*, **Richard Dawson** *Performer (1971–73)*, **Moosie Drier** *Performer (1971–73)*, **Tod Bass** *Performer (1972–73)*, **Brian Bressler** *Performer (1972–73)*, **Patti Deutsch** *Performer (1972–73)*, **Lisa Farringer** *Performer (1972–73)*, **Sarah Kennedy** *Performer (1972–73)*, **Jud Strunk** *Performer (1972–73)*, **Willie Tyler and Lester** *Performer (1972–73)*, **Donna Jean Young** *Performer (1972–73)*

Saturday Night Live

By Bruce Fretts

Broadcast History: NBC, 10/11/1975–
Runtime: 90 minutes
Genre: Sketch comedy

"I would like . . . to feed your fingertips . . . to the wolverines."

This was the first punch line in the history of *Saturday Night Live*, spoken by a professor (Michael O'Donoghue) teaching English to a European immigrant (John Belushi). While this unlikely colloquialism didn't sweep the nation, it launched a sketch-comedy franchise that transformed not just TV but the entire English language.

"But noooo!" you say. Well, we're TV GUIDE, and you're not. And we'll prove our point by summarizing the entire 30-plus-year history of *SNL* by using as many of the show's catchphrases as we can. So . . . live from New York, it's Saturday night!

After *SNL*'s October 11, 1975, debut, America began to consume mass quantities of the show's wicked humor. From the Coneheads to Roseanne Roseannadanna, it was always something. Blues brothers Belushi and Dan Aykroyd were two wild and crazy guys. (Wait, you tell us—Steve Martin and Aykroyd were actually the wild and crazy guys, and Martin was never an official cast member, just a frequent [*the* most frequent, actually] host. Well, *excuuuuse* us!)

All we know is that the original *SNL* cast was berry, berry good. Sharper than a samurai's sword. Deadlier than a killer bee. More delicious than a chee-burger, chee-burger and a Pepsi (no Coke—Pepsi!). And if you disagree with us, you're an ignorant slut.

Following a few lackluster years that we'll skip over because they didn't feature any memorable catchphrases, along came Eddie Murphy. He was Gumby, dammit—and Little Richard Simmons, Mr. Robinson and jailhouse poet Tyrone "C-I-L-L my landlord" Green.

But Murphy was far from *SNL*'s only master thespian in the '80s. We're no liars—yeah, that's the ticket. Billy Crystal was mahvelous during the '84–'85 season, which also boasted

---

TV and Film Connections

Has inspired 11 movies:

The Blues Brothers (1980)
Mr. Bill's Real Life Adventures (1986)
Wayne's World (1992)
Coneheads (1993)
Wayne's World 2 (1993)
It's Pat (1994)
Stuart Saves His Family (1995)
Blues Brothers 2000 (1998)
Night at the Roxbury (1998)
Superstar (1999)
The Ladies Man (2000)

Spin-off: *TV Funhouse*

Christopher Guest and, I must say, Ed Grimley himself—Martin Short. ("Of course I knew that," you say defensively. "What makes you think I didn't know that?")

Then along came Dana Carvey—isn't that special? He pumped us up as Hans (or was it Franz?). It wouldn't be prudent to forget his dead-on impression of the first President Bush, so we're not gonna do it. And we weren't worthy of his excellent work as Garth in the "Wayne's World" sketches with Mike Myers, who showed us it don't mean a thing if it ain't got that "Schwing!"

> ### Did You Know?
>
> Gilda Radner was once married to former *SNL* bandleader G. E. Smith.

Just thinking about all the great characters Myers created—from "Sprockets" host Dieter to "Coffee Talk" hostess Linda Richman—gets us a little *verklempt*, so talk amongst yourselves. (What's that, you say—don't we think the late, great Phil Hartman was *SNL*'s most versatile talent ever? Yes! You are correct, sir!)

During the mid-'90s, many critics wanted to say "Buh-bye" to *SNL*'s frat-boy humor. They wished Chris Farley really did live in a van down by the river. They greeted David Spade with a haughty " . . . and you are?" And nobody sang the praises of Adam Sandler's Opera Man.

Instead of going into a shame spiral, *SNL* decided it was good enough, it was smart enough, and doggone it, people liked it. It hired new female superstars like Molly Shannon, Ana Gasteyer and Cheri Oteri, and critics started to simmah down now. No one could resist the delicious dish of guest host Alec Baldwin's Schweddy Balls. Everybody cheered for Will Ferrell's impression of the second President Bush (a masterstroke of "strategery"), and there's no word to describe the perfection of his James Lipton spoofs, so we're forced to make one up: scrumtrilescent.

Top 3 Moments

- Never jumped.
- When the Not Ready for Prime Time Players departed.
- When Norm MacDonald got canned.

For more, visit www.jumptheshark.com.

We don't mean to be a Debbie Downer, but in the past few seasons, *SNL* hasn't specialized in catchphrases. So we'll just say good night, and have a pleasant tomorrow. And in the immortal words of Emily Litella, never mind.

Cast:

Chevy Chase *(1975–76)*, **John Belushi** *(1975–79)*, **Dan Aykroyd** *(1975–79)*, **Gilda Radner** *(1975–80)*, **Garrett Morris** *(1975–80)*, **Jane Curtin** *(1975–80)*, **Larraine Newman** *(1975–80)*, **Bill Murray** *(1977–80)*, **Albert Brooks** *(1975–76)*, **Gary Weis** *(1976–77)*, **Don Novello** *(1978–80; 1985–86)*, **Paul Shaffer** *(1978–80)*, **Al Franken** *(1979–80; 1988–95)*, **Tom Davis** *(1979–80; 1988–95)*, **Denny Dillon** *(1980–81)*, **Gilbert Gottfried** *(1980–81)*, **Gail Matthius** *(1980–81)*, **Joe Piscopo** *(1980–84)*,

Ann Risley *(1980–81)*, Charles Rocket *(1980–81)*, Eddie Murphy *(1981–84)*, Robin Duke *(1981–84)*, Tim Kazurinsky *(1981–84)*, Tony Rosato *(1981–82)*, Christine Ebersole *(1981–82)*, Brian Doyle-Murray *(1981–82)*, Mary Gross *(1981–85)*, Brad Hall *(1981–84)*, Gary Kroeger *(1982–85)*, Julia Louis-Dreyfus *(1982–85)*, Jim Belushi *(1983–85)*, Billy Crystal *(1984–85)*, Christopher Guest *(1984–85)*, Harry Shearer *(1984–85)*, Rich Hall *(1984–85)*, Martin Short *(1984–85)*, Pamela Stephenson *(1984–85)*, Anthony Michael Hall *(1985–86)*, Randy Quaid *(1985–86)*, Joan Cusack *(1985–86)*, Robert Downey Jr. *(1985–86)*, Nora Dunn *(1985–90)*, Terry Sweeney *(1985–86)*, Jon Lovitz *(1985–90)*, Damon Wayans *(1985–86)*, Danitra Vance *(1985–86)*, Dennis Miller *(1985–90)*, Dana Carvey *(1986–93)*, Phil Hartman *(1986–94)*, Jan Hooks *(1986–91)*, Victoria Jackson *(1986–92)*, A. Whitney Brown *(1986–91)*, Kevin Nealon *(1986–91; 1993–95)*, Mike Myers *(1989–95)*, Chris Farley *(1990–95)*, Chris Rock *(1990–93)*, Julia Sweeney *(1990–94)*, Ellen Cleghorne *(1991–95)*, Siobhan Fallon *(1991–93)*, Tim Meadows *(1991–2000)*, Adam Sandler *(1991–95)*, David Spade *(1991–96)*, Rob Schneider *(1991–94)*, Melanie Hutsell *(1991–94)*, Beth Cahill *(1991–93)*, Sarah Silverman *(1993–94)*, Norm MacDonald *(1993–98)*, Jay Mohr *(1993–95)*, Michael McKean *(1994–95)*, Chris Elliott *(1994–95)*, Janeane Garofalo *(1994–95)*, Mark McKinney *(1995–97)*, Laura Kightlinger *(1994–95)*, Molly Shannon *(1995–2001)*, Morwenna Banks *(1994–95)*, Jim Breuer *(1995–98)*, Will Ferrell *(1995–2002)*, Darrell Hammond *(1995–)*, David Koechner *(1995–96)*, Cheri Oteri *(1995–2000)*, Nancy Walls *(1995–96)*, Ana Gasteyer *(1996–2002)*, Chris Kattan *(1996–2003)*, Colin Quinn *(1995–2000)*, Chris Parnell *(1998–2001; 2002–06)*, Horatio Sanz *(1998–2006)*, Jimmy Fallon *(1998–2004)*, Rachel Dratch *(1999–2006)*, Tina Fey *(2000–06)*, Jerry Minor *(2000–01)*, Maya Rudolph *(2000–)*, Dean Edwards *(2001–03)*, Seth Meyers *(2001–)*, Amy Poehler *(2001–)*, Jeff Richards *(2001–04)*, Fred Armisen *(2002–)*, Will Forte *(2002–)*, Finesse Mitchell *(2003–06)*, Kenan Thompson *(2003–)*, Jason Sudeikis *(2005–)*, Andy Samberg *(2005–)*, Bill Hader *(2005–)*, Kristen Wiig *(2005–)*, Rob Riggle *(2004–05)*, The Saturday Night Live Band, Don Pardo *Announcer (1975–81; 1982–)*, Mel Brandt *Announcer (1981–82)*

Scrubs

By Nathaniel Hayes

Broadcast History: NBC, 10/2/2001–
Runtime: 30 minutes
Genre: Sitcom

February 15, 2005: *Cheers* **writer Charles** James (named after real-life creators Glen and Les Charles, and James Burrows) checks in at Sacred Heart hospital. When doctor and TV fanatic John "J. D." Dorian (Zach Braff) realizes his patient's identity he recommends a "surgical consult," in which he and colleague Turk (Donald Faison) fawn over him, making *Cheers* allusions and reciting catchphrases ("Nooooorrm!"). Unfortunately, sobering news spoils their fun: Mr. James has cancer. To escape the bleak situation, J. D. daydreams (as he is wont to do) about what life would be like if it resembled a sitcom.

Flash to fantasy sequence. The setting and tone mockingly imitate cheesy TV comedies, complete with bright, cheerful lighting, inappropriate outfits (nurses' shirts are cut too low, their skirts too high) and contrived plot lines (the staff performs in a talent show to raise money for a cafeteria worker). The acting is hammy (after J. D. cracks a corny one-liner he gives the audience a wide, dopey grin that would make *Three's Company*'s Mr. Roper proud) and the humor is groaningly insipid. Says James, when told he is dying: "Well, the good news is I won't have to eat my wife's cooking anymore!" Like that.

The studio audience, of course, finds it hilarious because it's coached to do so. I laugh because, like Turk and J. D., I grew up watching odious laugh-track sitcoms like *Night Court* and *Married . . . With Children* and remember how lame their jokes were.

Thankfully, *Scrubs* is nothing like this.

When the series debuted in 2001, there were a diminishing number of genuinely clever comedies. Reality shows seemed to be (then as now) flooding TV lineups and putting sitcoms on life support. From its inception, this series deftly combined the silly and the sophisticated. Though hardly a smash popular hit (it finished 34th in the Nielsen ratings its first year), it succeeded—at least creatively—from the start because of its unique style and tone. Unlike J. D.'s daydream, the lighting is subdued and more fitting of a hospital, jokes aren't artificially sweetened by a laugh track, and filming is done by a more personal, single-camera setup. (Ironically, J. D.'s sitcom-fantasy episode, titled "My Life in Four Cameras," earned *Scrubs* its only Emmy to date. The category: Outstanding Multi-Camera Picture Editing for a Series.)

Scrubs doesn't eschew *all* sitcom staples. The staff often sports outrageous outfits, like the sleeveless shirts (and occasional thongs) worn by high-five fan The Todd (Robert Maschio), a macho, sexually depraved surgeon; the acting is often exaggerated, such as the rants of Dr. Cox (John C. McGinley), who sarcastically e-nun-ci-ates ev-er-y syl-la-ble in his sardonic diatribes; and the humor is consistently, well, goofy. But these elements are deliberately and intelligently crafted with the intention of creating a loony, over-the-top surrealism usually reserved for cartoons. Indeed, the doctors and staff at Sacred Heart are the most absurdly preposterous characters on prime time this side of *The Simpsons*, *South Park* and *Family Guy*.

It's hard for me to pick a staff favorite, though J. D. is the obvious choice since he's regularly the center of attention. His nerdy, eager-to-please personality makes him a loyal friend—and an easy target. His mentor, Dr. Cox, described by a visiting psychologist as a "textbook closed-off Alpha male," takes pleasure in emasculating his protégé by calling him women's names, including Loretta, Nancy, Britney, Fantasia and Dorothy (appropriately used in the *Wizard of Oz*–themed 100th episode). J. D. is typically hurt ("Frankly, each time you call me a girl's name, I die a little inside") but remains joyfully undaunted in his attempts to impress.

While J. D. respects Dr. Cox, he fears the Janitor (Neil Flynn), an attention-starved custodian who wastes time working on wildly inane projects (he once built a life-size sandcastle in the parking lot) and tormenting the staff (he put wheels on a napping surgeon's shoes). A single, menacing look from the Janitor (cue sinister music) can put J. D. on edge for the rest of the day. Luckily, J. D. gets by with a little help from his friends. Turk, his best bud since college, has a confident surgeon's swagger, though he also shares his pal's childish affection for playing games (they love hide-and-seek), flamboyant nicknames (J. D. is Gizmo, Turk is Brown Bear), and spur-of-the-moment singing and dancing. Only two things keep me from labeling the inseparable duo as ambiguously gay: 1) Turk has a wife, Carla (Judy Reyes), a sweet yet feisty nurse who knows more about the patients than the doctors do, and 2) J. D. has an inexplicable ability to hook up with hot chicks despite his dorkiness.

Preview Review
September 15, 2001

As callow medical intern J. D. Dorian starts his first 36-hour shift, he boasts, "I'm the man." By the time it's over, he knows better. The nurses treat him like an obstacle, the doctors like an idiot, and his fellow scrubs, the alluring barracuda Elliot and the strutting "Turk," are looking out for No.1. Heaven help the patients.

We Say: If you like dark comedy seasoned with terror, irreverence and even a little pathos, the fast-paced *Scrubs* just might be the perfect tonic. The young cast is appealing, but John C. McGinley (*Platoon*) steals the show as a mercurial doctor who deep down actually gives a damn. So will you.

Scrubs

Among his former flames is Elliot (Sarah Chalke), or, as Dr. Cox calls her, Bambi, a quirky, neurotic blonde who looks ditzy but is remarkably bright. Sure, she's a doctor, but at Sacred Heart intelligence is not necessarily a given, no matter what the profession. Doug (Johnny Kastl) is a daft doc who has a penchant for losing patients and corpses, and Ted (Sam Lloyd), the hospital's lawyer, is a jittery, depressed doormat who once lost an intelligence contest to a dog. The cranky Dr. Kelso (Ken Jenkins), chief of medicine and Ted's chief adversary, is much smarter, though he's driven more by profit than by helping patients.

The element that bonds—and humanizes—this motley ensemble is their high-pressure, emotionally draining work. Though the humor veers between slapstick and the sublimely weird, *Scrubs* works precisely because—much like *M*A*S*H* decades earlier—the mood can change in a heartbeat. Death is common ("Each and every one of you is going to kill a patient," Dr. Cox ominously warns interns during a "pep talk"), and life, even in good times, always revolves around a place awash in sickness and suffering. When

> ### Did You Know?
>
> *Scrubs* is filmed on location at the North Hollywood Medical Center, a real decommissioned hospital in Sherman Oaks, California.

Elliot has to choose between caring for a patient and spending time with her boyfriend, Dr. Cox reminds her dourly, "The hospital comes first. Always. Forever and ever." Episodes typically descend into moments of beautiful sadness (most poignantly portrayed at the end of "My Lunch," when an inconsolable Dr. Cox breaks down after losing three patients); but they regularly end on a high note, with J. D. delivering a sugary, philosophical message. On occasion it's sappy, but most times it's remarkably uplifting.

As is the final act of "My Life in Four Cameras." Mr. James' flat-lining heart monitor jolts the daydreaming J. D. back to reality. Sadly, he's unable to save him. "Around here nice people don't always get better," he says in a voiceover as the scene jump-cuts from the emergency room to his living room. "And at times like that, it's comforting to know there's always one thing that can pick your spirits up." The ode-to-TV episode closes with a cheerful image of Carla, Turk and J. D. laughing in front of the television. They must be watching *Scrubs*.

Cast:

Zach Braff *John "J. D." Dorian*, **Donald Faison** *Chris Turk*, **Sarah Chalke** *Elliot Reid*, **Ken Jenkins** *Dr. Bob Kelso*, **John C. McGinley** *Dr. Phil Cox*, **Judy Reyes** *Carla Espinosa*, **Neil Flynn** *Janitor*

Seinfeld

By Todd Wakai

Broadcast History: NBC, 5/31/1990–5/14/1998
Runtime: 30 minutes
Genre: Sitcom

It's a show famously about "nothing." The network brass had so little faith in it that they picked it up for just three episodes . . . yada, yada, yada. Somehow it ended up, in a 2002 TV GUIDE article, ranking No. 1 among the Greatest Shows of All Time (*I Love Lucy* and *The Honeymooners* finished second and third, respectively).

Talk about your Festivus miracles!

"Nothing" best describes what went through my mind in 1989 when I first heard that stand-up comedian Jerry Seinfeld was getting his own series. It was trendy then for comics to get their own shows and I figured *Seinfeld* (or *The Seinfeld Chronicles*, as it was originally titled) was just more of the same. Bill Cosby and Roseanne Barr had already taken their acts and parlayed them into sitcom success. Seinfeld's shtick, which is based largely on daily observations, actually seemed harder to convert into ratings gold.

The concept is simple: Seinfeld, playing himself, goes about his everyday life in New York City with pal George Costanza (Jason Alexander), ex-girlfriend Elaine Benes (Julia Louis-Dreyfus) and across-the-hall neighbor Cosmo Kramer (Michael Richards). The essence of the show, according to co-creators Seinfeld and pal Larry David (who's the inspiration for George), is that it's about "nothing." Truth be told, the pilot was nothing special, and the series floundered early on. But in 1991, powered by episodes in which Jerry makes an unfortunate pony remark; Jerry, Elaine and George have a long wait in a Chinese restaurant; and the gang gets lost in a parking garage, *Seinfeld* started to generate some buzz.

In 1992, NBC moved *Seinfeld* to its powerful Thursday Must-See TV lineup and the show went on to produce six more seasons of classic comedy filled with nutty catchphrases and plots that were beyond bizarre. Long before product placement became so prevalent (and obvious) on TV, *Seinfeld* had entire episodes centered on a Pez dispenser, a Junior Mint and a Titleist golf ball.

> **Did You Know?**
>
> Steve Buscemi auditioned for the role of George Costanza.

Along the way we met hilarious peripheral characters like Newman, Frank Costanza, David Puddy, J. Peterman, Jackie Chiles—not to mention a memorable one-shot by a certain Soup Nazi.

There has never been a more pure situation comedy. It wasn't about a family or co-workers. It wasn't set in a police precinct, radio station or bar. It just took funny characters and placed them in situations that we can all relate to. As long as man walks this earth, he'll roam a parking garage looking for his car, struggle with post-swimming "shrinkage," contend with close talkers, try to maintain mastery of his domain (good luck) and contemplate the ultimate question: Are they real? (Of course, we've learned that when in doubt, assume that they are, "and they're spectacular!")

What made *Seinfeld* so great was that the humor was smart and its writers didn't care so much whether the entire audience understood a joke . . . what was more important was that those who *did* get the joke thought it was funny.

A case in point came in an episode from Season 7 titled "The Caddy." George's employer, the New York Yankees, mistakenly thinks that he has died and Yankees owner "George Steinbrenner" (whose face we never see and who was voiced by Larry David) shows up at the Costanza household to break the bad news to George's parents. After hearing from Steinbrenner that his son has passed, Frank gathers himself . . . and then blurts out: "What the hell did you trade Jay Buhner for?!" Steinbrenner's quick, defensive response: "My baseball people loved Ken Phelps' bat. They kept saying 'Ken Phelps, Ken Phelps.'"

Jay Buhner went on to be a rock-solid player for the Seattle Mariners, but hardly a household name. To be kind, let's just say that Ken Phelps's career was slightly less successful—and his name even more

> ## Classic Episode Close-Up
> ### "The Outing"
> *(Original telecast: February 11, 1993)*
>
> Elaine's practical joke was the foundation for this unforgettably funny episode. Aware that a woman in the next booth is eavesdropping on her restaurant conversation with George and Jerry, Elaine pretends the guys are gay, unaware that the woman (Paula Marshall) is a college reporter about to interview Jerry. Later, Jerry and George bicker "like an old married couple" in the writer's presence, fueling her mistaken impression. They vehemently deny they are homosexuals, while neurotically adding, "not that there's anything wrong with that." That phrase is uttered a total of eight times . . . and maybe a few million times since by those who've enjoyed the results of this wonderful Larry Charles script.

obscure. But those viewers who were baseball fans loved Frank ripping into Steinbrenner about this boneheaded Yankee trade—even if the timing was less than appropriate.

During its run *Seinfeld* was more than just watercooler fodder—it could also be a topic of conversation at parties (don't "double-dip" that chip!) or at the in-laws' ("Serenity now!") or even in the restroom ("I can't spare a square."). It's been nearly a decade since the series finale was broadcast in 1998, but *Seinfeld* continues to air constantly in syndication and on basic cable. The tiresome complaint about TV that there are "500 channels and nothing to watch" can't be true when a *Seinfeld* repeat is normally just a click away.

Today, so many elements of *Seinfeld* have become a part of our everyday lives. Think about how many times who've heard someone say, "Giddy-up!" "No soup for you!" or even "Maybe the dingo ate your baby." Have you ever accused someone of "regifting"? For goodness sake, there are now kids in this world named Seven (let's hope that there aren't any girls named Mulva).

In reality, *Seinfeld* wasn't a show about nothing. It was a show about *anything*. And I'm amazed at how many times I think of a *Seinfeld* reference when going about my day:

Every time I eat muffin tops, nonfat yogurt, a big salad or babka (preferably cinnamon), I think of *Seinfeld*.

Every time I lick an envelope, I think of *Seinfeld*.

Every time I read the sign at the bookstore that says books can't be taken into the restroom, I think of *Seinfeld*.

Every time I see footage of the Zapruder film I think of Keith Hernandez . . . and *Seinfeld*.

Every time I see a face painter, an orchestra conductor, a cigar-store Indian, a woman with "man hands," or a man in need of "an upper-body support undergarment," I think of *Seinfeld*.

Heck, every time I see a Fall Preview issue of TV GUIDE, I think of *Seinfeld*.

Not that there's anything wrong with that.

Cast:

Jerry Seinfeld *Jerry Seinfeld*, **Jason Alexander** *George Costanza*, **Julia Louis-Dreyfus** *Elaine Benes*, **Michael Richards** *Cosmo Kramer*

Sesame Street

By Raven Snook

Broadcast History: NET, 1969; PBS, 1969–
Runtime: 60 minutes
Genre: Children's educational

For those of us who were brought up on Sesame Street—and that's pretty much everyone born post-LBJ—the series' colorful human and Muppet characters are part of our extended family. The longest-running children's show in the United States and a well-known franchise worldwide, *Sesame Street* still feels as culturally relevant as it did back in 1969 when puppet pioneer Jim Henson teamed up with the Children's Television Workshop (later rechristened Sesame Workshop) to create this groundbreaking edutainment series. It's no surprise that through the years seemingly every big name has dropped by, ranging from First Ladies Barbara Bush, Hillary Rodham Clinton and Laura Bush to activists Ralph Nader and Rev. Jesse Jackson to entertainment heavyweights such as Harry Belafonte, Carol Burnett, Jim Carrey, Johnny Cash, Bill Cosby, Ellen DeGeneres, Robert De Niro, Destiny's Child, Burt Lancaster, Spike Lee, Natalie Portman, Ben Stiller, R.E.M. (singing "Furry Happy Monsters"), Robin Williams and Stevie Wonder. Who *wouldn't* want to visit? *Sesame Street* is, in a word, cool. Set in a multicultural—and "multi-creatural"—urban community, *Sesame Street* has always embraced progressive social politics, encouraging tolerance and appreciation for different kinds of people along with teaching the basic 1-2-3s and A-B-Cs. The main human characters have included a black couple, Gordon and Susan (Roscoe Orman, Loretta Long) and their son, Miles (Olamide Faison);

> **Did You Know?**
>
> James Earl Jones was the first celebrity to appear on *Sesame Street.*

Maria and Luis (Sonia Manzano, Emilio Delgado), a Latino couple, and their daughter, Gabi (Desiree Casado); Bob (Bob McGrath), whose former girlfriend Linda (Linda Bove) was deaf; the befuddled Noodle brothers (mime Bill Irwin and the late Michael Jeter); and Alan (Alan Muraoka), the Asian proprietor of the corner store, formerly run by the senior citizen Mr. Hooper (Will Lee), whose death was addressed in a groundbreaking 1983 episode. But the beloved Muppet characters are even more important to the success of the series, including perpetual 3-year-old Elmo (voiced by Kevin Clash); the slightly neurotic Grover (performed by Eric Jacobson but originally played by director Frank Oz); Mexican immigrant Rosita (performed by Carmen Osbahr); fairy-in-training Abby Cadabby (performed by Leslie Carrara-Rudolph); mismatched roommates Bert and Ernie (performed by Eric Jacobson and Steve Whitmire, respectively); the elephant-like Snuffleupagus (performed by Martin Robinson); and the overgrown but childlike Big Bird and trash-can grump Oscar the Grouch (both performed by Caroll Spinney).

Sesame Street has changed quite a bit over the years, even if the Muppets have not. In the '70s, the episodes were mosaics made up of zany vignettes and catchy songs thrown together in haphazard fashion. While today the show remains giddily clever and continues to offer material that will also entertain parents and caregivers ("Survivor: Musical Chairs," "Grouch Eye for the Nice Guy," *The Sopranos*' James Gandolfini cowering in fear of the dark, a Kiefer Sutherland Muppet in a *24* spoof, "The Man of La Muncha," Harvey Fierstein singing "Everything's Coming Up Noses"), its segments are longer and come on schedule: after a few street scenes, Big Bird takes a "Journey to Ernie," 20 minutes later it's time for "Elmo's World," and in between Rosita delivers the "Spanish Word of the Day" and the Count reveals the "Number of the Day" (and while this may seem boring to us old fogies, its familiarity makes children feel secure). Modern technology has also been incorporated: Elmo reads e-mail and CGI effects are used throughout the show.

The series' impact on pop culture has been understandably huge. The irreverent Broadway tuner *Avenue Q*, which won the 2004 Tony Award for Best Musical, is a satirical take on the PBS staple, and comedian Dave Chappelle did a *Sesame Street*esque sketch about the decidedly adult subjects of venereal disease and drugs on his eponymous Comedy Central show. The show's pioneering use of other languages, particularly Spanish, is now par for the course on newer kids' shows like *Dora the Explorer*. *Sesame Street* has also spawned a number of international incarnations, tailored to the needs and issues of each region (the South African version has an HIV-positive Muppet).

TV and Film Connections
Spin-off:
Hey Arnold!
Play with Me Sesame

As a journalist, I can talk about *Sesame Street*'s stats—109 Daytime Emmy Awards, 74 million "graduates" and versions in 120 countries as of 2006—until I'm as blue in the face as Cookie Monster. But that alone won't communicate what makes the show so special. I can't encapsulate 37 years (and counting) of such an iconic and interactive series without explaining the impact it's had on my life, because in the end, *Sesame Street* entered our communal consciousness because of its profound personal influence on us all.

I'm a thirtysomething woman raised on *Sesame Street* who is now watching the show with my own young daughter. When I turn on *Sesame Street* for her, I can't help but smile. I don't feel like a kid again—I feel more akin to Bob and Maria and the other adults than Elmo and his preschool pals. Yet the minute the unmistakable theme song starts, "Sunny day, chasing the clouds away," my insides become as warm and fuzzy as Grover's fur. The folks on Sesame

Street were my first friends and my first teachers. I remember how giddy I was when I was able to identify the number or letter of the day; how frustrated I was when Big Bird's buddies dismissed Snuffleupagus as his imaginary friend (thank god everyone can see him now); and how sad I was whenever the credits started to roll.

I rarely watched the show between 1979 and 2004, although I did catch the episode in which Big Bird came to terms with Mr. Hooper's death with a little help from the community. I still recall the sorrow in his voice when he asked, "Who's going to make my birdseed milk shakes and tell me stories?" Even though I was on the cusp of being a teenager, I broke down in sobs. Big Bird's realization brought the permanence of death home for me in a way that I had never experienced before. Mr. Hooper had been my friend, too. Now I'd never see him again.

I felt that same overwhelming sense of loss when Jim Henson died in 1990. I was in college at the time and my teary-eyed classmates and I kept asking each other, "What's going to happen to the show? Who's going to voice Ernie and Kermit the Frog now?" We were convinced that we had lost our childhood companions. But we had nothing to worry about. It's a testament to Henson's genius that *Sesame Street* was able to continue—and thrive—without him, although he remained in spirit and vision (if not in voice; Ernie and Kermit never quite sounded the same). Humans can come and go (indeed, a lot of the actors and puppeteers have changed over the years), but the Muppets never die. They stay young and curious and cute, able to enchant and instruct generation after generation. And my family and I are part of that cycle. Watching my daughter fall under *Sesame Street*'s spell is magical for me. She's meeting Mommy's oldest friends.

Cast:

Bob McGrath *Bob*, **Loretta Long** *Susan*, **Will Lee** *Mr. Hooper (1969–82)*, **Matt Robinson** *Gordon (1969–72)*, **Hal Miller** *Gordon (1972–74)*, **Roscoe Orman** *Gordon (1974–)*, **Carroll Spinney** *Performer: Big Bird/Oscar the Grouch*, **Jim Henson** *Performer: Kermit the Frog/Ernie (1969–90)*, **Frank Oz** *Performer: Bert/Grover/Cookie Monster (1969–2001)*, **Jerry Nelson** *Performer: Count von Count (1970–)*, **Fran Brill** *Performer: Prairie Dawn (1970–)*, **Emilio Delgado** *Luis (1971–)*, **Sonia Manzano** *Maria (1971–)*, **Northern Calloway** *David (1971–89)*, **Linda Bove** *Linda (1974–2003)*, **Alaina Reed Hall** *Olivia (1976–88)*, **Richard Hunt** *Performer: Elmo (1984–85)*, **Kevin Clash** *Performer: Elmo (1985–)*, **Alison Bartlett** *Gina (1987–)*, **Desiree Casado** *Gabriela (1989–)*, **Steve Whitmire** *Performer: Ernie/Kermit the Frog (1990–)*, **Carmen Osbahr** *Performer: Rosita (1991–)*, **David Langston Smyrl** *Mr. Handford (1992–98)*, **Imani Patterson** *Miles (1992–2002)*, **Ruth Buzzi** *Ruthie (1993–99)*, **Eric Jacobson** *Performer: Bert/Grover (2001–)*, **David Rudman** *Performer: Cookie Monster (2001–)*

Sex and the City

By Sabrina Rojas Weiss

Broadcast History: HBO, 1/6/1998–2/22/2004
Runtime: 30 minutes
Genre: Sitcom

The Manolos, the Cosmopolitans, the über-trendy nightclubs, the outrageous designer get-ups created by stylist Patricia Fields. There are so many superficial trappings one associates with *Sex and the City*'s legacy. And while one can't deny their fabulous impact, that's not even half the story of why, years after the show ended its six-season run on HBO, I can hardly go a day without hearing it referenced. And something tells me that's not just because I'm female and living in the titular city.

Carrie Bradshaw, Miranda Hobbes, Charlotte York and Samantha Jones were gorgeous, three-dimensional characters Darren Star miraculously adapted from the shallow sketches in Candace Bushnell's book of the same name. Carrie (Sarah Jessica Parker), clearly based on Bushnell, wrote a weekly sex column for a local paper, had a dangerous fashion addiction and wanted the kind of true love that wouldn't ask her to compromise her lifestyle. Miranda (Cynthia Nixon) was the fiercely independent lawyer who absolutely did not need a man, but she kind of would have liked to have one around. Though Charlotte (Kristin Davis) ran her own art gallery, she came from a very traditional, WASP-y upbringing and would have given anything for a husband and kids. Her polar opposite was Samantha (Kim Cattrall), a high-powered PR exec who shunned the very idea of a relationship and used men (many of them) only for sex. In the wrong hands, their stories could have been crass, trite and silly. Instead, it was quirky, smart and honest.

Some saw the four friends as realistic portraits of themselves or women they knew; others (like me) looked to them as fantasies, role models and cautionary tales all in one. As much as we knew we wanted to be glamorous professionals with our own Manhattan apartments, our own credit cards and our own terms for our relationships with men, there was clearly a price to pay for such independence. As Carrie dated Mr. Big (Chris Noth), a suave real-estate mogul, we saw her struggle to remain her own person in the face of his wealth and macho attitude. When Miranda fell in love with humble bartender Steve (Dave Eigenberg), she didn't know how to present him and his corduroy suit to her

> ### Did You Know?
>
> Instead of using the "555" telephone numbers as other TV shows do, the producers purchased two real phone numbers and used them repeatedly throughout the series' run.

stuffy colleagues. After Charlotte found that her perfect doctor husband came attached to a snooty, disapproving mother, she also discovered she couldn't conceive her perfect children. And Samantha was constantly finding no-escape clauses in her no-strings-attached policies. The plots were cleverly anchored with the broad questions Carrie asked in her column: "Why are there so many great, unmarried women and no great, unmarried men?" "Are threesomes the new sexual frontier?" "Are New Yorkers evolving past relationships?"

Then there were the dates and encounters that might sound hilariously fictional, but are sadly close to the real deal in today's dating world: the fetishists, the callous men, the bad lovers, the egotists, the ones with weird hang-ups, the damaged goods, the cheaters. The best part about these losers was the conversations the ladies had about them over brunch. And now I can't believe the fourth paragraph of this essay is the first time I mention the thing that really set this series apart from any other single-gal comedy before it: the shockingly frank sex talk. I'm hard-pressed to think of a sex act that wasn't discussed by Carrie and Co. over eggs or cocktails. At times, it was downright educational. It's the first time I remember seeing women speak so freely about sex on TV, where it previously seemed like only men were supposed to get raunchy. That's the beauty of HBO. (Though, amazingly, the syndicated version of the show that's now airing on TBS has managed to keep the bulk of the essential topics, with just a few words and images changed for the sake of the censors.)

Like most single young women in big cities, Carrie and her friends were far from their real families, so they relied on each other for every kind of support, not just for chats the mornings after bad dates. When Carrie was in financial straights after breaking off with her fiancé, Aiden (John Corbett), Charlotte gave Carrie her engagement ring to help her out. Samantha finally leaned on her friends when she was diagnosed with breast cancer. Miranda counted on them when she decided to be a single mother. I suppose that's why we rarely watched the show alone. It was often a social occasion on Sunday nights, complete with drinks and post-show analysis. (OK, I also didn't have HBO.) It was always an interactive event, as we hurled criticisms at the screen: Carrie should have stayed with sweet, down-to-earth Aiden! How does Smith stand being treated like that by Samantha? Who thought Mikhail Baryshnikov was a good casting choice? What in the hell is Carrie wearing this time?

Now that the series is over, every season a new show claims to be the next *Sex and the City*. But I'm not sure we're clamoring for that anymore. We still derive inspiration from the tales of Carrie, Samantha, Miranda and Charlotte, but we've got our own stories to share over Cosmos.

Cast:

Sarah Jessica Parker *Carrie Bradshaw*, **Kristin Davis** *Charlotte York*, **Cynthia Nixon** *Miranda Hobbes*, **Kim Cattrall** *Samantha Jones*, **Chris Noth** *Big*, **David Eigenberg** *Steve Brady (1999–2004)*, **Kyle MacLachlan** *Dr. Trey McDougal (2000–02)*, **John Corbett** *Aiden Shaw (2000–03)*, **James Remar** *Richard Wright (2001–03)*, **Evan Handler** *Harry Golden-blatt (2002–04)*, **Mikhail Baryshnikov** *Alexsandr Petrovsky (2003–04)*, **Jason Lewis** *Smith Jerrod (2003–04)*

The Shield

By Nathaniel Hayes

Broadcast History: FX, 3/12/2002–
Runtime: 60 minutes
Genre: Crime drama

Vic Mackey (Michael Chiklis) could hardly be mistaken for your typical detective. He says so himself as he tries to get a pedophilic kidnapping suspect to talk. "Good cop and bad cop left for the day," he explains ominously, moments after placing a lighter, a phone book, a box cutter and a bottle of whiskey onto the interrogation room table. "I'm a different kind of cop." A gruesome torture scene seems inevitable, but the suspect, who wisely confesses after getting smacked in the head with the phone book, gets off easy—relatively speaking, of course. At the end of the debut episode, the pugnacious, pate-shaven detective again demonstrates just how "different" he is by firing a bullet into the face of fellow officer—and snitch—Terry Crowley (Reed Diamond). Mackey's motive: to keep himself and his crew out of prison.

Welcome to *The Shield*. Viewer discretion is definitely advised.

FX's fiercely graphic series about an experimental police division is loaded with dirty cops, sleazy politicians, prostitutes, pimps, drug dealers, gangbangers, child molesters, rapists and killers. It ranks as one of the most violent, sexually explicit, foul-mouthed series in the history of basic cable. But it also happens to be one of television's boldest, most riveting dramas, fueled by bullet-paced directing; gritty, *Cops*-style cinematography; sharp writing; and explosive performances.

The Shield is set in fictitious Farmington, a crime-infested Southern California neighborhood nicknamed the Farm. Most of the division's officers, who work in a converted church called "the Barn," are respectable cops who sincerely want to improve the community—though they're not without their flaws. David Aceveda (Benito Martinez), the division's first captain and eventual city councilman, is often guided by career ambitions. Holland "Dutch" Wagenbach (Jay Karnes), an intelligent though socially inept detective, is sometimes more concerned with his "wins" (number of closed cases) than with the people he's helping. Julien Lowe (Michael Jace), a deeply religious though tragically misguided gay officer, struggles to accept his homosexuality. The two most honorable characters are women, Danielle "Danny" Sofer (Catherine Dent), an attractive officer whose tough-chick attitude earns respect in the mostly male workplace, and Claudette Wyms (the Emmy-nominated CCH Pounder), a crafty, straight-shooting detective with an impeccable sense of morality.

In stark contrast to their co-workers (especially the ladies) are the corrupt, testosterone-charged members of the Strike Team, the division's anti-gang unit. Shane Vendrell (Walton Goggins) is a reckless, racist redneck; Curtis "Lemonhead" Lemansky (Kenneth Johnson) is a fiercely loyal, spiky-blond-haired brute; and Ronnie Gardocki (David Rees Snell) is a low-key tech wiz skilled at surveillance. Mackey is the manipulative, hot-headed leader of the team, which regularly crosses legal and ethical lines in the pursuit of their par-ticular brand of "justice." They plant and steal evidence, use excessive force to question and subdue suspects, invade homes without warrants, and encourage vigilantism. Some of their transgressions are justified (in their eyes, at least) by a Machiavellian ends-justify-the-means rationalization. Invading a home illegally is OK, for example, if it leads to the recovery of a kidnap victim. But their more vicious actions lack any morality whatsoever. In addition to killing Crowley, the members singularly or collectively kidnapped a basketball star, conspired with drug dealers, locked rival rappers in a steel container until they worked out their differences (only one survived), blackmailed a fellow officer, stole millions from a money-laundering ring, and, most disturbing of all, killed a member of their own team with a grenade.

The Strike Team's aggressive and highly effective tactics electrify the series, but *The Shield* is more than a high-speed, shoot-'em-up urban street adven-ture. It's a multilayered drama that draws you in with rich, character-driven story lines. The complex and volcanic Mackey struggles to provide for his three children, two of whom are autistic. The divorced Dutch desperately wants a woman to fill the void in his lonely life. Aceveda deals with physical and emo-tional impotence after getting sexually assaulted. Julien hides his homosexu-ality from his co-workers and wife. Shane, himself just an overgrown child, has a young wife and newborn. Wyms has lupus. The peripheral, out-of-uniform stories humanize the officers, who win sympathy (deserved or not) through their everyday struggles.

At times, the series is also a semi-cerebral detective thriller. Much like in real life, the most obvious suspect is usually the guilty one, but in contrast to

> **Did You Know?**
>
> Det. Claudette Wyms was originally written as a man, but CCH Pounder so impressed producers in her audi-tion that they decided to change the sex of the character.

the Strike Team's strong-arm methods, Dutch and Claudette use clever, psy-chological tactics to arrest criminals. The tag-team duo solves their cases using intelligence, intuition and logic to capture and mentally wear down suspects, leading them into a confession of their crimes.

Nevertheless, while the personal side stories are emotionally involving, and Dutch and Claudette's interrogation-room waltz is intellectually satisfying, nei-ther delivers the visceral, adrenaline rush of watching Mackey and his boys break down a drug dealer's door, pistol whip a gang member or crash an illegal arms operation with their guns blazing. *The Shield* is at its suspenseful best when Mackey seemingly has his back against the wall, yet ultimately manages to out-duel his enemies using a combination of cunning and violence. Since day one, both good guys and bad have been gunning to take him down. Aceveda tried to investigate Mackey and got Crowley killed. Sadistic Mexican drug lord Armadillo Quintero (Daniel Pino) ordered a hit on the Strike Team, got arrested and was stabbed by an inmate (Mackey's crew provided the knife). Sinister drug kingpin Antwon Mitchell (Anthony Anderson) tried to blackmail Shane into killing Mackey and wound up in jail. Investigating Internal Affairs lieutenant Jon Kavanaugh (Forest Whitaker) tried to get Lemonhead to rat on his partners, so a vengeful Mackey slept with Kavanaugh's wife, and Shane turned the loyal Lem into Swiss cheese.

The Strike Team's actions range from reprehensible to repulsive, yet you find yourself rooting for them, especially the magnetic Mackey. He's like the arrogant, cocky quarterback in high school who cheats on his tests, picks on the geeks and gets all the girls. He should be despised, but since he's extremely charming and never loses, you can't help but want to be his friend.

When the series launched in 2002, Chiklis, at the time best known as the affable Tony Scali from *The Commish* (1991–95), seemed a curious choice to play the morally bankrupt Mackey. Shaving his head, shedding pounds and adding muscle, Chiklis took a career gamble, and it paid off. He won an Emmy for Outstanding Lead Actor in a Drama that first year (the first such win for a basic-cable series) and also a Golden Globe. *The Shield*'s uncompromisingly gritty style has helped FX further push the envelope and led to their mounting other memorable series such as *Nip/Tuck* and *Rescue Me*. Vic Mackey may be no one's idea of a conventional hero, but he has an indelibly commanding, bulldog-like presence. Future antiheroes may want to acknowledge and thank him for opening—or, rather kicking down—the door. Trust me. You don't want to get on his bad side.

Cast:

Michael Chiklis *Det. Vic Mackey,* **Benito Martinez** *Capt. David Aceveda,* **CCH Pounder** *Det. Claudette Wyms,* **Walton Goggins** *Det. Shane Vendrell,* **Catherine Dent** *Off. Danny Sofer,* **Michael Jace** *Off. Julien Lowe,* **Jay Karnes** *Det. Dutch Wagenbach,* **Kenneth Johnson** *Det. Curtis Lemansky (2002–06),* **David Rees Snell** *Det. Ronnie Gardocki (2004–),* **Cathy Cahlin Ryan** *Corinne Mackey (2004–),* **Glenn Close** *Capt. Monica Rawling (2005),* **Forest Whitaker** *Lt. Jon Kavanaugh (2006–)*

The Simpsons

By Paul Wolfe
Broadcast History: FOX, 12/17/1989–
Runtime: 30 minutes
Genre: Animated cartoon

Sing along if you wish: Simpsons / Meet *The Simpsons* / They're a modern nuclear family / From the / Town of Springfield / They're a page right out of TV history.

With a concept recalling the first family of prime-time animation, *The Flintstones*, the colorful clan of Homer, Marge, Bart, Lisa and Maggie Simpson arrived in 1987 as a series of crudely sketched and lightly viewed shorts on *The Tracey Ullman Show*. Two years later, creator Matt Groening's family (all but Bart are named after his actual family members) got an animated makeover and moved into their own half-hour series. Two decades later, *The Simpsons* is not only TV's longest-running animated series, it's the longest-running comedy, period (400 episodes and counting as of 2007).

Giving life and enduring success to *The Simpsons* is a versatile cast of voice artists. The actors behind the characters have been together from the start, surviving highly publicized negotiations in 1998 and 2004 that resulted in richly deserved raises. Dan "D'oh!" Castellaneta is the voice of dim-witted dad Homer (and Krusty, Grampa, Barney, Itchy and dozens of others); Julie "Hmmm" Kavner, like Castellaneta a performer on Ullman's variety show, speaks for nurturing wife and mother Marge (and her sisters Patty and Selma); bratty, underachieving son Bart is actually a woman, Nancy "Ay Carumba" Cartwright, who also voices Bart's schoolmates Ralph Wiggum, Nelson Muntz and Todd Flanders; while the words of wise middle child Lisa are perfectly enunciated by Yeardley "I'll be in my room" Smith, who also occasionally babbles as baby Maggie. Equally vital to the cast are Hank Azaria (Moe, Apu, Disco Stu and Comic Book Guy) and Harry Shearer (C. Montgomery Burns, Smithers, Kent Brockman and Scratchy), who each have contributed more than a hundred recurring or one-off voices to the show's ever-expanding universe of characters.

Did You Know?
Homer studied nuclear physics in college.

The characters' rapid-fire dialogue comes from the silly and subversive minds of a talented army of writers, who leave no aspect of society or pop culture unturned, including—bravely and scathingly—the show's own network, Fox, and its corporate owner, Rupert Murdoch. From the familiar opening sequence featuring family couch photos and cheeky chalkboard sayings to closing credits ripe with inside-joke nicknames, every episode is filled with tiny verbal and visual details that make network repeats, syndicated showings and DVD replays as pleasurable as the first airing.

Presidents, preachers, teachers, athletes, cops, corporations and nations are always ripe for ridicule, but movies, musicals and TV shows are the primary targets for the show's memorable parodies. Do you remember 1995's "Who Shot Mr. Burns?" It was Maggie, following a struggle with Burns over her lollipop, in a two-part *Dallas* takeoff. Marge starred as Blanche DuBois in 1992's "A Streetcar Named Marge," the show's first major musical production (directed by Jon Lovitz's character, Llewellyn Sinclair). There was lots of trouble, right here in Springfield, in 1993's "Marge vs. the Monorail," in which the late Phil Hartman (as Lyle Lanley) channeled *The Music Man* while selling the city a doomed monorail project. In 1992's "Homer the Heretic," Homer gave up church and spent Sunday morning dancing in his underwear, à la Tom Cruise in *Risky Business*. Sideshow Bob terrorized the Thompsons (the new name assigned the Simpsons by the FBI) in 1993's "Cape Feare." *The Right Stuff* took center stage in 1994's "Deep Space Homer," in which NASA sent our favorite "blue-collar slob" into outer space. But my all-time favorite parody, as staged in 1996's "A Fish Called Selma," is the *Planet of the Apes* musical starring Hartman's signature character, former movie idol Troy McClure in Charlton Heston's role. You may remember McClure crooning, "I hate every ape I see, from chimpan-a to chimpan-zee!" but more than a decade later I still can't get "The Dr. Zaius Song" (sung to the tune of Falco's "Rock Me Amadeus") out of my head. Oops, now you can't either if you call yourself a fan.

> ## TV and Film Connections
> Spun off from
> *The Tracey Ullman Show*

Holidays are also *Simpson*-ized with regularity. The very first half-hour episode, 1989's "Simpsons Roasting on an Open Fire," fully introduces the family and their lone Christmas gift: rescued racing dog Santa's Little Helper. But no holiday plays a bigger role in *The Simpsons'* popularity than Halloween. Starting with the show's second season, the "Treehouse of Horror" trilogy episode has become an annual tradition that brings together casual viewers, hard-core fanatics and fans who may have strayed. In addition to providing a scare (and a showcase for aliens Kang and Kodos), the "Treehouse" episodes allow the writers to have some extra fun with the characters by putting them in supernatural situations, often in smart, semi-scary send-ups of classic horror movies or *Twilight Zone* episodes. Homer has been cast as King Kong, Bart as The Fly, Mr. Burns as Dracula and Groundskeeper Willie as Freddie Krueger.

Celebrities also play a special role, so much so that it seems like a *Simpsons* credit comes along with every SAG card. While many guests appear simply as themselves in brief cameos, the most effective celebrity sightings have been fully integrated supporting characters, especially love interests. Homer has fallen for cocktail waitress turned country crooner Lurleen Lumkin (Beverly

D'Angelo) and co-worker Mindy Simmons (Michelle Pfeiffer), while Marge was drawn to sensitive bowling instructor Jacques (Albert Brooks). Bart has been smitten with both Jessica Lovejoy (Meryl Streep) and 15-year-old babysitter Laura Powers (Sara Gilbert). Mandy Patinkin played Lisa's fiancé Hugh Parkfield in the standout episode "Lisa's Wedding" (1995), which detailed the future fortunes of the family in 2010. Lisa also had a crush on her substitute teacher Mr. Bergstrom, who was voiced by Dustin Hoffman. The King of Pop, Michael Jackson, voiced a mental patient who thinks he's Michael Jackson. Relatively speaking, Glenn Close has appeared twice as Homer's mom, and Danny DeVito occasionally pops up with a full head of hair as Homer's half brother, Herb Powell.

In addition to simultaneously entertaining millions of adults and kids during three different decades, *The Simpsons* revived animation outside Saturday morning. Some copycats sizzled (Groening's follow-up, *Futurama*, *King of the Hill*, *South Park*, and *Family Guy*); some fizzled (*Fish Police*, *Capitol Critters*, *Baby Blues* and *The Oblongs*). Along with NFL football, Groening's wonderful world of Springfield also helped fledgling Fox compete with the Big 3 networks and then filled the coffers of Murdoch's News Corp. with a merchandising business that would even make Disney blush. You name it, Homer or Bart is on it—from Homer's Cinnamon Donut cereal to multicharacter chess sets. Call me biased, but the ultimate honor may have been a special October 21, 2000, issue of TV GUIDE featuring 24 different character covers. For the creators, perhaps the ultimate tribute is enshrined on jumptheshark.com, where *The Simpsons* leads a short list of shows that online voters have certified as Never Jumped.

Classic Episode Close-Up
"Treehouse of Horror I"
(Original telecast: October 24, 1990)

While there are normally "specific rules to *The Simpsons'* universe," according to series creator Matt Groening, the annual Halloween episodes give the animators "the opportunity to go wild. It's a send-up of our favorite great and schlocky horror stories." The inaugural trilogy was built around Bart and Lisa swapping scary stories in his "Treehouse of Horror." In the opener, the Simpsons make the best of it after moving into a haunted house. Then, the family has a misunderstanding with aliens in a hilarious parody of the great *Twilight Zone* episode "To Serve Man." Finally, James Earl Jones lends his voice to an adaptation of "The Raven."

Voice Cast:

Dan Castellaneta Homer Simpson/Grandpa/Krusty the Clown/Barney/Mayor Quimby, **Julie Kavner** Marge Simpson/Patty Bouvier/Selma Bouvier, **Nancy Cartwright** Bart Simpson/Nelson Muntz/Todd Flanders/Ralph Wiggum/Kearney, **Yeardley Smith** Lisa Simpson, **Hank Azaria** Apu/Carl/Comic Book Guy/Snake/Moe Szyslak/Chief Wiggum, **Harry Shearer** Mr. Burns/Lenny/Ned Flanders/Seymour Skinner/Waylon Smithers, **Marcia Wallace** Edna Krabappel (1990–), **Phil Hartman** Lionel Hutz/Troy McClure (1991–98)

Six Feet Under

By N. F. Mendoza

Broadcast History: HBO, 6/3/2001–8/21/2005
Runtime: 60 minutes
Genre: Comedy-drama

This was superlative life-and-death drama in more ways than one.

Before the summer of 2001, it seemed impossible that a show centered on a family who owned and lived at a mortuary could prove so compelling, so capable of eliciting the kind of strongly visceral emotions usually reserved for, at least in my own experiences, actual relatives. But HBO's artfully conceived *Six Feet Under* was such a series, pushing the envelope in images and storytelling, offering what is rarely seen on television.

The proprietors of Fisher & Sons Funeral Home of Los Angeles were hardly the typical TV family. If anything, Oscar-winning creator Alan Ball (*American Beauty*)—inspired by the death of his sister to create the series—presented the very antithesis of the happy nuclear family.

At the series opening, father Nathaniel Sr. (Richard Jenkins), while driving a new hearse, reaches for a cigarette and gets hit by bus. It's an introduction that repeated itself throughout the series: each episode opened with a death. Those deaths were never the same and varied greatly in tone. Some were gruesome: a worker falls into a giant dough mixer (body pieces later go missing); a recently divorced woman standing out of a limo sunroof has a fatal meeting with a street sign. Other deaths were quiet, maybe even peaceful. But all were disturbing in their own way.

The family Nathaniel Sr. left behind includes his repressed, unfulfilled, initially mousy wife, Ruth (Frances Conroy); oldest son Nate (Peter Krause), charmingly selfish, but spiritual and rudderless; middle son David (Michael C. Hall), hyper-responsible and tightly wound; and change-of-life daughter Claire (Lauren Ambrose), who grows from insecure teen to unsure adult. These characters and the others in their orbit are defined in shades of gray; they possess good qualities and bad—just like real people.

> **Did You Know?**
>
> Frances Conroy is just 12 years older than Peter Krause, who played her son on the show.

These are fascinating, often conflicted multilayered characters. Take Rico (Freddy Rodriguez), a hard-working Fisher & Sons employee with a young family to support. Once he proves himself invaluable to the Fishers—he becomes one of their best restorative artists—he experiences his own life-altering battles with morality. Or Ruth's second husband, the compassionate George (James Cromwell), through whom the insecure Ruth eventually finds inner strength.

Nathaniel's death in that initial episode is the impetus for a Fisher family reunion. After years of separation, they begin living under the same roof— sharing the three-story, sprawling old craftsman (which in real life is L.A.'s Filipino Historical Society building). Each of the Fisher children lived uneasily in that space. David kept it fastidiously neat, Nate turned it hippie with first wife Lisa and daughter Maya, and finally Claire brooded in it, hid in it and smoked weed both alone and with art-school friends in it.

There was plenty to explore through the Fishers and those who stepped into their circle. By the series' end, no family taboo was left unexplored. Among the most hauntingly vivid snapshots that I remember:

- The memorable pilot episode in which Nate, during a plane flight, meets—and has sex with—Brenda Chenoweth (Rachel Griffiths), thus beginning a tumultuous relationship and marriage.

- Brenda's strained relationship with her loopy psychiatrist parents, her almost-consummated incestuous relationship with her mania- cal brother, Billy (Jeremy Sisto), and her awful Season 1 foray into promiscuity. Brenda could be horrifyingly toxic, but Nate took her back and gave her a second chance, just like Brenda continued to give the scary Billy second and third chances, right up to the moment of her death.

- The ultimately triumphant coming-out at the end of Season 1 of once-repressed choir boy David Fisher and his tempestuous rela- tionship with policeman Keith (Mathew St. Patrick).

- David's abduction and torture at the hands of a masochist in an episode so graphically relentless, it's almost unwatchable. The intensity was amplified as the plot focused on the menacing terror David encountered. The event was so traumatic, David continued to have nightmares right up until the series ended. So did we.

- Nate's painful relationship with new-age chef Lisa (Lili Taylor), once his roommate and occasional lover. Her pregnancy resulted in a reluctant marriage, which subsequently ended with her dis- appearance and brutal murder.

The Internet boards for *Six Feet Under* were always active and it's for the very reason I've stressed here: these are people in situations that you would never want to be in, never want to wish anyone you loved in, but throughout each richly provocative episode, they were somehow so real, so credible. You knew them.

In Season 5, when Ruth's stepdaughter, Maggie (the poignant Tina Holmes), befriends Nate, some of us rooted for them: we wanted Nate to find someone more balanced, less narcissistic than Brenda, and yet there were others who found Maggie (whose child had died) whiny. It's Maggie who was with Nate when he suddenly died, at the start of their affair.

Nate may have been the show's emotional core, and for him to die so unexpectedly was again *Six Feet Under* thinking out of the box (or, if you will, the casket). My husband's reaction was that they must be bringing back Nate as a spectre (as they had with Nathaniel, who was nearly as much a regular character as the other Fishers); he couldn't imagine him dying and going away from the show forever. He dies, but, of course, he wasn't gone.

Lisa, Nate's overbearingly earnest first wife, also returned, but while the show never presented it explicitly, it became evident to anyone paying attention that when the person's "ghost" appeared to chat, mock or lecture, it was actually the inner voice of the live person, infused with their lasting impression of the deceased.

Alternately wrenching and wry, and filled with surprises, the brilliantly written and performed *Six Feet Under* knew when to pull the plug; five seasons was just about right. It infused itself into my consciousness so that I became wrapped up in these characters' decisions and fates. Who knew a series with corpses could have such vibrant, dramatic life?

Cast:

Peter Krause *Nate Fisher*, **Michael C. Hall** *David Fisher*, **Frances Conroy** *Ruth Fisher*, **Lauren Ambrose** *Claire Fisher*, **Rachel Griffiths** *Brenda Chenowith*, **Freddy Rodriguez** *Federico Diaz*, **Richard Jenkins** *Nathaniel Fisher*, **Mathew St. Patrick** *Keith Charles*, **Justina Machado** *Vanessa Diaz*, **Jeremy Sisto** *Billy Chenowith (2001–02)*, **Lili Taylor** *Lisa Kimmel Fisher (2002–03)*

60 Minutes

By Roger Leister
Broadcast History: CBS, 9/24/1968–
Runtime: 60 minutes
Genre: Newsmagazine

What would television be like without the tick-tick-tick-tick of that stopwatch every Sunday evening? Would upsetting the decades-old rhythm of the TV week cause sets to explode the way that hatch did on *Lost*? Cataclysmic or not, an era will end when (and if) we say farewell to *60 Minutes*, a vinyl LP in the age of the iPod. The way the show has evolved, thrived and survived for nearly 40 years—with its distinctive three-story format, lack of frills and reputation as the quintessential newsmagazine—the ticking stopwatch is more than a signature, it's the pulse for TV as we used to know it.

The brainchild of executive producer Don Hewitt in 1968, *60 Minutes* made the documentary program popular to the masses and became a rather unlikely smash hit. Former pitchman Mike Wallace was a star from day one alongside Harry Reasoner, with Morley Safer sliding in when Reasoner (temporarily) left for ABC in 1970. It didn't find traction on the schedule and ripen ratings-wise until the arrival of Dan Rather and a switch to 7 p.m. ET in 1975–76. A season later it cracked the Top 25, and has been bearing fruit for CBS (an estimated $2 billion in earnings) ever since. It's been the season's most-watched show four times (1980, '83, '92, '93), one shy of the mark held by *All in the Family* and *The Cosby Show*. The same level of entertainment Archie Bunker and Cliff Huxtable gave us, the family of *60 Minutes* correspondents deliver by keeping us glued to fresh, stimulating stories about our world.

While considered a first ballot shoo-in for this list, *60 Minutes* has its share of followers who respect the show more than they watch. Some years I'd tune in about as often as I'd read a print magazine like *Time* (i.e., when I'm in a waiting room). But in its favor is year-round promotion on CBS Sports coverage of golf, college basketball and perhaps the greatest Sunday lead-in ever, the National ... Football ... League. Nearly as routine as the two-minute warning is the announcer's reminder that "*60 Minutes* will be seen in its entirety following our game, except on the West Coast."

True enough, if I stick around, it's usually for all three stories—and Andy Rooney. Lo and behold, I feel better informed after doing so. Whether exposing scandalous behavior in government and corporate America or profiling newsmakers and celebrities, the diversity of the stories fulfills Hewitt's intention to "package news stories as well as Hollywood packages fiction."

One reason it's so easily digestible is the presentation. No theme music. No graphics. Because the interviewee's name is not provided on-screen, we're forced to pay closer attention. Like leaving a laugh track off of a sitcom, it lends realism to the interviews. As TV GUIDE wrote in a 1984 cover story, one of the great joys of watching *60 Minutes* is seeing "something that does not appear often in nonfiction television: the process of watching the correspondents discover the story at the same time that we do." Another production trademark is the *extreme* close-up (sometimes we see nothing but a subject's eyes, nose and mouth). Roone Arledge may have revolutionized Olympic coverage with "Up

> ### Did You Know?
>
> Mike Wallace, who stepped down in 2006, had been with *60 Minutes* since its inception in 1968—a phenomenal 38 seasons.

Close & Personal," but Hewitt got closer and a lot more personal with his subjects, be they athletes, world leaders or odometer-rigging car salesmen.

Of course, Wallace—and what came to be called his "ambush interviews"— made his subjects sweat, or at least squirm. In one-on-one situations, Wallace could break down his man better than Michael Jordan.

When Wallace, Safer, Reasoner and Ed Bradley were a Murderer's Row of investigative journalism (when subjects would literally flee from *60 Minutes* cameras), the tone of the show was as hard-hitting as Muhammad Ali at his peak. But like Ali, things have softened over the years. The show's identity swerves too often toward chummy celebrity features aimed at young viewers and interviews with authors-of-the-week (too often ex-jocks like Jose Canseco and Bill Romanowski), solely to promote their books. It's the kind of fluff formerly reserved for lesser newsmagazines.

Imitated in some fashion by virtually every major cable-network news department, the *60 Minutes* format even spawned the midweek *60 Minutes II* in 1999. Two years later, the original's run of 22 out of 23 years in the Nielsen's seasonal Top 10 came to an end as the franchise faced a changing TV landscape and began what has been a permanent ratings drop to the bottom half of the Top 25. In 2005, less than a year after Dan Rather's botched report on George W. Bush's National Guard record, *60 Minutes II* was scrapped. Its producer, Jeff Fager, took the *60 Minutes* reins from Hewitt. Throw in Wallace's retirement as a full-time correspondent, along with what seemed to

> ### TV and Film Connections
> Spin-off: *60 Minutes II*

be an increasing dependence on light features and the tragic passing of Ed Bradley, and the tick-tick-tick sounds more like a time bomb.

Yet it keeps on ticking. Thanks, in part, to *60 Minutes II* holdover Bob Simon, he of the measured, almost-haunting delivery. A 40-year CBS News correspondent who seems to have reported from everywhere but the moon, Simon contributes mostly internationally based stories that routinely highlight the show.

Easing the burden on fellow sixtysomethings Steve Kroft and Leslie Stahl, Simon and Scott Pelley are now bright lights of Sunday night, having reported on three of the four Emmy-winning features from 2005 to 2006 (bringing the show's Emmy tally to 78, to go with 11 Peabody Awards).

Of course, beyond the tried-and-true three feature stories, a pair of entertaining sidebars has further set *60 Minutes* apart from others newsies. The "Point/Counterpoint" segment between a righty and lefty—an all-too-common concept in today's cable universe—thrived in the '70s before giving way to the commentary of curmudgeonly everyman Andy Rooney, who puts a not-so-cheery cherry on top of our Sunday, if you will.

With help from satirists (from Joe Piscopo to Frank Caliendo) who sustain the Rooney phenomenon, Andy gets more mileage out of "a few minutes" than anyone really has a right to. His observational snippets can range wildly from serious to silly, but usually leave me echoing his high-pitched trademark query: *Now, WHY is that?* In the fall of 2006, an E coli scare produced some classic Andy: "For years mothers have been telling kids to eat their spinach, now they're telling them not to. I never liked spinach much, anyway."

While the show fades to black in TV's archives, *60 Minutes* remarkably maintains its identity as the gold standard. Continuing to deliver "those stories, and Andy Rooney," like clockwork.

Cast:

Mike Wallace *Reporter (1968–2006)*, **Harry Reasoner** *Reporter (1968–70; 1978–91)*, **Morley Safer** *Reporter*, **Dan Rather** *Reporter (1975–81)*, **Andy Rooney** *Commentator (1978–)*, **Ed Bradley** *Reporter (1981–2006)*, **Diane Sawyer** *Reporter (1984–89)*, **Steve Kroft** *Reporter (1989–)*, **Meredith Vieira** *Reporter (1989–91)*, **Lesley Stahl** *Reporter (1991–)*, **Katie Couric** *Reporter (2006–)*

The Sopranos

By Joe Friedrich

Broadcast History: HBO, 1/13/1999–
Runtime: 60 minutes
Genre: Crime drama

I was born, raised and spent most of my life in New Jersey, so you'll understand why I've developed a thick-skinned imperviousness to all manner of jokes, insults and complaints about the Garden State. At what "exit" was I born? Very original. How about that industrial stench along the New Jersey Turnpike? Big deal—hold your breath for a few miles. Beach tags? Give me a break. There is of course one thing about the place that just about everyone—except perhaps natives defensive about the spotlight on the state's organized crime—praises: *The Sopranos*. Ever since Tony Soprano emerged from the Lincoln Tunnel for the first time, to the infectious strains of A3's "Woke Up This Morning," the groundbreaking drama has employed a choke hold on popular culture.

Moreover, it may only be the slightest of hyperbole to state that, at the time, it single-handedly changed the way the television industry does business. For instance, how many cable offerings secured promotional spots on broadcast networks, as this one did on CBS before the second season began? And as CBS president Leslie Moonves told *The New York Times* in 1999, "All you have to do is see a show like *The Sopranos*, where the lead character is a murderer, the language is extreme and it's accepted as one of the finest hours on television. It's almost like networks are forced to deal with a new network standard."

The centerpiece is conflicted mob boss Tony Soprano (James Gandolfini), whose anxiety brought on by the incessant demands of two families—one at home, the other at "work"—landed him in the worst possible place, besides jail or the cemetery, a macho *mafioso* could be: therapy. Those first 13 episodes of Season 1 played like nothing audiences had ever seen, each one unfolding like a painstakingly crafted, stunningly original 60-minute feature film. Here we were, cheering for a chillingly violent criminal, for crying out loud, and empathizing with his utter deflation when, at the end of that delectable first season, his spur-of-the-moment decision to smother his own mother, Livia (Nancy Marchand)—a response to her ordering a hit on *him*—was scuttled by her neatly timed stroke. *Sopranos* mania had officially begun. HBO subscriptions jumped, and each new batch of episodes became the TV event of the season. Alarms were sounded about the graphic nature of the sex, violence and language, and protests were lodged from ethnic groups about stereotyping Italian-Americans as skirt-chasing, foul-mouthed, felonious goombahs, but clearly this show had the kind of momentum that is not easily arrested.

Along with Gandolfini, who's won three Emmys, the superb cast includes three-time Emmy winner Edie Falco as Tony's put-upon wife, Carmela, who gives as good as she gets; Lorraine Bracco as Tony's psychiatrist, Dr. Jennifer Melfi, who is alternately repulsed by and drawn to her patient; and Michael Imperioli as Tony's impulsive nephew, Christopher, whose loyalty to his uncle has survived Hollywood fever, drug addiction and a girlfriend (Drea de Matteo) whacked for talking to the Feds. Over the course of six seasons, several supporting players have also had a major impact, among them Joe Pantoliano as a Mafia captain and constant thorn in Tony's side, and Steve Buscemi as Tony's ex-con cousin whose efforts to go straight went for naught.

This is compelling stuff, poignant one moment and mordantly hilarious the next, but that's not to say I don't have occasional issues with the show. Take "Pine Barrens," for example, a celebrated episode from the third season that earned Emmy nominations for Steve Buscemi's direction and Terence Winter's script. It focuses on Christopher and Paulie Walnuts (Tony Sirico), one of Tony's captains, who get lost in the famed New Jersey pinelands after being outsmarted and eluded by the Russian mobster they had brought there to kill. Imperioli and Sirico do a terrific job portraying their characters' petty selfishness (and increasing panic) as a freezing winter night drags on. My problem is not with the direction, performances or story, but rather with the sloppy attention to detail. Call it nitpicking, but when Paulie pumps his own gas—which is illegal in New Jersey—on the Garden State Parkway or refers to an exit nowhere near the area in question, and rolling hills and bare *deciduous* trees are clearly visible in the flat-as-a-pancake *Pine* Barrens, well, that's just lazy. I don't think it's out of the question to expect a little bit of consistency. After all, if so much time and effort is spent on the big picture, why skimp on the fine print?

Apart from that, and the nagging question—never, to most folks, satisfactorily answered by HBO or series creator David Chase—about why fans had to wait ridiculously long periods between *Sopranos* seasons (21 months

Classic Episode Close-Up

"College"

(Original telecast: February 7, 1999)

A runaway hit from the start, the first season of the peerless drama hit new creative heights in its fifth episode, when Tony takes care of business far from his usual haunts. While on an innocent college-visitation trip to Maine with his daughter, Meadow, Tony spots a former associate who left the Witness Protection Program after ratting to the Feds. What follows is a remarkable tale that juxtaposes scenes of Tony Soprano as the devoted father and as the merciless mob enforcer. It's one of James Gandolfini's finest performances, and an episode, director Allen Coulter says, that "forces the audience to deal with its feelings about this nice guy who also has a monstrous side. Our intent was to make that as chilling as possible." It worked. The episode earned a Best Writing Emmy for James Manos Jr. and series creator David Chase.

separated five and six), there have been a multitude of series moments, astonishing, absorbing or simply endearing, that I continue to remember vividly: Tony strangling that Mafia turncoat in Maine while on a college visit with his daughter, Meadow (Jamie-Lynn Sigler); Big Pussy (Vincent Pastore) meeting a gruesome fate at sea; the revealing sessions between Tony and Dr. Melfi; an anguished Tony blowing away his cousin (Buscemi) or beating Ralphie (Pantoliano) to death; selected outbursts from the irritable Uncle Junior (Dominic Chianese); Carmela's evolving rationalizations for the gaudy lifestyle she could illicitly afford;

> ## Did You Know?
>
> Lorraine Bracco was offered the part of Carmela Soprano, but felt the role was too similar to her *Goodfellas* character, Karen Hill.

Tony's matter-of-fact farewell to his sister Janice (Aida Turturro) after she shot her coldhearted husband, Richie Aprile (David Proval); Christopher's drug-induced haze at a religious festival; the oddly coiffed capos Paulie Walnuts and Silvio Dante (Bruce Springsteen and the E Street Band's Steven Van Zandt); the profane baked-ziti lament by Tony's son, A. J. (Robert Iler); and just about any scene with the menacing (and for my money, too-seldom featured) Johnny Sack (Vincent Curatola).

Yes, there have been some gripes in recent seasons about presumed slumps, loose ends (for example, what ultimately *did* happen to the Russian in the Pine Barrens?), anticlimactic finales and a paucity of mob-related story lines. So what if every episode wasn't memorable. When you add it all up, *The Sopranos* endures as an unforgettable drama populated by complex and impeccably defined characters; an addictive one-of-a-kind masterwork.

Cast:

James Gandolfini Anthony Soprano, **Lorraine Bracco** Dr. Jennifer Melfi, **Edie Falco** Carmela Soprano, **Michael Imperioli** Christopher Moltisanti, **Nancy Marchand** Livia Soprano (1999–2000), **Jamie-Lynn Sigler** Meadow Soprano, **Dominic Chianese** Corrado "Uncle Junior" Soprano, **Robert Iler** Anthony Soprano Jr., **Steven Van Zandt** Silvio Dante, **Tony Sirico** Paulie "Walnuts" Gualtieri, **John Ventimiglia** Artie Bucco, **Vincent Curatola** Johnny "Johnny Sack" Sacramoni, **Vincent Pastore** Salvatore "Big Pussy" Bonpensiero (1999–2000), **Drea de Matteo** Adriana La Cerva (1999–2004), **Sharon Angela** Rosalie Aprile, **Kathrine Narducci** Charmaine Bucco, **Aida Turturro** Janice Soprano (2000–), **David Proval** Richie Aprile (2000), **Steven R. Schirripa** Bobby "Bacala" Baccalieri (2000–), **Federico Castelluccio** Furio Giunta (2000–02), **Joe Gannascoli** Vito Spatafore (2000–06), **Dan Grimaldi** Patsy Parisi (2000–), **Joe Pantoliano** Ralph Cifaretto (2001–02), **Ray Abruzzo** Little Carmine Lupertazzi (2002–), **Steve Buscemi** Tony Blundetto (2004), **Frank Vincent** Phil Leotardo (2004–)

South Park

By Sabrina Rojas Weiss

Broadcast History: Comedy Central, 8/13/1997–
Runtime: 30 minutes
Genre: Animated cartoon

Four round-faced, innocent third-grade boys learn life's important lessons from the adults they meet in their Colorado town. The premise is too sappy and thin even for a sitcom. Which is why it's so perfect when juxtaposed with biting social satire, potty jokes and inappropriate sexual innuendo. Without the appeal of *South Park*'s adorable little kids and idyllic setting, creators Trey Parker and Matt Stone probably wouldn't get away with most of their show's content, let alone keep it on Comedy Central for 10 seasons and counting. Comedy Central, said its president Doug Herzog, "is the house that Trey and Matt built. Before Jon Stewart, before Dave Chappelle, there was *South Park*."

Jesus vs. Frosty, the primitive stop-motion short created by University of Colorado film students Parker and Stone in 1992, was clever and cute. Versions of the *South Park* kids build a snowman that comes to life and kills two of them before Jesus saves the day by using his halo as a weapon. The timing of this birth couldn't have been better: A generation raised on a daily diet of cartoons was ready for more mature fare, as the popularity of *The Simpsons* proved, and the Internet coming into use by the general public. So when a Fox exec somehow got hold of the film, he commissioned Parker and Stone to create a new version, which the exec sent to his friends as a video holiday card. In "The Spirit of Christmas," Jesus fights Santa, the boys are torn about whom to cheer for, and Brian Boitano skates by to offer enlightening advice. Blasphemy, anti-Semitism, fat jokes, the accidental death of a kid, the callous reaction of his friends—it makes your jaw drop, until you laugh at yourself for being so shocked by a silly little cartoon. Thanks to e-mail, it spread like a virus, in much the same way all things *South Park* would circulate the Web. To this day, there are still fan sites devoted to making "The Spirit of Christmas" available for download.

> **Did You Know?**
>
> *South Park*'s opening theme song is an original musical score performed by the band Primus.

Then again, as a cable-less college student in 1997, when the series first aired on Comedy Central, I heard about *South Park* through word of mouth, so let's give credit to the infectious charm and mischievous, sick humor of the show—and to those four relatable, foulmouthed third-graders who hold up a mirror to the ridiculous truths of the world. Stan, the most normal of the group, is often the worrier and the voice of reason. Cartman is the mean, chubby one with a doting, promiscuous single mother. Kyle is a stereotypically neurotic, smart Jew. Kenny is the poor, neglected kid who mumbles through his parka and gets killed in every episode. Well, maybe they're not *just* like you and me, but even in outrageous situations, they acted just like the kids I knew when I was 9. And most of the other characters in their universe are twisted versions of people I knew growing up (or maybe it's just me, since I went to elementary school in small-town Colorado, too): closeted gay teacher Mr. Garrison, Kyle's overprotective mother, the crazy bus driver, the bumbling cop, Stan's mean older sister, eager-to-please nerd Butters, physically disabled aspiring comedian Jimmy. Even soul-singing, womanizing Chef is an exaggerated version of those grown-ups who were way cooler than our parents and didn't talk down to kids.

Then again, why have an animated show if you can't play with reality? In the pilot episode, Cartman was abducted and anal-probed by aliens. The kids have befriended a pot-smoking towel, a cyborg from the future and Mr. Hanky the Christmas Poo. Satan had a gay love affair with Saddam Hussein. The town has been attacked by a monster Barbra Streisand and by a *Dawson's Creek* Trapper Keeper. Kenny's frequent death—and his friends' nonchalant reaction, "Oh my god, they killed Kenny! You bastards!"—raised many eyebrows early in *South Park*'s history. There were those usual outcries about the show being a bad influence on children, especially because it is a cartoon. But the protests boosted the show's profile higher than a late-night basic-cable show could otherwise ever expect. Since then, it seems the writers try to offend as many potentially sensitive groups as possible, from Mormons to the disabled, possibly trying to stir up controversy. Then again, they made fun of such stunts (while still exploiting one) in Season 5's "It Hits the Fan," in which the word "shit" is said 162 times uncensored. As funny as most of these episodes are, we're also tuning in to see what they'll get away with next.

Among other hypocritical grown-ups, celebrities have always been a favorite target for *South Park*'s barbs. Count Ben Affleck, Jennifer Lopez, Roger Ebert, Michael Jackson, Mel Gibson, Rosie O'Donnell, Oprah Winfrey and Tom Cruise among the people who'd never make *Simpsons*-style guest appearances. Isaac

Preview Review
September 13, 1997

Comedy Central has received both critical raves and big ratings for its riskiest offering, *South Park*, a cartoon series that would give even Beavis and Butt-head pause. Comedy Central president Doug Herzog admits there has been an episode or two of the animated series that have "caused me to do a lot of nail-biting and my ulcer to act up." It's worth the indigestion: *South Park* is Comedy Central's highest-rated original show. For Herzog, there's also a certain amount of competitive pleasure in the cable channel's current upswing. "Oh, I know MTV would have loved to have gotten *South Park*," he says. "It's been a while since they've had a *Beavis and Butt-head*."

Hayes, the voice of Chef, was reported to have quit in March 2006 because Season 9's "Trapped in the Closet" episode harshly made fun of Scientology, also Hayes's religion. (Stan is mistaken for the reincarnation of L. Ron Hubbard, we get a brief summary of Scientology's mythology, and a depressed Cruise locks himself in Stan's closet because the boy doesn't love his acting. This, of course, gives everyone an excuse to declare that "Tom Cruise won't come out of the closet!") Hayes later denied that this was the reason for his retirement, but that didn't stop Parker and Stone from subjecting Chef to a violent death by grizzly bear and mountain lion in the premiere of Season 10.

After so many years, it appears that *South Park* is losing its steam. They're still trying pretty hard to shock us (countless child-molestation jokes, a weird episode about Oprah's gun-toting genitals), and to freshen things up by promoting the kids to fourth grade and shifting the focus to the peripheral characters once in a while. Maybe the show's impact is lessened because pop culture has become so saturated with bold political satire on Comedy Central and elsewhere, gross-out humor in the theaters, and the witty animated shows of the Cartoon Network's Adult Swim. Or perhaps it's time for *us* to grow up and move on. It would be a shame to sully the pristine memory of that satellite dish coming out of Cartman's butt, or the love scene between the elephant and the pig, with anything less inspired.

Voice Cast:

Matt Stone *Kyle/Kenny*, **Trey Parker** *Stan/Cartman/Mr. Garrison/Timmy*, **Mary Kay Bergman** *Principal Victoria/Liane/Sharon/Sheila/Nurse Gollum*, **Isaac Hayes** *Chef (1997–2006)*

SpongeBob SquarePants

By Megan Walsh-Boyle

Broadcast History: Nickelodeon, 7/17/1999–
Runtime: 30 minutes
Genre: Animated cartoon

Are you ready, kids? Ohhhh ... Who lives in a pineapple under the sea?

Unless you have been residing under a rock since 1999, chances are you undoubtedly know the answer is the absorbent and yellow and porous SpongeBob SquarePants, whose phenomenal (for cable) ratings have continued to soar since making his Nickelodeon debut on July 17, 1999.

Sort of an animated version of Pee-wee Herman, SpongeBob is the quintessential oddball underdog with his little brown suit, bright innocent eyes and goofy gap-toothed grin. He's square, both literally and figuratively. Working as a spatula-wielding fry cook at the Krusty Krab, "the finest eating establishment ever established," is SpongeBob's lifelong-dream-come-true and he takes mindless joy in being named Employee of the Month every month.

An innocent childlike hero surrounded by more cynical beings, SpongeBob (whose high-pitched, nasally voice is provided by Tom Kenny) is gleefully oblivious to all naysayers as he floats merrily through life. SpongeBob's best friends are dim-witted but loyal Patrick Starfish (voiced by Bill Fagerbakke, who played Dauber on *Coach*) and the thrill-seeking girl squirrel Sandy Cheeks (Carolyn Lawrence). Employed by the Krusty Krab's penny-pinching owner, Mr. Eugene H. Krabs (Clancy Brown), SpongeBob works alongside head cashier Squidward Tentacles (Rodger Bumpass), a clarinet-playing squid who's grouchy and sarcastic and constantly annoyed by SpongeBob's antics.

SpongeBob SquarePants is created and executive produced by Stephen Hillenburg, who previously worked on the Nickelodeon cartoon *Rocko's Modern Life*. Hillenburg, a former marine science teacher, came up with the concept as a way to combine his career as a marine biologist with his love of animation. While *SpongeBob* isn't exactly educational, the wacky cartoon series does provide life lessons about the importance of friendship and loyalty. And SpongeBob's ability to remain upbeat in the face of any and all obstacles offers a positive role model for kids and adults alike.

Not your ordinary children's cartoon, *SpongeBob* has reeled in a following among all age groups and has been consistently one of the top-rated kids' shows on television. Even critics like the series: In 2002, TV GUIDE ranked the endearing sea sponge the ninth-greatest cartoon character of all time, just behind Charlie Brown and Snoopy, and beating out Mickey Mouse (No. 19) and Scooby-Doo (No. 22). *SpongeBob* has scored several Nickelodeon Kids' Choice Awards, a Television Critics Association award and has been nominated for a few Emmys. Pretty impressive for a walking, talking yellow kitchen sponge.

Savvy grown-ups can also enjoy the sly pop-culture references that fly right over young heads, along with hip cameos made by the likes of indie director Jim Jarmusch and alternative band Ween. Other guest stars who have lent their voices to the show include Charles Nelson Reilly, John O'Hurley, Marion Ross, John Rhys-Davies, Amy Poehler, and Ernest Borgnine and Tim Conway from *McHale's Navy* as retired superheroes Mermaid Man and Barnacle Boy, respectively.

Although devotees of the happy-go-lucky sea sponge find his optimism and enthusiasm endearing, there are those—they might be called real-life Squidwards—who consider his bubbly personality as irritating as fingernails scraping a chalkboard. SpongeBob's fans, however, far outnumber his detractors (and rightly so) as evidenced by the fact that he's not only the star of a much-watched TV show but also a hot-selling commodity, with his smiling face plastered on everything from breakfast cereal to board games and apparel. In 2004, SpongeBob and his pals made the leap to the silver screen with the release of *The SpongeBob SquarePants Movie*, which had some big names attached, including Alec Baldwin, Scarlett Johansson, Jeffrey Tambor and a self-deprecating cameo by *Baywatch* star David Hasselhoff.

Did You Know?

Tom Kenny, the man behind the voice of SpongeBob, often appears on the show in human form as SpongeBob's No. 1 fan, Patchy the Pirate.

So why has *SpongeBob* remained so appealing to TV audiences over the years? It's probably because it's so unapologetically *silly*, with no pretext of anything remotely sensible. The rules of the ocean do not apply to SpongeBob's colorful deep-sea community of Bikini Bottom. After all, SpongeBob's pet snail, Gary, meows like a cat. Fire burns underwater. SpongeBob's neighbors drive boats, not cars. It's absurd, but very, very entertaining.

Just as the theme song promises, if nautical nonsense be something you wish, look no further than the delightful humor of *SpongeBob SquarePants*.

Voice Cast:

Tom Kenny *SpongeBob SquarePants*, **Bill Fagerbakke** *Patrick Starfish*, **Rodger Bumpass** *Squidward Tentacles*, **Clancy Brown** *Mr. Krabs*, **Carolyn Lawrence** *Sandy Cheeks*

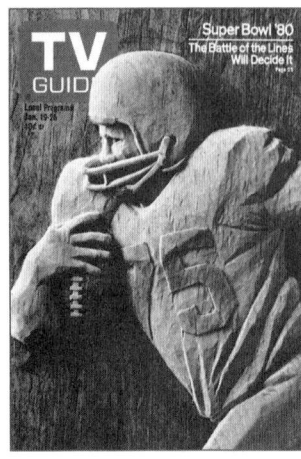

SportsCenter

By Todd Wakai

Broadcast History: ESPN, 9/7/1979–
Runtime: Varied
Genre: Sports program

Looking back, it seemed almost medieval. There was once a time—long, long ago—when sports fans were at the mercy of the local sports anchor, an overly enthusiastic talking head who had a mere four minutes or so during the 11 o'clock news to provide all the sports scores and highlights.

As a young kid growing up in southern New Jersey, I somehow became a huge fan of the run-and-gun San Antonio Spurs (George "Iceman" Gervin's Nike poster in which he's sitting on blocks of ice hung on my wall). Sports coverage on my local newscasts mainly focused on the Philly teams. I was lucky to get even a score from a Spurs game—I knew seeing a highlight from that game was out of the question. Many times, particularly if the Spurs were playing a late game on the West Coast, I had to wait until I read the newspaper the next morning to find out whether they won or lost.

Oddly, when cable TV started invading the country in the late 1970s and early '80s, I wanted my parents to subscribe for the uncut, commercial-free movie channels. I had heard of the 24-hour sports channel called ESPN, but knew that it only aired events like Australian Football and World's Strongest Man competitions. However, when I looked in TV GUIDE (yes, my parents were subscribers long before I started working here) I was intrigued by a single title on the ESPN schedule:

11 PM (ESN) **SPORTSCENTER** *1:00*

Could this really be what I think it is? A full hour of sports scores and highlights? That's pure genius. Forget MTV. I want my ESPN!

It wasn't until 1984 that my neighborhood was wired for cable and my parents plunked down the money for a cable box. It was five years since the first *SportsCenter* telecast in September 1979. Chris Berman was already making celebrities out of athletes by giving them unique nicknames—and he was well on this way to becoming a household name himself. (A little bit of trivia: Frank Tanana "Daiquiri" was Berman's first nickname; Bert "Be Home" Blyleven is my personal favorite.)

SportsCenter was everything that I hoped it would be. It was chock-full of scores, stats and highlights. And more importantly, it didn't talk down to viewers. This was an hour for hardcore sports fans, not novices who were still spending four minutes a night with their local sports anchor, right before they got their five-day weather forecast.

But *SportsCenter* was becoming more than just a godsend for sports fans. Athletes began to see the series as a way to gain more exposure, which could make them more popular with fans, and in turn get them more endorsement opportunities. By 1987 the Iceman had passed the crown of NBA scoring king to Michael Jordan. Jordan was still a few years away from his first NBA title, but he was already making more money pitching products than he could ever earn shooting hoops. Jordan's acrobatic dunks and flair for dramatics made him a *SportsCenter* darling, and clearly other athletes (and perhaps their agents) began to see regular appearances on *SportsCenter*'s highlights as a way to improve marketing Q ratings and get endorsement deals.

For good or bad, *SportsCenter* has helped create a sports world in which athletes play to the camera in a way that goes far beyond the standard "Hi Mom!" salute. Does Terrell Owens pull a Sharpie from his sock and autograph a football if there isn't a *SportsCenter* to show that highlight over and over again? Same for Joe Horn and his cell phone? Dikembe Mutombo and his finger wagging? Ickey Woods and his shuffle?

When ESPN2 launched in 1993, the Bristol, Connecticut–based company really was becoming the "worldwide leader in sports." The ESPN and ESPN2 schedules were now filled with NFL football, MLB baseball, PGA golf, big-time college basketball and college football, and more and more airings of *SportsCenter*. And by now *SportsCenter* wasn't just making national celebrities out of athletes, it was making celebrities out of the hosts themselves.

Berman was *SportsCenter*'s first big star, but Dan Patrick and Keith Olbermann were the ones who made *SportsCenter* the "Big Show." The program was never better than when they anchored the nightly 11 p.m. telecast. Patrick's understated quick wit played perfectly off of Olbermann's smark-aleck smarminess.

In 1994, all of the hosts were able to show off their acting chops when ESPN launched its hilarious "This Is SportsCenter" ad campaign, a series of comical commercials based on the premise that the ESPN office is the center of the sports world. The hosts are seen going about their daily activities while mingling with athletes, coaches and mascots in the ESPN parking lot, cafeteria, hallways—even the restrooms. Charley Steiner emerged as the star of many of the top entries, particularly one in which he suffers the ignominy of being traded from *SportsCenter* to *Melrose Place* in exchange for actor Andrew Shue (he shows up on the *Melrose* set as Bobby the pool boy and asks a disgusted Laura Leighton to rub cocoa butter on his back).

The arrival of ESPNews in 1996 signaled that viewers couldn't get enough of what ESPN has to offer. The channel basically uses the *SportsCenter* format nearly 24 hours a day (save for the occasional press conference). Indeed, the *SportsCenter* influence is everywhere. Sports-specific offshoots like *Baseball Tonight*, *NBA Fastbreak* and *NFL Primetime* allow for a deeper dive into those leagues' games. The reality series *Dream Job* provided aspiring anchors with the chance to audition for a gig on *SportsCenter* (Al Jaffe, ESPN's VP of Talent Negotiation and Production Recruitment, served in the Simon Cowell role of "tell-it-like-it-is" judge). And the game show *Stump the Schwab* gave sports-trivia nuts a chance to go one-on-one against Howie Schwab, ESPN's first, and best, fact researcher.

Of course, the influence isn't limited to ESPN. *SportsCenter's* bottomline ticker concept is now commonplace on the cable news channels. Competitors like CNN's *Sports Tonight* and Fox Sports Net's *National Sports Report* come and go. And in 1998 executive producer Aaron Sorkin used *SportsCenter* as the basis for the critically acclaimed, though short-lived, ABC comedy series *Sports Night*, which starred Peter Krause, Josh Charles and Felicity Huffman.

As is often the case with any TV show that lasts so long (the 30,000th episode aired in February 2007) and experiences so many changes, *SportsCenter* has become a target for some criticism. Older fans pine for the pre-*SportsCenter* days when athletes didn't turn routine plays into celebratory dances and refer to themselves in the third person. While alums such as Craig Kilborn, Robin Roberts, Kevin Frazier (and to a degree, Olbermann himself) have enjoyed crossover success to other genres of TV, ESPN has yet to find a pair of hosts that have the chemistry of the great Patrick-Olbermann tag team. Instead, it seems that many of today's hosts, like the athletes, try to draw attention to themselves by inserting their signature catchphrases into as many highlights as possible.

One of the more amusing criticisms I've heard is that *SportsCenter* now spreads itself too thin: It covers *too* many sports. Or more specifically, it covers events that maybe shouldn't really be considered sports at all. It was bad enough, the carping went, when ESPN legitimized extreme events like skateboarding and street luge, but now it gives air time to the likes of poker, spelling bees and, get this, rock paper scissors tournaments.

When I hear this, I just smile and think, "Have we forgotten how far we've come?" I'd rather be saddled with hearing superfluous news like Dave McGill winning the first-ever USA Rock Paper Scissors Championship, than having to wait to read in the morning paper that Ice dropped 42 on the Sonics last night.

Clearly *SportsCenter* is a pop-culture institution. The show's longevity and its impact on sports and television make a strong case for its inclusion on any "best of TV" list. But what makes it so special? I think about how often something heard on *SportsCenter* is referenced in a lunch conversation or during a phone call with family or friends. When I travel on business I make sure to

---

Did You Know?

SportsCenter has aired every day since its inception on September 7, 1979, including 9/11. That day, they considered not airing, but instead did a show overviewing how the sporting events scheduled for that week would be affected by the attack.

---

tune in to *SportsCenter* in my hotel room—and not just to get sports scores. The familiarity of the show actually makes me think of home and helps me feel connected. And I know I'm not alone when I say there is something curiously enjoyable about spending a lazy morning watching the previous night's *SportsCenter* repeats air over and over again.

What makes it so special is that at least one new episode has been broadcast every day since September 7, 1979, and I've come to think of *SportsCenter* as a reliable friend that's always there ready to spend another hour talking sports with me.

Cast:

Chris Berman Anchor (1979–), **Bob Ley** Anchor (1979–), **Lee Leonard** Anchor (1979), **Tom Mees** Anchor (1979–93), **George Grande** Anchor (1979–89), **Greg Gumbel** Anchor (1980–86), **Sharon Smith** Anchor (1980–90), **Gayle Gardner** Anchor (1983–88), **Tim Brando** Anchor (1986–94), **Eric Clemons** Anchor (1987–91), **Charley Steiner** Anchor (1988–2002), **Chris Fowler** Anchor (1989–), **Dan Patrick** Anchor (1989–2006), **Chris Myers** Anchor (1989–94), **Robin Roberts** Anchor (1990–2002), **Gary Miller** Anchor (1990–2004), **Jack Edwards** Anchor (1991–2003), **Mike Tirico** Anchor (1991–2003), **Linda Cohn** Anchor (1992–), **Keith Olbermann** Anchor (1992–97), **Suzy Kolber** Anchor (1993–96; 1999–), **Steve Levy** Anchor (1993–), **Bill Pidto** Anchor (1993–), **Karl Ravech** Anchor (1993–), **Stuart Scott** Anchor (1993–), **Craig Kilborn** Anchor (1993–96), **Brett Haber** Anchor (1994–97), **Rece Davis** Anchor (1995–), **Kenny Mayne** Anchor (1995–), **Jason Jackson** Anchor (1995–2002), **John Buccigross** Anchor (1996–), **Mike Greenberg** Anchor (1996–), **Chris McKendry** Anchor (1996–), **Larry Beil** Anchor (1996–99), **Dave Feldman** Anchor (1996–2000), **Pam Ward** Anchor (1996–2004), **Rich Eisen** Anchor (1996–2003), **Brian Kenny** Anchor (1997–), **Trey Wingo** Anchor (1997–), **Whit Watson** Anchor (1997–2002), **John Anderson** Anchor (1999–), **Dave Revsine** Anchor (1999–), **Kevin Corke** Anchor (1999–2003), **Steve Berthiaume** Anchor (1999–2005), **Cindy Brunson** Anchor (1999–2000; 2002–), **Cara Capuano** Anchor (2000–04), **Scott Reiss** Anchor (2001–), **Scott Van Pelt** Anchor (2001–), **Matt Winer** Anchor (2001–), **Kevin Frazier** Anchor (2002–04), **Dana Jacobson** Anchor (2002–05), **Neil Everett** Anchor (2004–), **Stan Verrett** Anchor (2004–), **Jay Harris** Anchor (2004–), **Fred Hickman** Anchor (2004–), **Mike Hall** Anchor (2004–05), **Michelle Bonner** Anchor (2005–), **Josh Elliott** Anchor (2006–), **Robert Flores** Anchor (2007–)

St. Elsewhere

By N. F. Mendoza

Broadcast History: NBC, 10/26/1982–8/10/1988
Runtime: 60 minutes
Genre: Medical drama

Hospital settings have historically been healthy for television, right up to the present with *Grey's Anatomy*, *House* and *ER* continuing to score in the ratings.

Back in the day, of course, doctors like James Kildare, Ben Casey and Marcus Welby were pretty much saint-like and infallible, kindly figures (although, in Casey's case, with a surly edge) who seemed to know precisely what ailed their patients and usually cured them. *St. Elsewhere*, described at the time as *"Hill Street Blues* in a hospital," changed all that. Here, the doctor was no longer god, and many patients, frankly, were somewhat lucky to survive. The setting was Boston's run-down and over-burdened St. Eligius Hospital, where doctors also treated criminals, the homeless and the downtrodden. It was a place, one doctor kidded, where "you wouldn't send your mother-in-law." Some patients in *St. Elsewhere* died, and not always by natural causes. One was accidentally taken off life support. ·

Idiosyncratic and intense, wildly inventive and filled with scathing satire, *St. Elsewhere* was unpredictable to the end. In the series finale, for example, there were shades of *Citizen Kane*, when it was suggested that St. Eligius may have only existed inside, of all things, a snow globe and that 137 episodic stories were a figment of autistic youngster Tommy Westphall's imagination.

M*A*S*H, with its Korean-battlefield setting, was a sitcom with pathos. Like that classic series, *St. Elsewhere* used humor brilliantly and occasionally to surreal effect. My favorite example is when Dr. Elliot Axelrod (Stephen Furst) performs an autopsy while chatting with his dad (Louis Nye), who'd brought along his dog. As they visited, Alexrod Sr. was nonchalantly tossing bits of the cadaver's liver to the dog as treats.

In another episode, Dr. Wendy Armstrong (Kim Miyori)—plagued by bulimia, a misdiagnosis and an attack by a serial rapist—commits suicide. It's played opposite a scene in which Mark Harmon's Dr. Robert Caldwell, in the throes of passion with Nancy Stafford's Joan Halloran, gets his penis caught in his zipper.

Creators Joshua Brand and John Falsey (*Northern Exposure*) left after the first season, and Tom Fontana and John Masius took over through Season 5. Fontana's known for the gritty realism of his acclaimed *Homicide: Life on the Street* and *Oz*, and the darker tonal change is evident with them at the helm.

For the kind of fan who anticipates Alfred Hitchcock's cameos in his films, *St. Elsewhere* provided plenty of inside jokes (e.g. "Paging Dr. Howard, Dr. Moe, Dr. Fine"; *M*A*S*H*'s B. J. Hunnicutt is referred to by Dr. Craig as a drinking buddy in Korea.)

This was one of the all-time finest ensemble casts. While David Morse's Dr. Jack Morrison was the moral center, as the series progressed, audiences grew to know and understand and care for sharp-tongued Dr. Mark Craig (Emmy winner William Daniels), kindly Dr. Donald Westphall (Emmy winner Ed Flanders), sexy Dr. Phillip Chandler (Denzel Washington) and ladies' man Dr. Bobby Caldwell (Mark Harmon). It was here, too, that comedian Howie Mandel demonstrated considerable acting chops as Dr. Wayne Fiscus. The great Alfre Woodard was twice nominated for Emmys for her role as Dr. Roxanne Turner; Helen Hunt had a recurring role as Morrison's girlfriend; and Ed Begley Jr. and Christina Pickles garnered high praise for their portrayals of Dr. Victor Ehrlich and head nurse Helen Rosenthal (with six and five Emmy nominations, respectively).

When pompous, often unforgiving Dr. Craig quotes the end of Dr. Seuss's *Green Eggs & Ham* right after his son dies, it elicits an emotion fans still remember, more than 20 years later. Daniels later played George Feeny on *Boy Meets World*, and a whole generation may only associate him with that sitcom, but in *St. Elsewhere*, Daniels offered audiences some of the series' most powerful moments. One that comes to mind is a holiday show in which a grim and miserable Dr. Craig comes face to face with the very last people he wants to see at that particular moment—joyful revelers. His acting here, and throughout the series, is spot on. Daniels had to step into the shoes Flanders once filled, when Dr. Westphall famously quit (and mooned the boss). Some argued that Craig was just not as sympathetic as Westphall. Agreed. But that shouldn't take away from Daniels's importance to the series.

As for Dr. Morrison, he always struck me as the kind of doctor I never seem to encounter in real life. Actually, Dr. Morrison, Mandel's Dr. Fiscus and Cynthia Sikes's Dr. Annie Cavanero had much more personality than any real doctor I've been to (my doctors

> ## Did You Know?
>
> St. Ellglus (the name of the hospital in *St. Elsewhere*) is the patron saint of, among other things, veterinarians, sick horses, metalsmiths and cabbies.

are generally humorless and rote). Personal tragedy upon tragedy plagued Morrison. His beloved wife, Nina, who had recently given birth, slipped in the bathtub and died. Right after her death, Morrison had to pick up baby Pete from day care. He brings Pete home and collapses, sobbing, on the sofa in a memorably wrenching scene.

I also vividly remember the visceral moment when, after Dr. Craig used Nina's heart on a transplant patient, Morrison goes into the patient's room and, with his stethoscope, listens to her heart. And later, Pete is kidnapped and when he's finally returned to Morrison, the doctor, reaching to hug his son, chokingly whispers, "Oh, Nina!" Even Pete cannot escape unscathed.

And can any fan forget Dr. Peter White, played by Terence Knox? A regular for 50 episodes, the deeply troubled doctor was revealed to be the serial rapist who terrorized the hospital (with several of his victims being staff members, including Barbara Whinnery's Dr. Cathy Martin).

It's just as surprising today as it was then that, during its six-season run, the Peabody-winning *St. Elsewhere* never ranked above No. 49 in the ratings. It was nominated for 63 Emmys and won 13, and a good case can be made that it paved the way for more graphically realistic medical series such as *ER*. At this writing, *St. Elsewhere* was not yet available on DVD, so fans and fans-to-be must look, well, elsewhere—perhaps for syndicated or cable reruns. *St. Elsewhere* was a total original that respected the intelligence of its audience and was not shy about taking creative chances. What ails television today is that there aren't more series like it.

Cast:

Ed Flanders *Dr. Donald Westphall,* **William Daniels** *Dr. Mark Craig,* **Norman Lloyd** *Dr. Daniel Auschlander,* **Ed Begley Jr.** *Dr. Victor Ehrlich,* **David Morse** *Dr. Jack Morrison,* **Howie Mandel** *Dr. Wayne Fiscus,* **Christina Pickles** *Nurse Helen Rosenthal,* **Denzel Washington** *Dr. Phillip Chandler,* **David Birney** *Dr. Ben Samuels (1982–83),* **Cynthia Sikes** *Dr. Annie Cavanero (1982–85),* **Terence Knox** *Dr. Peter White (1982–85),* **G. W. Bailey** *Dr. Hugh Beale (1982–83),* **Kavi Raz** *Dr. V. J. Kochar (1982–84),* **Kim Miyori** *Dr. Wendy Armstrong (1982–84),* **Mark Harmon** *Dr. Robert Culdwell (1983–86),* **Stephen Furst** *Dr. Elliot Axelrod (1983–88)*

Star Trek: The Franchise

By Raven Snook

Star Trek
Broadcast History: NBC, 9/8/1966–6/3/1969
Runtime: 60 minutes
Genre: Sci-fi

Star Trek: The Next Generation
Broadcast History: Syndicated,
9/28/1987–5/23/1994
Runtime: 60 minutes
Genre: Sci-fi

Star Trek: Deep Space Nine
Broadcast History: Syndicated,
1/3/1993–6/2/1999
Runtime: 60 minutes
Genre: Sci-fi

Star Trek: Voyager
Broadcast History: UPN,
1/16/1995–5/23/2001
Runtime: 60 minutes
Genre: Sci-fi

Star Trek: Enterprise
Broadcast History: UPN,
9/26/2001–5/13/2005
Runtime: 60 minutes
Genre: Sci-fi

"Space, the final frontier." Not only is that the iconic opening line to *Star Trek*, it also sums up my impossible mission: to write about this unstoppable sci-fi franchise in 1,500 words or less. (Oh, how I wish I were the ever-efficient Data right now.) Never mind its cult following; this sci-fi series, which was only moderately successful in its first incarnation, spawned *five* small-screen spin-offs (not including online webisodes); 10 (and counting) films; tons of merchandise including novels, video games and toys; countless conventions; millions of acolytes; and even a bona fide language (say "Qapla" with me, my Klingon brothers!). Although you may not be the sort of person to don your homemade Starfleet uniform while watching reruns of *Star Trek*, you've undoubtedly heard of Kirk, Spock and the Starship Enterprise. *Star Trek* is, in short, a phenomenon, and it was created by an idealistic visionary named Gene Roddenberry.

A World War II pilot and ex-cop, Roddenberry was already a successful television writer when he came up with the idea for *Star Trek*, which he pitched as "*Wagon Train* to the stars." The series got off to a rocky start. Deemed "too cerebral," the first pilot (which starred Jeffrey Hunter as Capt. Pike in an episode titled "The Cage") was rejected by NBC execs. Roddenberry only kept one actor after retooling the show: Leonard Nimoy as the half-Vulcan/half-human science officer Mr. Spock. (Even Roddenberry's future wife, Majel Barrett, got the ax, although she later returned as Nurse Chapel and was involved in all the subsequent series, often supplying the voice of the ship's computer.) Beginning in 1966, Nimoy—along with William Shatner as the brash Capt. James T. Kirk and DeForest Kelley as the irascible Dr. Leonard "Bones" McCoy—led the USS *Enterprise* on its mission "to boldly go where no man has gone before." Along the way, they encountered strange and sometimes hostile alien life-forms, not to mention a galaxy of fascinating characters (including, in one episode, Abe Lincoln) and some provocatively clad beauties who invariably locked lips with Kirk.

Although set in the 23rd century, this seminal series pushed the 20th-century envelope. A humanitarian and futurist, Roddenberry wanted the series to be a catalyst for social change. In addition to tackling interstellar problems analogous to the struggles of the '60s (racism, class divisions, the cold war with the Klingons standing in for the Russians), it delivered a utopian vision of Earth's future in which people of all colors, creeds and cultures were ostensibly equal—even though women and minorities were usually relegated to subsidiary

Classic Episode Close-Up
"The Trouble with Tribbles"
(Original telecast: December 29, 1967)

A trash-talking Klingon, a living ball of fur that only wants to eat and reproduce, sly humor, Scotty throwing a punch, and some tongue-twisting dialogue make "The Trouble with Tribbles" a series classic. It first aired in 1967, but the episode was so memorable that footage from it was incorporated into an installment of *Star Trek: Deep Space Nine* almost 30 years later. Among the unforgettable moments: Kirk's exasperation when he finds the purring fur balls in his soup, his sandwich and even in his captain's chair; Spock's lame denial that he is "immune" to the creature; and Stanley Adams's performance as a jolly but relentless space-age salesman.

roles as evidenced by the supporting cast: James Doohan as Scottish engineer Montgomery Scott; Asian-American George Takei as helmsman Hikaru Sulu; Walter Koenig as Russian navigator Pavel Chekhov; and African-American Nichelle Nichols as communications expert Nyota Uhura, who was basically just a glorified secretary in a decidedly un-feminist miniskirt. Yet despite its limitations, *Star Trek* endorsed progressive politics and smashed taboos, even providing network television with its first interracial kiss—between Uhura and Kirk, of course—as well as lots of extraterrestrial love.

While the *Star Trek* prologue indicated that the Enterprise was on a "five-year mission," NBC unceremoniously dumped the Emmy-nominated show during its third season because of low ratings. Roddenberry didn't even get the chance to wrap everything up. But that changed when the series became a huge hit in reruns. In 1973, there was sufficient interest in the show to resurrect it as a cartoon, *Star Trek: The Animated Series*. Although the show was not officially part of the *Star Trek* canon, certain details were absorbed into its universe, including Kirk's middle name, Tiberius, and the invention of the Holodeck. But the true resurgence occurred later that decade, when plans for a new series, *Star Trek: Phase II*, were scrapped and ultimately transformed into *Star Trek: The Motion Picture*, starring the original series players. Although it was overlong and only moderately successful, three more movies followed before the franchise returned to the small screen—the awesome *Star Trek II: The Wrath of Kahn* featuring Ricardo Montalban's character from the "Space Seed" episode; the soporific *Star Trek III: The Search for Spock;* and the comical *Star Trek IV: The Voyage Home*, which took place on Earth in the 20th century.

Star Trek: The Next Generation, which launched in 1987 and lasted seven syndicated seasons, differed from its parent show in many ways. It was set a century later, boasted superior special effects and makeup, and featured a brand-new cast of characters, including Patrick Stewart as Capt. Jean-Luc Picard, who was less impulsive than Kirk; Jonathan Frakes as second-in-command William Thomas Riker, a Kirk-like ladies' man; Brent Spiner in the Spock-like role of Data, an android who longed to be human; and a host of multicultural supporting players. Minorities certainly had more authority on *ST: TNG* than they did on the original, a reflection of the social changes that had taken place between the '60s and the '80s. But *ST: TNG* had a lot less action, too. Whereas Kirk would subdue an enemy with a photon torpedo or karate chop, Picard and his crew always erred on the side of diplomacy. Yet Trekkers were rewarded with nuanced scripts that posed fascinating ethical and moral questions mirroring late 20th-century issues.

Although the original *Star Trek* actors appeared in two more movies—*Star Trek V: The Final Frontier*, ill-advisedly directed by Shatner, and *Star Trek VI: The Undiscovered Country*—they were, frankly speaking, a bit long in the tooth, and in 1994, Kirk officially passed the baton to the *ST: TNG* cast by passing away in the feature *Star Trek: Generations*.

Three more films starring the *ST: TNG* cast followed (the brilliant time-travel epic *Star Trek: First Contact*, and the lackluster *Star Trek: Insurrection* and *Star Trek: Nemesis*) as did three more series: *Star Trek: Deep Space Nine*, *Star Trek: Voyager* and, a prequel to the original series, *Star Trek: Enterprise*. While each show was unique, boasting its own particular premise and cast, they all fit into the palpable and complex universe created by Roddenberry. Although he died in 1991, his *Star Trek* legacy lived on thanks to reruns and continued to attract new generations of fans. Unlike *Star Wars*, which was a

---

TV and Film Connections

Has inspired a franchise of films
Spin-offs:
Star Trek: The Animated Series
Star Trek: The Next Generation
Star Trek: Deep Space Nine
Star Trek: Voyager
Star Trek: Enterprise

Did You Know?

Star Trek: The Next Generation was the first syndicated series to be nominated for a Best Drama Emmy, an honor the show received for its seventh and final season.

mythic, black-and-white, good-versus-evil saga, *Star Trek* morality was much more complicated and ambiguous. There was not one enemy to identify and defeat. Instead, every crew encountered multiple conflicts and was constantly challenged to come up with tailor-made resolutions. Sometimes they involved self-sacrifice—Spock giving his life in *Wrath of Kahn* because "the needs of the many outweigh the needs of the few . . . or the one." Sometimes they involved trickery—Kirk feigning death in "Amok Time" to help Spock through a Pon Farr ritual. And they often involved disobeying Starfleet's bureaucratic orders.

With seemingly inexhaustible possibilities, the franchise has inspired an unbelievable amount of fan fiction (including the "Slash" subgenre featuring gay story lines, often pairing up Kirk and Spock) and an impressive series of webisodes called *Star Trek: New Voyages*, which continued the truncated "five-year mission" with an amateur cast. (The series garnered so many downloads and such positive buzz, professional *Trek* veterans including Koenig and Tim Russ, who played Tuvok on *ST: Voyager*, got involved.) And in 2006, news emerged that *Lost* creator J. J. Abrams would helm the 11th *Star Trek* film, rumored to focus on Kirk and Spock's early days as students at Starfleet Academy.

But more than anything, *Star Trek* continues to inspire the hope that one day the world will match Roddenberry's optimistic vision of togetherness. Although Trekkers are too often stereotyped as nerdy losers who probably live in their parents' basements (hilariously spoofed in the classic 1986 *Saturday Night Live* sketch starring Shatner), in reality the franchise attracts an incredibly diverse array of fans. Visit any convention and you'll be amazed at how *Star Trek* brings disparate groups together regardless of color, creed or culture. And ultimately, that's what *Star Trek* has always been about.

> ## Classic Episode Close-Up
> *Star Trek: Deep Space Nine*
> "Trials and Tribbleations"
> *(Original telecast: November 4, 1996)*
>
> More trouble with tribbles. Clever use of footage from a classic episode of the original series conjures a slyly humorous outing that finds Capt. Kirk still having problems with the adorable, furry creatures. A renegade undercover Klingon agent steals a Bajoran Orb and sends himself, along with the Defiant and its crew, back 105 years into the past. His objective: to kill Kirk. Sisko and company realize they must somehow board the *Enterprise* (and the tribble-filled K-7 space station) to stop him, while preserving the time line. The assassin's weapon of choice? An exploding tribble.

Cast for *Star Trek*:

William Shatner *Capt. James T. Kirk*, **Leonard Nimoy** *Mr. Spock*, **DeForest Kelley** *Dr. Leonard McCoy*, **George Takei** *Sulu*, **Nichelle Nichols** *Uhura*, **James Doohan** *Engineer Montgomery Scott*, **Majel Barrett** *Nurse Christine Chapel*, **Walter Koenig** *Ens. Pavel Chekov (1967–69)*

Star Trek: The Franchise

Cast for *Star Trek: The Next Generation*:

Patrick Stewart *Capt. Jean–Luc Picard*, **Jonathan Frakes** *Cdr. William Riker*, **LeVar Burton** *Lt. Geordi La Forge*, **Denise Crosby** *Lt. Tasha Yar (1987–88)*, **Marina Sirtis** *Deanna Troi*, **Brent Spiner** *Lt. Cdr. Data*, **Wil Wheaton** *Wesley Crusher (1987–90)*, **Michael Dorn** *Lt. Worf*, **Gates McFadden** *Dr. Beverly Crusher (1987–88; 1989–94)*, **Diana Muldaur** *Dr. Katherine 'Kate' Pulaski (1988–89)*

Cast for *Star Trek: Deep Space Nine*:

Avery Brooks *Cdr. Sisko*, **Rene Auberjonois** *Odo*, **Siddig El Fadil (a.k.a. Alexander Siddig)** *Dr. Bashir*, **Terry Ferrell** *Jadzia Dax (1993–98)*, **Cirroc Lofton** *Jake Sisko*, **Armin Shimerman** *Quark*, **Colm Meaney** *Miles O'Brien*, **Nana Visitor** *Maj. Kira Nerys*, **Michael Dorn** *Lt. Cdr. Worf (1995–99)*, **Nicole de Boer** *Lt. Ezri Dax (1998–99)*

Cast for *Star Trek: Voyager*:

Kate Mulgrew *Capt. Kathryn Janeway*, **Robert Beltran** *First Off. Chakotay*, **Tim Russ** *Security Chief Tuvok*, **Ethan Phillips** *Neelix*, **Robert Picardo** *The Doctor*, **Roxann Dawson** *Chief Engineer B'Elanna Torres*, **Robert Duncan McNeill** *Lt. Tom Paris*, **Garrett Wang** *Ens. Harry Kim*, **Jennifer Lien** *Kes (1995–97)*, **Jeri Ryan** *Seven of Nine (1997–2001)*

Cast for *Star Trek: Enterprise*:

Scott Bakula *Capt. Jonathan Archer*, **Connor Trinneer** *Chief Engineer Trip Tucker*, **Jolene Blalock** *Sub Cdr. T'Pol*, **Dominic Keating** *Lt. Malcolm Reed*, **Anthony Montgomery** *Ens. Travis Mayweather*, **Linda Park** *Ens. Hoshi Sato*, **John Billingsley** *Dr. Phlox*

Survivor

By Tim Holland
Broadcast History: CBS, 5/31/2000–
Runtime: 60 minutes
Genre: Reality competition

Executive producer Mark Burnett calls it a "nonscripted drama," while host Jeff Probst refers it as "a social experiment." Whatever it is, *Survivor* is *the* show that launched the reality craze, which has dominated much of television since 2000. Since its debut, the show has aired 14 editions, from such far-flung locales as Borneo, Africa, Australia, Panama's Pearl Islands (the setting for three contests), Guatemala and Palau. Along the way the series has become a bona fide cultural phenomenon and a ratings juggernaut, even though viewership is down somewhat from its heyday. It is still, arguably, the class of the genre and was the first reality show to win an Emmy, picking up 2001's Outstanding Non-Fiction Program (Special Class) award.

Survivor's setup is brilliant in its simplicity. Sixteen to 20 "castaways," equally divided between men and women, are stranded in a remote area, usually on a deserted island, where they attempt to "outwit, outlast, outplay" their competitors to win the $1 million grand prize. The players are divided into two to four tribes and compete against opposing groups in mostly physical challenges, such as obstacle courses and endurance tests, to win either a reward (often food or supplies) or immunity from elimination. The tribe that loses immunity must attend a tribal council where the members vote out one of their own. Generally, when there are eight to 10 players remaining, the tribes merge into one and the castaways, when they aren't conspiring against one another and forming and dismantling alliances, compete individually in challenges. When only two players remain, a number of previous members who were cast out form a jury that votes for the winner.

The key to winning *Survivor* is to form a strong alliance with three to four other players who remain true to each other. Richard Hatch, on the original Borneo edition, figured that out early. His four-person alliance picked off competitors one by one. Not only did Hatch make it to the finals, he was crowned the game's first champion. The game has pretty much been played the same way since. That's not to say there haven't been twists along the way. In Africa, players had to switch teams without warning (this oftentimes still occurs). The Amazon and Vanuatu editions divided its initial tribes by sex, while the Panama series mixed tribes up according to sex *and* age (younger men, younger women, older men, older women) and added to the mix Exile Island, a small, uninhabited island where individual players are banished for days on their own. The most controversial tribal splits occurred on Cook Islands where the four original tribes were divided by race (white, African-American, Asian-American, Hispanic). The eighth installment was an all-star version that pitted 18 of the show's most memorable players against one another, with Australian Outback castaway Amber Brkich being crowned the ultimate survivor.

Survivor was thought to be nothing more than a fun, experimental summer series when it debuted on May 31, 2000. That quickly changed when it achieved instant watercooler buzz. Spirited debates followed on whether the addictive show, with its Machiavellian strategies and bug-eating contests, marked a new low in TV programming or was simply a great soap opera starring regular folks who are, well, just like us. The debate still goes on, albeit with far less vigor since *Survivor* and reality shows in general are now as much a part of the TV landscape as dramas and sitcoms. In fact, a case could be made that *Survivor* is the most influential program of the past decade. Without it, there would be no *American Idol* or *Apprentice* or *Amazing Race*. Yes, reality television existed before *Survivor* (MTV's *The Real World* kicked off in 1992 and PBS's landmark *An American Family* dates back to 1973), but *Survivor* brought reality into the mainstream and made it a programming staple to be reckoned with. Its first edition was so successful that CBS moved it from Wednesday to Thursday nights in early 2001 to anchor TV's most financially lucrative evening. The switch, along with *CSI* also moving over to Thursdays, sounded the death knell for NBC's Must-See comedy lineup and allowed the perennially older-skewing CBS to attract the significantly younger audience that advertisers craved.

Did You Know?

Contestant Jon Dalton lied about his grandmother passing away in order to win a reward challenge. CBS executives actually called his grandmother's home to offer condolences, but she herself answered the phone.

The thrill of watching ordinary people make utter fools of themselves, engage in backstabbing or attempt extraordinary challenges isn't anything new. Nor is voyeurism, for that matter. "We've become a race of Peeping Toms," Thelma Ritter says in Alfred Hitchcock's 1954 suspense thriller *Rear Window*. She is, of course, talking to James Stewart, who spends his days and nights in a wheelchair spying on his neighbors (a lonely woman, a sexy girl, a newlywed couple, a suspected murderer) through his apartment's rear window. He just can't pull himself away. More than 50 years later not much has changed, except the *way* we peep. Thanks largely to *Survivor* and its astonishing cultural impact, TV and computers are our preferred rear windows that allow us to peek in on each other 24/7. No wonder TV GUIDE once named Mark Burnett No. 1 on its Most Valuable Players list and *Time* selected him as one of the 100 most influential people in the world.

In 1968, Andy Warhol famously predicted that "in the future everyone will be famous for 15 minutes." Now we know how. Some *Survivor* alumni stretched their newfound fame a bit longer, like Jeri Manthey and Jenna Morasca who each posed for *Playboy*, and Colleen Haskell who co-starred in the 2001 big-screen comedy *The Animal*. But the castaway who capitalized the most on her *Survivor* popularity is Elisabeth Hasselbeck. She parlayed her final-four finish and girl-next-door good looks from the Australian Outback into a co-hosting gig on ABC's morning chatfest *The View* in 2003.

Most of her reality cohorts are long forgotten, but the show that made her a celebrity has definitely remained one of the medium's sturdiest survivors.

Cast:

Jeff Probst *Host*

Taxi

By Stuart Michaelson

Broadcast History: ABC, 9/12/1978–6/10/1982;
NBC, 9/30/1982–7/27/1983
Runtime: 30 minutes
Genre: Sitcom

Winner of three straight Outstanding Comedy Emmys, *Taxi* was fuel-injected with one of TV's great ensemble casts and turbo-charged by MTM Productions, conjurers of such classics as *Bob Newhart* and *The Mary Tyler Moore Show*.

It was also director James Burrows's toughest ride because, he once said, "all of the actors were from another planet, and the writers were from another galaxy."

One, I'd think, that no GPS navigation system could find.

Emmy voters, it would seem, hailed *Taxi* more frequently than viewers: It was canceled twice during its 1978–83 run, first by ABC, then by NBC. Star Judd Hirsch, accepting an Outstanding Actor in a Comedy Series Emmy the year of its final cancellation, commented that since "you got to keep giving some kind of laurels to us, then you should really put us back on the air."

Maybe, maybe not: Could be it's best that, like the Beatles, the folks behind *Taxi* (including Burrows and producers Ed Weinberger, James L. Brooks, and Glen and Les Charles) left behind a brief, unblemished streak of greatness that never faded into self-parody.

Life in New York's tiny, unforgettable Sunshine Cab Co. garage was wonderfully etched, with its blue-collar antiheroes who basked (or baked) in hysterical camaraderie and often waited with mixed feelings for their ships to come in. I can still almost taste bitter coffee from the machine where Hirsch's hangdog Alex Rieger had countless philosophical chats with Sunshine folks, confidently dispensing wisdom and good advice to others, but oddly unable to significantly better himself. He was like Andy Griffith before him, only here he was the straight man to myriad Barney Fifes.

Those half (and sometimes whole) loonies who tried to gain the world without losing their souls (not to mention their jobs) also included good-natured sexpot/struggling art dealer Elaine Nardo (Marilu Henner); affable boxer Tony Banta (Tony Danza); floppy-haired fledgling actor Bobby Wheeler (Jeff Conaway); signals-crossed '60s casualty Reverend Jim Ignatowski (Christopher Lloyd); warmly bizarre mechanic Latka Gravas (Andy Kaufman), who spoke an unidentifiable foreign language; Lakta's spunky love, Simka (Carol Kane); for one season, John Burns (Randall Carver); and TV GUIDE's No. 1 Television Character of All Time, bullying dispatcher Louie De Palma (Emmy winner Danny DeVito).

DeVito's infamous audition for the role of the tiny tyrant consisted of the actor taking his acid-tongued character literally: DeVito tossed down the script and demanded, "Who wrote this s—t?" "We were all hysterical," recalled original casting director Joel Thurm. "He left, and everybody just turned to each other and said 'I guess that's Louie.'" Louie's underlings wouldn't have been so blasé in describing him. For while DeVito had once played Hirsch's dog in a regional theater production, Louie clearly held the leashes at the garage, compulsively barking orders ("Rieeeegah!!! Nahhdohh!!!") from a cage above his minions and sparing no one in harsh put-downs.

Even Louie, though, had some flirtations with humanity, such as his turn in the episode "I Wanna Be Around" (January 7, 1982), in which he couldn't go through with plans to boot Reverend Jim from a bomb shelter that Louie put together after watching a frightening episode of *Donahue*.

That was one of countless *Taxi* outings that spew from fans' memories like smoke from the radiator of an old cab. Others include:

- "Reverend Jim: A Space Odyssey" (September 25, 1979), featuring Ignatowski's driving test. After reading the first question, he asks the cabbies what a yellow light means. "Slow down!" Bobby tells him. "OK," says Jim. "What . . . does . . . a . . . yellow . . . light . . . mean?"

- "Latka the Playboy" (May 21, 1981), in which Kaufman (one of TV's most original and strangest comics) takes on a self-centered, skirt-chasing alter ego, Vic Ferrari, whom he reprised in subsequent episodes.

- "Latka's Cookies" (February 5, 1981), featuring a guest appearance by cookie mogul Famous Amos during Latka's brief fling marketing suspiciously popular cookies . . . which turn out to be drugged.

- "Guess Who's Coming for Brefnish?" (January 15, 1980), highlighted by the debut of Kane in her Emmy-winning role. She and Latka click after he hears her speaking in the same ersatz Eastern European language ("Tenk you veddy much") as his; their characters eventually wed.

- "Come As You Aren't" (October 10, 1978), in which Elaine hopes to quicken her ascent in the New York art world by hosting a cocktail party, to which she invites Alex . . . but asks him to lie about his occupation, for fear hers will be discovered.

Within the confines of a network sitcom, *Taxi*—thanks to wonderful acting, writing that put character ahead of plot, and sophistication ahead of lowest-common-denominator predictability—played more like a series of short plays than TV episodes. Its memorably dingy set made viewers truly feel they were in that garage with those people, and the cabbies' dreams, often so out of reach, were palpable.

In most cases, for its actors, of course, dreams weren't so elusive. Hirsch went on to more success on TV (*Dear John*, *Numb3rs*), movies (the acclaimed *Running on Empty* and the popular *Independence Day*) and stage (winning Tonys for *I'm Not Rappaport* and *Conversations with My Father*); Henner was on TV's *Evening Shade*, such films as *L.A. Story* and the play *Chicago*; former real-life boxer Danza again succeeded in a role in which he used his real first name, starring on the sitcom *Who's the Boss?*, and hosted a talk show; Lloyd went on to more fame, notably in the *Back to the Future* film franchise; Kaufman's comedy became even more offbeat until his untimely death, and he was immortalized both in the R.E.M. song "Man on the Moon" and a Jim Carrey film of the same name; Kane acted in such films as *The Princess Bride*; and DeVito, so adept then as now at being both appealing and appalling, proved that you needn't be a hunk to be a star, taking on lead roles in films like *Throw Momma from the Train*, *The Rainmaker* and *Get Shorty*.

I'd like to think, while watching episodes today, that all the ex-cabbies, alive in some parallel TV world, succeeded, too, and can look back at their scuffling days, their beers at Mario's, and their battles with Louie and themselves, with affection.

As for its fans, all we can say is, "Tenk you veddy much."

Cast:

Judd Hirsch *Alex Rieger*, **Jeff Conaway** *Bobby Wheeler (1978–81)*, **Danny DeVito** *Louie De Palma*, **Marilu Henner** *Elaine Nardo*, **Tony Danza** *Tony Banta*, **Andy Kaufman** *Latka Gravas*, **Randall Carver** *John Burns (1978–79)*, **Christopher Lloyd** *"Reverend Jim" Ignatowski (1979–83)*, **Carol Kane** *Simka Gravas (1981–83)*

thirtysomething

By Trish Wethman

Broadcast History: ABC, 9/29/1987–9/3/1991
Runtime: 60 minutes
Genre: Drama

I was 16 on September 29, 1987, when *thirty-something* made its debut—a veritable lifetime ago when I was thoroughly unacquainted with the impending realities of adulthood that were being explored on the series. Yet this superlative drama about baby boomers in Philadelphia resonated with me in a way no television show had before and, truthfully, only a few have since. Perhaps it was the simple fact that the show exuded a wrenching intimacy that even a teenager could discern. No question, this was quality television, but quality doesn't always translate into viewer loyalty—look no further than the classy but not especially successful subsequent collaborations of *thirtysomething* creators Marshall Herskovitz and Edward Zwick (*My So-Called Life*, *Relativity*, *Once and Again*). This was one of those shows that got under your skin and, for better or worse, stayed there.

Say what you will about its angst-ridden band of yuppies and all that (much parodied) introspective dialogue, there was something about these people that was undeniably compelling and utterly watchable. Maybe it was because they were so human—flawed, neurotic, possessing equal amounts of self-awareness and self-loathing. Or maybe it was because their day-to-day situations were so recognizable—work acquaintances merging awkwardly with college friends; family tensions bubbling to the surface; marriages on the brink of disaster, tenuously strung together by children and mortgages; the romantic wanderlust of the twenties that, for many, gives way to the realities of adult responsibilities and expectations. There was something about these people that made you feel like you knew them . . . that in many ways, you *were* them.

This little universe revolved around the Steadmans—Michael, the artistically unsatisfied writer trapped in the life of a precariously self-employed advertising breadwinner; and Hope, his accomplished, conflicted stay-at-home wife. Both struggled with the demands of a new family, a new home and a marriage in flux. Played to endearing, maddening perfection by Ken Olin and Mel Harris, the Steadmans embodied the hopes and dreams of every young couple wishing for financial success unfettered by compromise.

Emmy winners Timothy Busfield and Patricia Wettig offered nuanced portrayals of philandering, immature Elliot Weston, Michael's partner in their ill-fated advertising company, and his long-suffering wife, Nancy. The demise and subsequent rebuilding of their marriage packed an emotional wallop and provided a realistic counterpoint to Michael and Hope's seemingly perfect coupling. Nancy's diagnosis with cancer in the show's third season brought her and Elliot's distinctive, tumultuous love story to the forefront.

Polly Draper embodied Ellyn, Hope's successful, self-conscious childhood friend. Her bond with Hope was laced with a competitive streak that provided a context for Hope's ambivalence over abandoning her career for motherhood. There was also Michael's witty, bohemian photographer cousin, Melissa, portrayed by Emmy winner Melanie Mayron. Melissa's disappointment with Michael's life choices—turning his back on his artistic aspirations to ascend the corporate ladder—was always an undercurrent of their sibling-like relationship. But it was Melissa's vulnerability and humor that were most frequently on display and made her character so appealing and relatable. Adding to the incestuous vibe of this crowd, Melissa's onetime love and current platonic crush was Michael's best friend from college, the roguish, irresponsible Gary (Peter Horton). The character of Gary could have easily slid into cliché, but instead the writers, and Horton himself, imbued him with an earnest likeability, intelligence and charisma. Gary's death in the show's last season was all the more wrenching because it came on the heels of his tentative first steps into maturity via a committed relationship and fatherhood.

There were other memorable characters as well—Susannah (Patricia Kalember), Gary's edgy foil; the deliciously venal Miles Drentell (David Clennon), Michael's DAA boss (a character who later returned in episodes of *Once and Again*); Lee (Corey Parker), Melissa's much younger soul mate; and Billy (Erich Anderson), Ellyn's patient, soft-spoken husband-to-be. And there was also controversy, such as the advertiser boycott spurred by the inclusion of a scene featuring two consenting male adults enjoying some post-coital bliss. But for me, one of the most memorable aspects of the show was the music. Frequently penned by W. G. Snuffy Walden and Stewart Levin, the music in each episode, starting with the spry, lilting guitar and piano-tinged theme song, was carefully used to match the story that was being told, resulting in a signature sound that was evocative and soulful, much like the characters themselves.

Did You Know?

Thirtysomething was also responsible for the coinage of the word "twentysomething," to describe Generation X.

A recent review of some of my favorite episodes (lovingly videotaped in the pre-TiVo era since the show is not yet available on DVD) reminded me once again of not only how much I love this show but why. Each episode of this series was filled with thought-provoking, tear-jerking, head-nodding glimpses into the ways that friends become family and vice versa, and how it is not what we do, but how we do it and with whom, that ultimately defines who we are. I am still genuinely moved by these people and the journeys they took. I laughed while revisiting "Mr. Right," which chronicled Melissa and Ellyn's misadventures in video dating. "A Second Look" again brought me to tears as Nancy's recovery from ovarian cancer was juxtaposed against the sudden, shocking car accident that ended Gary's life. "I'll Be Home for Christmas" showcased the strife of celebrating the holidays in a two-religion household with a dose of melancholy thrown in for good measure.

However, my single favorite episode remains "The Wedding," in which Ellyn's pre-matrimonial doubts threatened to overtake her long-awaited walk down the aisle. This episode aired during the last season and came close on the heels of Gary's death—which was still an open wound for many of the characters and series fans. But for devotees of the show, Ellyn's wedding provided the closest thing to closure that we would get. After a series of romantic missteps, Ellyn finally got her happily ever after, with Hope and Michael presiding over the festivities like proud parents, Melissa rekindling her romance with Lee, Nancy and Elliot basking in the glow of her remission, and Gary's apparition making an appearance, assuring his friend Michael that "It's all gonna be OK."

Top 3 Moments
- Never jumped.
- When Gary died.
- Bad from Day 1.

For more, visit www.jumptheshark.com.

Looking back now, I can see why my 16-year-old self responded to this show in such a visceral way. At a time in my life when uncertainty about the future loomed large, I could look at these characters and see that no one is handed a roadmap for the future. The only things we have any control over are the choices we make and the company we keep. Despite the uncertainty, there was something reassuring about that idea that this show encapsulated. *Thirtysomething* "is a show about creating your own family," Zwick and Herskovitz wrote. For a much-too-brief run of four years, I felt, in a sense, a part of this particular TV family. And, in the process, learned a good deal about myself.

Cast:

Mel Harris *Hope Steadman,* **Ken Olin** *Michael Steadman,* **Polly Draper** *Ellyn,* **Peter Horton** *Prof. Gary Shepherd,* **Timothy Busfield** *Elliot Weston,* **Melanie Mayron** *Melissa Steadman,* **Patricia Wettig** *Nancy Weston,* **Patricia Kalember** *Susannah Hart (1989–91),* **David Clennon** *Miles Drentell (1989–91)*

Today

By Paul Droesch

Broadcast History: NBC, 1/14/1952–
Runtime: Varied
Genre: Newsmagazine

It's the most profitable show on television.

Today's no stranger to superlatives, seeing as how it is TV's longest-running show (it's five and a half months older than *Guiding Light*). But most profitable? That's a superlative you can take to the bank: in the television industry, nothing says *ca-ching* like *Today*. It earns NBC some $250 million a year. It also leads the way during the only time of day that has proven impervious to the inroads of cable. You have to get up pretty early in the morning to beat that.

The concept behind *Today* is simplicity itself—just a mix of news; news-maker, celebrity and author interviews; health and lifestyle advice; plus an occasional singer (and weather and traffic during local cut-ins). But while no backs were broken in thinking it up, mountains were moved because of it. Just think about it and you can see how *Today* begat, say *Oprah* (it was first with "infotainment," and that led to the development of talk shows). Local news, too. Someone in Kankakee or Houston had to fill those local cut-in segments. Many stations created news departments to do so, and their advertising departments would come to love that because they got to sell ads during the cut-ins.

The NBC exec behind it all, Sylvester ("Pat") Weaver—Sigourney's dad—was the same guy who thought up its enormously profitable bookend on NBC, *Tonight*. Weaver's brilliance (he's also credited with developing Sid Caesar's *Your Show of Shows*) was that he knew how to mix the sacred and the profane, with a slight but definite tilt toward the latter. In Weaver's day, *Today* was a place where Eleanor Roosevelt could coexist with a chimp named J. Fred Muggs. And today, it's a place where Hillary Rodham Clinton can sit for a seri-ous interview and Kevin Federline can turn up an hour later. True, newscasts are likely to spend more time on runaway brides or Michael Jackson's latest mishap than on the goings-on of the International Atomic Energy Agency, but if the IAEA's up to something important, you'll know about it first thing in the morning on *Today*. The overall aim: to "put you in touch with the world," as *Today*'s first anchor Dave Garroway put it, "without being stuffy about it."

Weaver also knew that he had to create an on-air "family" that would be welcomed into people's homes at a time of day when folks aren't always at their cheeriest. The talent had to supply the cheer, of course, and some wit, but be low-key enough so that their cheer and wit didn't seem histrionic. They had to be likable—particularly in the softer-focused second hour of the show, when more of the hosts' personalities were on display. After all, the bankable beauty of a morning show is that its all-things-to-all-people approach can attract a much wider array of advertisers than evening newscasts can ever hope to. And with two (and, as of 2000, three) hours to fill, there's plenty of time for commercials. But viewers must keep watching, and they won't do that if they don't like the people they're watching.

The horn-rimmed, bow-tied Garroway, a one-time Chicago jazz-and-variety-show host, would prove to fill the daddy role nicely. But on *Today*'s first day, January 14, 1952, NBC had fewer than 30 affiliates and only one sponsor on board. Things didn't get much better that first year as pacing problems, technical glitches and an American public unaccustomed to turning on the TV first thing in the morning (those who had TV sets, that is, and not many did) combined to make it a rough one indeed. Wrote one critic: "Do yourself a favor, NBC, roll over and go back to sleep."

Enter J. Fred, who brought in kids and their moms. He's credited with selling a lot of television sets, too, so Weaver and Garroway had more and more company as they worked out the kinks during the first five years. They did lose a newscaster, Jack Fleming, who didn't like working with a monkey, but Fleming was replaced by Frank Blair, who stayed with the show for 22 years.

Also in the mix was announcer Jack Lescoulie, who schmoozed with folks in the crowd outside the studio and served as Garroway's Ed McMahon (there were *Tonight*-style comedy sketches in those days, too). Lescoulie was also the sportscaster, and while sports wasn't particularly important to *Today*, which has always appealed largely to women, what was important was that Lescoulie was funny—he was the first guy to hold down the "jolly" slot that Joe Garagiola, then Willard Scott and now Al Roker fill so well.

J. Fred, never an especially cuddly chimp, became downright nasty as he grew up and, after biting Martha Raye one morning in 1957, was history (although, as of 2006, he was still alive). His Trivial Pursuit–worthy successor, Kokomo Jr., lasted only a year and by 1961, when *Today* was placed in NBC's news division, the skits were history, too.

> ## Did You Know?
>
> In its first year, ratings were not good. However, once *Today* added the chimp J. Fred Muggs to the cast, ratings improved because kids begged their parents to watch it.

Garroway left in 1961, and whatever shenanigans still remained were not brooked easily by his replacement, John Chancellor, a bad fit for the program if ever there was one. "*The Today Show* was awful," he once told Larry King. "I found myself introducing musical acts at 7:45 in the morning and that was too much for me. I wanted to get back to work." Not surprisingly, Chancellor lasted only a year before being rescued by the more easygoing Hugh Downs.

Another important change of the '60s was the emergence of women. In the '50s they were "the *Today* Girls." Estelle Parsons was the first, and others included Lee Meriwether, Helen O'Connell, Florence Henderson, Maureen

O'Sullivan and Betsy Palmer. Barbara Walters came on board in 1961, and soon the times began a changin'. Hired as a writer, Walters was pressed into on-air duty around the time of the JFK assassination and became the unofficial co-host in '64. Ten years later her status was made official.

But Walters's arrival wasn't as big a deal as her departure, in 1976, would prove to be. Walters left for a co-anchor slot (with a grumbling Harry Reasoner) on ABC's evening news, a first for a woman at a time when network evening newscasts mattered a lot more than they do now. Her departure coincided with the birth and rapid rise of *Today*'s only meaningful competition, ABC's less newsy, more casual *Good Morning America*. One of Walters's replacements, Tom Brokaw, wasn't much happier a camper than Chancellor had been (he refused to do commercials), and while his co-anchor, Jane Pauley, proved to be an enduring success (she lasted 13 years), by the early '80s *GMA* had dethroned *Today*. Pauley and the less-than-cheery Bryant Gumbel would wander in the second-place wilderness for most of the '80s.

Katie Couric righted things after she signed on in 1991, of course, and by '95 *Today* was back on top. Couric was warm and witty (though a tough interviewer when she had to be), but what was most important was that she had an everywoman appeal. People, women particularly, could relate to her. Witness the national grief when her 42-year-old husband, lawyer Jay Monahan, died of colon cancer in 1998. And witness the upsurge in colonoscopies shortly thereafter when Couric had one on *Today*. Couric also hit it off famously with Matt Lauer, the affable newsreader who was promoted to co-anchor in 1997, and by '99, *Today* had some two million more viewers a day than *GMA*.

But this essay won't end happily ever after because who knows how *Today* will end? It should be noted that the first half of the 2000s hasn't been kind to the longest-running show on television. Diane Sawyer and Charles Gibson reinvigorated *GMA*, while executive producer after executive producer has walked the plank at *Today*. There were even Q rating signs indicating that Couric was beginning to wear out her welcome after 15 years on the job.

So her move to CBS was likely good for her and NBC. Her replacement, Meredith Vieira, demonstrated compellingly on *The View* that she relates to viewers (women particularly) with the best of them, and words like "smooth" and "seamless" were used to describe her transition to *Today*. But still, Vieira has no small challenge facing her. After all, there's no place to go but down for TV's most profitable show.

Cast:

Dave Garroway Host *(1952–61)*, **John Chancellor** Host *(1961–62)*, **Hugh Downs** Host *(1962–71)*, **Frank McGee** Host *(1971–74)*, **Jim Hartz** Host *(1974–76)*, **Barbara Walters** Host *(1974–76)*, **Tom Brokaw** Host *(1976–81)*, **Jane Pauley** Host *(1976–89)*, **Bryant Gumbel** Host *(1982–97)*, **Deborah Norville** Host *(1989–91)*, **Katie Couric** Host *(1991–2006)*, **Matt Lauer** Host *(1997–)*, **Meredith Vieira** Host *(2006–)*

The Tonight Show Starring Johnny Carson

By Jeff Gemmill

Broadcast History: NBC, 10/1/1962–5/22/1992
Runtime: 60 minutes
Genre: Talk show

During his last *Tonight Show* **monologue** on May 22, 1992 (a farewell seen by 55 million people, making it still the highest rated *Tonight* of all time), Johnny Carson confessed that NBC approached him with the suggestion of turning the finale into a prime-time special. "I said, well, I would prefer to end like we started [in 1962]—rather quietly, in our same time slot, in front of our same shabby little set." However, he added, "I am taking the applause sign home—putting it in the bedroom. And maybe just once a week turning it on." *Ba-ram-bump*.

Each night, as the title and opening credits scrolled across the screen, the band—led by Skitch Henderson (from '62 to '66), Milton DeLugg ('66 to '67) and Doc Severinsen (from '67 to the end)—launched into a jaunty theme song that Carson himself co-wrote with Paul Anka. Then, the venerable Ed McMahon's deep voice boomed in, announcing the night's guests before introducing the star with a roll of the tongue as distinct as any Buddy Rich drum fill: "Heeeeere's Johnny!"

With that, the man himself walked to center stage and did a few solid minutes of stand-up. He targeted politicians and others in the news with deft jabs, commented on the economy and crazy fads, and did it all with a twinkle in his eye. During a mid-'70s recession, for instance, he observed "the bad news is that unemployment lines are getting longer and longer. And the good news is that by the time you get up to the clerk you'll be old enough to qualify for Social Security." After the first President Bush apologized for breaking a vow not to raise taxes, Carson joked, "Read my lips: no new promises." The 20-or-so jokes ran the gamut from hilarious to (intentional or not) cringe-worthy bad, but the bombs were always followed by that classic Carson doubletake or a zinger that more than made up for the comic affront. The key, of course, was flawless timing. Like Jack Benny (one of his idols), he waited for the groans to stop before tossing out a self-deprecating line that brought down the house.

> **Did You Know?**
>
> Carson never appeared on *The Tonight Show* following his retirement, but did appear twice on *The Late Show with David Letterman*.

When the show returned from commercial break, Johnny and Ed might engage in unscripted banter; or Johnny might star in a skit as fast-talking movie host Art Fern, the formidable Aunt Blabby or that mysterious soothsayer from the East, Carnac the Magnificent. In Ed McMahon's warm memoir of working with and for his longtime boss, *Here's Johnny: My Memories of Johnny Carson, The Tonight Show, and 46 Years of Friendship*, he recalls how Johnny set the guiding principle for the program with a simple comment moments before their first show: "Let's just go down and entertain the hell out of them." It may seem obvious, but following in the footsteps of the emotional and unpredictable Jack Paar, his *Tonight Show* predecessor, it needed to be said. Carson understood that his viewers were either in bed or on their way to bed; and that it was his job to send them to dreamland with smiles, not frowns. Another point he insisted upon: "Don't make it feel too planned." By relying on his, McMahon's and their guests' innate charm, wit and eccentricities, he created a facsimile of a cocktail party that everyone wanted to attend.

As with any good party, success often rested with the guests—and what Johnny had was a great skill in putting them at ease and drawing them out. Just as important, he knew when to let *them* take control—Robin Williams taking flight on any of his visits comes to mind, as does Bob Hope and Dean Martin creating havoc with George Gobel in 1969. The two turned the crew-cut comedian into a human punch line, with Martin (back in the days when guests smoked on-air) using Gobel's drink as his personal ashtray, which led Gobel to observe, to much laughter and applause, "Do you ever get the feeling that the world was a tuxedo and you were a pair of brown shoes?" And when the unexpected happened, few could toss off an ad-lib like Johnny. For example, everyone—or most everyone of a certain age—remembers the highlight clip from 1965 of Ed Ames (who played a Native American named Mingo on *Daniel Boone*) tossing a tomahawk with circumcision-like precision at a man-shaped target. Carson's reaction was priceless, as was his riposte: "Ed, I didn't know you were Jewish!" Through it all, Carson was confident, dapper and pleasant, even when dumping ice down Burt Reynolds's shirt. He seemed completely unflappable and never appeared to lose his cool.

Well, maybe once. First understand: in the '70s, the *Tonight Show* aired from 11:30 p.m. to 1 a.m. five nights a week, but Johnny himself only worked Tuesdays through Fridays. Mondays, guest hosts filled in. (It wasn't until '83 with Joan Rivers that a "permanent" guest host was named.) On Tuesday,

Preview Review
September 15, 1962

The Tonight Show will rely mostly on the new host and replacement for Jack Paar, Johnny Carson, veteran TV comic and most recently emcee of ABC's *Who Do You Trust?* The content will be the same—guests who will sing, dance, tell jokes and just talk. But the style will be different. Carson is more incisive, sharper, quicker than Paar. But will the ladies love him? *Debut: October 1 (color).*

December 14, 1976, he returned to work to discover that comedian Don Rickles, who'd appeared the previous night with Bob Newhart, had broken one of Johnny's most treasured possessions—a cigarette box he'd brought with him when the show moved from New York to "beautiful downtown Burbank." Outraged, he broke off his monologue and, with camera in tow, stalked onto the stage of Rickles's sitcom *CPO Sharkey*—during its taping, no less! He confronted the quick-witted comic before two studio audiences, plus the viewers back home. The result: for perhaps the only moment in his career, Rickles was left speechless. He was too busy cracking up, and so were we.

Over his three decades on the air, Carson interviewed more than 22,000 guests, from heavy-hitters like Frank Sinatra to such "up-and-comers" as Woody Allen, Roseanne Barr, Ellen DeGeneres, Jerry Seinfeld and Barbra Streisand. Yet whether he was paired with a celebrity, a baby orangutan or a fitness instructor, this much was certain: with Johnny, you'd laugh, and then you'd laugh some more. Many hilarious bits, in fact, came with guests that might best be described as "eccentric"—such as Myrtle Young, who collected odd-shaped potato chips. In what TV GUIDE ranked in 1999 as TV's all-time funniest moment, one night in 1987 she found herself sharing her prized collection with Johnny. Distracted by Ed, she turned her head—and a *crunch* was heard. As she prepared to faint, an impish Carson showed her the bowl of decidedly mundane chips he'd just eaten from.

Johnny brought *everyone* in on the joke; no one was left behind. Through three decades, two wars, seven presidents, umpteen economic slowdowns and many good times, he let us wind down from the day, laugh and fall asleep a little happier than before we tuned in. There's no better legacy for an entertainer than that.

Cast:

Johnny Carson *Host*, **Ed McMahon** *Announcer*, **Skitch Henderson** *Conductor (1962–66)*, **Milton DeLugg** *Conductor (1966–67)*, **Doc Severinsen** *Conductor (1967–92)*, **Tommy Newsom** *Conductor (1968–92)*

24

By Matt Webb Mitovich

Broadcast History: FOX, 11/6/2001–
Runtime: 60 minutes
Genre: Drama

On November 11, 2001, viewers of Fox's *24* began a wild, crazy (and fantastically implausible) thrill ride that, for six seasons and counting, shows no signs of slowing down with former member of the '80s Brat Pack-turned-TV action hero Kiefer Sutherland in the driver's seat racing against time to save the world. The concept of each addictive and suspenseful season has the events of a 24-hour period in the life of U.S. counterterrorism agent Jack Bauer unfolding in real time, with each hour a separate episode. Sutherland offers a gripping, gritty performance as *24*'s seemingly indestructible hero, a man who will bend the rules to get the baddies, and puts serving his country before everything else—his family, loved ones and himself. In 2006, Sutherland won two Emmys for his work on the show, one for Outstanding Lead Actor in a Drama Series and one as producer of the Outstanding Drama Series. Since the show began, Jack has had some pretty horrific days, facing the worst possible threats with no sleep and a clock ticking down to some alarming disaster scenarios for the United States. What's a bad day for Jack, however, makes pulsating entertainment for TV audiences.

It was clear from the onset that Fox's *24* was out to break the rules, be it with a ground-breaking real-time format (rather strictly adhered to during that debut season, less so as the series ran on), the abrupt and often deadly dispatch of series regulars (Edgar, we hardly knew ye), or a wonderfully serpentine take on what is, let's face it,

> ## Preview Review
> *September 15, 2001*
>
> **Premise**: This man is running out of time. In 24 hours—each hour a separate episode—counterterrorist agent Jack Bauer must stop an assassination attempt on a popular African-American presidential candidate. He and his chief of staff must also find a "mole" in the agency who's in on the plot. What's more, Jack's teenage daughter has broken curfew to go partying, and his wife has gone to find her, putting them both in harm's way. And the clock keeps ticking.
>
> **We Say**: Time flies when you're having fun. One of the most exciting and confidently executed opening nights ever, *24* takes a great concept and delivers a tense, twist-filled, sensational adventure. You'll be checking your watch in amazement that the hour is already over and then setting your timer for the next nerve-racking installment.

often just a game of capture the flag. (And by flag, I mean missile/presidential football/disk/microchip/laptop/document/incriminating tape recording.)

Just how resolved were *24*'s creators, Joel Surnow and Robert Cochran, to upping the suspense-drama ante? For the very coda of Season 1—a point at which no one would have faulted anyone for resting on their laurels after Jack has saved the first of many a bad day—what do they do? Up and have master villainess Nina Myers put a bullet in Teri, leaving Jack to cradle his dead wife in his arms. The gloves were off, folks. Subsequent season-ender cliffhangers would find President David Palmer (Dennis Haysbert) on the receiving end of a toxic handshake from recurring bad girl Mandy (I still have that one saved on my TiVo); Jack faking his death and disappearing into the sunset; and Jack literally imprisoned on a slow boat to China, still hungry for its pound of flesh from a season prior.

Compelling in such new and exciting ways, the budding success of *24* was actually at first seen as an anomaly by industry insiders—even those at Fox, who years later hesitated to green light the similarly styled *Prison Break* (that is, until ABC's serialized *Lost* opened big). But to this day, the digital clock keeps on ticking, as the ratings surge higher and stronger with each new "day" in Jack's life.

More than pushing the envelope with its style of storytelling, however, *24* can be credited in large part with ushering in a bold, new thinking in prime-time programming. Beginning with Season 4 (which premiered January 9, 2005), *24* unspooled its entire season in repeat-free, always-a-new-episode fashion, recognizing the series' particularly unique need to deliver uninterrupted storytelling —a maneuver sampled by *NYPD Blue* years earlier. But in this instance, the over-whelming result was that mid-season sud-denly meant something. Mid-season was the new fall.

> ### Did You Know?
>
> For continuity's sake, the cast must have their hair trimmed every five days.

What's more, *24*, like *The West Wing* which preceded it, gave the American television audience a warm and honorable presidential figure to embrace and believe in—during, perhaps not coincidentally, turbulent real-life times. David Palmer, but a contender during the first season's assassination arc, rose to power, joining Jed Bartlet in the ranks of genuine do-gooders we dream to have lording over the White House.

Yet the same *24* also gave us a commander-in-chief as villain—is there a scarier thought?—in Season 5's Charles Logan. As the sixth season began, 20 months after a bloodied Jack was taken away by Chinese government agents, several high-powered actors joined the cast, including Ricky Schroder as a CTU operative and James Cromwell as Jack's estranged father. Supporting cast members may come and go, but this much never changes: Each and every day is a guessing game for Jack and his CTU support network, as true agen-das more often than not lay buried deep beneath the surface. In the world of *24*, where even sometimes-rogue agent Jack's endgame is questioned by high-ranking doubting Thomases, no one's allegiance can be certain. But, like viewers' love for this high-octane series, Jack's determination to snuff the latest threat to our country can never be questioned.

Cast:

Kiefer Sutherland *Jack Bauer*, **Dennis Haysbert** *President David Palmer (2001–06)*, **Elisha Cuthbert** *Kimberly Bauer (2001–04; 2006–)*, **Carlos Bernard** *Tony Almeida (2001–06)*, **Leslie Hope** *Teri Bauer (2001–02)*, **Sarah Clarke** *Nina Myers (2001–04)*, **Penny Johnson Jerald** *Sherry Palmer (2001–04)*, **Xander Berkeley** *George Mason (2001–03)*, **Eric Balfour** *Milo Pressman (2001–02; 2007–)*, **Reiko Aylesworth** *Michelle Dessler (2002–06)*, **Sarah Wynter** *Kate Warner (2002–03)*, **James Badge Dale** *Chase Edmunds (2003–04)*, **DB Woodside** *Wayne Palmer (2003–04; 2006–)*, **Mary Lynn Rajskub** *Chloe O'Brian (2003–)*, **Alberta Watson** *Erin Driscoll (2005)*, **William Devane** *James Heller (2005–06)*, **Kim Raver** *Audrey Raines (2005–)*, **James Morrison** *Bill Buchanan (2005–)*, **Lana Parrilla** *Sarah Gavin (2005)*, **Roger Cross** *Curtis Manning (2005–06)*, **Louis Lombardi** *Edgar Stiles (2005–06)*, **Gregory Itzin** *President Charles Logan (2005–07)*, **Jean Smart** *Martha Logan (2006–07)*, **Jayne Atkinson** *Karen Hayes (2006–)*, **Carlo Rota** *Morris O'Brian (2006–)*, **Peter MacNicol** *Thomas Lennox (2007–)*, **Regina King** *Sandra Palmer (2007–)*, **Marisol Nichols** *Nadia Yassir (2007–)*

The Twilight Zone

By Maitland McDonagh

Broadcast History: CBS, 10/2/1959–9/1964,
  9/27/1985–4/15/1989; UPN, 9/18/2002–5/21/2003
Runtime: 30 minutes (1959–62, 1963–64, 1988–89);
  60 minutes (1963, 1985–87, 2002–03)
Genre: Sci-fi

In this world nothing can be certain, except death and taxes and that somewhere someone's watching an episode of *The Twilight Zone*. Long before there were hundreds of channels with endless hours of airtime to fill, before boomer nostalgia and DVD shook the cobwebs off TV shows that were old when they were new, Rod Serling's anthology series was quietly worming its way into the collective unconscious. It wasn't the first TV anthology to tell serious stories about human nature with a consistent sci-fi/horror spin—the obscure, live-broadcast *Tales of Tomorrow* debuted in 1953, and *One Step Beyond*, a collection of purportedly fact-based weird tales hosted by John Newland, started airing nine months before *Twilight Zone* and ran concurrently until 1961. But *The Twilight Zone* was the keeper. It only ran for five seasons, from 1959 to 1964, but I can't remember a time when it wasn't on. Those crisp, dark stories—156 in all—always seemed to be lurking somewhere, waiting to snare you with their moody photography and striking sense of foreboding, then zap you with a zinger ending you couldn't wait to share with someone: "And then they take off the masks and . . ."

And yet five decades ago, *The Twilight Zone* looked more than a little like slumming for Serling, a golden boy of television drama's golden age. The medium's own Clifford Odets, he was a poet of disparate types ranging from driven executives in big business ("Patterns") to egomaniacal TV performers ("The Comedian") to washed-up boxers ("Requiem for a Heavyweight"). Serling could tackle controversial social issues—racism, political corruption, mob mentality—in the guise of genre fiction. "I found that it was all right to have Martians saying things Democrats and Republicans could never say," he was often quoted as saying. *The Twilight Zone*, a place Franz Kafka might have imagined if he'd harbored the slightest hope of cosmic justice, is now Serling's claim to fame—people talk about his groundbreaking work for *Playhouse 90* or his movie work (*Seven Days in May*, *Planet of the Apes*), but they watch *The Twilight Zone*.

> ### Did You Know?
>
> Rod Serling once asked viewers to submit scripts for the show, which resulted in 14,000 screenplays. Of those, Serling believed only two were good enough, but they were never produced because they didn't fit the show's format.

Long before I realized Serling's sensibility was O. Henry by way of EC horror comics, I got sucker punched by the episode "Time Enough at Last." You know, the one where the meek, near-sighted bookworm who wants nothing more from life than time to read in peace survives a nuclear holocaust. Rescued from despair by the realization that he can spend the rest of his life in the library reading, he accidentally smashes his glasses. I was hooked. I feel as though I've seen every episode of *The Twilight Zone* a dozen times, though in fact there are several I've never seen at all. A grab bag of cautionary tales, cheeky "what if . . . ?" riffs, ghost stories, psychological mind-benders, righteous allegories and occasional comic goofs, *The Twilight Zone*'s episodes unfolded as close to home as the house next door and as far away as outer space, but kept circling back to a handful of themes: You can't go home again; second chances come at a price; and you should be very, very careful what you wish for.

Serling never directed an episode of *The Twilight Zone*, but try to tell the work of television veterans and established feature-film directors like Robert Florey, Mitchell Leisen, Robert Brahm, Don Siegel and Ida Lupino from the efforts of up-and-comers. You can't. Story ideas came from all over—published and unpublished sci-fi and horror tales, existing and original teleplays—and the show's writers included luminaries like Reginald Rose ("The Incredible World of Horace Ford"), of *Twelve Angry Men* fame, and sci-fi legend Ray Bradbury ("I Sing the Body Electric"). Earl Hamner Jr., future creator of *The Waltons*, contributed eight original episodes (including the haunting "Jess-Belle," a backwoods variation on *Cat People*), most of which put a dark spin on the homespun storytelling that made him

---

Classic Episode Close-Up

"To Serve Man"
(Original telecast: March 2, 1962)

"Respectfully submitted for your perusal: a Kanamit," intones Rod Serling. "Height: a little over 9 feet. Weight: in the neighborhood of 350 pounds. Origin: unknown. Motives? Therein hangs a tale." The alien Kanamits' motives are unclear even though a "spokesman" says they've come to Earth to help. This seems to be confirmed when a cryptographer (Lloyd Bochner) translates the title of a Kanamit book as "To Serve Man." Encouraged, Bochner prepares to board a ship bound for Kanamit, and what follows is one of the series' most memorable punch lines.

---

famous. But Serling's distinctive sensibility—equal parts tight-lipped righteous outrage and sardonic amusement at what fools these mortals be—ruled; he personally scripted a whopping 92 episodes, and the like-minded Richard Matheson and Charles Beaumont accounted for another 35 between them.

I'm not a huge fan of Serling's famous homilies, especially the closers; I find them a tad purple and I'd rather figure out the moral for myself. I'd be lying, though, if I pretended immunity to the spookily incantatory power of Serling's clipped, somber voice, or the glimmer of glee that lurks beneath every portentous lead-in to the object lesson du jour. That place "that lies between the pit of a man's fears and the summit of his knowledge?" No walk in the park. And the theme music—not the quietly unsettling one Bernard Herrmann wrote specifically for the show, but the mash-up of French avant-garde composer Marius Constant's Etrange no. 3 (the insistent doo-doo-doo-doo part) and Milieu no. 2 (the insinuatingly discordant bit for bongos, flute and brass) that was pulled from the CBS stock-music library for Season 2 and just might be the most recognizable TV show theme of all time. Be honest—can you hear it without getting a teeny-tiny frisson?

The Twilight Zone struck out with some regularity: it could be obvious and preachy; most of the hour-long episodes from the show's fourth season are sluggish and labored, and the funny episodes aren't. But when *The Twilight Zone* got it right, it nailed it. From the once seen, never forgotten file:

- The reveal at the end of "The Eye of the Beholder," in which a hideously deformed girl undergoes one last, desperate plastic surgery: The bandages come off and—whew!—she's a beauty (*The Beverly Hillbillies*' sexy Donna Douglas, in fact), except in the world of pig-faced grotesques she calls home.

- The sweaty panic of "Nightmare at 20,000 Feet" as salesman William Shatner, fresh off a nervous breakdown, looks out the window of his plane to see a gremlin grimly worrying at the wing.

- The mounting panic of lovely Anne Francis, trapped in a department store with a gaggle of living mannequins during "The After Hours."

- The sorry spectacle of longtime suburban neighbors turning on each other when an unexplained power outage sparks rumors of an alien invasion in "The Monsters Are Due on Maple Street."

- The true subject of the book "To Serve Man," the one brought by the incredibly nice aliens who say they just want to help us end war, famine and disease.

- The ordeal of mute, middle-aged, increasingly panicked Agnes Moorehead as she defends her isolated country shack from "The Invaders," tiny aliens from . . . Earth.

- The tight-lipped hysteria of "It's a Good Life," where a 6-year-old boy (*Lost in Space* moppet Billy Mumy) who can kill and maim with his thoughts, holds an apparently idyllic town hostage to his casually cruel whims.

- The bleak fate of a Civil War soldier whose all-too-brief reprieve from hanging, courtesy of a broken rope, constitutes "An Occurrence at Owl Creek Bridge." (This is, incidentally, the only episode not made for the series; a stand-alone, Oscar-winning French short film adapted from Ambrose Bierce's short story, it was only aired twice.)

I could go on, but there's no need. *The Twilight Zone* is rooted so deep in our shared imagination that humming those first four notes can put a roomful of strangers on notice that things are taking a turn for the weird, and its ironic lessons are as familiar as fables or recurring dreams. Above all, the *Zone* is always waiting: Stray from the blinkered path and its shadows are there to swallow us up—none of us can say we weren't warned.

Cast:

Rod Serling *Host (1959–64)*, **Forest Whitaker** *Host (2002–03)*, **Charles Aidman** *Narrator (1985–87)*, **Robin Ward** *Narrator (1987–88)*

Twin Peaks

By Paul Wolfe

Broadcast History: ABC, 4/8/1990–6/10/1991
Runtime: 60 minutes
Genre: Drama

In hindsight, the provocative and highly stylized cult favorite *Twin Peaks* could have been a masterpiece as a miniseries. What started as an engrossingly quirky small-town whodunit quickly devolved into a surreal good vs. evil serial that struggled to answer a simple question: Who killed Laura Palmer? By the time the show's fading fandom found out that the killer was BOB, an abusive spirit that inhabited her father, Leland, most viewers screamed, "Who cares?"

Director David Lynch's first foray into television (a co-creation with Mark Frost) piqued the curiosity of viewers and critics on April 8, 1990, when it debuted as the season's highest-rated TV movie. A soundtrack alternating between whimsical and haunting, impressive big-screen-style cinematography showcasing Washington State and a cast of fascinatingly weird characters (hello, Log Lady) were all seductive draws to viewers drowning in cookie-cutter sitcoms and past-their-prime prime-time soaps. But always at its heart was the puzzle of Laura Palmer's death—and her life. As Special Agent Dale Cooper slowly learned, Laura was much more than a homecoming queen in the Pacific Northwest lumber town of Twin Peaks.

The obsessive FBI agent, brilliantly played by Kyle MacLachlan, meticulously dictated into a tiny tape recorder details of the case ("Ring finger, under the nail. Let's see what he left us. It's an R.") and his travels ("24-hour room service must be one of the premier achievements of modern civilization"). He ultimately discovered that Laura was a drug user, a sex addict and a victim of abuse. With help from Sheriff Harry S. Truman (Michael Ontkean), Cooper also learned that Laura had ties to nearly every one of the town's 51,201 inhabitants, from psychiatrist Lawrence Jacoby to best friend Donna Hayward to boyfriend Bobby Briggs to a list of secret lovers that included James Hurley, Leo Johnson, Josie Packard and Jacques Renault. The mystery deepened and the list of suspects grew steadily throughout the first season's eight-episode run, concluding with a frustrating cliffhanger that not only failed to reveal Laura's killer (though Jacques was arrested) but also introduced another huge mystery (Who shot Cooper?). Despite already declining ratings, the much-discussed and heavily hyped series was nominated for 14 Emmys (it won only for editing and costumes) and secured a second season of 22 more episodes.

Twin Peaks

After a summer of speculation and merchandising (which included a soundtrack, Agent Cooper's audiotapes and *The Secret Diary of Laura Palmer*, written by Lynch's daughter, Jennifer—all of which suckers like me bought), remaining fans expected a resolution when *Twin Peaks* returned in September. The second-season premiere did reveal the identity of the killer—nightmare-inducing BOB—but then strung fans along until December, when Cooper finally discovered during a "magical" gathering of suspects at the Roadhouse that BOB was the demon that lurked within Laura's father. (Would you believe that chewing gum was the biggest clue?) BOB, by the way, first appeared as a vision to Laura's mother in Episode 2. So, technically speaking, the killer was unmasked at the very start. Lynch later stated that he never wanted to reveal Laura's killer but ultimately bowed to network pressure to do so. Instead, he originally envisioned a series in which Laura's unsolved death served as a plot device to introduce the evil that potentially lurks within seemingly quaint towns.

The legacy of *Twin Peaks* remains strong. In addition to increasing our appreciation for damn-good coffee, cherry pies and donuts, the series introduced a slew of young stars: Sherilyn Fenn and Mädchen Amick, who both graduated to guest roles on *Dawson's Creek* and *Gilmore Girls*; and Lara Flynn Boyle, who went on to date MacLachlan and Jack Nicholson (and star in *The Practice*). Heather Graham and David Duchovny made early career appearances. *Twin Peaks* also paved the way for similarly off-kilter TV series (*Northern Exposure* and *Picket Fences*) and towns (Sunnydale, Stuckeyville and Stars Hollow). But most importantly it led many producers and writers of future series to reveal their mysteries and questions earlier, rather than later. Or not at all. Would *Desperate Housewives* or *Veronica Mars* have wrapped up their initial murders in the first season if *Twin Peaks* had never aired? Probably not. Then again, with *Lost*'s creators still generating more confusion than clarity, perhaps *Twin Peaks* just taught TV fans to wade gently into future mysteries . . . or better still, close their ears and eyes and wait for the DVD set. It's less suspenseful, but at least you know there's a conclusion.

> **Did You Know?**
>
> The photo of Laura Palmer is Sheryl Lee's real homecoming photo.

Cast:

Kyle MacLachlan *Agent Dale Cooper*, **Michael Ontkean** *Sherrif Harry S. Truman*, **Joan Chen** *Jocelyn "Josie" Packard*, **Piper Laurie** *Catherine Martell*, **Jack Nance** *Pete Martell*, **Ray Wise** *Leland Palmer*, **Grace Zabriskie** *Sarah Palmer*, **Sheryl Lee** *Laura Palmer/Madeline Ferguson*, **Dana Ashbrook** *Bobby Briggs*, **Everett McGill** *Big Ed Hurley*, **Wendy Robie** *Nadine Hurley*, **James Marshall** *James Hurley*, **Richard Beymer** *Benjamin Horne*, **Sherilyn Fenn** *Audrey Horne*, **Lara Flynn Boyle** *Donna Hayward*, **Warren Frost** *Dr. William Hayward*, **Madchen Amick** *Shelly Johnson*, **Eric Da Re** *Leo Johnson*, **Chris Mulkey** *Hank Jennings*, **Peggy Lipton** *Norma Jennings*, **Kimmy Robertson** *Lucy Moran*, **Russ Tamblyn** *Dr. Lawrence Jacoby*, **Catherine E. Coulson** *Margaret, "The Log Lady"*

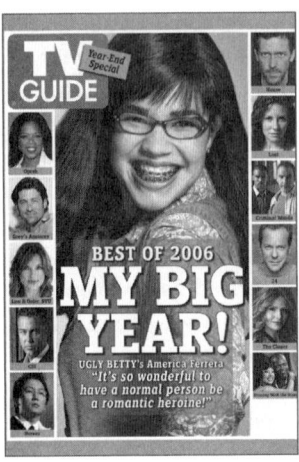

Ugly Betty

By Damian J. Holbrook
Broadcast History: ABC, 9/28/2006–
Runtime: 60 minute
Genre: Comedy-drama

In the summer of 2006, TV GUIDE magazine sent me to L.A. to do a piece on an awful-titled comedy for our 2006 Fall Preview issue. Escorted by a helpful ABC publicist, I walked into a cavernous soundstage off Melrose Avenue—Hollywood's asphalt canal of all things cool—to meet a five-foot-nothin' mess with less style than a celebrity mug shot and the biggest heart of the season.

And that's how I fell in love with *Ugly Betty*.

Based on the *muy caliente* Colombian telenovela *Yo Soy Betty la Fea*—already adapted to mondo success in such far reaches as Russia, Germany and the Netherlands—the charmingly Americanized version follows homely Betty Suarez through the shiny, starving halls of the haute-y *Mode* magazine after the publisher handpicks her as the only assistant his newly in-charge son would never sleep with. Of course, a dorky sad sack who lives at home with her Spanish-speaking family in Queens would at first seem to be the girl least likely to win over millions of viewers, but here in front of me, dwarfed by an enormous neon-orange set and an unforgiving pair of Coke-bottle glasses, stood proof that fabulous was overrated.

"Betty's not *entirely* normal either," laughed the show's breakout star, America Ferrera (*The Sisterhood of the Traveling Pants*). "She's a little bit of an exaggeration." She's also not what we were used to seeing as the lead character on network TV, although as Ferrera—ironically 100% adorable under all of the hair don'ts and makeup mishaps—put it back then, there's a little bit of Betty in everyone. "The story is going to relate to people more than anything else because most of us are just normal people . . . you root for Betty because you're rooting for yourself."

And boy, did we root for her. Even before airing, the series had generated enough buzz to make its original Friday night time slot a head-scratcher. If the network had a show worth watching, why put it on a night when nobody was? Critics rose up in *Betty*'s defense, eventually leading ABC to rejigger its schedule and move their *Ugly* duckling into the much more attractive Thursdays-at-8 slot.

Knowing that a *few* pretty faces were needed to surround Betty's bushy eyebrows and braces, producer Salma Hayek—who should know from telenovelas, having started out on the serialized hoots *Teresa* and *Nuevo Amencer*—jammed *Mode*'s masthead with lookers who could also act. *The L Word*'s Eric Mabius slipped into the bicep-hugging suits of Betty's playboy boss-with-a-semi-heart Daniel Meade; *The O.C.*'s dapper Alan Dale signed on as his icy publishing mogul daddy, Bradford; and relative newcomer Becki Newton made a tart foil to sweet Betty as Amanda, the hard-shell receptionist with a soft spot for Daniel. Topping it off—and taking chewed bits of scenery with her—was certified beauty Vanessa Williams as Wilhelmina Slater, the Prada-wearing devil who wants editorial reign over *Mode* . . . and may be willing to kill for it.

Because, you see, *Betty*'s not just about who's hot and who's not. It's also about who's hiding what beneath their lacquer-perfect veneer. Kicking off with the *seemingly* random hit-and-run demise of the magazine's previous honcho, Fey Somers, the first season decked itself in a slow-boil subplot involving a bandage-encased mystery person that gave the ladies of Wisteria Lane a run for their money. Not to mention the Thursday night competition. With NBC's Must-See schedule mustier than ever and CBS's *Survivor* showing its age, the time was prime for a new show to romance those picky Nielsen viewers and *Betty* did just that. It didn't hurt that she also got a little help from Hayek.

"I don't think anything is being lost in the translation," the Oscar-nominated actress told TV GUIDE of reimagining *Betty* for U.S. audiences. "It's definitely been a conscious decision to change some things so that it can become something on its own." Those changes included toning down the original's over-the-top flavor and beefing up Betty's home life to provide an emotional antidote to the often-heartless machinations going on at *Mode*. "That is what I am most proud of," revealed Hayek. "That it has an identity of its own."

That identity—camp comedy crossed with soapy story arcs, Betty's determination to do the right thing and that potentially killer subplot—became all the more fiery after Hayek cast herself as both the temperamental maid on Betty's favorite telenovela *and* as Daniel's enigmatic love interest for a short-term arc. And while A-listers slapping their name onto a vanity project is nothing new for TV, Hayek's devotion pretty much verified what fans already knew by the time she showed up during November sweeps: that the triumphant *Ugly Betty* truly was a thing of beauty.

> ### Did You Know?
>
> The series won two Golden Globes in its first season (2007): one for star America Ferrera (Best Actress in a Television Series, Musical or Comedy) and one for the show itself (Best Television Series, Musical or Comedy).

Cast:

America Ferrera *Betty Suarez*, **Eric Mabius** *Daniel Meade*, **Ana Ortiz** *Hilda*, **Vanessa Williams** *Wilhelmina Slater*, **Tony Plana** *Ignacio*, **Ashley Jensen** *Christina*, **Mark Indelicato** *Justin*, **Alan Dale** *Bradford Meade*, **Michael Urie** *Marc*, **Becki Newton** *Amanda*

Veronica Mars

By Angel Cohn

Broadcast History: UPN, 9/22/2004–5/9/2005;
  CW, 10/3/2006–5/22/2007
Runtime: 60 minutes
Genre: Comedy-drama

It may sound like the makings of a science-
fiction show—the title character is named Veronica Mars, she lives in a town called Neptune and
drives a Saturn—but while this show has many
out-of-this-world qualities, it is anything but a
spacey drama.

I have to admit to initially being a bit skepti-
cal of this series. I heard the comparisons to *Buffy the Vampire Slayer* easily bandied about and then also heard it described as a teen show about a
crime-solving girl that had the look of an old noir film. Honestly, it sounded
a little pretentious to me, which is why I dragged my feet to start watching
it. I recorded about six episodes, then decided it was make or break time, I
was either going to give the show a shot or just ignore it. Choosing to hit play
on the VCR instead of recording over the tape was one of the best decisions
I've made in my TV-addicted life. I sat and stared at the television, instantly
obsessed with this incredibly written and well-crafted show. With my appetite
only whetted for more, I kicked myself for waiting so long and made it my
personal mission to convert more people to this series. Every time someone
comes to me and thanks me for convincing them to give it a chance, I smile
with glee.

And I'm not the only member of this show's small but loyal fan base. There
are many devotees, who banded together and raised money out of their own
pockets in order to rent a plane with a banner begging CW execs to save
this beloved program, despite its lackluster ratings, when the WB and UPN
merged. Their efforts didn't go unnoticed and CW president Dawn Ostroff even
told advertisers about the stunt during the spring upfront presentation of the
new network. The struggling series gained support from critics, as well as horror legend Stephen King and *Buffy* mastermind Joss Whedon.

But comparing *Buffy* and *Veronica* is like comparing *Star Wars* and *Star
Trek*; while fans can enjoy both, they are very different. Sure the shows both
have sassy blonde heroines who fight evildoers, both are intelligently written, but while *Buffy*'s Sunnydale was a monster-infested community filled with
supernatural beasties, *Veronica*'s Neptune is a gritty real-life town that has
human beings committing dastardly crimes. For Veronica (played by the petite
Kristen Bell) it's not so straightforward when it comes to doling out punish-
ments. Buffy would kill demons, plain and simple, but Veronica has to deal

with the uncomfortable realities of the legal system, and she does it all with no super-strength or powers—just her trusty Taser and her loyal pooch, Backup.

One of the most unique aspects of this drama is the relationship that Veronica has with her father, Keith (Enrico Colantoni), a private investigator. The two have been relying on each other since her mom, Lianne (Corinne Bohrer), took off on the run. Keith has been a solid presence, trying to provide her with a normal life of college and friends, and attempting in vain to keep her away from solving crimes. Unfortunately, his daughter inherited his stubborn streak, along with his knack for cracking cases. While they bicker and banter, it's always with love and she's as fiercely protective of him as he is of her. She staunchly defended him when he was ostracized by many in the community when, as sheriff, he failed to convict a likely suspect in the Lilly Kane murder investigation (he believed the suspect was innocent). Their uncomfortable relationship with Neptune's current sheriff, Don Lamb (Michael Muhney), is an ongoing bone of contention.

Of course one of the most buzzed-about portions of the show is Veronica's romantic entanglements. She's been a bit unlucky in love, falling for the troubled sorts, but all of her boyfriends have at least been easy on the eye. Her first boyfriend, Duncan Kane (Teddy Dunn), was sweet, but things got rocky when, during her investigation into his sister's death, Veronica started to suspect Duncan. They briefly reconciled after the case was solved, but just when things started getting serious, he skipped town with the child he had with his former (and now deceased) girlfriend Meg (Alona Tal). This opened the door for her to rekindle her on-again-off-again relationship with town bad boy Logan Echolls (Jason Dohring). When they're together, sparks fly, and he's described their story as "epic" —but it's never smooth sailing. He's got issues, he's had run-ins with the law, and he was recently orphaned when his actress mother (Lisa Rinna) jumped off a bridge in an

---

Preview Review

September 12, 2004

The Setup: High-school student Veronica Mars helps her private-eye dad get to the bottom of secrets swirling around the small town of Neptune. The biggest mystery: the murder of Veronica's best friend.

The Twist: There are puzzles in Veronica's own past, including a date-rape incident and an alcoholic mom who split several months ago. Or did she?

We Say: *Mars* is a teen noir with a moody blend of adolescent angst, family drama and mystery. As Veronica, Bell is tough, funny and resourceful but also vulnerable. You'll root for her.

---

apparent suicide and his famous but abusive father, Aaron (Harry Hamlin), was found killed. Aaron's death wasn't an entirely terrible thing since he was guilty of murdering Lilly Kane (but later exonerated, exposing the true power of money in this small town). However, his parents' back-to-back deaths left a mark on the rich but alone Logan. This all may sound a little melodramatic, but the nuances and details add to the impact.

Veronica also has a few pals who help her with cases, keep her grounded and prevent her from becoming a complete social misfit. There's Wallace (Percy Daggs III), the affable jock who goes along with most of Veronica's schemes; computer genius Mac (Tina Majorino); and the former leader of the PCH motorcycle gang Eli "Weevil" Navarro (Francis Capra). These three may not always agree with their flawed friend—and they surely don't always make life easy for her—but they've managed to break through her guarded exterior and proved their loyalty. Her relationship with Weevil is most often on the fritz since he (like her) is from the less-than-wealthy side of the tracks in a town that is truly split by class and he frowns upon her fraternization with the upper-crust kids. In fact, former mayor Woody Goodman (Steve Guttenberg) even wanted to split the town in half keeping the rich in a safer and more protected community. Weevil has a bitter sense of resentment toward the wealthy and entitled Logan, who's part of the exclusive 09er zip code of rich kids who often take delight in tormenting the less privileged kids who live along the Pacific Coast Highway.

> **Did You Know?**
>
> According to creator Rob Thomas, the title character for this series was originally going to be a boy.

Tough, flawed and sometimes downright surly with a smile, Veronica's one of the most complex characters on network television. Unfortunately that complexity and the often extremely complicated story arcs and mysteries might be what hindered this show in the ratings. Each season it struggled to find a larger audience. In its third season, the show's executive producer, Rob Thomas, attempted to make shorter mysteries (the first being the rapes and head shavings of young women at Hearst College) in order to grab and keep the attention of new fans. In the end, the series was canceled in 2007. I'll still proudly keep my huge poster beautifully displayed in my living room, so that when new people come over to my house and ask what *Veronica Mars* is about, I can tell them, and hopefully introduce at least one other person to the wild world of Neptune, California, and all of its charms.

Cast:

Kristen Bell *Veronica Mars*, **Enrico Colantoni** *Keith Mars*, **Percy Daggs III** *Wallace Fennel*, **Teddy Dunn** *Duncan Kane (2004–06)*, **Francis Capra** *Weevil*, **Jason Dohring** *Logan Echolls*, **Ryan Hansen** *Dick Casablancas*, **Tessa Thompson** *Jackie Cook (2005–06)*, **Tina Majorino** *Mac*, **Chris Lowell** *Piz (2006–)*, **Julie Gonzalo** *Parker (2006–)*

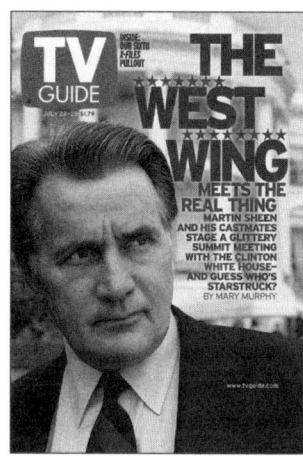

The West Wing

By Paul Droesch

Broadcast History: NBC, 9/22/1999–5/14/2006
Runtime: 60 minutes
Genre: Drama

As blue-state fantasies go, *The West Wing* **was** about as good as it gets, for the first few seasons at least: popular liberal president Josiah ("Jed") Bartlet (Martin Sheen) was Clinton without the ideological ambiguities or the moral lapses. He was also very, *very* smart.

So were his senior staffers—old friend Leo McGarry (John Spencer), the chief of staff, who persuaded Bartlet to run in the first place; Toby Ziegler (Richard Schiff), the brooding communications director; Josh Lyman (Bradley Whitford), Leo's workaholic deputy; C. J. Cregg (Allison Janney), a press secretary who actually liked reporters (and ended up marrying one); and chief speechwriter Sam Seaborn (Rob Lowe), the series' first-season fulcrum. They weren't exactly shy about showing off their erudition, either, casually weighing in on everything from Gilbert and Sullivan to colliding superconductors with a snap-crackle-pop wit that was rare indeed on the TV landscape.

And Bartlet (a Catholic) could do it in *Latin*. What's more, his vast knowledge of the Bible (his first line uttered in the series' pilot: "I am the Lord thy God . . . ") served him well when pesky conservative preachers needed a smiting. Just to listen to these folks, and appreciate what they had to say, actually made you feel smart, important and trendy. It was geek-chic, and no political or intellectual fantasy, no matter what color your state turns on Election Day, can get any better than that.

They were also remarkably idealistic, considering that they were running the world. Their biggest scandal involved Bartlet's health: he had neglected to disclose that he had multiple sclerosis while running for president. True, VP John Hoynes (Tim Matheson) resigned in the wake of a sex scandal (he had also once slept with C. J., who regretted it deeply). But Hoynes, a conservative Texas senator Bartlet had defeated for the nomination, was always regarded with suspicion in the White House: he represented the sort of nasty *realpolitik* that these guys wanted to rise above.

And even when they couldn't—most notably when Leo talked Bartlet into allowing the assassination of a Persian Gulf–state defense minister with ties to terrorists—the decision-making process was almost melodramatically tortured. Besides, if they hadn't killed the guy the terrorists would have blown up the Golden Gate Bridge. But overall, Jeb's watch was remarkably free of "ethics problems." There was no Nixon-type enemies list in this administration, and when a major campaign contributor whose company was in trouble came to Leo, he *didn't* spend the night in the Lincoln Bedroom. As series creator Aaron Sorkin put it, *The West Wing* was "a valentine to public service."

It was also a public-policy primer. Sorkin, who wrote the 1996 film *The American President* and oversaw the well-received ABC dramedy *Sports Night* before launching *The West Wing* on NBC in 1999, was a master at mining drama from the sort of stuff you'll find on the news pages of *The New York Times*. Tobacco-industry lawsuits, the estate tax, gun control, seat-belt laws, weapons testing on the Puerto Rican island of Vieques, you name it. And the Bartlet administration (Toby in particular) went after drug companies over their AIDS-drug patents with a ferocity that Clinton no doubt wishes he would have when he was president.

Almost immediately, the geek-chic translated into plain old non-hyphenated chic. *The West Wing* was never a monster hit (the highest it made it to was No. 8 in 2001–02), but it was a more-than-solid performer for the first three years, and it always attracted one of network TV's best-educated and most demographically desirable audiences. All this, of course, made it a show that actors with reputations clamored to appear on. Semi-regulars included John Amos, Marlee Matlin, Mary-Louise Parker, Ron Silver, Anna Deveare Smith and Lily Tomlin. And then there were the "guest stars." Who was that cantankerous old State Department East Asia hand warning the White House about North Korea? He was Hal Holbrook. Bartlet's shrink? Adam Arkin. The White House counsel? There were two: John Larroquette and Oliver Platt (and Matthew Perry was an assistant counsel). The Republican House Speaker who became acting president when Bartlet was incapacitated by MS? John Goodman. And Roger Rees, as British ambassador Lord John Marbury, was a policy wonk and comic relief rolled into one.

> ## Preview Review
>
> *September 11, 1999*
>
> **Premise**: More backstage White House activity from Aaron Sorkin, writer of *The American President*. Martin Sheen, who has played his share of Kennedys, stars as President Josiah Bartlet, whose harried yet loyal staff includes a photogenic deputy communications director, a gruff chief of staff, a hotheaded deputy chief of staff who often has to eat his words, and a wry press secretary. Let the crises and scandals begin.
>
> **We Say**: The ultimate workplace series, expertly melding comedy and drama in an intoxicating and sophisticated rush of sharp writing and canny acting. The show deservedly has taken heat for not casting minorities among the president's staff, and *Sports Night* fans will recognize Sorkin's tendency toward speechifying, but this is solid, slick, irresistible entertainment. Even those with C-SPAN phobia might get hooked.

The West Wing was also an Emmy machine: its nine first-season awards is a record, and its 26 overall ties it with *Hill Street Blues* for first place among dramas; it won for Best Drama in its first four seasons; and Sheen, Spencer,

Janney, Schiff and Whitford all won, as did Stockard Channing as Bartlet's wife, Abigail, a high-powered physician, and executive producer Thomas Schlamme, who directed many of the important episodes and whose Steadi-cam "walk and talk" tracking shots were the series' flashy visual signature. Sor-kin et al. also won Peabody and Humanitas Awards.

But nobody's perfect, not even Sorkin, and *l'affaire MS* came to haunt Bartlet in Seasons 2 and 3. As scandals go, it never rose to the level of impeachment, though as it began to unfold it seemed like it might. But Sorkin, who said he gave his president the disease in Season 1 because he wanted a reason to put Bartlet in bed for a scene, must have realized that this was a wrong turn, because scripts soon took on a "row-back" character. It was as if he had said to himself: "I've gotten Bartlet into this mess; how do I get him out of it?" With an unconvincing whimper: Bartlet accepted a congressional censure and the very complicit Abbey lost her medical license for a year.

> **Did You Know?**
>
> Among those considered for the role of the President were Alan Alda, Jason Robards and Sidney Poitier.

Of course, critics noticed. They had already taken Sorkin to task for the melodramatic assassination-attempt cliffhanger that ended the first season, and by the time Bartlet's daughter Zoey (Elisabeth Moss) was kidnapped in the fourth season's next-to-last episode, they were piling on. Too much, perhaps, and that wasn't Sorkin's only problem. The change from blue to red in the real White House caused by the 2000 presidential election turned *The West Wing*'s "parallel universe" (as Schlamme called it) into an alternate universe, and scripts lost much of their verisimilitude. Now it was sheer fantasy, and fewer fans were buying it.

It also didn't help that the competition had become stiffer when ABC put *The Bachelor* on against it on Wednesday night, but there wasn't much overlap in the show's fan base, so the real problem lay elsewhere: *The West Wing* had ceased to be trendy. Sorkin, meanwhile, had gotten himself arrested for possession of hallucinogenic mushrooms in 2001, and he left the series after the fourth season.

Enter John Wells, a producer whose remarkable success with *ER* points to a special talent for keeping old hits on the air long after watercooler conversation has moved on to the next big thing. The scripts Wells wrote or oversaw had less literary bite than Sorkin's, but still had more than you'd find in most other shows. And while he couldn't get many viewers to come back, he did keep his ship of state afloat for another three years. During the final season he even got the critics back on board.

He did it with what amounted to a two-year audition for Bartlet's job, pitting in the end Republican Arnold Vinick (Alan Alda), a wily, gnarled and slightly cynical (but not too cynical) California senator, against Democrat Matt Santos (Jimmy Smits), an obscure Latino congressman from Houston whom Josh persuaded to run. Leo McGarry was his running mate. (This caused real-life complications when Spencer died in December 2005, during the filming of the final season.)

Santos was every bit as idealistic as Bartlet was (even if his wife, played by Teri Polo, was much more stylish in her Jackie-style pillbox hats than Abbey Bartlet could hope to be), and the campaign was as issue-driven as if Sorkin had written it. In the end Santos won (this *is* a blue-state fantasy after all), but Vinick did get a consolation prize: he was named secretary of state. And Alda got a prize of his own: he won *The West Wing*'s final Emmy.

Cast:

Martin Sheen *President Josiah "Jed" Bartlet,* **John Spencer** *Leo McGarry,* **Rob Lowe** *Sam Seaborn (1999–2003),* **Richard Schiff** *Toby Ziegler,* **Allison Janney** *C. J. Cregg,* **Bradley Whitford** *Josh Lyman,* **Stockard Channing** *First Lady Abigail Bartlet,* **Janel Moloney** *Donna Moss,* **Dule Hill** *Charlie Young,* **Moira Kelly** *Madeline Hampton (1999–2000),* **Emily Procter** *Ainsley Hayes (2000–02),* **Mary-Louise Parker** *Amy Gardner (2001–03),* **Joshua Malina** *Will Bailey (2002–06),* **Mary McCormack** *Kate Harper (2004–06),* **Kristin Chenoweth** *Annabeth Schott (2004–06),* **Jimmy Smits** *Matthew Santos (2004–06),* **Alan Alda** *Arnold Vinick (2005–06)*

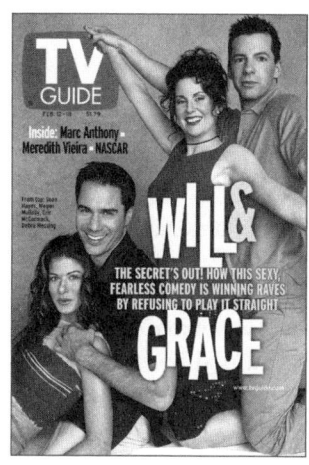

Will & Grace

By N. F. Mendoza

Broadcast History: NBC, 9/21/1998–5/18/2006
Runtime: 30 minutes
Genre: Sitcom

While a last-minute escape from an ill-conceived marriage was the story line that launched the undeniably successful *Friends*, it also worked effectively four years later to establish the theme and tone for a sitcom about another group of Manhattan friends, *Will & Grace*. This time, however, the runaway bride would *not* be hooking up with her closest pal.

In the series opener, Debra Messing's manic Grace Adler, an interior designer, leaves her fiancé and subsequently moves in with buddy Will Truman (Eric McCormack), a lawyer who's gay. In effect, she chooses her unattainable best friend over her lover. This quickly establishes the duo's strong bond—and you don't even need their backstory to spell out their connection. You just get it.

Thanks to terrifically witty writing, Messing's Lucille Ball–inspired antics and the breakout performances of the "supporting" players, the series evolved into a weekly delight. Theirs was not a show or a relationship that could be easily explained. Will and Grace, we learned early on, met in college. By the time the mullet-coiffed Will stepped out of the closet, the straight Grace was already in love. These were wonderfully compatible and loving friends . . . except for that sex thing, of course.

And as comfortable as Will and Grace were, their pals Jack and Karen were equally unconventional. Their story lines may have been secondary, but Sean Hayes's flamboyantly narcissistic Jack McFarland and Megan Mullally's high-pitched, boozy, breezy

Preview Review
September 12, 1998

Premise: Gay and Stacey. A buddy comedy with a post-*Ellen* twist, pairing Will, a lawyer, and Grace, an interior designer, who would be perfect for each other except for the fact that he's gay—although he's so low-key about it you might not initially notice. These soul mates become roommates, both nursing broken hearts after ending long relationships.

We Say: This looks to be the best of NBC's new comedies, with appealing stars, snappy writing and polished direction from the masterful James Burrows. Yet there's a strange double standard at work here. While its refreshing to see a gay character like Will who doesn't wear his sexuality as a banner, his good friend (Sean Hayes) is a flamboyant queen who makes entrances with a birdcage and a hatbox, seeming to reinforce the stereotype that Will quietly shatters. Still, Hayes is screamingly funny, and so is Megan Mullally as a scatterbrained socialite who works with Grace.

Karen Walker registered immediately with audiences. From the moment they met (lifting shirts and coyly bumping bellies), Jack and Karen stole every scene they were in. They shared a, well, queer sense of camaraderie: gossiping together, bathing together, depending on each other. They were the proverbial yin to the other's yang. Yes, it was completely outrageous and ridiculous, but you just couldn't get enough of them.

Jack's job arcs were legendary, including his long-running ambition to star in musical theater (we still do the "Just Jack" pose), and forays into nursing and massage therapy (which Karen much benefited from), just to name a few.

Meanwhile, Karen, who "worked" as Grace's assistant, was married to the ultra-rich, obese (and never seen on-camera) Stan. She flaunted her millions, her Birkin bag full of prescription meds and bottles of booze, and frequently bellowed for her long-suffering housekeeper, Rosario (Shelley Morrison, in a role that was a far cry from her *Flying Nun* days as Sister Sixto).

There were recurring jokes, not without some meanness, but always funny: Grace's flat chest, bad-luck relationships and horrible singing voice; Will's fastidiousness; Karen's perennial state of intoxication; and Jack's gnat-like attention span.

> ### Did You Know?
> Debra Messing beat out Nicolette Sheridan for the role of Grace Adler.

But the series was not without its watershed moments. While *Ellen* may have carried the torch for gay characters on the TV landscape, it was *Will & Grace* that made it burn brighter. Times were changing, and this series was smart—and funny—enough to lampoon sexuality and stereotypes. I remember, for example, the episode in which a disgruntled Will and Jack, protesting the editing out of a gay kiss in a prime-time series, go to the *Today* show's outdoor set and enact their own lip-lock on live television.

A-listers clamored for guest spots on this sitcom, which reveled—sometimes to mixed results—in stunt casting. Stars who appeared included Kevin Bacon, Alec Baldwin, Jack Black, Cher, Glenn Close, Joan Collins, Macaulay Culkin, Matt Damon, Geena Davis, Ellen DeGeneres, Taye Diggs, Michael Douglas, Minnie Driver, Andy Garcia, Janet Jackson, Jennifer Lopez, Madonna, Demi Moore, Rosie O'Donnell, Suzanne Pleshette, Sydney Pollack (as Will's father), Debbie Reynolds (as Grace's mother), Parker Posey, Mira Sorvino, Britney Spears, Eric Stoltz, Sharon Stone, Lily Tomlin, Tracey Ullman and Gene Wilder (as Will's nutty boss Mr. Stein).

Sure, the stunt casting may have been excessive, but it was a lot of fun. There were also many less heralded, minor characters who further enhanced the series. Super-talented Leslie Jordan, for example, won a Guest Actor Emmy in 2006 for his recurring role of Beverley Leslie, Karen's friend and sometimes nemesis, a closeted conservative married to an older wealthy socialite. All in all, the guests on this show racked up 14 Emmy nominations and three wins (for Jordan, Wilder and Bobby Cannavale).

Throughout the series' eight years, it was nominated for a whopping 83 Emmys (including wins for the series and all four principals), 24 Golden Globes, 14 SAG Awards and six People's Choice Awards. In 2002, 2003, 2005 and 2006, *Will & Grace* boasted more Emmy nods than any other sitcom.

After being a regular viewer, I still DVR favorite episodes, and nearly always find a moment, a line, a look that I may have missed the first time. But each viewing continues to generate laughs. *Will & Grace* is classically memorable in its own screwball way. It's genuinely funny, laced with terrific pop-culture references and, despite the rapid-fire quickness of the delivery and lines (and perhaps incredible situations), it is beautifully paced.

Was there a misstep along the way? Probably (did we *really* need Harry Connick Jr.'s Leo Markus to marry and then split from Grace?). But in its prime, and at its best, this was a bona fide sitcom classic.

Cast:

Eric McCormack *Will Truman*, **Debra Messing** *Grace Adler*, **Megan Mullally** *Karen Walker*, **Sean Hayes** *Jack McFarland*, **Shelley Morrison** *Rosario*

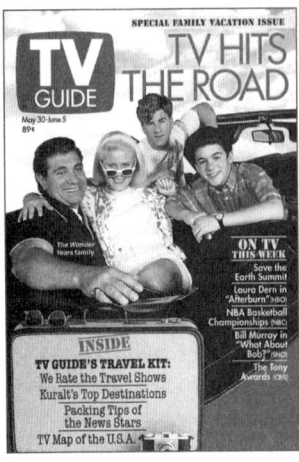

The Wonder Years

By Jeff Gemmill

Broadcast History: ABC, 3/15/1988–/1/1993
Runtime: 30 minutes
Genre: Comedy-drama

Growing up happens in a heartbeat. One day you're in diapers, the next you're scanning baby photos of yourself for a digital family album. Watching *The Wonder Years* is akin to a friend sharing such snapshots. For six seasons, it mined gentle humor and heartfelt insights while charting the path of "everyboy" Kevin Arnold (Fred Savage) through the rocky years of adolescence; and added perspective via the narration of the adult Kevin (an uncredited Daniel Stern). Beside him in many pictures are his monosyllabic, intimidating dad, Jack (a scene-stealing Dan Lauria); his patient homemaker mom, Norma (Alley Mills); his eldest sibling, hippie Karen (Olivia d'Abo); and bullying older brother, Wayne (Jason Hervey). Other faces appear as well, including best friend Paul (Josh Saviano) and Winnie (Danica McKellar), Kevin's on-again, off-again girlfriend.

When it debuted after the 1988 Super Bowl, the show was hailed as a baby-boomer confection because of the era in which it was set—the 1960s—and its soundtrack, which employed popular songs from that decade. It was also, importantly, placed in the suburbs, a sprawling terrain of tract houses for the burgeoning middle class. These communities seemed safe, a perfect place to both raise children and be a child; to paraphrase the adult Kevin, back then a kid could walk the streets at dusk without ending up on a milk carton.

The story opens in 1968, a turbulent year that saw growing unrest over the Vietnam War, the assassinations of Rev. Martin Luther King Jr. and Bobby Kennedy, and a contentious presidential election won by Richard Nixon. Yet, for 12-year-old Kevin, the single biggest issue on his mind was . . . junior high. In the pilot, he, Paul and Winnie see this as a time to reinvent themselves but, for Kevin, *everything* goes wrong. At lunch, when lunkhead Wayne teases him about liking Winnie—in front of her, no less—it's the last straw and, with a toss of an apple, he winds up in the vice principal's office alongside his miffed mom and angry dad.

If the episode ended there, it would have achieved what every series pilot basically seeks: introducing the major characters while telling a story that compels viewers to tune in again. But creators/writers Carol Black and Neal Marlens had a twist that told us immediately that this was no ordinary sit-com. Arriving home, Kevin and his parents learn some awful news—Winnie's brother has been killed in Vietnam. At dusk, Kevin walks to an old haunt of his and Winnie's, and finds her looking up at the stars. There's so much he wants to say, to make go away, but he can't manage much more than "I'm sorry," and not just because he's a kid. Words of those sorts don't come easy, ever. As Percy Sledge's "When a Man Loves a Woman" swells on the soundtrack, they kiss—their first. It's bittersweet, to be sure, but it's exactly such moments that make *The Wonder Years*, time and again throughout its run, hit home.

I also fondly remember the fourth-season episode "The Candidate," when a reluctant Kevin ran for student-council president against Becky Slater (Crystal McKellar), a girl he once spurned who's now savoring this chance to stomp him. The campaign quickly spirals into a series of dirty tricks, culminating with his acquisition of the speech she's to give at a school assembly. Since he's due to speak first, if he delivers it not only will he steal her thunder, but—best of all—he won't have to write his own. Of course, thanks to an ample push from Paul, his conscience wins out when he steps to the podium. Seconds later, a stink bomb hits, clearing the auditorium. It's hilarious, and says much about politics then and now.

Two episodes from its fifth season rate among the series' best. In "The Lake," a memorably rueful snapshot of a summer romance, Kevin's and Paul's families are on a summer vacation and the boys are, in a word, bored. Soon, Kevin finds excitement in the form of a sultry teen named Cara (Lisa Gerber). On their final night together, Kevin expresses his desire to stay with her and not go home. But, of course, he must. "Back to the Lake" takes place the next summer, when not only is Kevin's dad insisting he get a job, but girlfriend Winnie's suggesting the same! Kevin can't help but recall his carefree days with Cara, whom he never wrote, and in a rash moment heads back to her to try and recapture a little of the magic that they once shared.

The series' finale is perhaps its most bittersweet entry. It's the summer of 1973 and 17-year-old Kevin's working for his dad while Winnie's a lifeguard at a far-away resort. After a fight with his father, he quits and seeks out the one person he thinks will make everything okay. But Winnie's not exactly thrilled to see him, particularly when he takes a job at the resort. After he spies her kissing another boy (in a deft touch, "When a Man Loves a Woman" swoops in), he hits the road as a hitchhiker, having lost his car in a poker game, and finds himself in a backseat with none other than his ex-girlfriend. They argue and are quickly deposited by the roadside as a result. When a rainstorm hits, they seek shelter in a barn and, before the night's out, in each other's arms. As they return home the next morning—Independence Day—the adult Kevin informs us of the fates of his family and friends, the most surprising of which is the death of his dad in two years' time, and concludes: "Growing up happens in a heartbeat. One day

Did You Know?

Oops! In one episode, Kevin came home from school to watch the *Apollo 13* launch. Seems unlikely, since *Apollo 13* lifted off on Saturday, April 11, 1970, and splashed down on Friday, April 17.

you're in diapers, the next day you're gone. But the memories of childhood stay with you for the long haul . . ."

In the series (as in real life), sometimes the dots don't quite connect, and it's one achievement of this beloved Emmy-winning series that loose ends are allowed to dangle. As the "simpler" days of our youth evolve into more complex, even tumultuous times, certain life events remain constant. Somewhere a 12-year-old boy comforts a friend over a brother's death; a teen romance blooms; and teenagers defy their parents. In artful, ironic and at times haunting fashion, *The Wonder Years* articulates all of that, plus this: one day those kids, too, may think wistfully of their own childhood experiences as the wonder years.

Cast:

Fred Savage *Kevin Arnold,* **Daniel Stern** *(Narrator) Kevin Arnold as an adult,* **Danica McKellar** *Gwendolyn 'Winnie' Cooper,* **Jason Hervey** *Wayne Arnold,* **Dan Lauria** *Jack Arnold,* **Alley Mills** *Norma Arnold,* **Josh Saviano** *Paul Pfeiffer,* **Olivia d'Abo** *Karen Arnold* *(1988–92)*

The X-Files

By Matt Roush

Broadcast History: FOX, 9/10/1993–5/19/2002
Runtime: 60 minutes
Genre: Sci-fi

Sounds like a tabloid headline: "I Was a Part of *The X-Files* Mythology."

Strange, but true. It happened without warning in the fall of 1997, while screening the gripping two-part opener of the fifth season, when *X-Files* fever was at its peak. Amid a swirl of intrigue—Scully fighting a mysterious cancer, Mulder faking his own suicide (it was that kind of show)—I watched as a character, being grilled by an FBI panel, admits that he's on the payroll of a congressional lobbying firm. "Something called Roush."

"Any idea what that is?" grumbles Assistant Director Skinner, as he scratches the name (spelled correctly!) on a legal pad. Later in the episode, Skinner refers to Roush as a "biotechnology company" that's funneling funds into the coffers of the all-mighty alien-colonization conspiracy. And that's the last anyone ever heard of Roush.

What gives? Who knows? On *The X-Files*, who ever knew? (Series creator Chris Carter later told me it was a tip of his cap for my championing of the series in its earliest days, when it was nearly invisible on Fox's Friday lineup and had yet to achieve even cult status.)

This was just one of countless enigmas buried deep in the show's forbiddingly dense, hauntingly creepy mythology. *The X-Files* was at its best raising the big questions, not answering them (as if we'd understand, anyway). The show's most enduring slogan, "The Truth Is Out There," may really have been saying that it would be best for all of us if the truth *stayed* out there.

That *The X-Files* was "out there" can never be denied. Like Rod Serling's *The Twilight Zone*, the landmark anthology that most clearly inspired its obsessions, *The X-Files* transcended genre with its deft juggling of fantasy, horror, humanism and whimsy. You never knew in any given week what sort of story would be told. But you could be sure the telling would leave you with a sense of wonder, perhaps laced with a frisson of terror. At heart—and despite all of the graphic mayhem, this show had a soul and searched it regularly—*The X-Files* was a celebration of the imagination.

Anything went, and where it went, it was impossible not to follow.

> ### Did You Know?
> Gillian Anderson resumed her role of Agent Scully just four days after the birth of her daughter, Piper.

In the simplest terms, this was the story of an outsider's epic quest for elusive truths, many of which hit perilously close to home, and of a classic opposite-sexes partnership that evolved into the most profound of friendships (with every glance, hug and kiss endlessly analyzed by fanatical so-called "relationship-pers").

"I Want to Believe," read the poster (with an iconic image of a UFO) in the subterranean office of FBI Agent Fox "Spooky" Mulder (David Duchovny), a likably forlorn loner assigned to the infamous "X-Files," a repository for unsolved, unexplainable, possibly paranormal events. Mulder believed, all right. He believed his sister had been abducted by aliens when they were kids, and he wouldn't stop until he learned what had become of her, and why. (The answer would involve both government and family secrets.)

Joining him on the hunt was Dana Scully (Gillian Anderson), a medically trained scientific skeptic whose task was to debunk Mulder's findings. Disarmed by his boyishly vulnerable charms, Scully soon succumbed to Mulder's enthusiasm for all things inexplicable. She didn't want to believe her eyes, but eventually she had to.

Fans of the fantastic, so often starved by network TV's more formulaic leanings, couldn't believe what they were seeing, either. Here was the show we had long been waiting for: a weekly exercise in sustained supernatural suspense, unafraid of explicit horror or metaphysical ambiguity, defying us to suspend our disbelief as it took us on a thrill ride into darkly paranoid waters.

> ## Classic Episode Close-Up
>
> "Small Potatoes"
> *(Original telecast: April 20, 1997)*
>
> Fans waiting for the sparks between Mulder and Scully to ignite are rewarded— sort of—in "Small Potatoes." A loser named Eddie uses his "striated muscle tissue" to bed women after morphing into the men they love. When Mulder uncovers the scam, Eddie knocks him out and assumes his shape. What follows spoofs every hallowed *X-Files* tradition, as Eddie becomes Mulder and ridicules him. After he's busted while putting the moves on Scully (as Mulder), Eddie tells him, "I was born a loser, but you're one by choice."

Lavishly cinematic in its production values, blessed with instant and electric chemistry between its lead actors, *The X-Files* was cult nirvana with blockbuster potential, which it finally achieved when Fox moved it to Sundays in its fourth year. This was the rare fantasy genre show to be taken seriously by the Emmys, nominated several times for Best Drama. (Major wins included Gillian Anderson as Best Actress and an award for writing.) To exploit the growing phenomenon, a big-budget *X-Files* movie was released between the fifth and sixth seasons, addressing some of the mythology questions while baffling the more casual fan.

I had been hooked since the third episode: a flesh-crawling vignette titled "Squeeze," about a grotesque mutant who could slither into the tiniest of spaces as he hunted human livers every 30 years. What a refreshing rush to realize that, as fascinating and intriguing as the government conspiracy and alien-invasion angles were, *The X-Files* was also content just to scare the socks off you every now and then. There were times it could also be frighteningly funny, as in the "Rashomon"-like "Jose Chung's 'From Outer Space'."

Depending on the episode, the show could feel as timeless as a campfire story about things that go bump (or worse) in the night, or as timely as today's headlines about institutional and political corruption. *The X-Files* was perfectly timed to tap into end-of-millennium anxieties about our place in the cosmos, and it had the good fortune to arrive just as the Internet was exploding into the culture at large. This was among the first series to develop an intense online following, with *X*-philes parsing every oblique twist for clues about what it all meant.

As the series evolved, iconic characters took root, most memorably the villainous Cigarette-Smoking Man (William B. Davis). A cancer on humanity, this ever-lurking shadow figure had close family ties to Mulder as well as inside info about the secret conspiracy between humans and aliens, which involved genetic tampering, a toxic black-oil virus dating back to the Ice Age, a secret vaccine and alien bounty hunters. (Lost? You're not alone.) In one memorable episode, Cigarette-Smoking Man's murky past was revealed, linking him to the assassinations of JFK and Rev. Martin Luther King Jr.

On the side of good were three wacky conspiracy theorists known as the "Lone Gunmen," who in a misguided act of hubris were briefly given their own spin-off series.

Also unfortunate: the decision to continue producing *The X-Files* after Duchovny quit following the seventh season, in a cliffhanger that whisked Mulder away in a spaceship, leaving Scully behind, mysteriously pregnant with an implanted "miracle baby" (the series' worst idea ever).

TV and Film Connections

Spin-off: *The Lone Gunmen*

With Mulder gone, replaced by Robert Patrick as ex-marine John Doggett (solid work in a thankless role), the show stumbled on for two more seasons. Mulder did return for the grand two-hour finale, standing trial for the murder of an alien super-soldier and tying up many loose ends of the conspiracy.

Fans were rewarded with a tender coda of Mulder and Scully snuggling in a motel room. His, and the show's, final words: "Maybe there's hope."

Hope for humanity, sure. But *The X-Files* also restored one's hope in TV as a canvas for visionary storytelling on a grand scale. It took a few years, but *Lost* and the reimagined *Battlestar Galactica* are now fulfilling that promise. The truth is still out there. You just have to know where to find it.

Cast:

David Duchovny *Fox Mulder*, **Gillian Anderson** *Dana Scully*, **Mitch Pileggi** *Walter Skinner*, **Robert Patrick** *John Doggett (2000–02)*, **Annabeth Gish** *Monica Reyes (2001–02)*

Your Show of Shows

By Nathaniel Hayes

Broadcast History: NBC, 2/25/1950–6/5/1954
Runtime: 90 minutes
Genre: Sketch comedy
Black and White

Alphabetically, the New York–based *Your Show of Shows* falls last on our list, though its influence and impact on American TV comedy places it among the most significant series in television history. It was, as one of its celebrated writers, Larry Gelbart, wrote in his memoir *Laughing Matters*, a "template for all that followed in the field of TV variety."

Guided by legendary producer Max Liebman during TV's Golden Age, *Your Show of Shows* was a live, Saturday-night extravaganza—39 weeks a year and no repeats—featuring big-name guest stars, song-and-dance routines, and, most memorably, inventive comedy sketches. Audiences were treated to an appearance by a celebrity host (Jackie Cooper, Robert Cummings, Eva Gabor, Rex Harrison, Charlton Heston, Veronica Lake, Angela Lansbury and Burgess Meredith, just to name a few), musical performances that ranged from classical (Marguerite Piazza sang operatic arias) to contemporary (Bill Hayes, Jack Russell and Judy Johnson sang pop tunes), ballet and ballroom dancing, and versatile artists like Lena Horne, Pearl Bailey and Nat King Cole.

The production numbers added an air of sophistication, but *Your Show of Shows* is best remembered for its great skits that spoofed foreign and American movies (fans can never forget the send-up of *From Here to Eternity* that had stars Sid Caesar and Imogene Coca drenched repeatedly by buckets of water), TV shows, personal relationships and social situations. At the center of the circus were Caesar and Coca. Brought over from Liebman's previous variety creation, *The Admiral Broadway Review* (1949–50), they rarely spent time together off the set, but once the cameras started rolling they displayed a remarkable chemistry. "I never went with jokes," Caesar said. "The situation made it funny, not the joke."

The imposing Caesar was a master of tongue-twisting, double-talk linguistics, no matter if his character had a German, French, Japanese or Italian accent. He could also play henpecked husbands, goofy jazz musicians (like Progress Hornsby), and loquacious, know-it-all "experts," including a doctor, a professor, a mountain climber and a fisherman. When interviewed, they revealed that they actually knew nothing at all.

Coca, his petite, rubber-faced co-star, had a flair for both wry humor and outrageous physical comedy and was equally adept at playing an opera diva, a nagging housewife, a sheltered spinster or a snooty socialite. Together, the creative sparks flew as they transformed themselves into uproarious characters like the Hickenloopers, a quarreling, mismatched married couple, or performed elaborate pantomime routines, such the "The 1812 Overture," in which the pair played cards and bickered between exaggerated acts of pounding on drums, crashing cymbals, loading and firing a cannon and throwing grenades.

Joining Caesar and Coca onstage were *Admiral Broadway Review* alum Howard Morris, a squirrelly, energetic performer, and venerable funnyman Carl Reiner, who regularly played the straight man to Caesar's collection of buffoons. (Several years later, Reiner drew on his writing experiences on *Your Show of Shows* and the follow-up series, *Caesar's Hour*, to create *The Dick Van Dyke Show*.) The actors' unique talents were best showcased in the show's popular sketches. In "This Is Your Story," for example, a hilarious parody of the 1950s realty series *This Is Your Life*, Caesar was an initially reluctant audience member who, after being dragged onstage, became overly emotional during hysterical reunions with long-lost family members. A lively Morris played Uncle Goopy, who leaped into Caesar's arms and clung to his leg, while Reiner took the role of the jovial Ralph Edwards–like host with the plastic smile, who gamely tried to maintain order amid the escalating chaos. In the timeless skit, "The Clock," Caesar, Morris, Coca and Reiner played mechanical figures on a town clock in Bavaria. At the top of each hour, the foursome, clad in lederhosen and a dirndl, toddled out to perform an intricate blacksmith routine, which got increasingly bungled as the clock's internal mechanisms malfunctioned. Though simple in concept, the skit showcased the ensemble's exquisite timing—vital for a series that didn't allow second takes.

Did You Know?

Sid Caesar insisted that no cue cards be used on this live show.

Of course, feeding them material was a veritable Hall of Fame of comedy writers, including Gelbart, Mel Brooks, Mel Tolkin, Neil Simon and his brother Danny, Sam Denoff, Lucille Kallen, Michael Stewart and Bill Persky

Your Show of Shows had four magnificent years before the curtain fell on June 5, 1954—exactly 21 years and three months before I was born. Today, we commend the show for setting the standard for subsequent variety and sketch series (perhaps most notably, *Saturday Night Live*). More important, though, we can watch the series (some of us for the first time) and laugh and marvel at one-liners, running gags and colorful characters that remain as fresh and funny as when they first aired more than a half century ago.

Cast

Sid Caesar Performer, **Imogene Coca** Performer, **Carl Reiner** Performer, **Tom Avera** Performer (1950), **Robert Merrill** Performer (1950–51), **Margaret Piazza** Performer (1950–1953), **Bill Hayes** Performer (1950–53), **Howard Morris** Performer (1951–1954)

INDEX

A

Index

Index

Index

Index

Index

Index

Index

Index

Index

Index

Index

Index

Index

T

Tabitha, 32
Takei, George, 256, 258
Tal, Alona, 287
Talbott, Michael, 173
Tales of Tomorrow, 278
Tamblyn, Amber, 107
Tamblyn, Russ, 283
Tambor, Jeffrey
  on *Arrested Development,* 19, 21
  on *The Larry Sanders Show,* 150, 151
  in SpongeBob movie, 247
Taming of the Shrew, The, 183–84
Tanana, Frank, 248
Tarantino, Quentin, 114
Tarkenton, Fran, 178
Tartikoff, Brandon
  Cheers as championed by, 46
  The Golden Girls, as originator of, 114
  Law & Order, airing of, 154
  Miami Vice, as originator of, 171
  Michael J. Fox, impression of, 92
Tata, Joe E., 29
Taxi, 47, 263–65
Taylor, Buck, 121
Taylor, Clarice, 48
Taylor, Lili, 235, 236
Taylor, Liz, 104
Temptations, the, 212
Teresa, 284
That 70's Show, 122
Theron, Charlize, 20
Thiessen, Tiffani-Amber, 28, 29
Thinnes, Roy, 106
thirtysomething, 266–68
This Is Spinal Tap, 195
This Is Your Life, 303
Thomas, Betty, 129
Thomas, Danny, 77
Thomas, Philip Michael, 171, 173
Thomas, Rob, 288
Thomas, Tony, 114
Thompson, Andrea, 191
Thompson, Fred Dalton, 156, 157
Thompson, Jason, 107
Thompson, Kenan, 216
Thompson, Scott, 151

Thompson, Tessa, 288
Thorne, Callie, 132
Thorne-Smith, Courtney, 5, 7, 169, 170
Three Dog Night, 212
Three's Company, 217
Throw Momma from the Train, 265
Tierney, Maura, 82, 84
Till Death Us Do Part, 2
Tilton, Charlene, 61, 62
Time Bandits, 182
Time Tunnel, The, 168
Tinker, Grant, 76, 147, 162
Tirico, Mike, 251
T. J. Hooker, 183
Toast of the Town, 78, 79
Tobias, George, 32
Today, 269–71, 294
Tolkin, Mel, 303
Toma, 207
Tomlin, Lily
  on *Homicide,* 131
  on *Laugh-In,* 212, 213
  on *The West Wing,* 290
  on *Will & Grace,* 294
Tonight Show, The
  funniest moment on, 43, 274
  Late Show with David Letterman,
  compared to, 152
  Leno as host on, 149
  Today, compared to, 269, 270
  tribute to, 272–74
  See also Carson, Johnny
Top Gun, 82
Torn, Rip, 150, 151
Tortellis, The, 47
Towers, Constance, 107
Townies, 111
Tracey Ullman Show, The, 231, 232
Trachtenberg, Michelle, 41
Trading Spaces, 14, 89
Trapper John M.D., 165
Travanti, Daniel J., 127, 129
Travolta, John, 13
Trebek, Alex, 47, 144–45
Trinneer, Connor, 259
Truesdale, Yanic, 113
Truth or Consequences, 143
Tucker, Michael, 146, 148

Index

Index

About the Authors

Alan Appel, who edited this book and contributed the essay for *The Honeymooners*, is a 40-year TV GUIDE veteran who most recently served as Manager of Editorial Projects. His other positions with the magazine have included Associate Listings Editor and New York Bureau Chief.

Sue Tuttle, who edited this book, has been with TV GUIDE for 17 years, most recently as Manager of Data Quality Assurance. She has also edited the *TV GUIDE Book of Lists* and the television encyclopedia *TV GUIDE Guide to TV*.

Karina Reeves, who managed this project and contributed the essay for *Frasier*, is a lifelong TV lover who's been able to parlay that into a career. She has been TV GUIDE's Director of Licensing for more than 4 years.

Angel Cohn works for TVGUIDE.com, is part of the weekly podcast, writes commentary on way too many shows, pens the popular Surfer Girl blog and can't live without her TiVo.

Writer-editor **Michael Davis** spent eight years at TV GUIDE, serving terms in both the Radnor and New York offices. He left in 2007 to complete his first book for Viking, a definitive history of *Sesame Street*.

A 30-year TV GUIDE veteran, **Paul Droesch** served as Close-up Editor in the 1980s. He also wrote the magazine's "This Week" and "Hits and Misses" columns.

For 13 years, **G. J. Donnelly** has made people jealous by telling them he gets paid to watch TV. This obsessive Monty Python fan is currently a Writer in TV GUIDE's Radnor bureau.

General editor **Greg Evans** joined TV GUIDE in 1998. His earliest childhood memory is of crawling away from the TV set during a commercial break.

Bruce Fretts is Editor at Large for TV GUIDE. Since joining the magazine in 2003, he's written the popular "Cheers & Jeers" column, as well as numerous cover stories.

Joe Friedrich became a writer for TV GUIDE in 1997, working in New York and Pennsylvania, and began covering HBO in 1999. Undaunted by Y2K, he's been doing so ever since.

Ali Gazan is a writer for TV GUIDE, penning feature articles and overseeing the "Behind the Scenes" and "Moment of the Week" sections. Ali is also a frequent guest on television and radio shows where she comments on popular shows and trends. Ali joined the New York office in April 2005.

About the Authors

Jeff Gemmill has written for various publications, including TV GUIDE, since 1990. He admits to liking *The Donny & Marie Show* as a kid; his wife, Diane, loves him anyway.

Nathaniel Hayes graduated from St. Joseph's University (B.A.) and Temple University (M.J.). He started at TV GUIDE in 1999 as a Make-up Editor, transitioned to Listings in 2003 and is currently a Copy Writer for the Sports Team.

TV GUIDE Writer **Damian Holbrook** covers every guilty pleasure imaginable and counts meeting Aaron Spelling as the greatest moment of his life. He's currently teaching his Chihuahua, Pepito, to program the TiVo.

Tim Holland is a native South Carolinian who presently lives in Berwyn, Pennsylvania, with his wife and two children. He is a Senior Text Writer at TV GUIDE.

Robin Honig is a contributing writer for TV GUIDE and was the magazine's Research Chief for seven years. She also writes the *Gilmore Girls* blog for TV GUIDE Online. Currently, she is a writer and editor in New York City.

Joseph Hudak is an Associate Editor for TV GUIDE. Prior to beginning his career as a wordsmith, he installed lawn-sprinkler systems throughout Pennsylvania's Wyoming Valley. His favorite television series of all time is *The Honeymooners*.

Roger Leister is a veteran of TV GUIDE's sports desk and has a special place in his heart for Oscar Madison, Slap Maxwell and *Sports Night*, 2000's "Best Show You're Not Watching."

Shawna Malcom is a Los Angeles-based Senior Correspondent for TV GUIDE and a frequent on-air contributor to the TV GUIDE Channel. When she's not writing or talking about TV, she's watching it.

Daniel Manu is the Editorial Director for TVGUIDE.com in New York. He was previously an editor at AOL Entertainment, Sony Online Entertainment and *Sound & Vision* and *Stereo Review* magazines.

Jon McDaid, a sports copywriter, began working at TV GUIDE's offices in Radnor, Pennsylvania, in 2000. He lives with his wife and two children in nearby King of Prussia.

Senior Editor **Maitland McDonagh** is TVGUIDE.com's FlickChick columnist, movie reviewer and the author of four books, including *Movie Lust: Recommended Viewing for Every Mood, Moment and Reason*.

N. F. Mendoza is a Los Angeles-based Senior Correspondent for TV GUIDE.

About the Authors

Stuart Michaelson is an Editorial Supervisor in the Data Operations department in Radnor, Pennsylvania, and has worked for TV GUIDE since 1995.

Matt Webb Mitovich joined TV GUIDE in June 2005, serving as TVGUIDE.com's News Editor. Raised in Stamford, Connecticut, he lives with his wife and twin sons in Woodcliff Lake, New Jersey.

Mary Murphy is the Senior Writer for TV GUIDE. She has covered the TV industry for the past 15 years, authoring major investigative pieces and obtaining interviews with celebrities and such luminaries as Presidents Bill Clinton and George Bush. Mary appears frequently on such shows as *The Today Show*, *The O'Reilly Factor* and *Entertainment Tonight*, where she worked for two years as an on-air personality.

Before she spent 13 years working as a TV GUIDE Writer, **Donica O'Bradovich** spent her teenage years obsessively checking the magazine's listings for ABBA TV appearances. She now works as a freelance writer.

Rebecca Paley has been the Deputy News Editor at TV GUIDE since January 2006. Prior to that, she wrote about culture and celebrity for such publications as *The New York Times*, *People* and *Mother Jones*.

Tracy Phillips was a writer and editor for TV GUIDE Magazine for more than 10 years, a Professional TV Lover forever. Mom and Dad are *really* proud!

TV GUIDE Associate Editor **Nerina Rammairone** still misses Brandon, Dawson and Buffy, so what's a girl to do? Write poetry. Her collection of poems *But Ice Cream Melts* was released in 2003.

Matt Roush has been the Senior TV Critic at TV GUIDE since 1998, when the Indiana native (and Phi Beta Kappa graduate of Indiana University) joined the magazine from *USA TODAY*. He lives and works in New York City.

Ileane Rudolph is a veteran staff writer in TV GUIDE's New York office, who has happily interviewed stars ranging from Mary Tyler Moore to Brad Pitt in her years at the magazine.

Rich Sands is a Senior Editor at TV GUIDE, overseeing the magazine's coverage of sports, science fiction and soaps. He joined the staff in 1995.

After a lifetime of her mom complaining about the amount of time she spent in front of the tube, **Raven Snook** is thrilled to be making her living off her obsession as the Database Editor for TV GUIDE.com.

About the Authors

Ray Stackhouse, a Senior Writer and 25-year TV GUIDE veteran, has been covering television for more than 30 years. He previously was on the entertainment staff of the defunct *Philadelphia Evening Bulletin* (but it wasn't his fault they closed!).

Associate Editor **Rochell D. Thomas** is TV GUIDE's quirky "Is It Just Me?" columnist. A native Hoosier, she resides in Brooklyn where she keeps an impressive To-Do List collection.

Sue Tiedeck is an Editorial Supervisor in the Data Operations department in TV GUIDE's Radnor, Pennsylvania, office. She has worked for the company for 19 years in various positions, including Copy Editor, Writer and Associate Listings Editor.

Craig Tomashoff is the West Coast Bureau Chief for TV GUIDE. He has previously written for *People* magazine, *US Weekly* and television shows including VH1's *Behind the Music*.

Todd Wakai counts Sports Editor and Director of Program Listings among his many roles at TV GUIDE. He lives in Wilmington, Delaware, with his wife (who *thinks* he watches too much TV) and two kids (who watch too much TV).

Megan Walsh-Boyle is a Writer and television fanatic who has been with TV GUIDE for 7 years. When not glued to the tube, she's with her husband, Laughlin, and daughter, Sadie.

Trish Wethman has worked at TV GUIDE in Radnor for 10 years, most recently as a Training Manager, always as an entertainment fiend. She lives in Chester Springs, Pennsylvania. with her husband, Chris, and their son, Jake.

Associate Editor **Sabrina Rojas Weiss** has spent her five years at TVGUIDE.com attempting to recover from a strict childhood TV-diet of nothing but PBS, MTV and Mexican telenovelas.

Paul Wolfe has been writing and editing since 1995 at TV GUIDE in Radnor, Pennsylvania, where he fell in love with his future wife and also continued his passion for sports, reality TV and drama queens ranging from Buffy to Veronica Mars.